Book Markets for Children's Writers

2016

The Most Comprehensive Directory of Book Publishers for and about Children

THE WRITER'S BOOKSTORE

www.WritersBookstore.com

www.InstituteForWriters.com

Acknowledgments

The editors of this directory appreciate the generous cooperation of the publishers who made clear their policies and practices, as well as the contributions from our instructors and students.

Marni McNiff, Editor in Chief

Michele Coppola Ames, Copy Editor

Sarah Goldie, Assistant Editor

Abbey Salamon, Assistant Editor

Grace Hewlitt, Proofreader

Cover image from *Sleepytime Me* written by Edith Fine and published by Random House Children's Books
©2014 Christopher Denise

To learn more about Christopher Denise visit
www.christopherdenise.com
https://www.facebook.com/Christopher-Denise-Illustrator-385062757194/

International Standard Book Number ISBN: 978-1-944743-01-7

203-792-8600. www.writersbookstore.com
email: StudentServices@InstituteChildrensLit.com

Printed and bound in Canada

Table of Contents

Submissions

Standing on Your Platform: Write and Publish in a Changing Marketplace

New This Year

The year 2015 was decidedly fast-paced and eventful in book publishing. The young adult market continues to grow with more publishers including teen horror and real-life stories in their mix. And because of technology, self-publishing presents even more new opportunities.

Other miscellaneous news of the year to keep in mind:

- Publishing giant MacMillan hired Erin Stein, formerly of Tokyo Pop and HarperCollins to start a new imprint, simply titled Imprint, which targets kids 0–12.
- The children's nonfiction market continues to surge with Lerner Books' new imprint Hungry Tomato.
- The YA romance market is still growing strong with new imprints including: Teen Crave and Teen Crush from Entangled Publishing, and Spencer Hill Contemporary and Tulip Romance from Spencer Hill Press.
- Comic-Con continues to drive the comic book market including new publisher, Oni Press.
- Check for other new or changing publishers or imprints on pages 536-537, including Pavilion Children's Books, Angry Robot Books, and Wido Publishing.

The Writing & Publishing Process

Mnemonic devices helped many of us remember essential facts during our school days, elementary through collegiate. Mary's Violet Eyes Make a John Stay Up Nights, Period: Mercury, Venus, Earth, Mars, Asteroids, Jupiter, Saturn, Uranus, Neptune, Pluto. Or, from Western history class, the ditty that tells the fate of the six wives of Henry VIII: Divorced, beheaded, died. For those looking to make a success of writing for children, this adaptation might work to reinforce the process:

Inspired, researched, devised.
Queried, sold, revised.

You have the inspiration already, or you would not be using this book. You may know the subject or genre that most interests you and what you want to research. You may have identified the audience that most appeals to you (kindergartners? teens?) and have a plot or a plan for structuring a book. You may even know your writing career goals (hobbyist? professional? part-time? full-time?) and be ready to put together queries and energetically sell your work. But you may not know how to put the whole together, or you may be looking for advice on one or two aspects of the whole. You most certainly will need to know the markets and how they change from month to month, year to year.

Knowing the markets and pulling the whole together is what *Book Markets for Children's Writers* is all about. It has all the information you need to improve your resources and knowledge. In this 2016 edition:

- *Listings are organized into sections for practical use.* You can easily find publishers that focus on children's or teen books only (Children's Trade). Or, if you have a teaching background, search the Classroom section for educational publishers. Perhaps you want to expand the possibilities and increase your income; look for additional opportunities under Parenting, or publishers "of interest" to children and teens.

- *Listings reflect the online presence of publishers,* from their guidelines to products to specializations in new media.

- *Cross-references among parent companies, divisions, and imprints* will help you navigate the marketplace, know who is related to whom, and better target your submissions.

- *An extensive agents section* will help you to impress agents as well as editors.

All these features will help you build your *platform*, the buzz word that refers to how you present yourself as a writer via the writing itself, networking, professional appearances, websites, social media, and more. You are, or want to be, a writer, and more specifically, a published writer for children. How do you pursue that goal, while simultaneously refining your craft, carving a career, and earning a living? How do you create a voice and a visible identity—your platform as a writer?

Book Markets for Children's Writers 2016 is here to help you become an author who knows your reader, knows where you want to go with your writing, and knows how to sell your work to the markets best-suited for your books and your aspirations.

Inspired

Writing may have always been your aspiration. Perhaps you've been told you have a gift for language or storytelling. You may want to write to please your children, family, or just yourself. *Book Markets for Children's Writers 2016* is for those who want to go beyond the dream and carve a writing career. It is all about finding places to sell the writing that you put your heart and head into.

Whatever your aspiration, it will inform and help you accomplish: the idea generation, research, interaction with editors and agents and audience, even your technology and tax decisions.

Idea Generation

Along with the desire to write comes an attraction to certain subjects and genres. But most beginning writers are quick to ask the more experienced: "Where do you get your ideas?" The answer is almost always, "Everywhere." You get ideas from what you have experienced, from what you see in daily life, from personal interests, from the news, from listening to children and adults. Practicalities of career may at some point inspire you too, when you identify a hole in the marketplace waiting to be filled by your writing.

When you are in the inspiration stage, ask yourself:

- What do I want to write about? Will it interest editors? Do have a passion for the subject or story that will inspire others?
- Am I ready to write this? Have I honed my writing skills with practice, classes, workshops, writers' groups?
- Do I know my audience? What is its age range? Interests? Skills? Will these readers be interested in my idea, topic, or story?
- Is the idea substantial enough? Is it worth researching further, developing more deeply?

To explore an idea you already have in hand, or find one that makes you enthusiastic and ready to jump into researching and writing, try some of the idea generation strategies on page 9.

Researched

Inspiration and research are chicken and egg. The motivation to write on a subject prompts research, but research unearths ideas. Research is a journey that embraces a subject, audience, books, and markets.

Idea Generation Strategies

Ideas for subjects on which to write or stories to develop come in many ways, perhaps as many ways as there are writers. But ideas may generally be grouped into those born of experience, brainstorming, research, or even editor assignments. Here are ways to help you add to your potential idea pile.

- Do brainstorming exercises. Brainstorming is an important creative tool. Today, a variety of resources beyond the tried-and-true pencil and paper can help you brainstorm. But first, here are a few ways to loosen up your creativity:
  - Play children's games; generate memories.
  - Take a bus, ride a subway, sit in a park or a museum atrium, and observe the people. Create backgrounds and story lines for individuals you see. For nonfiction, ask yourself questions based on your observations.
  - Explore mind maps. Use books or electronic sources if you like, such as:
    - Mind Tools: www.mindtools.com/brainstm.html
    - Free Mind: http://freemind.sourceforge.net/wiki/index.php/Main_Page
  - Try writing prompts, such as Hatch's Plot Bank (www.angelfire.com/nc/tcrpress/plots1.html); Creative Writing Prompts (creativewritingprompts.com); or Easy Street Prompts (www.easystreetprompts.blogspot.com).
- Keep a journal or commonplace book. For centuries writers and others have journaled or kept commonplace books. They are places to record random ideas and life experiences related to family, schooling, hobbies, personal events (good and bad), jobs, volunteer work, neighborhood, places of worship, and beyond.
- Scour the media. Daily newspapers, magazines, and specialized and aggregate websites all have stories that range from serious and fascinating to bizarre and funny. Clip or bookmark stories with potential interest for research. You can also use services such as Google Alerts (www.google.com/alerts) to have online news and articles on specific topics emailed to you.
- Probe your family history. Beyond daily events in your life, is there something in your family history that would make for a good children's story or an intriguing nonfiction subject? Are there relatives or family friends you might pump for interesting information?
- Cultivate creative habits. Meditate, listen to music, knit or embroider, take a walk, journal, free-write, go to an Internet cafe (not unlike a certain English billionaire children's author who sat in a coffee shop writing about a wizard). Focus on developing a series of questions, and then let the answers unfold or lead you in other directions.
- Review the curriculum for your state and other states. School subjects can help you develop ideas for classroom books, and generate possibilities for trade titles too.
- Read, read, read! It may sound strange, but the more quality children's books you read, the more ideas you're likely to generate for your own stories.

Subject Research

Topical research is core to nonfiction but can be as important in creating authentic fiction. Long gone are the days when children's books were publishing's stepchildren and the research behind them could be seen as secondhand. Accuracy and an appropriate level of information are essential in children's literature today. Editors won't stand for anything less.

Living in an age when any museum, university, organization, or expert can be found and often accessed freely with a few clicks of a mouse, research is easier and infinitely more wide-ranging than a generation ago. The quantity of thin, inaccurate information online is also great. Be very cautious about the quality of your sources in this technological age, when anyone can write virtually anything they want on a website without verification.

Research rule number one: Know the value of your sources.

- *Primary sources:* firsthand information in the form of original documents (letters, diaries, statistics, maps, legal papers, and so on), photographs, artwork, film, audio recordings, witness testimonies, diaries, journals, and even objects like clothing or crafts. They are the most highly valued resource in terms of objectivity and accuracy because they date to the time, place, event, or person being investigated. That could involve a historical period, a contemporary event, or even a scientific experiment.

- *Secondary sources:* information that is one or more steps removed from the topic's point of origin. Secondary sources include scholarly studies, biographies, databases, encyclopedias, commentaries, textbooks, newspapers, magazines, or other media that contain secondary accounts. These sources analyze and interpret. They can be very accurate and objective, or they can be highly subjective. It is up to the writer to judge and use these sources appropriately.

- *Interviews with experts:* a writer's personal research with an individual. Experts are often professionals in a field—scientists, historians, businesspeople—but they can also be the local kid, an ordinary person who had an interesting experience, or anyone who is knowledgeable and has firsthand information about a given subject. Thus, experts can be either primary or secondary sources.

Fiction: Don't think fiction can simply do without research because it is "made up." True, some picture books, chapter books, and novels taken largely from personal and observed experience may not need extensive research, but details must be right. The most obvious genre calling out for research is historical fiction, but even in contemporary novels characters, places, and environments all need to be right too. Otherwise, readers will not have what Samuel Taylor Coleridge called the "willing suspension of disbelief."

Consider how character traits and setting might be researched. Perhaps your protagonist has Tourette's, or has moved to a small town in southern Florida from Santiago, Chile—what do you need to know and convey to readers about those qualities and settings? How will your characters' names reflect the time and place of the story? Perhaps some political event in Chile's past helped create an apparent villain in the story. Or maybe the story is a mystery, and you want to find a clever resolution based in science.

Fact Checking: At the end of the writing process you will need to fact check your own research, so keeping good records of what you learn along the way is vital.

For every fact you include, whether in nonfiction or fiction, try to have three reliable sources to support it, if possible. For interviews, record them when you can as backup. When you get to the revision stage for your writing, fact-checking should confirm your accuracy. Publishers require such accuracy of writers; some publishers—by no means all—do additional fact checking on their own.

The last thing you want to do is undermine your authority in nonfiction or believability in fiction. Who hasn't had a book or movie ruined by some wrong tidbit that misrepresented the truth of an event or shattered the necessary suspension of disbelief?

Audience Research

You may have been drawn to write for a particular age group even before you honed in on a subject area or genre of interest. Picture books for preschoolers or kindergartners might appeal to you, or perhaps writing for beginning readers excites you. Middle-graders in love with reading—or reluctant to read—may be the audience for you. YA writing has never before appealed to quite so many readers, from teens themselves to adults, and it continues to evolve. Whichever age group is your desired audience, study it, know it well, and remember the variations within it.

Learn by reading the literature already published, and acknowledged as strong. Talk to teachers, coaches, mentors, and librarians. Look at curricula to see what is being taught in school. Keep up with age-related websites, and check professional resources, such as those for the American Library Association (ALA). Learn about vocabulary and reading levels. Is it an age that wants its books in chapters? Does rhythm have little or great value at this age?

For a sense of the developmental stages among young people, see the sidebar on pages 16–17, Authentic Kids.

Internet Research Sources

The Internet has made the number and range of research sources limitless; here is a sampling that reveals how broad they are.

- Archives
  - Internet Archive: www.archive.org. Includes audio, moving images, live music, and texts.
  - United States National Archives: www.archives.gov/research. States and localities also may have collections.
  - Bibliotheque Nationale de France: http://gallica.bnf.fr. A very wide-ranging collection (access is available in English as well as French), including books, manuscripts, maps, periodicals, images, sound recordings, and more.
  - Look for other national archives around the world, including: United Kingdom, nationalarchives.gov.uk; Russia, www.russianarchives.com; Egypt, www.nationalarchives.gov.eg/nae/home.jsp; and so on.

- Experts
  - All Experts: www.allexperts.com. Divided into subject categories, All Experts is a Q&A site manned by experts.
  - ProfNet: https://profnet.prnewswire.com/ProfNetHome.aspx. Journalism site that helps find professionals and experts to interview or help develop leads.
- Gateway Sites
  - Infomine: http://infomine.ucr.edu. Scholarly resources from the University of California. Subjects include the sciences and humanities, government, business, and cultural diversity.
  - Intute: www.intute.ac.uk. Specialized research links across many categories.
  - ipL2: www.ipl.org. A virtual library.
  - Library Spot: www.libraryspot.com: A virtual library.
  - NoodleTools: www.noodletools.com. Data on many topics, and guidance in using statistics and graphs.
  - Refdesk.com: http://refdesk.com. A virtual library.

- Government Sites
  - Federal Resources for Educational Excellence: http://free.ed.gov. Categories covered are the arts, health, history, language, math, science.
  - Library of Congress: www.loc.gov. The largest library in the world makes many collections and avenues of research available.
  - NASA: www.nasa.gov
  - National Institutes of Health: http://nih.gov
  - National Science Foundation: http://nsf.gov
  - Smithsonian: www.si.edu
  - United States Geological Survey: www.usgs.gov
  - USA.gov: www.usa.gov. Focuses on governmental issues, including the economy, consumer protection, environment, health, public safety, transportation, and culture.

Internet Research Sources

- Media
  - NewsLibrary: http://nl.newsbank.com. Links to thousands of U.S. newspapers.
  - NewspaperARCHIVE: www.newspaperarchive.com. Claims to be the world's largest historical newspaper archive. It focuses on people and history. Subscription-based, $72/year.

- Museums
  - Museums: www.umich.edu/~motherha/museums.html. A list of museums, large and small, around the world, with links. They range from the Museum of Decorative Arts in Prague, London's Tate Gallery, and the Vatican Collections to Taipai's Museum of World Religions and the Institute of Egyptian Art and Archaeology in Memphis, TN.
  - Museum Stuff: www.museumstuff.com. Guide to international museums, from air and space to the arts and the history of pharmacy.

- Professional Organizations
  - American Library Association: www.ala.org/ala/mgrps/divs/rusa/sections/history/resources/pubs/usingprimarysources/index.cfm. A helpful introduction to primary sources, how to use them, and where to find them.

- University Collections
  - Princeton: www.princeton.edu/~refdesk/primary2.html
  - University of Chicago: www.lib.uchicago.edu/e/spcl/arch.html
  - Voice of the Shuttle: http://vos.ucsb.edu. A gateway database for scholarly resources, maintained by the University of California, Santa Barbara.
  - Yale: www.yale.edu/collections_collaborative/primarysources/primarysources.html#manuscripts_a

- Select Specialized Sources
  - Artcyclopedia: www.artcyclopedia.com. Information on artists, art sites, and related links.
  - BioMedCentral: www.biomedcentral.com. An "open access publisher" with articles from 243 medical journals.
  - History Sourcebooks: www.fordham.edu/Halsall/index.asp. From ancient to medieval to modern, from East Asian to African to Islamic to Women's studies, sources for historical resources, from Fordham University.
  - Sportscience: www.sportsci.org. Research about all areas of sports, from performance and training to health.

- Search Engines and Other Useful Sites
  - Dogpile.com: A metasearch site that gathers results from multiple search engines.
  - Technorati.com: Search engine for blogs.

Competitive Title Research

Publishers often want competition or market research as part of nonfiction book proposals. Some may also want to know something about the competition for fiction. Imagine if just a few years ago you were writing a novel about wizards or vampires. What you would have to report today and what you would have found in a pre-Potter or pre-Twilight universe would have been very different.

When you include information about competitive titles into your submission to an editor or agent, it signals that you are a professional, and are serious about not just your writing but about creating a platform for yourself—knowing the markets and doing something to distinguish yourself in them.

On page 18 is a form to help you list and analyze competitive titles. You should also note in the listings in *Book Markets for Children's Writers 2016* exactly which publishers want competition or market reports, and the details of how they want them

Age Targeting Resources

- American Academy of Pediatrics: www.healthychildren.org. Provides extensive information about child development and other child-related issues.
- American Academy of Child & Adolescent Psychiatry: www.aacap.org. Look for child development resources and a page of helpful links.
- American Library Association: www.ala.org. The ALA website includes many resources about children and reading. The Young Adult Library Services Association (YALSA) section is particularly active.
- Bright Futures: www.brightfutures.org. A national health promotion initiative.
- Childcare.gov: www.childcare.gov. A U.S. government resource site for parents, educators, and policymakers.
- International Reading Association: www.reading.org. A nonprofit organization focused on literacy.
- Child & Family WebGuide: www.cfw.tufts.edu. Child development topics.
- Guysread.com: www.guysread.com. A site promoting reading among boys, who generally read less than girls, from author Jon Scieszka.
- ReadKiddoRead: www.readkiddoread.com. A literacy site sponsored by author James Patterson.
- Search Institute: www.search-institute.org. A nonprofit research and service organization for children and families. See the What Kids Need to Succeed section.
- Teenreads.com: www.teenreads.com. Encourages teen reading.
- Zero to Three: www.zerotothree.org. A national nonprofit focused on early learning.

structured, if available. Note the other items that are expected in the submission package. For example:

- Fulcrum Publishing, a small press looking for nonfiction queries related to nature, the environment, Native American culture, and history, wants a competition analysis along with a synopsis and sample chapters.
- Magical Child Books prefers stories that have modern-day children as main characters.
- Skyhorse Publishing, which has a children's imprint called Sky Pony Press for upper elementary readers, requests a market/competition analysis, as well as a cover letter, synopsis, annotated outline, and sample chapters.
- Sourcebooks publishes more than 300 books a year and wants competition reports in nonfiction proposals.

For educational publishers producing classroom and library books, competition reports can be particularly important. Some have extensive series of books focusing on curriculum areas and related subjects. Among the classroom publishers that request competition reports are Benchmark Books, Creative Teaching Press, History Compass, Nelson Education, and Prometheus Books.

So how do you do this competitive title research? Using *Book Markets for Children's Writers 2016,* begin by noting which of the listings sections cover subjects and forms of interest to you: trade, classroom, religious, regional, etc. Even easier, start with the Category Index, beginning on page 530, to find publishers whose books are similar to yours. Then look at their catalogues or websites for relevant titles.

- You can get considerable information on sites like Amazon and search engines like Google. Do subject and age searches on Amazon or Barnesandnoble.com to help compile a list of titles. Pay attention to reviews and sales rankings, and to other titles the sites automatically suggest. This process may help you shift your angle of approach as you research and compose the book. Again, check publisher websites in case more information is available about the competitive titles you have identified.

- When you find the titles that are competitive to yours, use the library to read and review as many of them as possible. Or, buy the books you want to own at a bookstore, or download them to your electronic reader. A brief description and some reviews on Amazon won't give you the full flavor and necessary details to know your competition well.

-

What are you looking for as you do the research and put a report together?

Authentic Kids

If you're going to write for kids, it's crucial that your child characters talk and act like real kids. Young people want to read about kids their own age (or just a little older) and they want to read about kids they can relate to, even if those characters live in a fantasy world or somewhere in the past.

To make your kids authentic, you'll have to do some research. If you're a parent or a teacher, you'll have easy access to kids on a daily basis. If not, find ways to enter their world. Watch them at the mall, which gives you the advantage of being able to see what they do and say when they feel they are unobserved by an adult. Check out their culture by reading their books and magazines and watching popular movies, and become familiar with YouTube and social media like Snapchat. Access your own childhood memories by looking at childhood photographs and interviewing people who knew you as a kid.

Children's books are usually separated into various age categories. Here are some very basic developmental outlines about those ages:

Ages 0-3

Babies are naturally egocentric. They can't see things from someone else's point of view, and they don't yet have the language skills to express their needs. Babies and toddlers aren't quite ready for full-blown stories with vivid characterization. They care more for colors, shapes, and sounds in their books.

Ages 3-5

Preschoolers are beginning to use more complicated sentences and to learn that they can use specific words to say what they mean. "No" and "Why" become important words. They are fascinated by everything. Where does milk come from? What makes a shadow? How do birds fly? Family is their world, but they are also growing aware of people outside their family—teachers, the other kids in nursery school, their neighbors and friends.

Ages 5-8

Kids in this age range are taking on more independence. They go to school, participate in sports, and learn to read and write and ride bicycles without training wheels. They now realize they are no longer the center of the universe. They move from being more concrete thinkers to more reflective ones, as they begin to look at causes and ask more challenging questions. School age kids feel alternatively dependent, resistant, or rebellious toward their parents. Friends become important. They enjoy telling jokes, appreciate puns, and love to be silly.

Authentic Kids

Ages 8-12

Kids this age are developing specific interests, and they're eager to learn all about them, whether it's sports or music or movies. This is when their lives outside the home start to compete with their lives inside the home. Kids in this age range are becoming aware of hierarchies at school and who is okay to hang out with and who isn't. This is also when the opposite sex becomes more intriguing.

Ages 12-16

Puberty sets in during this stage, and kids' bodies seem to change overnight. This is also when the center of activity shifts fully away from home, over to school and activities and hanging out with friends. To their dismay, parents find they've become uncool and often a source of embarrassment to the child who was once attached to them like flies to flypaper. Some other kids are uncool, too, and social status and being in the right clique becomes all consuming. And for the older teens, so does getting into the right college. For a lot of kids, the teen years can be filled with pressure and angst.

Know the Difference: Middle Grade vs. Young Adult

Many people confuse these two categories of children's books, but there are key differences between them:

Middle Grade (for ages 8-12)
• 30,000 – 50,000 words
• No profanity, graphic violence, or sexuality
• Protagonist is typically 10 years old for younger middle grade, or up to 13 for more complex books. Kids like to read up, so don't make your protagonist younger than 10.
• Content: Fantasy, humor, and focus on friends, family, and school

Young Adult (for ages 13-18)
• 50,000 – 75,000 words
• Profanity, graphic violence, sexuality are acceptable.
• Protagonist is typically 14-15 years old, or up to 18 for edgier fiction.
• Content: Stories that are emotionally true to teens' experiences (often in first person). Often tend to be "dark" and can cover topics like murder, date rape, alienation, and sexual identity.

Competitive Title Research Form

My Book: real-life stories of a service dog and an autistic girl, ages 8–10

Title	Author	Publisher	Pub. Date	Description
Helping Dogs	Hoffman	Gareth Stevens	January 2011	library market series, grades 2-3
Assistance Dogs	Tagliaferro	Bearport	January 2007	hi-lo, library market, grades 3-4
Service Dogs	Schuh	Capstone/Pebble	August 2010	school/library market, grades K-1

- Ask yourself, what titles look similar to the concept I have in mind, or the book I have outlined or written?

- Who published the title, and how many other titles of this kind or category are included on the publisher's list? When were they published?

- Is it an overcrowded list, or is this publisher likely to be open to another title on a similar subject? Are the books old enough that a newer treatment might be welcome?

- How are the books similar to or different from mine? What is the slant, and can I adapt mine if needed? How is my slant better? Similarly, what's the target age and book structure?

Then do an analysis of what you have discovered, for yourself first, but also to help convince an editor or agent. Is a new book needed on the topic? Why is one or another publisher the right one for you to approach? How can this book be marketed in the framework of the publisher's other titles? Why are you the one to write and help sell it, and *how* will you help sell it? (Remember, selling is a big part of your platform.)

Market Research

With all your idea generation and research, you have also been gathering market research along the way—that is, determining the best publishers for your particular book.

One of the advantages of the new organization of *Book Markets for Children's Writers 2016* is that it can help you target your research more easily and accurately from your very first steps. Are you interested in writing nonfiction that will be read in classrooms or taken off the shelf in libraries? Or in writing historical fiction that will complement the state curriculum? Look in the Classroom Publishing section. Is your novel going to focus on a particular region (Texas in the 1860s), or have a Christian perspective? Begin with the Regional or the Religious Publishing sections. Don't limit yourself—the Category Index will help you find relevant genres, categories, and publishers across all the sections—but you can take better aim by using the new structure of this market directory.

Gather a list of potential publishers and look at each of them more closely. How do you evaluate publishers most likely to be interested in your book? Ask and analyze:

- Has the company published other books related to this subject, this audience, this format?

- Does your book fit, and bring something fresh to the list?

- How big is the company? How many new titles does it publish annually? Does it have a strong backlist?

Potential Publisher Form

My Book: real-life stories of a service dog and an autistic girl, ages 8–10

Category	Publisher	Notes
Special Ed	Autism Aspergers Pub Co.	Some children's books, middle-grade, fiction and non-fiction. Niche for parents. 30 books a year. Open to submissions.
	Carolina Wren	Small press, under-represented writers, disabilities. Note: not currently reviewing but see Doris Bakwin Contest.
	PowerKids Press	Large, educational. 200+ books a year. K-6. Covers social, emotional, health issues. Nonfiction only. Open.
	Star Bright Books	Books on animals, and disabilities. No middle-grade, but does chapter books. 15–20 books annually. Open to queries.
Online search:	Picture Window Books	Has series called Friends with Disabilities. Part of Rosen Pub. Group. K-6, high-interest.
	Albert Whitman	1998 title, *Ian's Walk: A Story About Autism*

- Are the company's books literary, commercial, mass-market, educational? Can you see your work fitting into that type? If you think your fiction is meant to be a literary hardcover, don't send it to a mass-market paperback publisher.

- Is it a company that specializes in a genre or niche (for example, multicultural authors or a strong line of fantasy)? Remember, the one complaint editors make over and over again is that so many writers submit books of a type the company has never published—YA novels sent to a picture book publisher, or nonfiction texts submitted to a dedicated fiction imprint.

- Do you want the wide-ranging and large-scale support of a big publishing house, or the more personalized support of a small press?

- If you're a new author, does the company (or agent) appear to be open to new voices? In *Book Markets for Children's Writers 2016,* pay attention to the description of interests, the freelance potential, and the categories of interest in particular.

- Find other titles the company has published (as you would do for the competition report), and read some. Representative titles of this kind are annually updated in *Book Markets for Children's Writers 2016.*

When you feel confident you've identified a half-dozen or so good markets for your fiction or nonfiction, make use of your research in your query, cover letter, proposal, or whatever materials the publisher requests. Convince the editor, as you would a potential employer in another industry, that you have the work that is best-suited to the company.

Be sure you have the quality of goods to sell! Stay aware of changes in the industry through trade publications such as *Publishers Weekly.* Find blogs and websites by publishing industry insiders. Join the Society of Children's Book Writers and Illustrators (SCBWI) and stay aware of its publications and conferences. Follow news on editors, agents, and other writers. And make others aware of you through networking, a website, and more. Stand on your platform.

Devised

You've been inspired, you've researched, but you still have to do it—write the book, find your voice, and fit the doing of it into your life. The devising of the book can be broken down into two components: (1) the characteristics of writing that need to be developed—voice, style, and structure, and (2) the practicality of accomplishing the writing task—goal-setting, time management, and organization. The first must evolve out of the book you want to write. But here are tips for the latter.

Does Your Manuscript Stand Out?

An editor is swamped with manuscripts on a daily basis and often, after perusing just the first few pages, knows whether an idea is fresh and interesting—or stale as yesterday's bread. While there's no such thing as a completely original idea, there are ways to make sure that your story idea captures an editor's attention.

• Don't follow a trend. If you do, you're likely to lose your voice. Strike out and find new territory to write about.

• Be honest. Make sure your child characters talk and act like real kids. See the sidebar "Authentic Kids" to find out more about what kids are like at different stages.

• Don't preach. All good books impart a message, but if your story is didactic, you'll turn off the reader. Make sure your theme is subtly drawn through your characterization and plot.

• Stay away from anthropomorphic animals. If you're going to include animals in your story, make sure they behave like real animals.

• Don't rhyme. It's very hard to rhyme as well as Dr. Seuss, so if you're writing picture books, try to give your text rhythm and incorporate wordplay without rhyming.

• Have a vision. Strong characters, and a unique way of approaching an idea, creates a book with vision.

Goal Setting

Whatever the projected length or complexity of your book, to become a writer with a successful career you will need to set goals for completing your projects, as well as for approaching editors, revising accepted manuscripts, and so on. Setting goals for your career itself is also important.

• How much do you want to write in a week, a month, three months, six months, a year?

• What kinds of books do you want to write? Do you aspire to write one picture book or three in the coming year? A picture book and a middle-grade novel? Do you want to branch out into plays or mix books with short stories? Add parenting articles to the mix?

• How many submissions or queries do you want to send out in a week, month, and so on?

• How do you deal with rejection when a submission is declined, and how long does it take you to get back on your horse?

• How much income do you want—or need—to generate, in what time frame?

- Can you set aside time to take a children's writing course, either at a local university or writing institute? Many places now offer online courses that allow you to have your work critiqued by class participants and the instructor.

Time Management

Many writers live a dual existence, with a day job as they build their writing careers. They have families and other responsibilities. People doing freelance work such as writing have to be self-starters who know how to manage their time well. Here are some questions to help you determine how you might best use your time.

- How much time can you give to developing concepts, to research?
- How do you balance kids and writing, spouse/partner and writing, home and writing, day job and writing, school and writing?
- What are you willing to give up in order to give more time to your writing? Some television or computer time? Time-consuming meals? Lunch with friends or acquaintances? Volunteer work?
- How can you create a support group for your writing? From your family, fellow writers?
- What amount of time are you willing or able to devote to the business side of a writing career—creating and maintaining a website, networking, attending conferences, making appearances to support your books, tracking submissions, following up with editors, doing financial tasks, and so on?

Use a calendar or PDA to schedule your day, including making appointments with yourself to do the writing and the marketing.

Organization

The workspace: To accomplish your goals and manage your time, you need some practical mechanisms in place.

- Do you have a truly workable space—desk and files devoted to your writing?
- Is your research well-organized? Create a system, whether it's paper or electronic or both. Make notes on sources. Remember those bibliographic skills your English teacher worked hard to drill into your brain.
- Do you have a system for tracking submissions and accounting for finances, like expenses and income?

• Is your technology working for you? Is the hardware in good shape, and does your software help you write and maintain the business side too?

The writing: Everyone has their own techniques for writing. Some write straight through a chapter or section, and go back later for revisions. Others must begin with an outline for the whole piece. Some allow their voice and tone to flow. Others craft these elements carefully.

Prolific author Dean Koontz has revealed in interviews that he still writes on an old Commodore word processor. He doesn't send, or know how to send, emails. He writes out messages and gives them to an assistant to email. The method certainly works for him! But think about the most efficient way for you to optimize the quality and production of your writing. Whether you use index cards, an old typewriter, a Commodore, or the latest Apple product, make sure your method truly works for you.

Organization contributes to your platform. The presentation of your work—in your writing, your communications with editors and colleagues, on your website or blog, in speaking engagements—becomes part of your voice and professional persona.

Queried

When it comes to becoming a *published* writer, queries are quintessential. They represent the bridge from your creative endeavors to becoming a professional. Sure, some submissions require cover letters or website forms, but every writer must conquer the query above all. And the query is a key part of a writer's platform. This section will look at queries, cover letters, and the other elements that make up submission packages.

Queries

In addition to a great book, you also need a great query letter. The query letter is your calling card. It's essentially a pitch. You know what it's like to read a great blurb on a book jacket? Think of your query letter as great jacket copy. Use it to sell your story and your talent.

The basic query consists of these parts:

• Introduction
• Pitch
• Writer (about yourself)
• Closing

Sample Query

Here's what a sample query letter for this Caldecott Honor-winning picture book might have looked like:

Dear Mr. Parker,

Enclosed please find my children's picture book, *When Sophie Gets Angry – Really, Really Angry*. We recently met at the Society of Children's Book Writers and Illustrators conference in Los Angeles, and you invited me to send it to you.

"I want to smash the world to smithereens," says Sophie when her sister takes her stuffed gorilla away from her. She's so angry, in fact, that she kicks, screams, and eventually runs into the woods where she climbs a huge beech tree, looks out over the water, and is comforted by the "wide world." Calm, she returns home, ready to participate in family life.

Tantrums and angry outbursts are common among preschoolers, but, unfortunately, there are very few books that treat this issue in a sensitive – and entertaining – way. *When Sophie Gets Angry* fills a need in the marketplace for real stories that can help small children process their feelings and to understand that anger is a natural emotion. This book will be useful not only to parents but also to educators or anyone who works with children and cares deeply about their emotional needs.

I am a member of the SCBWI and have studied my craft at Gotham Writers' Workshop, a respected writing school based in New York City. I have had several short stories published in *Highlights* magazine for children.

As per your request, I will not submit this work to anyone else while you have it. Thank you for your time and consideration.

Sincerely,

Daphne Davis

Let's look at these four elements.

Introduction (paragraph 1)
This is where you state the basics about your project – the title and type of book. It's also where you mention whatever connection you may have to the editor to whom you're sending it (e.g., you met a conference, were referred by a friend) and also state that the editor had requested the manuscript.

Pitch (paragraphs 2 and 3)
This is the most important part of the query. This is where you sell the idea to the editor. These paragraphs encapsulate the characters and plot of your story. You should establish that your idea is new and compelling and the right concept for that publisher. Indicate your understanding of the marketplace and how your book fills a need within that marketplace.

Writer (paragraph 4)
This is where you'll describe any pertinent background information or writing credits.

Closing (paragraph 5)
Close gracefully and professionally by thanking the editor for her time and consideration. If you've included other materials requested by the publisher, mention that here. The publisher may have requested the complete manuscript, especially if it's a picture book, or perhaps a partial manuscript if it's a longer piece of fiction. Send exactly what's required or requested.

What not to do:

• Don't use fancy paper or fonts. Make sure your query is single-spaced on white paper and use a basic 12-point typeface.

• Don't overtalk or provide excess information. Publishers do not want to hear that your kids and friends love your book. This telegraphs to publishers that you're a beginner.

• Don't misspell the editor's name. Misspellings and questionable grammar are surefire ways to turn off an editor.

Cover Letters

The technical difference between a cover letter and a query, both of which can take a variety of forms, is that the former accompanies a manuscript and the latter does not.

Good cover letters remain the most common accompaniment to fiction. They are simple in both senses of *form*: in their structure, and in custom or professional purpose. Cover letters are a

Sample Cover Letter

Address
Phone Number
Email Address
Date

Editor
Publishing Company
Address

Dear (Editor's name):

I would like to submit the enclosed manuscript for your consideration.

The Light in the Shadows is mystery novel targeting young adults where the main character, Hannah, finds a quartz amulet while staying with her grandmother. Finding the amulet's original owner takes Hannah on a journey that leads to her own past.

After doing some research, I found that Baen Books is currently accepting mystery manuscripts. While the current market is filled with YA mysteries, I think you will find that this book will hook readers right from the start with its strong, relatable characters and elements of real-life drama.

Thank you for your time and consideration. Please note that I am not sending this to other editors until I hear from you.

Sincerely,

Noelle Marin

Sample Outline

Title: *Spies Yesterday and Today*
Audience Age: 12+

Introduction

Chapter I. Good Spy, Bad Spy
    A. Why Spy?

Chapter II. Spies in History
    A. Ancient Egypt
    B. Ancient China
        1. Sun Tzu and *The Art of War*
    C. Elizabethan England
        1. Sir Francis Walsingham's spy network
    D. American Revolution
        1. Nathan Hale
        2. Benedict Arnold
    E. Intelligence Collection
        1. The Pinkerton Agency
    F. Writers Who Spied
        1. Chaucer
        2. Christopher Marlow
        3. T. E. Lawrence

Chapter III. Modern Espionage
    A. Wartime Spies
        1. World War I
        2. World War II
        3. Cold War
            a. CIA
            b. KGB
            c. Alger Hiss, Whittaker Chambers, and
               the Rosenbergs
            d. Gary Powers
    B. Peacetime Spies
    C. Counterintelligence
    D. When Spies Are Caught

Chapter IV. The Science of Spying
    A. Early spy techniques
    B. Spying in space
    C. Modern technology

Chapter V. Future of Espionage

Sample Synopsis

Foolish John

Synopsis

A retold folktale based on a Highlands legend.

There was once a king in ancient Ireland with three sons, the youngest named John. He was taken for a fool by many. When the king's eyes dimmed and he could not see to walk alone, the king sent his two older sons to bring three bottles of water from a well that was said to heal the eyes. John was left behind but decided to travel out on his own.

In the first town he reached, John came upon his two older brothers, who threatened to harm him if he did not return home. Afraid of being lost in the woods at night, John climbed a tree in a green glen, to be safe from the animals and his brothers. Soon, he saw a large brown bear coming toward him. The bear called to John to come down, but John said, "Do you, too, think me a fool?"

"Then let us chat," said the bear and they began to talk. John revealed that he was the king's son, and that he was very hungry. The bear hunted down a buck, and said, "For the son of the king of Ireland, here is a dinner to fill you and keep you warm." John was coaxed down. They roasted the deer and ate. John told the Bear of the Green Glen how his brothers would not let him gather the water to cure their father's sight. Soon, John was so full he fell asleep. He woke in the morning between the paws of the great bear.

The bear told John of the home of a giant who loved the king and would help him. When John and the Bear of the Green Glen told the giant of the king's blindness, the giant put out food that would attract a giant eagle with a painful growth on its head. The giant told John to draw his sword, cut off the growth, and the eagle would do John a service. The grateful eagle picked up John and flew him across the sea, to the Green Isle. There, John filled three bottles of blessed water, and met a girl as beautiful as a gem, called Gemma. After adventures on the Green Isle, the eagle flew John toward home. They saw the two brothers below them.

When the empty-handed brothers saw John on the back of an eagle, with the three bottles of water, they decided to steal the water and take credit for their father's cure, expecting to be given the kingdom to divide. The brothers threw John in a ditch where he stayed for three days. But the eagle, the Bear of the Green Glen, and Gemma, the daughter of the King of the Green Isle, came to John's aid. Gemma opened the water and washed the king's eyes until he could see almost across the sea to the Green Isle.

When the king of Ireland learned what the older sons had done, he asked John, "What are you willing to do to your two brothers?" John replied, "The very thing they wished to do to me," and from that day the brothers were known to be fools. John married the daughter of the king of the Green Isle, and when the ancient king died in peace, they ruled over Erin and the Green Isle together for seventy years and seven.

courteous introduction, and when done properly, can lead you to acceptance in the right circles.

A cover letter should give the basics, but not much more. If it is too long, an editor may see it as wastefully eating into time or as reflective of a writer who can't quite focus or self-edit. Cover letters should indicate:

- That a manuscript is enclosed.
- The basic facts: word length, genre, whether or not the manuscript is a simultaneous submission.
- Other attachments, such as your résumé or a bibliography for certain kinds of fiction.
- Your contact information.

Cover letters may also include:

- The particular needs met by the enclosed manuscript—a theme, topic, hole in the marketplace—and why it works for that publisher and a given readership.
- A short synopsis, perhaps a paragraph.
- Your publication history or relevant background.
- Any other information requested in the publisher's submission guidelines.

A cover letter may include a synopsis of a paragraph or two but technically remains a cover letter because it *covers* an attached manuscript. A query would not, but would ask an editor if the manuscript might be sent along. For book submissions, a longer synopsis is often attached to the cover and manuscript.

Proposals

A proposal is a form of submission package that goes beyond a query alone. Paying attention to writers' guidelines is essential in pulling a proposal together because publishers may have very specific requirements. For those that don't, take hints from others that do. Here are some examples of what is requested by publishers listed in *Book Markets for Children's Writers 2016*.

- Bancroft Press requests a cover letter, résumé, and market analysis.
- Boyds Mills Press, the trade book division of *Highlights for Children* requests a detailed biography and a detailed explantion of competitive titles for nonfiction submissions.
- Charlesbridge, a trade publishing company requests a pro-

posal with synopsis, chapter outline, and first three chapters.

- Children's Book Press, an imprint of Lee & Low, requests a table of contents, market analysis, and projected date of completion.

- Dawn Publications requests a proposal with cover letter, yor vision for the book, and credentials.

Synopsis: When publishers or agents request a synopsis—a summarizing narration of the story or of the information to be included in a book and how it is structured—they may want something as brief as a paragraph in a cover letter or as long as several pages. Some publishers request chapter-by-chapter summaries.

Synopses can be daunting. How much can you convey in so little a space that will present an impactful picture of your book in both substance and style? You must condense but represent, painting a miniature portrait of your work.

Fiction: For fiction, a synopsis should reveal the main characters, point-of-view, setting, basic plot line, conflict, motivation, and theme. Briefly describe pivotal scenes, and include the story's resolution. Convey your book's tone and voice, but do not make your protagonist or narrator speak. You are doing the talking, but write the synopsis in the third person.

Nonfiction: Cover all the major points of the book and let the synopsis make clear your primary purpose or approach in writing the book, the scope of your subject, and why you have structured the information the way you did. If you do this well, it should become clear why you are the right person to write the book.

Aim for clarity when putting together a synopsis, but without sacrificing a style that reflects your book. Look at the blurbs on book dust jackets for some inspiration. These are almost an art form, whose purpose it is to make a book's contents clear and highly appealing.

Outline: In general, publishers look for synopses for fiction and outlines for nonfiction. An outline is a more formal, enumerated list of topics and subtopics to be covered in a book. Outlines may vary by level of detail; in an annotated form they can be not dissimilar to chapter-by-chapter synopses.

Outlines highlight organization, and through that, substance. Whether or not they use the traditional school-taught roman numeral structure, outlines indicate main thoughts or arguments (and sometimes counter-arguments), and supporting detail. Like synopses, they should indicate the theme, angle, or overall approach to the book and to each of the book's major parts, as well as the book's conclusions. As always, check a targeted publisher's submission requirements to see if they give guidance on the level of detail preferred.

Bibliography: As the children's book publishing industry grew over recent decades, its expectations of research quality increased, as discussed in earlier pages. A wise author will be sure that a solid bibliography, or list of sources, accompanies nonfiction submissions, and some fiction as well (think historical fiction). A good bibliography need not be as scholarly as an accompaniment to a graduate school thesis, but it should be pointedly compiled, comprehensive, and accurate in its form. That is, you want to use high-quality sources that are relevant, and not just pile them on randomly to impress; they won't.

Build a strong bibliography (which reflects the quality of your proposed manuscript) with primary sources—original documents, expert interviews—carrying the most weight. Secondary sources should be solid. Avoid encyclopedias, with few exceptions.

A strong bibliography convinces editors that you have done the research, thought through the project, and can back up what you've written. It indicates that you are likely to put a premium on accuracy, and that you can create your own book out of a synthesis of wide-ranging information. It reassures editors and their legal departments that plagiarism of ideas or language will not be an issue. In this age of James Frey, Jayson Blair, and others, that is an important concern across the industry.

The bibliography you send an editor may not be the one you include in an appendix in your finished book, but parts of it could be, depending on the age of your targeted audience. That's a plus.

Don't forget to use appropriate bibliographic formatting. See page 34 for a sample bibliography.

Résumés and author biographies: Résumés can be the coin of the realm in publishing, as in any industry, and should be well-constructed and regularly updated. Sure, your manuscript will ultimately be evaluated for itself, but a résumé may be the token you pay to get it read. Editors judge résumés or author biographies not just for experience and qualifications, but for writers' ability present themselves.

Résumés should include your contact information (name, address, phone, email), work experience, education, and relevant professional organizations to which you belong. For writers, this might include the Society of Children's Book Writers and Illustrators (SCBWI). Résumés may also include an objective, which should highlight what you want to accomplish with your writing and especially the particular book or project you are proposing.

Tailor one résumé specifically to writing, even if you are employed in another field. One-size-fits-all does not work well. For your writing résumé, emphasize your relevant credentials and, depending on the book you are proposing, your background in given topics. For example, if you're looking to write a book on health for children, it's a plus if you've been trained as a nurse or dietician. If you're writing a novel that takes place in India in the time of Gandhi, a degree in Asian history counts for much.

An author biography is basically a narrative version of your background. Some publishers want a very brief (one-paragraph) biography included in the cover letter; others want a longer one (one or two pages), attached.

For writers who have been published, the résumé should be accompanied by a list of publishing credits. If you have credits in a wide variety of categories, tailor them to the work you are currently pursuing. So, if you've written middle-grade novels and articles for the local newspaper on zoning regulations and recent town elections, you don't need to include the latter.

Sample chapters or clips: If you have sent a query and been invited to forward sample chapters, or if the publisher you are targeting accepts proposal packages that include samples, select either those that the publisher requests—often, the first three chapters—or those that best represent your book and style of writing. If the book is still in the idea or outline stage, you might send clips. These too should be reflective of the kind of writing you are now proposing, in terms of target age, style, and subject.

Competitive titles and market research: Publishers increasingly ask prospective authors to look for competitive titles already published (see pages 15–19) and also for suggestions about where and how the proposed book may be sold, especially if it is a special interest title. A science title might be appropriate for gift shops at children's museums across the country; a regional novel should be marketed to local independent bookstores and regional Barnes & Noble stores; perhaps sports organizations would be interested in a baseball book.

Manuscript Formatting

Whether you send your manuscript as hard or electronic copy, formatting is an important issue for editors. They don't want to spend time adjusting their procedures to the idiosyncrasies of a writer's software or struggle through a manuscript that's hard to read because the type is too small or crowded or fuzzy.

Show your professionalism by always following the best manuscript formatting practices. Always retain a copy for yourself. See page 38 for an example of how to format a book, and follow these guidelines:

- Use high-quality 8½x11 white bond paper.
- Double-space manuscript text; leave 1- to 1½-inch margins on the top, bottom, and sides.
- Create a title page:

Sample Bibliography

The Northwest Passage and Arctic Warming
<u>Audience</u>: Middle-grade

Arctic Drift.. Clive Cussler and Dirk Cussler. Waterville, ME: Paragon, 2008.

Arctic Labyrinth: The Quest for the Northwest Passage. Glyn Williams. Berkeley, CA: University of California Press, 2011.

Arctic Passages: A Unique Small-boat Journey Through the Great Northern Waterway. John Bockstoce. New York: Hearst Marine Books, 1991.

Arctic Warming Unlocking A Fabled Waterway. Jackie Northam. First in a six-part series, National Public Radio. www.npr.org/2011/08/15/139556207/arctic-warming-unlocking-a-fabled-waterway.

Changes in the Arctic Environment and the Law of the Sea. Edited by Myron H. Nordquist, et al. Martinus Nijhof, 2010.

Interview with Dr. Vladimir Romanovsky of the Geophysical Institute, University of Alaska, Fairbanks, AK. January 2009. Arctic Warming, web-site collection of interviews with experts on Arctic warming, www.arcticwarming.net/node/70

"The North Pole Is Melting." David Biello. *Scientific American.* September 21, 2007. www.scientificamerican.com/article.cfm?id=the-north-pole-is-melting

The Northwest Passage. Documentary by Sprague Theobald. Hole in the Wall productions. Newport, Rhode Island, 2009.

The Search for the Northwest Passage, Great Journeys series. Jill Foran. Weigl Publishers, 2005.

"Will the Opening of the Northwest Passage Transform Global Shipping Anytime Soon?" Anne Casselman. *Scientific American.* November 10, 2008. http://www.scientificamerican.com/article.cfm?id=opening-of-north-west-passage

Sample Resume

Ellen Brooke
Address
Telephone Number
Email

Experience
- Published author of children's stories, articles, and books, and adult nonfiction articles
- Fifth-grade teacher, Mytown Intermediate School, 1998–present
- Sales associate, Baa Baa Black Sheep Bookstore, Mytown, Ohio, 1994-1998

Education
- B.A., English and Education, Greene College, cum laude, 1997
- M.F.A candidate, Greene College School of Fine Arts

Published Credits
- *Girls: Aces in Sports* (Kiddo Publishing, 2011)
- *A Secret Passage* (Fiction Company, 2008)
- "Circle the Wagons" (*U.S. History for Kids Magazine,* September 2007)
- "Why the Library's Children's Section Must Grow" (series of three articles, *Mytown* weekly paper, spring 2003)
- "Teaching Etiquette in a Third-Grade Classroom" (*Teachers Share Magazine,* November 1999)

Professional Memberships
- Society of Children's Book Writers and Illustrators
- National Council of Teachers of English

Awards
- Kids' Choice Award, Ohio, for *A Secret Passage*

- In the upper left corner, type your name, address, phone number, and email address.
- In the upper right corner, indicate the page count, or for a picture book, the word count.
- About 5 inches down, centered, type the title of your book in capital letters.
- Two lines below the title, type your byline.
- Create a chapter opening page:
  - Type your last name, and the title (in shortened form, if necessary) in the upper left corner.
  - Type the page number in the upper right corner.
  - Start the chapter halfway down the page.
- On following pages, continue to type your name/title in the left corner and page number in the right corner.

Picture Book Formatting

Publishers who accept picture books usually request the complete manuscript, but editors do not expect—nor want—to see artwork unless the author is also the illustrator. If you are not a professionally trained artist, an editor will likely prefer to find the illustrator separately.

Picture book manuscripts may be prepared in the same way as other manuscripts, except you may begin the book on the title page, about four lines down from the byline. On following pages, continue to type the story without breaks.

Many publishers do not request picture book dummies, but some do. Send one only if requested. For a standard 32-page picture book, take eight sheets of paper, fold them in half, and number them as on page 40; this will not include the end papers that line the book's front and back cover. Lay out your text and a brief description of the accompanying illustrations, being sure that the words and pictures fit together as they should. Picture books also come in other lengths, from 16 to 64 pages.

If you are an author-illustrator and plan to submit artwork, never send the original art. Send copies only, and the appropriate size self-addressed, stamped envelope (SASE) if you need the materials returned.

Mail or Electronic Submissions

Increasingly publishers prefer electronic submissions, some using email messages only, some with attachments, some using website forms. Other publishers prefer to continue receiving hard copy. Follow the submission guidelines closely. *Book Markets for Children's Writers 2016* includes extensive research on these preferences, but always double-check publisher websites for updates.

Picture Book Dummy

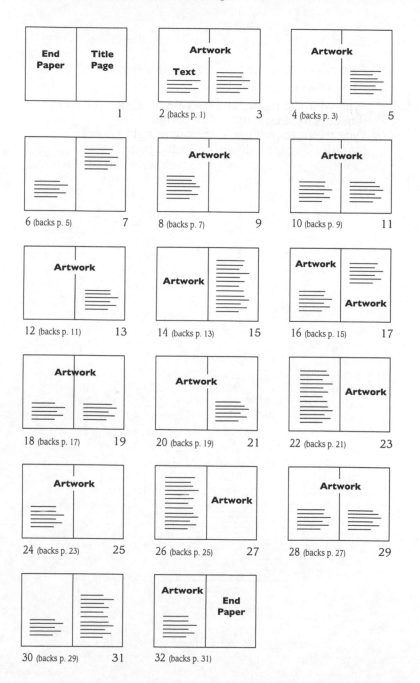

Manuscript Format

Title Page

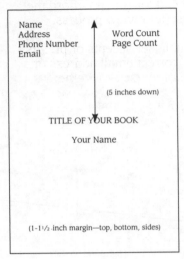

Name
Address
Phone Number
Email

Word Count
Page Count

(5 inches down)

TITLE OF YOUR BOOK

Your Name

(1-1½-inch margin—top, bottom, sides)

New Chapter

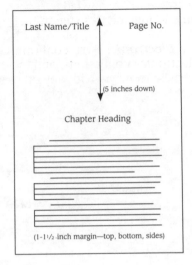

Last Name/Title   Page No.

(5 inches down)

Chapter Heading

(1-1½-inch margin—top, bottom, sides)

Following Pages

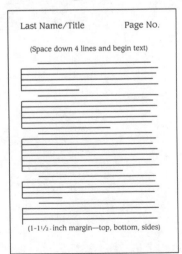

Last Name/Title   Page No.

(Space down 4 lines and begin text)

(1-1½-inch margin—top, bottom, sides)

Mail: With a cover letter on top, gather the pages. Do not staple them. To mail the manuscript, use a 9x12 or 10x13 manila envelope and send it First Class or Priority. Do not use certified or registered mail. If the publisher returns manuscripts (many do not), include an SASE marked First Class, or, for foreign markets, enclose an International Reply Coupon (IRC) for return postage.

Some editors will return an enclosed self-addressed, stamped postcard to acknowledge receipt; many no longer can afford the time to include this step in their manuscript review process.

Electronic: First, confirm that a publisher accepts or prefers electronic submissions, and locate the correct email address or website form. As with any other submission, check whether the editor wants a query, complete manuscript, or proposal package.

Then, confirm what form is acceptable: email messages with no attachments, or, if attachments are allowed, what kind.

- Unless otherwise indicated in the publisher's submission guidelines, make the email message—your electronic cover letter—brief.

- Make sure that you check your spelling and grammar. Don't use fancy fonts or colors or anything that would complicate reading your email.

- Be sure to include your contact information: name, adress, phone number. Your email address is already included when sending an electronic message.

- Guidelines sometimes request specific information in the email subject line, for example: "Query, YA fiction."

- Don't be informal in style because you're sending an email. Remain professional.

- If attachments are preferable, confirm which kind: Micrsoft Word documents (check if .doc and/or .docx is accepted); Adobe PDF; or RFT (Rich Text Format). Attach documents as directed by your email program.

Sold

As exciting as it is to receive a positive response to a submission, your job is far from over once you've sold your idea or the book itself. You'll interact with an editor, abide by a contract, work on publicity. You will manage your own business concerns, by developing online and print promotional materials; tracking your submissions and work that's been sold; monitoring income, taxes, office expenses; and so on. You'll be working on the whole package of being a published writer.

The Platform: Promote!

Having a platform is all the rage in the age of Twitter and Facebook. A platform is about presenting yourself to the world at large. Small as your credentials may seem at first, writers who truly want to find a market and be published must *brand* themselves today. Editors, marketing staff, agents, other writers, teachers, librarians, and especially your young readers should know who you are and what you write—and, of course, buy your books.

This is not to say you should be friending and tweeting and linking every day. Begin building a platform gradually, after some self-examination as a writer. First, identify yourself with genres, subjects of interest, a style, a voice, a perspective, and eventually how these are expressed in your specific writing credits. Next, determine how best to communicate your abilities, what you have to offer, and why others should be interested. Finally, create ways, reflective of you, for others to find you and your work.

The components of a writers' platform today might be divided into three parts, and they take place before and after you've sold your book(s): submissions, electronic, and traditional.

Submissions: The materials you submit are core. They represent you and your capabilities. What is it that interests you in writing? What subjects, what form, what voice, what goals, what readers? How do you want to present yourself to editors and readers, and how do you match your work with editors who are likely to be responsive to your particular platform? How do you write that right query or proposal?

Electronic: Use electronic media to connect and promote in the form of a website, blog, online articles, social media, online forums and groups, even podcasts.

Websites: If a business doesn't have a website today, we may very well question its solidity. That is increasingly true for writers too. A website is a virtual business card, a résumé, and a marketing tool rolled into one. Developing and maintaining an effective site will help draw readers to you by highlighting you and your books.

When developing a website, you will need to consider the creative side and the numbers side. Creatively, look at the information to include, the kind of design that represents you, what works on the landing/home page, how interactive it should be, whether you want to develop it yourself or hire someone with website design expertise. On the numbers side, you will want to know how much traffic the site gets, from where, the most popular features, the keywords that best allow search engines to find you (SEO, or search engine optimization), and how much time you can give the site without taking away from your writing. Here are some other suggestions for your website:

- Include a brief biography, publishing credits, and contact information.

- Emphasize connection. Reflect your personality. Give the website some depth and make it well-rounded and easy to use.

- Consider including *extras*, especially for child or teacher use, such as games or activities related to your writing, or a free ebook or stories. Perhaps you might compose a free newsletter to which readers can subscribe.

- Do you want a comments or forum page? A page of FAQs? Links to publishers' or other writers' websites?

- Remember to refresh or create new content regularly.

- When you publish a new title, add links to Amazon or other booksellers.

Blogs: If you're going to write a blog—potentially a great mechanism for a publishing platform—commit to doing it well.

- Decide what it should contain. Will it be all about your writing or your subjects of interest, or will it be more wide-ranging?

- Will it target readers of your books, other writers, and the publishing community? Teens, children, adults?

- Will you bring in content from other people by doing interviews, for example, with writers or editors?

- Consider participating on other writers' blogs or websites, and inviting them to contribute to yours.

- How often can you post to it—daily, weekly, biweekly?

Other high-tech routes: Many other technological means of promoting and building your platform are possible. Among them:

- Create a presence on Amazon.com for you and your book— explore Amazon Advantage to promote yourself, or Create Space to self-publish.

- Use Facebook, Twitter, or other social media to talk about your writing and publishing.

- Connect with other writers on online forums or sites dedicated to literature, writing, books, or publishing, such as Absolute Write.

- Check for blogs and other sites specifically about children's writing and keep up to date on people and publishers.

- Write online articles to showcase your areas of expertise, on sites such as Demand Media and About.com. Upload to

Websites, Blogs, and Social Media

Webhosting
- Bluehost.com
- Dreamhost.com
- Godaddy.com
- Hostmonster.com
- Justhost.com
- Yahoo: www.webhostingconsumer.com

Blog Platforms
- Blogger.com (Google)
- Tumblr.com
- Wix.com
- Wordpress.org

Miscellaneous Writing and Publishing Sites
- Absolute Write: http://absolutewrite.com
- Authonomy.com
- Cynsations: www.cynthialeitichsmith.com
- Gather.com
- Goodreads.com
- Verla Kay: www.verlakay.com
- Kidlit.com
- The Purple Crayon: www.underdown.org

Online article opportunities:
- About.com
- Demand Media: www.demandmedia.com
- How To Do Things: www.howtodothings.com

Scribd.com, "the world's largest social reading and publishing company."

Traditional: While electronic may trump print for promotion in some ways, there's no substitution for old-fashioned networking. Publishing promotion has long consisted of distributing print materials such as business cards, postcards, brochures, or bookmarks; attending conferences to network; doing bookstore readings, school visits, and other speaking engagements; participating in professional organizations; developing connections with the press, and so on.

- Join professional organizations. The premier children's writer group, SCBWI, has been mentioned earlier. Consider joining organizations related to your subject area. If you're a science writer for children, for example, look at the National Association of Science Writers (www.nasw.org). Mystery writers might join Mystery Writers of America (www.mysterywriters.org).

- Develop a presentation about your book and/or related subjects for schools, bookstores, and libraries.

- Print materials are still important when you attend conferences or speaking engagements, and for general personal networking. Have business cards, bookmarks, postcards, brochures, or flyers to hand out. Make sure they are well-designed, appealing, and professional in appearance. Ask local bookstores to make some of your materials available.

- When you've published a book, arrange school visits and bookstore or library readings, or speak at a writers' conference.

- Send press releases to local and regional publications or radio programs. Put together a press kit about your book, including a brief biography and credits if any, an excerpt from the book, synopsis, a picture of the cover, a picture of you, and your print promotional material (business card, postcard, etc.) with information on price and availability. If you have reviews, add those. Offer these to local reporters and editors and let them know you're available for an interview.

- Some writers cross-promote with groups of other writers: "You talk about my book on your blog or when you're at a conference, and I'll do the same." So, network away with a critique group, online groups, and so on.

- Between your online connections (website, blog, forums, social networking, etc.) and your real-time connections (critique group, conferences, presentations, school visits, etc.), start gathering email and/or regular addresses for a mailing list to send information to promote your publications.

The Business: Rights, Contracts, and Payment

Before you're fully promoting your sold book, you will have been offered and signed a contract. It will include the purchase of certain rights, payment, deadlines, and other legal issues. New writers signing book contracts without the aid of a literary agent would be wise to seek legal or other business advice from someone who specializes in intellectual property law and knows the publishing industry. At the very least become well-read on the subject, should you go into contract negotiations on your own. Another place to get advice is the Authors Guild (www.authorsguild.org), whose legal staff will review book contracts as part of

Guild membership benefits. For a discussion and list of agents, see pages 461.

Here we offer just the basics of book contracts.

Copyright: Even without registering, you own the copyright to your book. Unless the publisher is offering to buy the book outright (unlikely) or it was commissioned as a work-for-hire (see page 49), you hold the copyright. Once your book is sold, however, the publisher often registers the copyright and pays the fee for you.

Rights granted: The contract will include language that says you guarantee your book is completely original. You grant the publisher certain rights to your book, including the primary right to produce and distribute it as a bound book, whether hardcover or paperback, trade or mass-market, or, increasingly today, electronic.

Subsidiary rights include reprint rights, foreign rights, electronic rights, audio rights, film/TV/dramatic rights, merchandising rights, and book club rights. Subsidiary rights should be handled very carefully. Among the most argued issues in publishing today is electronic rights. As new publishing formats like electronic readers have developed, publishers have tried to extend their reach under contracts signed before the media even existed.

The kind of book you've written will affect the rights you'll be asked to convey, and at what payment rate. You won't be selling film rights for a concept book, but you might just hit the jackpot and see your teen novel become a TV show, like Cecily von Ziegesar with *Gossip Girl*. Picture books with great characters could give rise to product licensing arrangements. Think Olivia and Fancy Nancy. Remember that picture book authors may have different arrangements because they split rights and royalties with an illustrator.

Rights generally may be held as long as the copyright, which under U.S. law is the lifetime of the author plus 70 years.

Payment: For the right to produce and sell your book, you receive a payment in return. For books, this usually means a royalty, and sometimes an advance. The royalty may be a single percentage across the life of the book (7.5, 10, 12.5, or 15 percent of the cover price), or it may be graduated—a sliding scale that depends on the number of books sold (10 percent for the first 5,000, and 12.5 percent for the next 5,000). Royalties vary between paperbacks and hardcovers, trade and mass-market.

An advance is "taken against royalties." That is, the author is given an amount before the book goes on sale that is subtracted from the royalties earned from actual sales.

The contract will include when and how often royalties are paid. They may be paid quarterly, semi-annually, or annually.

Finally, note that the royalty system can be quite complicated and varies among publishers. Royalty calculations may include printer costs, discounts to booksellers, returns, and sometimes other costs. This is another reason to have legal and business advice when negotiating a book contract.

Reversion and out-of-print clauses: The publisher's part under the contract is to print, produce, and distribute the book. If it does not perform these tasks, it has not honored the contract and the rights may revert to the author. A reversion clause includes a time frame for publication, and if that deadline is not met, the author may also usually keep any advance.

If a publisher produces a book but lets it go out of print after some time, an out-of-print clause says the rights return to the author, who may take the book to another publisher for reprint. Many authors make an effort to find new publishers for out-of-print books or to offer them in another form. Today, that can mean self-publishing through print-on-demand (POD), or offering an electronic version through an ebook publisher.

Option clause: The option clause gives the publisher the right to have the first opportunity to read the author's next book and make an offer to publish it, within a reasonable amount of time. This clause has many variations, and many people are cautious about it. Some argue it is unnecessary.

Electronic rights: Electronic rights are changing practically before authors' and publishers' eyes, as the pace of technology continues to quicken and ebook publishing has begun to overtake print publishing. In May 2011, Amazon sold more Kindle books than print books for the first time ever.

Electronic rights have been at the center of arguments between authors and publishers of many kinds, from newspaper publishers to book publishers, for a decade and more now. New book contracts handle these rights more directly, but the question "What is a book?" is still being hammered out. Get good legal advice about selling these rights; the Authors Guild has a strong viewpoint and some basic recommendations:

- An author should be fairly compensated whether his or her work is in print, an ebook, on the Internet, in a database, or in any other digital form.

- Check the Grant of Rights clause carefully to see how it covers electronic rights. Publishers try to get the broadest rights they can.

- Check the royalty clause to see if electronic formats have a different payment structure than print.

- Publishers may want to assign digital versions of your book to another company. Decide whether that is in your best interest.

For more advice from the Authors Guild on this complex topic, go to www.authorsguild.org/services/legal_services/electronic_rights.html.

Work-for-hire: Some publishers want to purchase books outright, with the author surrendering any claim to copyright. Educational publishers in particular may assign books in series to authors, and want to retain the rights to all the titles in the series. Books written as works-for-hire are developed either by employees as part of their job, or by freelancers (independent contractors) who are specifically commissioned and must sign a specific work-for-hire agreement.

The advantage of work-for-hire arrangements can be that a writer is asked to do a series of books for a publisher. Another advantage is that, because all rights are being purchased, the payment—a flat, project fee in many cases—may be relatively high. Unlike a royalty arrangement, payment is received on completion of the project, rather than as books are sold. Many authors consider this possibility an assurance of steady income.

Self-publishing, subsidy, and POD: If you're considering self-publishing, understand that you will assume the cost and responsibility of printing, publishing, and promoting your book. You can write your book, design it, find a printer, work out a marketing plan, and sell it. As difficult as it is, there have been some major self-publishing success stories, including *Eragon*.

Ebook self-publishing is growing rapidly. Amazon is at the forefront with its Digital Text Platform (DTP), but other companies are also making strides in this field. They include FastPencil, Lulu, Publish Green, Scribd, and Smashwords.

Some companies—subsidy publishers—will take on some of these tasks for a fee; they produce the book, and do a limited degree of marketing and distribution.

Print-on-demand (POD) publishers will print and ship limited numbers of your book, and may handle a few other services, for a fee. The advantage of POD is that costs can be controlled through limited printings. Even some mainstream publishing companies are now using POD.

While these publishing choices may be viable for writers who are committed to seeing their work in print, self-publishing, subsidy publishing, and POD publishing all have pitfalls. Be cautious. Authors may be taken advantage of, or end up taking on more than they know how to handle. Do extensive research on what services companies offer (whether an independent printer down

Parts of a Contract

Book contracts can be very complex and include many more clauses than listed here. These are the basic clauses found in most publishers' contracts.

- Grant of Rights: This clause near the beginning of the contract says you "grant and assign" or "convey and transfer" specified rights to your book. The rights include the primary right authorizing the company to publish your work in a designated form. Later clauses may cover subsidiary rights.
- Subsidiary Rights: These may include reprint rights, electronic rights, audio, foreign, book club, merchandise, film/TV/dramatic, and others.
- Author's Representation and Warranties: You guarantee that the manuscript is your original work, and yours alone; it does not infringe on another copyright; it has not been published elsewhere; and it contains nothing libelous, obscene, or in violation of privacy. While the latter is not much of an issue for children's writers, the confirmation that your work is completely original and not owned by anyone else is very important in this day of plagiarism claims.
- Manuscript Delivery: You guarantee to deliver an acceptable manuscript to the publisher in an agreed-upon form by a certain date.
- Acceptance of Manuscript: The publisher acknowledges that you have developed the manuscript as required, and accepts it.
- Editing: With this clause, the writer gives consent for a certain degree of editing. The clause sets out a schedule for editing, and the review and return of the manuscript by the author.
- Obligation to Publish: Under the contract, the publisher is committed to publishing a book within a certain period of time.
- Payment: The royalty clause sets out the arrangements for the advance and royalty, whether fixed or on a sliding scale. It may also indicate that the author has a right to request a review of the publisher's "books," as in accounting statements; this is sometimes included in an Accounting Statements clause. A Statements and Payments clause may also detail when payments and accountings will be made.
- Marketing: The publisher agrees to promote and market the book. It may include the size of the print run, and other specifics about how marketing will be done.
- Reversion: A reversion clause says that if the publisher does not produce and sell the book within a set time, the rights revert to the author, who may take the book elsewhere and possibly keep any advance. Reversion clauses may also indicate that after publication, should the publisher intend to discontinue the book, the publisher will give notice and rights will revert to the author within a given time period.
- Option: An option clause, sometimes a focus of dispute, gives the publisher the right to look first at the author's next book.

the street or a full-blown subsidy publisher) and what they don't, and costs. Have any contracts reviewed by a lawyer or a knowledgeable business advisor.

Revised

It's the end of the day: You've sold an editor on an idea and the manuscript, and you've signed a contract. You're ready to turn to revisions. Any successful writer will tell you how important they are. Revisions are the last step before putting a polished book—your best efforts—out into the world.The revision process is also important in terms of your career: Developing a strong writer-editor relationship can mean the difference between being a one-hit wonder and extending your publishing success.

May authors suggest putting the manuscript down for a few days before beginning revisions. At times authors become too close with their manuscript, and editing your own words can be a difficult process. A few days and a fresh mind will allow you to look at the manuscript more objectively.

One suggestion is to read the manuscript out loud to check for sentence flow. Sometimes hearing things spoken allows you to hear when things are too wordy.

And so now you've been inspired. You've researched. You've devised your book and queried. The book sold and the revisions are done. You've put together a complete creation and others will soon share it. On to the next . . . and a promising writing career.

Articles

The Year in Review: A Recap of Children's Publishing in 2015

by Michelle McCormick

It's time again to reflect on the notable accomplishments of the last twelve months. Those in the world of children's publishing can sit back and relax, because it was a good year! Company profits were up; new imprints welcomed new talent; independent booksellers enjoyed a resurgence in popularity; diversity stayed on the short list of industry goals; and social media and the digital universe continued reshaping the old guard. So without further ado, here are the highlights of the year in children's publishing.

Vloggers, Bloggers, and Bears...Oh, My!

If location is everything in real estate, promotion is everything in publishing. Celebrities, with their built-in legions of followers, have long been courted by publishers. Now, thanks to our ever-expanding digital world, celebrities aren't just created in Hollywood anymore. YouTube and personal blogs have made stars out of many a common folk, and the publishing companies are paying attention.

Indeed, the first publishing imprint devoted entirely to "digital innovators" launched in late 2014. Keywords Press (a division of Simon and Schuster's Atria Publishing Group) cranked out its first tentative title in November of 2014 and went full bore with six titles in 2015. "There are a lot of superstars out there who have everyone's attention," says Senior Editor Jhanteigh Kupihea. "The way we figure out who to pursue for book deals is finding people who have a story to tell beyond whatever work they're doing on the platform that they're best known for. For us, it's more about creating a book that makes sense for that author or for that voice and for that readership" (*Publisher's Weekly*, February 2015).

The jury is still out on the success of creating book authors from scratch or making readers out of people who prefer videos, but the 2015 results are promising, with respectable sales by the likes of YouTube royalty PewDiePie, Connor Franta, and Zoe Sugg, as well as blog sensations such as Jessica Shyba. Heads up, writers! This may be the back door into the publishing world you're looking for.

FanFiction (yes, it's one word)

Plagiarism is such an ugly word. Let's just call it FanFiction instead. Long present in the dark, back alleys of the Internet, FanFiction— the practice of adopting another author's characters and rewriting his or her stories to make them one's own—can present a hornet's nest of legal issues for traditional publishing houses. However, like bloggers and vloggers, the better authors of FanFiction have a large and loyal following, which makes them an untapped and potentially huge market for publishers.

With the release of Rainbow Rowell's YA bestseller *Fangirl* in 2013, the concept of FanFiction was effectively introduced to the mainstream reading public. Her fictional FanFic characters Simon and Baz (Harry Potter and Draco Malfoy) were so popular that Rowell created a spin-off novel starring the two. In September 2015 *Carry On* hit the bookstores with great fanfare (pun intended).

More publishers are now beginning to embrace FanFiction. Grosset & Dunlap, Disney Publishing Worldwide, and Amazon's Kindle Worlds have each stuck a cautious toe in these murky waters by securing licenses from the parent product, be it book, toy, or movie. Macmillan Children's Publishing Group, who owns *The Lunar Chronicles*, used FanFiction to promote the final book in the series by hosting a 2015 FanFic contest. The originator of the series, Marissa Meyer, launched her own career by creating FanFiction and FanArt and whole-heartedly supports the fandom her series has generated: "The great thing about being in a fandom is that you're not alone in your room with books that you love. You have access to the Internet, and you can share and connect with others who feel the same way you do about books, and a great community grows over time" (*Publishers Weekly*, November 2015).

Free to Be You and Me

Celebrating diversity is nothing new in children's publishing. However, in 2015 diversity became even more diverse, and the proponents of it even more outspoken.

Who can forget J.K. Rowling publicly outing Dumbledore eight years ago? In 2015 she reiterated her position in a tweet heard 'round the world: Q: Why did you say Dumbledore is gay? I just don't see him that way. JKR: Maybe because gay people just look like....people. Rowling has clearly lost her patience with the narrow minded of the world, and she is not alone in her opinions. In 2015 David Pilkey, author of the Captain Underpants series, enthusiastically revealed that Harold, one of his main characters, grows up to marry a man.

A host of other respected children's authors, with Ellen Oh at the forefront, staged a Twitter coup in April 2014 when BookCon announced an all-white author line-up for its annual convention. From the uproar rose the We Need Diverse Books (WNDB) Initiative, which continued to gain momentum throughout 2015. BookCon got the point, and at this year's gathering there were not one, but two panels addressing diversity.

"Outside forces are changing publishing; now it's up to publishers to change it from the inside," says award winning YA author Sherman Alexie. "Something's wrong when television is more diverse than publishing." He also made it clear that the responsibility doesn't just lie with publishers. "It's up to us to go to the bookstores and buy shitloads of multicultural books. If you can't afford to do that, go your library and demand they stock them" (*Publisher's Weekly,* May 2015).

BookCon wasn't the only event around the country to respond to the concerns of WNDB. At this year's Society of Children's Book Writers and Illustrators (SCBWI) winter conference in New York City, the moderator of the marketplace panel urged the publishers in attendance to address diversity in children's publishing. At ALA's annual conference in San Francisco, authors of graphic novels led a discussion on gender, sexuality, and racial diversity in their genre. Independent booksellers around the country have started their own WNDB initiatives, as well. Internationally, Pope Francis got in on the action in his support of

Piccolo Uovo (Little Egg), an Italian children's book featuring gay penguins, lesbian rabbits, a single parent hippo, a mixed race dog couple, and kangaroos that have adopted polar bears. "His holiness is grateful for the thoughtful gesture and for the feelings which it [the book] evoked, hoping for an always more fruitful activity in the service of young generations and the spread of genuine human and Christian values," wrote Peter B. Wells, Assessor for General Affairs of the Secretariat of State (*The Guardian*, August 2015).

It's definitely a brave new world out there, and publishers are responding in kind. In 2015 Interlude Press, a boutique publisher of LGBTQ (Lesbian, Gay, Bisexual, Transgender, Queer) romantic fiction, launched a new YA imprint, Duet.

"Since the day we started building a business plan for Interlude Press, we wanted to develop an imprint appropriate for teenage readers featuring new voices and fresh perspectives on LGBTQ characters," said Annie Harper, managing editor of Interlude Press and Duet. "Our goal is to publish compelling stories by various authors featuring diverse characters any reader can identify with" (*Publisher's Weekly*, February 2015).

Bye-Bye, E-Book

Ok, maybe it's not as dramatic as all that, but in 2015 we watched the novelty of e-books continue to wear off. At the SCBWI winter conference this year, Stephanie Owens Lurie, associate publisher at Disney Hyperion, summed up the industry-wide trend: "E-books aren't doing as well as they used to; last year they plateaued and this year we're seeing them trend downward. People are abandoning their Kindles for phones. Barnes & Noble is abandoning the Nook business." Referencing a recent Nielsen survey, she added, "Kids prefer real books, and that's the kind of disruption I like" (*Publishers Weekly*, February 2015).

E-books for the average reader may be diminishing in popularity, but ink-on-paper hasn't. Indeed, 2015 finishes on a note of optimism for authors, publishers, and booksellers alike. Children's sales are up across the board, particularly in YA. Laura Godwin, vice president and publisher of Henry Holt Books for Young Readers, stated at the SCBWI winter conference, "Unlike the music business, which has seen a huge drop in revenue, we have not. The perceived value of the physical book has held up. Picture books have rebounded from the retreat of previous years to something that feels like a renaissance. The growth of social media, and the very active children's community on it, provides opportunities we've never had before" (*Publishers Weekly*, February 2015).

I Tweet, Therefore I am

Social media has taken on a life of its own. No one is exempt from its reach, including the publishing industry. "Ten years ago, prognosticators were sure social networks would usher in a new era for publishing. Five years later, social media spelled doom for the industry as a whole. Yet, instead of transforming publishing into a mass of niche blogs and feeds or bringing about the end of the business, social media has become a set sophisticated tools for matching content to reader interests, growing communities and building brands" (Joe Hyrkin, *Entrepreneur*, April 2015).

Writing good books isn't enough anymore—authors are expected to build brands through social media, as Stephanie Owens Lurie explains: "Fans now expect to be able to interact with writers. An author like Rick Riordan goes where the kids are online, and feeds their insatiable appetite for content"(*Publisher's Weekly*, February 2015). Like it or not, authors have to digitally mingle with their fans. John Green, for example, has a whopping 4.7 million followers on Twitter; J.K. Rowling, 5.9 million. You get the idea. And so do publishing companies.

In 2013 Little, Brown Books For Young Readers launched Novl, a sort of centralized website for the social media activities of its authors. It was so successful that in 2015 LBYR turned Novl into a digital imprint that sells short-form, low-priced content on a monthly basis. Tina McIntyre, executive director of strategic planning and digital publisher for LBYR, oversees Novl. She notes that the imprint will offer a mix of established and new talent, but that any who are represented must be active on social media. Why? Because that's where the kids are!

When I Grow Up, I Want An Imprint Named After Me

A handful of new imprints emerged in 2015, some of which were named after the talent appointed to head or inspire them:

- Little, Brown launched James Patterson's children's imprint, called (and cutely uncapitalized) jimmy patterson.

- Simon and Schuster Children's Publishing launched an imprint under Atheneum Books called Caitlyn Dlouhy Books, headed by—you guessed it—Caitlyn Dlouhy!

- Macmillan Children's Publishing Group gave a new imprint to publisher, Erin Stein, who ingeniously named it Imprint.

- Quarto Publishing, USA, has appointed Josalyn Moran to head its new imprint, Seagrass Press.

- Little Pickle Press, headed by publisher, Rana Diorio, launched Relish Media, its YA imprint.

- Quarto Publishing Group selected Charles Nurnberg to develop a new children's imprint called Moondance Press, which is slated for launch in 2016.

- The New York Review of Books launched a new paperback imprint, NYRB Kids.

- And last, but certainly not least, bestselling children's author and illustrator Cornelia Funke went beyond heading an imprint to starting her own publishing company called Breathing Books.

And the Award Goes to.....

We would be remiss if we didn't celebrate some of the great hits of 2015. But where to start? Literary awards are plentiful (a more daunting list to summarize there never was). That said, we must certainly give a shout out to this year's Newbery and Caldecott winners: author Kwame Alexander for *The Crossover,* and illustrator Dan Santat for *The Adventures of Beekle: An Unimaginary Friend.* Well done, gentlemen.

Of course, there are plenty of other worthy titles to mention, but how does one narrow it down? Well, it is all about children's publishing, so why not ask the kids themselves? Started in 2008 by the Children's Book Council (CBC) and Every Child a Reader (ECR), the annual Children's and Teens Choice Book Awards program is the only national award voted on by children and teens. Here are their picks for 2015:

- Kindergarten to 2nd Grade Book of the Year: *Eva and Sadie and the Worst Haircut EVER!* by Jeff Cohen, illustrated by Elanna Allen (HarperCollins)
- 3rd to 4th Grade Book of the Year: *Kali's Story: An Orphaned Polar Bear Rescue* by Jennifer Keats Curtis, illustrated by John Gomes (Arbordale)
- 5th to 6th Grade Book of the Year: *The Dumbest Idea Ever!* by Jimmy Gownley (Scholastic/Graphix)
- Teen Book of the Year: *The One* by Kiera Cass (HarperTeen)
- Children's Choice Debut Author: J.A. White for *The Thickety: A Path Begins* (HarperCollins/Tegen)
- Teen Choice Debut Author: Jennifer Mathieu for *The Truth About Alice* (Roaring Brook)
- Children's Choice Illustrator: Chris Appelhans for *Sparky!*, written by Jenny Offill (Random/Schwartz & Wade)

Gone But Not Forgotten

Finally, our recap of the year in children's publishing would not be complete without saying goodbye to those who made an indelible impression on all of us who love children's books. In Memoriam:

- George McHugh Nicholson, literary agent and celebrated publishing executive
- Ellen Conford, author
- Vera B. Williams, author and illustrator
- Marcia Brown, illustrator
- Margaret Bloy Graham, illustrator
- Mal Peet, author and illustrator
- Ann McGovern, author and illustrator

Well, that's it. With any luck, 2016 will be just as successful as 2015. See you in the bookstores!

E-Books: The Future of Education?

by Isabel Thottham

We live in a technology-heavy world, and, as it becomes more advanced, more and more aspects of the physical world are being digitized. Just as retail shopping now exists through e-commerce, the book industry is experiencing its own digital revolution through electronic or e-publishing. Though print may never truly die, as many people still enjoy being able to hold a physical book, products like Amazon Kindle and iPads allow for easy access to hundreds of thousands of books.

In particular, e-books have had a huge impact on how we teach students, especially in grades pre-K through eight. Technology now provides more hands-on learning experiences, since devices like iPads and laptops have become so prevalent in the classroom. With e-books offering access to hundreds and thousands of books on a variety of topics, the teachings and assignments become endless.

Anil Hermrajani, CEO of Big Universe, an engaging online reading and writing community for grades pre-K through eight, believes that e-books are the future.

"That's the only way people going to schools are going to use books in the long term," he says. "Even in high school and colleges. It's only a matter of time before everything goes digital."

Expanding School Libraries

In particular, technology makes it increasingly easier for students who spend too much time – and money – carrying around heavy, bulky books to obtain their reading materials. In the education sector, e-books are taking over the common school library as more and more schools seek to provide computers for students. In fact, according to Hermrajani, some states have dictated that schools have to be totally digital. Though every school district handles it differently, many schools are moving to this one-to-one model, in which each student has his or her own computer, iPad, or other tablet. This allows for an expansive library, whereby students and teachers are able to find everything they need in one place.

This makes a lot of sense, considering all the books students are required to purchase in high school or college—in some cases, multiple books for each subject. Hermrajani says he'd rather have his own kids carry a Kindle, especially if it helps avoid hurting their backs.

"It's so much easier to carry a Kindle as opposed to a heavy backpack. Plus, you're able to annotate and search for text right there on the tablet," explains Hermranjani. "The benefits of e-books for students are endless."

Tracking Student Progress

Moreover, teachers also benefit from using e-books. It gives them the ability to track how students are progressing as well as monitor to make sure they are doing the readings assigned in their online accounts. Big Universe allows teachers to assign software and assignments to students through their online accounts, which helps keep everything in one place and allows for tracking improvements.

In addition to their ease and access, e-books are more cost-effective. Hermranjani explains that many schools love using e-books because they would never be able to afford this many books.

"For $2,000 we offer unlimited access, and we have thousands of books available on our platform," he explains. "If they have to buy a single copy of each book, it's so much more expensive. They wouldn't be able to afford it."

Cheryl Tardif, owner of Imajin Books, which publishes children's books in addition to other genres, doesn't believe print will ever die, but that the future looks more tech-savvy for students.

"I think it's exciting to see how many schools are getting kids to learn with tablets," she says. "Our kids are going to go to school and if they have a backpack at all it'll be with a laptop and a pen. That, to me, is exciting and schools will be more prepared."

Tardif wrote and published her first book at sixteen, so she knows the industry well and has seen it change over the years. When she started her own publishing company in 2003, before Amazon came out with their platform, electronic publishing didn't really exist yet. By 2009, friends saw that Tardif was doing well as a self-published author and asked if she'd help them market their own work; she began to publish a variety of titles under the name Imajin Books.

"When I started in 2003, we didn't have e-books as an option. That came out around 2005 or 2006," Tardif explains. "E-books became a big thing and then we had all the devices released. Now, we publish trade paperback and e-books. Our main focus is e-books though, because that is the future."

Tardif remembers being a student and going to the library to find a book you were assigned in school. She explains that you were lucky if you got a book with color photos because everything was so dry.

"Now you get so much more information and more visual stuff. I think it helps [students] learn and engage more with the visuals," says Tardif. "It's really exciting the ways they teach kids now because it's more hands-on work, as well as computer work."

Tardif makes a valid point. If you give students the option of reading a black and white textbook or having access to video and interactive photographs to bring history or science to life, chances are they're going to choose the tablet version.

Bye-Bye Enclyclopedias

Think about how obsolete the encyclopedia has become. That used to be a comprehensive reference book for all the information we needed. Now, encyclopedias are already out of date by the time they're printed. They can't capture the up-to-date information that we can access instantly on the Internet.

Educational E-Book Publishers

The *Book Markets for Children's Writers 2016* features several educational e-book publishers including:

Edcon Publishing, p. 445, produces learning materials for grades K–12, adult/special education, homeschooling, English-as-a-Second Language, and English language learners.

Go Teach It!, p. 267, publishes original curriculum related to grades K-12 on the following subjects: civics, geography, history, language, literature, math, science and wellness.They prefer curriculum related to established works in print (e.g. literary classics).

Guardian Angel Publishing, p. 133, uses books to create a safe and fun environment for children to learn and grow. Its talented authors have pioneered to create a new dynamic form of eBooks and print paperback and hardcover books.

Incentive Publications, p. 321, an imprint of World Book, produces supplemental resources for student use and instruction. With more than 400 titles available, this company specializes in resources for middle grade students, as well as teaching strategies for grade K–12.

Pieces of Learning, p. 287, uses innovative ideas and unique ways to present enrichment activities and thinking skills to students. It offers a broad range of books across all core subjects, including language arts, math, science, and social studies, that support standardized assessment criteria. It also offers titles geared to staff development.

Familius, p. 343, dedicates itself to a wide piece of the family-life spectrum. Its mission is to help families be happy by creating beautiful books that teach, inspire, and bring families together.

Both Hermranjani and Tardif believe e-books are the future and are excited to see more schools pick up on the trend. Though print will probably always exist and might have a stronger hold in the fiction area of publishing, e-books are growing in the education market and their impacts are enormous.

"I don't believe print will ever totally be gone; there still are a lot of people who prefer to read paperback and hardcover," says Tardif. "However, we're all trying to be environmentally conscious and though cutting down trees to turn into books seemed like a good idea at first, we're going to pay for that if we're not careful."

Tardif also notes that e-books allow publishers to offer books at a lower price.

"I see [e-books] over $15 and that's unnecessary," she says. "You don't have all the unstocking and re-stocking that you have to pay for. The sales on all different e-readers are still going strong. People enjoy that experience. No more lugging thick paperbacks on a plane. There are still needs for print so it will still be around for a while, or until we see any kind of major disaster that wipes out forests."

As e-books take on the education sector, more and more publishers are looking for material that is more than just straight text. We're going to see more enhanced e-books for the industry, which will give young people the ability to connect and learn in ways we've never imagined.

Listings

How to Use the Listings

One of the most essential—and we believe, useful—qualities of *Book Markets for Children's Writers* is the division of publisher listings into sections: trade, classroom, educators, parents, regional, religious, and of interest. These listings number 665 in total, with 31 *new* trade markets, and 5 in classroom publishers. This edition also lists 68 literary agents (36 new) and 62 contests and awards.

You can approach this book three ways: (1) Use the alphabetical index beginning on page 593 to find a particular publisher, agent, or contest listing. (2) Browse through a given section of the book to review the needs of the companies of most interest to you (maybe you want to write a religious picture book, for example, so begin with the religious section of the listings). (3) Go to the category index, page 538, and search out publishers in specific genres and categories.

We have reviewed and updated every listing in the book through research, and multiple rounds of surveys and fact-checking. Also included are cross-references among parent companies, their divisions, and imprints, to help you hone in on exactly the right place for your submissions. Note, however, that it is not uncommon for contact names, addresses, and editorial needs to change suddenly. After deciding to approach a company, agent, or contest you've found in *Book Markets for Children's Writers 2016,* follow the advice often given in the book: Check the publisher's website for updates to guidelines before submitting a query letter or manuscript.

To help you judge a publisher's receptivity to submissions, we include a Freelance Potential section in each listing. This is where you'll find the number of titles published yearly, and other figures available about unpublished writers, authors new to the publishing house, and agented authors. We also provide numbers of query letters and unsolicited manuscripts received.

Use this information and the other information included in the listing to locate publishers that are looking for the type of material you have written or plan to write. Become familiar with the style and content of the house by studying its catalogue and several recent titles.

Bloomsbury Spark

New Listing
Agented
Submissuins

1385 Broadway, New York, NY 10018
www.bloomsburyusa.com,
www.bloomsburykids.com

Website

Submissions Editor

Contact

Bloomsbury Spark is a one-of-a-kind, global, digital imprint from Bloomsbury Publishing. It is dedicated to publishing a wide array of exciting fiction eBooks to teen readers. It offers a wide array of fiction including sci-fi, paranormal, mystery and thriller.

Profile of
Publisher &
Readership

Freelance Potential: Publishes about 25 titles annually: all by agented authors; 1–10% by previously unpublished writers. Receives 50 queries monthly.

Number of
Books Published
and Freelance
Statistics

Fiction: YA. Genres: mystery, thriller, paranormal, sci-fi, and romance.

Categories of
Current Titles

Titles: *Pride Unleashed*, by Cat Kalen (YA). *Hollywood Witch Hunter*, by Valerie Tejeda (YA).

Recent Titles
to Study

Submissions and Payment: Guidelines and catalogue available at website. Accepts agented submissions only. Responds in 6 months if interested. Publication period varies. Royalty; advance.

How to Submit

Parents, Divisions, Imprints

Cross-reference
to Related
Publishers

Bloomsbury Children's Books, See page 86

 New Listing   Agented Submissions Only

 Overseas Publisher   Not Accepting Submissions

 A percentage of material is subsidy/vanity

Children's Trade Publishers

Trade publishers are the companies that most people think of when they think of books in general, and children's books in particular: Trade publishers sell their books primarily through bookstores or other profit-making businesses, and target the general consumer market. This is in contrast to classroom or educational publishers, who sell their books to the institutional market made up of schools and libraries.

The big companies with large lists and well-known titles, including many best-sellers, are usually trade publishers: Scholastic with Hunger Games, HarperCollins with Fancy Nancy, Abrams Books with the Wimpy Kid series. But small, *independent* publishers may be trade publishers as well, as long as they sell through the same consumer publishing channels.

The larger trade companies can be difficult to break into, and often work with agented writers primarily. But this is far from universal. Some big houses remain open to unsolicited submissions. Smaller publishers are often more open, but they can also be more limited in what they publish. Study the listings in this section to become more informed about the publishing industry in general, which is very important for a writer serious about selling a book. You will begin to learn about the extraordinary range of publishers, their needs, the styles of their books, their editorial perspectives—and where you might fit in. Every publisher wants to find a gem of a new writer.

Abbeville Family

137 Varick Street, 5th Floor, New York, NY 10013
www.abbevillepress.com

Editorial Director: Susan Costello

Headquartered in New York, this independent publisher offers fine art
and illustrated books. The Abbeville Family imprint publishes parenting manuals and a variety of fun and educational books for kids.

Freelance Potential: Publishes 10–12 titles annually: about 30%
by authors who are new to the publishing house.

Fiction: Toddler books, early picture books, picture books, story
picture books, middle-grade. Genres: multicultural, fairy tales,
folklore, mystery.

Nonfiction: Concept books, board books, novelty books, toddler books, preschool, picture books, story picture books, middle-grade, young YA. Topics: animals, the arts, counting, letters,
dinosaurs, vehicles, families. Also publishes parenting books.

Titles: *Flop-O-Saurus*, by Sara Ball and Britta Drehsen (ages 3–8).
Brave Wolf and the Thunderbird, by Joe Medicine Crow (ages 4–8).

Submissions and Payment: Not currently accepting queries or
manuscripts at this time because its list is full for the next several
seasons. Check the website for policy changes.

Abrams Books for Young Readers

115 West 18th Street, 6th Floor, New York, NY 10011
www.abramsbooks.com/childrens.html

Editor: Maggie Lerman

Abrams Books for Young Readers publishes picture books and
illustrated nonfiction for preschool through midde-grade children.
Its fellow imprints are Amulet Books, which focuses on middle-grade and YA, and Appleseed Books, which publishes books
for infants to age five.

Freelance Potential: Publishes 50–75 titles annually: 100% by
agented authors; 10–25% by authors who are new to the publishing house; 10–25% by previously unpublished writers. Receives
100 queries monthly.

Fiction: Early picture books, picture books, early readers, middle-grade. Genres: adventure, fantasy, contemporary, multicultural, historical, horror, humor, mystery, fairy tales, stories about nature and animals, graphic novels, poetry.

Nonfiction: Early picture books, picture books, early readers, middle-grade, YA. Topics: animals, the arts, biography, nature, science, holidays, activity books.

Titles: *The Bear Report*, by Thyra Heder (ages 4–8). *Hot Pink: The Life and Fashion of Elsa Schiaparelli* (ages 8–12).

Submissions and Payment: Guidelines and catalogue available at website. Not accepting unsolicited fiction submissions (picture books or novels) at this time. For nonfiction picture books of up to 20 pages, send complete manuscript. For longer nonfiction, query with table of contents, sample chapter, and chapter-by-chapter synopsis. Include your biography with all submissions, indicating what makes you qualified to write the proposed book, and a list of competitive titles and what will distinguish your book. Accepts hard copy only; no email submissions or disks. Responds within 6 months. Publication period varies. Royalty; advance.

Parents , Divisions, Imprints

Abrams ComicArts, See page 436
Amulet Books, See page 75
Appleseed Book, See page 77

Accord Publishing

1404 Larimer Street, Suite 200, Denver, CO 80202
www.accordpublishing.com

Submissions Editor

This division of the general trade nonfiction company Andrews McMeel Publishing (AMP) specializes in innovative, colorful board books for babies and toddlers, and story picture books for young children, many of them interactive. It also publishes puzzle and activity books.

Freelance Potential: Publishes 20 titles annually. Receives 10+ unsolicited manuscripts monthly.

Fiction: Board books, toddler books, story picture books, comics.

Genres: contemporary, multicultural, animal and family stories, humor.

Nonfiction: Board books, novelty books, concept books, toddler books, story picture books, puzzle/activity books. Topics: animals, concepts, families, toys, holidays, seasons, vehicles.

Titles: *The Adventures of Max the Minnow*, by William Boniface. (ages 3–8). *Mouse Goes to School*, by Paula Hannigan (ages birth–4). *Bugs: A Mini AniMotion Book* (ages birth–4).

Submissions and Payment: Catalogue available at website. Andrews McMeel guidelines available at website. Prefers agented submissions, but accepts queries with proposals, or complete manuscripts, if the guidelines are followed. No simultaneous submissions. Accepts hard copy. SASE. Response time, publication period, and payment policy vary.

Adventure Publishing

820 Cleveland Street South, Cambridge, MN 55008
www.adventurepublications.net

Submissions Editor

Great books, great sales, great service is the tagline of this publisher. It offers high-interest fiction and nonfiction titles that feature a strong outdoor component or backdrop. It also publishes regional activity books.

Freelance Potential: Unavailable.

Fiction: Story picture books, early readers, middle-grade, YA. Genres: adventure and mystery set in the great outdoors.

Nonfiction: PreK, picture books, early readers, middle-grade, YA. Topics: animals, birds, the outdoors, nature, wilderness skills and recreation.

Titles: *Do Beavers Need Blankets?*, by Stan Tekiela (ages 4–8). *The Cutest Critter*, Marion Dane Bauer (ages 4–8).

Submissions and Payment: Guidelines and catalogue available at website. Query with cover letter, sample chapter, and outline, or send complete manusctript. Also include target audience and author credentials. Accepts email submissions to custservice@ adventurepublications.net (include "submission" in the subject) and hard copy. Submissions not returned. Responds in 6 months. Publication period varies. Royalty.

Aladdin

Simon & Schuster Children's Publishing, 1230 Avenue of the Americas, New York, NY 10020
http://imprints.simonandschuster.biz/aladdin

Assistant Editor: Alyson Heller

From picture books to chapter books, from middle-grade fiction to nonfiction, the Aladdin imprint from Simon & Schuster has something for everyone. Its titles build worlds that kids don't want to leave and establishes characters that feel like old friends.

Freelance Potential: Publishes 100 titles annually: all by agented authors.

Fiction: Early readers, story picture books, chapter books, middle-grade. Genres: contemporary, historical, suspense, mystery, fantasy, adventure, graphic novels.

Nonfiction: Picture books, middle-grade. Topics: America's national monuments, natural wonders, biographies of world figures, humor.

Titles: *The Monstore*, by Tara Lazar (ages 4–7). *Dinosaurs Love Underpants*, by Claire Freedman (ages 3–7).

Submissions and Payment: Catalogue available at website. Agented authors only. Offers some work-for-hire assignments on certain series. Response time, publication period, and payment policy vary.

Parents, Divisions, Imprints

Simon & Schuster, See page 207

Algonquin Books for Young Readers

225 Varick Street, New York, NY 10014
www.algonquinyoungreaders.com

Editor: Elise Howard

This imprint from Workman publishing features books for children and teens ages 7 to 17. From short, illustrated novels for the youngest independent readers to topical crossover young adult fiction, the books from Algonquin offer unforgettable characers, absorbing stories, and superior writing.

Freelance Potential: Publishes 4–6 juvenile titles each year.

Fiction: Early reader, Middle-grade, YA. Genres: contemporary, current events, fantasy.

Nonfiction: Middle-grade, YA. Topics: biography, memoir, social issues.

Titles: *Anton and Cecil: Cats on Track*, by Lisaa Martin and Valerin Martin (ages 3–7). *If You're Lucky*, by Yvonne Prinz (YA).

Submissions and Payment: Guidelines and catalogue available at website. Query with cover letter and 15- to 20-page sample of the manuscript. Accepts hard copy only. SASE. Response time, publication period, and payment policy vary.

Parents Divisions, Imprints

Workman, See page 243

Allosaurus Publishing

3711 Brassfield Oaks Drive, Greensboro, NC 27410
www.allosauruspublishers.com

Editor

Connecting the past to the present through history, science, and reading comprehension, this indepenedent publisher produces educational matierals for students in grades K–12. All of its titles are published in both print and ebook formats.

Freelance Potential: Unavailable.

Fiction: Early readers, story picture books, middle-grade, YA. Genres: science and historical fiction.

Nonfiction: Story picture books, middle grade, YA. Topics: history, science, regional titles on North Carolina and workbooks.

Titles: *North Carolina's Geography & Geology* (ages 10–12). *Asia* *and Its Many Cultures* (8–10).

Submissions and Payment: Catalogue, guidelines, and editor list with specific genres they seek, available at website. Send 1-page query letter only; include brief synopsis of manuscript and author publishing credits (if any). Accepts hard copy. SASE required. Responds in 4 months if interested. Publication in 1+ years. Royalty; advance.

Alma Little

8362 Tamarack Village, Suite 119-106, St. Paul, MN 55125
http://www.elvaresa.com/almalittle.html

Acquisitions: Elizabeth Snow

This children's imprint of Elva Resa Publishing offers meaningful picture books, nonfiction books, and novels on general interest topics for young children through teens. Its goal is "to bring children a diverse world of possibilities, opportunities, and wonder through books that make a positive difference in readers' lives." A portion of all book sale proceeds is donated to charity.

Freelance Potential: Publishes about 5 titles annually: 10–25% developed from unsolicited submissions; 75–100% assigned; 25–50% by authors who are new to the publishing house; 10–25% by previously unpublished writers. Receives 100–150 queries, 15+ manuscripts monthly.

Fiction: Story picture books, chapter books, middle-grade. Genres: contemporary, historical, inspirational.

Nonfiction: Chapter books, middle-grade. Topics: self-help, current events, activities, biography, politics, inspirational, real life/problems, religious, reference, parenting, military life.

Titles: *Scarlet Says Good-Bye*, by Christine Thompson (ages 4–8). *Perch, Mrs. Sacket's and Crows Nest*, by Karen Pavlicin-Fragnito (ages 8–12).

Submissions and Payment: Guidelines and catalogue available at website. Accepts submissions on a call-for-manuscript basis only; check website for updates. Query with outline. Accepts email queries (Word or PDF attachments) to submissions@elvaresa.com. Accepts queries for work-for-hire assignments. Responds in 3–6 weeks. Publication in 12–24 months. Royalty; advance. Flat fee.

Elva Resa, See page 342

American Girl Publications

www.americangirlpublishing.com

Submissions Editor

American Girl Publications has a deep understanding of girls' wishes and dreams. From exciting adventures to girlhood guides to playful crafts, the award-winning titles from this publisher increase confidence and self-respect in girls.

Freelance Potential: Publishes 30–40 titles annually. Receives 12 queries, 30 unsolicited manuscripts monthly.

Fiction: Story picture books, chapter books, middle–grade. Genres: historical.

Nonfiction: Picture books, story picture books, middle-grade. Topics: advice, self-help, activity books, games, puzzles.

Titles: *Beforever* by Kathleen Ernst (ages 8+). *A Smart Girl's Guide: Drama, Rumors & Secrets*, by Nancy Holyoke (ages 10+).

Submissions and Payment: Catalogue available at website. It is not accepting unsolicited submissions of fiction or nonfiction by adults at this time.

Amistad Press

10 E. 53rd St., New York, NY 10022
www.harpercollins.com

Editorial Director: Dawn Davis

Amistad Press, an imprint of Harper Collins, is the premier publisher of mutlicultural fiction and nonfiction. Its list show-cases award-winning authors, celebrated cultural figures, and esteemed critics and scholars.

Freelance Potential: Publishes about 20 titles annually.

Fiction: Picture books, chapter books, middle-grade. Genres: multicultural, historical, contemporary, social issues.

Nonfiction: Picture books, chapter books, middle-grade. Topics: biography, history, sports, social issues.

Titles: *The Other Side of Truth,* by Beverly Naidoo (ages 8–12). *After the Dance*, by Jan Gaye and David Ritz (YA–A)

Submissions and Payment: Guidelines and catalogue available at website. Accepts submissions through literary agents only. Publication in 18–36 months. Royalty; advance.

Parents, Divisions, Imprints

HarperCollins, See page 137

AMP! Comics for Kids

1130 Walnut Street, Kansas City, MO 64106. www.ampkids.com

Book Submissions

AMP! Comics for Kids is the graphic novel imprint from Andrews McMeel. It features fiction aimed at middle-grade readers. The line began with a combination of original work and material adapted from already published titles. New titles include digital versions of its titles with interactive elements.

Freelance Potential: Publishes about 5 titles annually. Andrews McMeel publishes about 250 titles annually.

Fiction: Middle-grade. Genre: comics.

Titles: *Phoebe and Her Unicorn*, by Dana Simpson (ages 8–12). *The G-Man Journal,* by Chris Giarusso (ages 8–12).

Submissions and Payment: Guidelines and catalogue available at website. Query with cover letter describing manuscript, target audience, and why AMP! is the best publisher for it, 1 or 2 sample chapters, brief author bio, and completion schedule for the manuscript. Prefers hard copy. SASE. Responds if interested. Publication period and payment policy vary.

Amulet Books

115 West 18th Street, 6th Floor, New York, NY 10011
www.amuletbooks.com

Assistant Editor: Erica Finkel

Amulet Books, a division of Abrams, publishes novels, graphic novels, and nonfiction for young adults and middle grade students.

Freelance Potential: Publishes 50–75 titles annually: all by agented authors; 10–25% by authors who are new to the publishing house; 10–25% by previously unpublished writers. Receives 100 queries monthly.

Fiction: Chapter books, middle-grade, YA. Genres: contemporary, historical, science fiction, fantasy, suspense, mystery, humor, graphic novels, poetry.

Nonfiction: Middle-grade, YA. Topics: art, multicultural, ethnic, history, natural history, the environment, nature, self-help.

Titles: *The Bamboo Sword*, by Margi Press (YA). *The Secrets to Ruling the School*, by Neil Swaab (ages 8–12).

Submissions and Payment: Guidelines and catalogue available at website. Not accepting unsolicited submissions at this time. Publication period varies. Royalty; advance.

Parents, Divisions, Imprints

Abrams Books for Young Readers, See page 67
Abrams ComicArts, See page 435
Appleseed Books, See page 77

Andersen Press

20 Vauxhall Bridge Road, London SW1V 2SA United Kingdom
www.andersenpress.co.uk

Picture Book Submissions Editor, Fiction Submissions Editor

This award-winning children's publisher offers picture books (approximately 500 words); juvenile fiction (approximately 3,000–5,000) words; and older fiction (to 75,000 words).

Freelance Potential: Publishes about 90 titles annually: 10% by agented authors. Receives 100 unsolicited manuscripts monthly.

Fiction: Early picture books, early readers, story picture books, chapter books, middle-grade, YA. Genres: historical, contemporary, humor, adventure, fantasy, folktales, horror, mystery, suspense, romance, animals, sports.

Titles: *The Adventures of Beekle: The Unimaginary Friend,* by Dans Santat (0+ years). *Abela: The Girl Who Saw Lions*, by Berlie Doherty (ages 12+).

Submissions and Payment: Guidelines and catalogue available at website. Query with synopsis and 3 sample chapters. Send complete manuscript for picture books only (500–1,000 words). Accepts hard copy. Label envelope with Picture Book Submission Department or Fiction Submissions Department. SASE. Responds in 2 months. Publication period and payment policy vary.

Annick Press

15 Patricia Avenue, Toronto, Ontario M2M 1H9 Canada
www.annickpress.com

Editors

Annick Press is recognized as one of the most innovative and cutting-edge Canadian publishers of fiction and nonfiction for toddlers to young adults. The publisher strives to create educational, entertaining books that will spark a lifelong love affair with the written word. At this time, Annick Press is closed to picture book submissions.

Freelance Potential: Publishes 20+ titles annually: 50% by authors who are new to the publishing house; 30% by previously unpublished writers. Receives 350 queries monthly.

Fiction: Picture books, middle-grade, YA. Genres: contemporary, fantasy, humor.

Nonfiction: Middle-grade, YA. Topics: culture, history, science, biography, pop culture, contemporary issues.

Titles: *Not My Girl*, by Christy Jordan-Fenton and Margaret Pokiak-Fenton (ages 6–9). *Horrendo's Curse: The Graphic Novel*, by Anna Fienberg (ages 8–12).

Submissions and Payment: Canadian authors only. Guidelines and catalogue available at website. Query with synopsis and sample chapter. Accepts hard copy. SAE/IRC. Response time, publication period, and payment policy vary.

Appleseed Books

115 West 18th Street, 6th Floor, New York, NY 10011
www.abramsbooks.com/imprints/abramsappleseed

Publishing Director: Cecily Kaiser

Appleseed, formerly known as Abrams Appleseed, creates beautiful books for babies, toddlers, and preschoolers. By pairing the comfort of familiar objects with the introduction of something new or unexpected, each book is artfully conceived and developmentally appropriate.

Freelance Potential: Publishes approximately 20 books annually.

Fiction: Board books, novelty books, picture books.

Nonfiction: Board books, novelty books, picture books.

Titles: *Brave As Can Be*, by Jo Witek (ages 0–3). *Whose Truck?*, by Toni Buzzeo (ages 0–3).

Submissions and Payment: Agented authors only. Responds to queries in 2–4 months, to manuscripts in 3–6 months. Publication period varies. Royalty; advance.

Parents, Divisions, Imprints

Abrams Books for Young Readers, See page 67
Abrams ComicArts, See page 436
Amulet Books, See page 75

Atheneum Books for Young Readers

Simon & Schuster Children's Publishing, 1230 Avenue of the Americas, New York, NY 10020
http://imprints.simonandschuster.biz/atheneum

Editorial Director: Caitlyn Dlouhy

This imprint of Simon & Schuster offers hardcover and paperback books for children and teens. It is known for its enduring literary picture books and middle-grade and teen fiction, as well as a selection of graphic novels, nonfiction, and poetry. Simon & Schuster accepts agented manuscripts only.

Freelance Potential: Publishes 50–75 titles annually: most are by agented authors; some are by previously unpublished writers. Receives 2,500 queries monthly.

Fiction: Concept books, toddler books, early picture books, story picture books, chapter books, middle-grade, YA. Genres: fantasy, mystery, adventure, fairy tales, historical, contemporary, graphic novels.

Nonfiction: Story picture books, chapter books, middle-grade, YA. Topics: adventure, biography, the environment, science, nature, sports, history, multicultural issues.

Titles: *What Makes You Happy,* by Jimmy Gownley (ages 7–12). *Nothing,* by Martin Aitken (ages 12+).

Submissions and Payment: Catalogue available at website. Guidelines available. Accepts agented manuscripts only. Publication period varies. Royalty.

Parents, Divisions, Imprints

Simon & Schuster, See page 207

Autumn Publishing

1.07-1.09 The Plaza, 535 King's Harbour, London, SW10 0SZ, UK
www.autumnchildrensbooks.co.uk

Editor

A market leader in the field of children's activity and learning books, Autumn Publishing was established in the late 1970s. Its catalogue is filled with high-quality children's books with strong educational integrity that are equipped to help make learning fun. Autumn Publishing is an imprint of Bonnier Publishing.

Freelance Potential: Publishes 20 titles annually.

Fiction: Concept books, early picture books, early readers, story picture books, middle-grade. Genres: nature, reluctant readers, animals.

Nonfiction: Toddler books, story picture books, YA. Topics: animals, history, nature, science.

Titles: *Amazing Ancient Things* (ages 8–12). *Jack's Hair* (ages 3–6).

Submissions and Payment: Catalogue and guidelines available at website. Query. Accepts queries through an online submission form at the website. Responds if interested. Publication period and payment policies vary.

Baen Books

P.O. Box 1188, Wake Forest, NC 27588
www.baen.com

Editor: Toni Weisskopf

Baen Books is a publisher of science fiction and fantasy. It looks for manuscripts with powerful plots and firm scientific and philosophical foundations. For fantasy, it seeks originality and well-developed magical systems that are integral to the plot of the story. While many of its adult titles would be of interest to YA readers, it has recently started publishing titles specifically for young adults. Although an independent press, Baen's titles have long been distributed by Simon & Schuster.

Freelance Potential: Publishes 36–48 titles annually; publishes 2 to 3 new authors annually.

Fiction: YA and adult. Genres: fantasy, historical, hard science fiction, military science fiction, space opera, urban fantasy.

Titles: *The High Crusade*, by Paul Anderson (YA). *Interstellar Patrol*, by Christopher Anvil (YA).

Submissions and Payment: Guidelines and catalogue available at website. Prefers mss between 100,000–130,00 words. Send complete manuscript. Prefers electronic submissions using submission form at http://ftp.baen.com/Slush/submit.aspx. No email submissions. Accepts hard copy. Responds in 9–12 months. Publication period and payment policy vary.

Balzer & Bray

HarperCollins Children's Books, 10 E. 53rd St., New York, NY 10022. www.harpercollinschildrens.com

Co-Publishers: Alessandra Balzer, Donna Bray

Balzer & Bray publishes bold, creative, groundbreaking picture books and novels that appeal to kids in a fresh way. With this imprint from HarperCollins, authors have the freedom to take risks and fullfill their unique visions.

Freelance Potential: Publishes 25 titles annually. Agented only.

Fiction: Picture books, chapter books, middle-grade, YA. Genres: adventure, contemporary, historical, multicultural, mystery/suspense, nature, science fiction, fantasy, sports.

Nonfiction: Picture books, chapter books, middle-grade, YA. Topics: biography, history, the arts, nature, multicultural.

Titles: *Snoring Beauty*, by Sudipta Bardhan-Quallen (ages 4–8). *Cheetah Can't Lose,* by Bob Shea (ages 4–8)

Submissions and Payment: Agented submissions only. Publication in 18 months. Royalty; advance.

Parents, Divisions, Imprints

HarperCollins, See page 137

Bancroft Press

P.O. Box 65360, Baltimore, MD 21209-9945
www.bancroftpress.com

Editor: Bruce Bortz

In business for more than 25 years, Bancroft Press only publishes titles it feels strongly about. Its list includes fiction for young adults and middle grade readers, as well as nonfiction for young adults.

Freelance Potential: Publishes 4–6 titles annually: 50% by authors new to the publishing house; 30% by previously unpublished writers. Receives 170 queries, 800 unsolicited manuscripts monthly.

Fiction: Middle-grade, YA. Genres: mystery, history, sports, contemporary, multicultural.

Nonfiction: YA. Topics: sports, biography. Also publishes parenting and self-help books for adults.

Titles: *The Secrets of the Greaser Hotel*, by J. L. Herchenroeder (YA). *The Whole Kitt & Caboodle*, by Susan Laubach (YA).

Submissions and Payment: Guidelines and catalogue available at website. Query with résumé and 4–5 sample chapters; or send complete manuscript with cover letter, market analysis, and résumé. Accepts hard copy. SASE. Responds in 6 months. Publication period varies. Royalty; advance.

Barking Rain Press

www.barkingrainpress.org

Submissions Editor

Barking Rain Press is a nonprofit publisher of print and ebooks. Its goal is to publish novels or novellas of at least 20,000 words by new and mid-career authors and to maintain a commitment to artistic excellence and imaginative contemporary literature that is not profit driven. Titles are published both in print and electronic formats. It publishes young adult fiction as well as books for adults. It plans to start two new imprints this year: Nitis Books, publishing nonfiction; and Virtual Tales, featuring short fiction and collections of fiction ebooks.

Freelance Potential: Publishes 12–14 titles annually.

Fiction: YA. Genres: mystery, historical, contemporary, fantasy.

Titles: *The Anthropoligist's Daughter*, by Vanessa Furse Jackson (YA). *Winner Take None*, by Greg Comer.

Submissions and Payment: Guidelines and catalogue available at website. Send proposal, which includes: title, genre, word count, 40-word promotional blurb, promotional text for back cover (100–200 words), brief excerpt (no more than 300 words), the first 4 chapters, outline of whole story, short author bio (100–250 words), and a marketing plan. Accepts submissions through contact form at website only during the months of January, May, and September. Responds in 2 months. Publication period varies. Royalty, 50% of net sales paid monthly.

Beach Lane Books

http://imprints.simonandschuster.biz/beach-lane-books

Editor: Andrea Welch

Founded in 2008, this imprint from Simon & Schuster publishes books for all ages and across all genres, with a primary focus on lyrical, emotionally engagng, highly visual picture books for young children. Beach Lane Books only accepts submissions from literary agents.

Freelance Potential: Publishes about 20 books annually.

Fiction: Board books, novelty books, picture books, early readers, middle-grade. Genres: animals, adventure, fairy tales, multicultural.

Nonfiction: Board books, novelty books, picture books, early readers, middle-grade. Topics: animals, dinosaurs, concepts, multicultural.

Titles: *In the Canyon*, Liz Garton Scanlon (ages 4–8). *1-2-3 Zoo-Borns!*, by Andrew Bleiman and Chris Eastland (ages 4–8).

Submissions and Payment: Catalogue available at website. Simon & Schuster imprints accept agented submissions only. Publication period and payment vary.

Parents, Divisions, Imprints

Simon & Schuster, See page 207

Bell Bridge Books

P.O. Box 300921, Memphis, TN 38130. www.bellebooks.com

Acquiring Editor: Deborah Dixon

An imprint of BelleBooks, Bell Bridge is known for nurturing emerging fiction voices as well as being the "second home" for many established authors. Some of its notable authors include Sharon Sala, Anne Bishop, and Cheryl Reavis. Its list features books for children and young adults, as well as titles for adults.

Freelance Potential: Unavailable.

Fiction: Middle-grade, YA. Genres: mystery, suspense, horror, fantasy, science fiction, humor, urban fantasy.

Titles: *Astronaut Noodle and the Planet Velocity*, by Kerilyn Foster Spence (age 6–10). *How to Stop a Witch*, by Bill Allen (ages 6–10).

Submissions and Payment: Guidelines and catalogue available at website. Not currently accepting middle grade submissions. Query with full ms, brief synopsis and writers credentials. See website for specific editor needs and requirements. Accepts email only to queries@bellebooks.com. Responds in 1–3 months, publication period 12+ months, Royalty; advance.

Bellerophon Books

P.O. Box 21307, Santa Barbara, CA 93121
www.bellerophonbooks.com

Editor

Children from around the world have grown up with the books from this publisher. Its titles are visually appealing, entertaining, and edificatory. It also offers many coloring books with historical themes.

Freelance Potential: Publishes several titles annually.

Nonfiction: Story picture books, middle grade, YA. Topics: animals, history, nature, science, music, nautical, air and space.

Title: *Horses and Riding*, by Prof. Anderson.

Submissions and Payment: Catalogue available at website. Query. Accepts queries though the website only. Responds if interested. Publication period and payment policies vary.

Bilingual Books for Kids

P.O. Box 653, Ardsley, NY 10502. www.bilingualbooks.com

Editor

This publisher's catalogue is filled with bilingual books for children and young adults. Its books introduce bilingual skills, increase language learning, and introduce children to different cultures.

Freelance Potential: Publishes 10–15 titles annually.

Fiction: Concept books, early picture books, early readers, story picture books, middle-grade, YA. Genres: contemporary, adventure, mystery, fantasy, humor.

Nonfiction: Toddler books, story picture books, YA. Topics: animals, history, nature, science.

Titles: *Looking for Alaska*, by John Green (YA). *Sophomores and Other Oxymorons*, by David Lubar (YA).

Submissions and Payment: Catalogue, guidelines, and editor list with specific genres they seek, available at website. Send 1-page query letter only; include brief synopsis of manuscript and author publishing credits (if any). Accepts hard copy. SASE required. Responds in 4 months if interested. Publication in 1+ years. Royalty; advance.

Black Bed Sheet Books

www.downwarden.com

Editor

Black Bed Sheet Books specializes in fiction, especially dark fiction, fantasy, and thrillers. Its catalogue includes both books for children and young adults. It publishes both print and online titles.

Freelance Potential: Publishes 10–20 titles annually.

Fiction: Middle-grade, YA. Genres: Mystery, fantasy, dark fiction.

Titles: *Flatty Cat: Tales of an Urban Feline*, by Phyllis Graubert and Nicholas Grabosky (ages 8–12). *Electric Angel,* by Tom Sawyer (YA).

Submissions and Payment: Catalogue and guidelines available at website. Query with brief synopsis of manuscript and author publishing credits (if any). Accepts email submissions to BBSAdmin@downwarden.com. Responds if interested. Publication period and payment policies vary.

Black Dog & Leventhal Publishers

151 West 19th Street, New York, NY 10011
www.blackdogandleventhal.com

Publisher: J.P. Leventhal

This publisher specializes in books for children and adults that are meant to provide visual and reading pleasure. Its titles delve into art, history, natural wonders. Parenting titles are also found on its list.

Freelance Potential: Publishes several titles annually: most are by agented authors.

Nonfiction: Middle-grade, YA. Topics: history, nature, social issues, biography, history.

Titles: *National Parks: A Kid's Guide to America's Parks, Monuments, and Landmarks*, by Erin McHugh (ages 5+). *Mac King's Campfire Magic*, by Mac King (ages 9–12).

Submissions and Payment: Catalogue available at website. Send complete ms. Prefers to work with agented authors. Authors email queries to submissions@workman.com (PDF attachments). Response time, publication period, and payment policy, unknown.

Parents, Divisions, Imprints

Workman Publishing, See page 243

Blink

5300 Patterson Ave SE, Grand Rapids, MI 49530
http://blinkyabooks.com

Editor

Blink brings true stories and fiction to young adult readers. Its titles are a positive reflection of what is inspiring and heartening while maintaining a tradition of imaginative and exciting story telling that keeps teen readers on the edge of their seat.

Freelance Potential: Publishes 5–6 titles annually.

Fiction: YA. Genres: social issues, contemporary, mystery, fantasy, dystopian, paranormal.

Titles: *Both of Me*, by Jonathan Friesen (YA). *Like Moonlight at Low Tide*, by Nicole Quigley (YA).

Submissions and Payment: Guidelines and catalogue available at website. Agented submissions only. Manuscripts may be also be uploaded on HarperCollins's writing community site, Authonomy.com, for consideration. Publication period and payment policy, unknown.

Parents, Divisions, Imprints

HarperCollins, See page 137

Bloomsbury Children's Books USA

1385 Broadway, New York, NY 10018
www.bloomsburyusa.com, www.bloomsburykids.com

Submissions Editor

Bloomsbury is a leading independent publishing house, established in 1986. Its four divisions include Bloomsbury Academic and Professional, Bloomsbury Information, Bloomsbury Adult Publishing, and Bloomsbury Children's Publishing.

Freelance Potential: Publishes about 75 titles annually: all by agented authors; 1–10% by previously unpublished writers. Receives 300 queries monthly.

Fiction: Concept books, toddler books, early picture books, early readers, story picture books, chapter books, middle-grade, YA. Genres: adventure, fantasy, mystery, contemporary, science fiction, multicultural.

Nonfiction: Early picture books, middle-grade, YA. Topics: multicultural, ethnic, biography.

Titles: *Space Jackers*, by Huw Powell (ages 8–12). *The Double Cross*, by Jackson Pearce (ages 8–12).

Submissions and Payment: Guidelines and catalogue available at website. Accepts agented submissions only. Responds in 6 months if interested. Publication period varies. Royalty; advance.

Parents, Divisions, Imprints

Bloomsbury Spark, See page 87

Bloomsbury Spark

1385 Broadway, New York, NY 10018
www.bloomsburyusa.com, www.bloomsburykids.com

Submissions Editor

Bloomsbury Spark is a one-of-a-kind, global, digital imprint from Bloomsbury Publishing. It is dedicated to publishing a wide array of exciting fiction eBooks to teen readers. It offers a wide array of fiction including sci-fi, paranormal, mystery and thriller.

Freelance Potential: Publishes about 25 titles annually: all by agented authors; 1–10% by previously unpublished writers. Receives 50 queries monthly.

Fiction: YA. Genres: mystery, thriller, paranormal, sci-fi, and romance.

Titles: *Pride Unleashed*, by Cat Kalen (YA). *Hollywood Witch Hunter*, by Valerie Tejeda (YA).

Submissions and Payment: Guidelines and catalogue available at website. Accepts agented submissions only. Responds in 6 months if interested. Publication period varies. Royalty; advance.

Parents, Divisions, Imprints

Bloomsbury Children's Books, See page 86

Blue Apple Books

515 Valley Street, Suite 180, Maplewood, NJ 07040
www.blueapplebooks.com

Submissions

The catalogue from Blue Apple Press offers board books, picture books, activity books, and more for babies through age 14. The Publisher is Harriet Ziefert. Its books are distributed by Consortium.

Freelance Potential: Publishes about 50 titles annually: most from agented authors. Receives 300+ unsolicited manuscripts monthly.

Fiction: Board books, picture books, concept books, early readers. Genres: social skills, education, animals, family.

Nonfiction: Board books, picture books, concept books, early readers. Topics: numbers, colors, letters, language arts.

Titles: *Can You Whoo, Too?*, by Harriet Ziefert (ages 0–5). *Super Hero Food Doodles,* by Deborah Zemke (grades 4–8).

Submissions and Payment: Catalogue available at website. It accepts agented submissions only. Response time, publication period, and payment policy vary.

Blue Bike Books

11919–125 Street, Edmonton, Alberta T5L 0S3 Canada
www.bluebikebooks.com

Publisher: Nicholle Carriere

At Blue Bike Books, humor and trivia are serious business. This publishers caters to those among us that can't resist reading little factoids or funny anecdotes. It also publishes sports titles, history and biography, and books on outdoor recreation.

Freelance Potential: Publishes about 5 titles annually: most are assigned; about 60% by authors who are new to the publishing house; 40% by previously unpublished writers. Receives 15 queries monthly.

Nonfiction: Middle-grade. Topics: weird science, trivia for a general audience.

Titles: *Bathroom Book of Michigan Trivia*, by Andrew Fleming (ages 12+). *All Hat, No Horse*, by Willie Clement (ages 12+).

Submissions and Payment: Guidelines and catalogue available at website. Query with résumé and hobbies, outline, and 2–3 sample chapters (up to 50 pages). To be considered for in-house work, send résumé and 3 writing samples (preferably humorous). Accepts email submissions to info@bluebikebooks.com (Word or PDF attachments). Responds in 2 weeks. Publication in 6–12 months. Flat fee.

Blue Marlin Publications

823 Aberdeen Road, West Bay Shore, NY 11706
www.bluemarlinpubs.com

Publisher: Francine Poppo Rich

The main goal of this independent publisher is to promote quality children's and middle grade books that make children laugh as they learn. Established in 1999, Blue Marlin is a family owned and operated business.

Freelance Potential: Publishes 2 titles annually: most developed from unsolicited submissions; many by previously unpublished writers. Receives 40 unsolicited manuscripts monthly.

Fiction: Picture books, middle-grade. Genres: contemporary, historical.

Nonfiction: Picture books, middle-grade. Topics: biography, science, history, social issues.

Titles: *Hanni and Beth: Safe & Sound*, by Beth Finke (ages 4–10). *Sofia's Stoop Story: 18th Street, Brooklyn*, by Maria LaPlaca Bohrer.

Submissions and Payment: Guidelines and catalogue available at website. Send complete manuscript. Accepts hard copy. Responds in 3–9 months. Publication in 18 months. Royalty; advance.

Blue Sky Press

Scholastic, 557 Broadway, New York, NY 10012-3999
www.scholastic.com

Editorial Director: Bonnie Verburg

The Blue Sky Press imprint at Scholastic produces a wide variety of children's fiction and nonfiction with the goal of inspiring students and cultivating their minds. It features titles for children of all ages, from birth to YA. Products are designed to help enhance readers' understanding of the world around them. Among its best-selling titles are Dav Pilkey's Captain Underpants books, for ages 9 to 12.

Freelance Potential: Publishes 10–15 titles annually: all by agented authors. Receives 250 queries monthly.

Fiction: Toddler books, early picture books, easy readers, story picture books, chapter books, middle-grade, YA. Genres: historical, contemporary, multicultural, folklore, fairy tales, fantasy, humor, adventure.

Nonfiction: Story picture books, middle-grade. Topics: nature, environment, history.

Titles: *Alphabet Rescue,* by Audrey Wood (PreK-grade 1). *The Dumb Bunnies Go to the Zoo*, by Dav Pilkey (PreK-age 3).

Submissions and Payment: Agented authors only. Responds in 6–12 months. Publication in 2–5 years. Royalty, 5% hardcover trade; advance.

Parents, Divisions, Imprints

Scholastic Inc., See page 204

Boyds Mills Press

815 Church Street, Honesdale, PA 18431
www.boydsmillspress.com

Editorial Director: Mary-Alice Moore
Executive Editor: Elizabeth Van Doren

Boyds Mills Press is the trade book division of Highlights for Children. It publishes a wide range of high-quality fiction and nonfiction titles for young readers. Picture books, chpater books, novels and nonfiction are all included in its list.

Freelance Potential: Publishes 25 titles annually. Receives about 85 queries monthly.

Fiction: Story picture books, middle-grade, YA. Genres: adventure, contemporary, historical, multicultural, humor, seasonal, folktales, humor.

Nonfiction: Concept books, early picture books, early readers, story picture books, chapter books, middle-grade. Topics: history, science, nature, crafts, activities, reference.

Titles: *Bats: Space Boy and His Dog,* by Dian Curtis Regan (PreK-age 2). *Christina Katerina & the Box*, by Patricia Gauch (ages 4–8).

Submissions and Payment: Catalogue and guidelines available at website. For middle-grade and YA fiction, query with first 3 chapters and plot summary. Send complete manuscript for picture books and poetry books only. Nonfiction should have a strong narrative quality. For nonfiction, send the manuscript, a detailed bibliography, an expert's review of the manuscript, and a detailed explanation of competitive titles. Send cover letter with all submissions. Accepts hard copy. SASE. Responds in 3 months. Publication in 2-3 years. Royalty; advance.

Parents, Divisions, Imprints

Calkins Creek Books, See page 92
Wordsong, See page 242

Brandylane Publishers

5 South Street, Richmond, VA 23219
www.brandylanepublishers.com

Submissions

Brandylane's mission is to help previously unpublished writers and poets break into print. This independent press was established in 1985. It also has a cooperative publishing imprint titled Belle Isle Books.

Freelance Potential: Unavailable.

Fiction: Early readers, middle grade, YA. Genres: animals, humor, real-life problems, folktales.

Nonfiction: Early readers, middle grade, YA. Topics: biography, history, self-help, nature.

Titles: *Bubble Duck and Bubble Duck Does Hockey,* by Teresa Pistole (ages 4–7). *Remembering for Both of Us,* by Charlotte Wood (ages 7–10).

Submissions and Payment: Catalogue and guidelines available at website. Query with one-page summary/synopsis, author bio, and target audience. Accepts email queries to brandlane@gmail.com. Responds only if interested. Publication period varies. Royalty.

Buster Books

Michael O'Mara Books, 16 Lion Yard, Tremadoc Road, London
SW4 7NQ United Kingdom. www.busterbooks.co.uk

Submissions

Buster Books is the children's imprint of Michael O'Mara Books.
It specializes in entertaining commercial nonfiction for older
children, including the Girls' Book and the Boys' Book series, and
activity and doodle books. It has recently added fiction to its list,
with the first titles being published in 2012. In 2013 it began publishing activity titles in conjunction with Historic Royal Palaces
and The Science Museum.

Freelance Potential: Publishes 40–50 titles annually.

Fiction: Middle-grade, YA. Genres: fantasy, contemporary.

Nonfiction: Activity and puzzle books for ages 5–12. Topics: art,
doodling, drawing, science geography.

Titles: *5 Seconds of Summer* (ages 10+). *Where's the Zombie* (10+).

Submissions and Payment: Guidelines and catalogue available
at website. Query with synopsis and sample text. Accepts hard
copy and email to enquiries@mombooks.com. SASE. Response
time, publication period, and payment policy vary.

Calkins Creek Books

815 Church Street, Honesdale, PA 18431
www.calkinscreekbooks.com

Manuscript Submissions

This imprnt from Highlights for Children publishes both fiction
and nonfiction that introduces children to many people, places,
and events that have shaped U.S. history. Calkins Creek presents
many points of view through original and extensive research,
and each of its books uses primary sources, such as timelines,
bibliographies and historical notes.

Freelance Potential: Publishes about 7 titles annually. Receives
4 unsolicited manuscripts monthly.

Fiction: Story picture books, chapter books, middle-grade, YA. Genres: historical.

Nonfiction: Story picture books, chapter books, middle-grade, YA. Topics: U.S. history.

Titles: *Woodford Brave,* by Marcia Thornton Jones (YA). *Last-But-Not-Least Lola and the Cupcake Queens*, by Christine Pakkala (ages 8–12).

Submissions and Payment: Catalogue and guidelines available at website. Query or send complete manuscript with cover letter, and detailed bibliography for historical fiction and nonfiction. Accepts hard copy. SASE. Responds in 3 months. Publication period varies. Royalty.

Parents, Divisions, Imprints

Boyds Mills Press, See page 90

Candlewick Press

99 Dover Street, Somerville, MA 02144
www.candlewick.com

Editorial Director: Liz Bicknell

This independent publisher produces books for all ages, incuding board books, ebooks, and cutting edge fiction. Candlewick Press reviews work from agents or through conference appearances where editors meet authors. Check the website for changes to this policy.

Freelance Potential: Publishes 200 titles annually: almost all by agented authors; 1–10% by authors who are new to the publishing house; 1–10% by previously unpublished writers. Receives about 500 queries monthly.

Fiction: Toddler books, early picture books, early readers, picture books, chapter books, middle-grade, YA. Genres: contemporary, multicultural, historical, science fiction, fantasy, adventure, mystery, humor, poetry.

Nonfiction: Concept books, early picture books, story picture books, middle-grade, YA. Topics: history, nature, science, the environment, politics, geography, biography, music, visual arts.

Titles: *A Monster Calls*, by Patrick Ness and Siobhan Dowd (YA). *A Surprise for a Tiny Mouse*, by Petr, Horcek (ages 0–3).

Submissions and Payment: Agented authors only. Catalogue available at website. Response time, publication period, and payment policy vary.

Parents, Divisions, Imprints

Nosy Crow, See page 176
Toon Books, See page 228

Carolrhoda Books

Lerner Publishing, 241 First Avenue North, Minneapolis, MN 55401. www.lernerbooks.com

Editorial Director: Andrew Karre

Since 1969, Carolrhoda has been publishing award-winning picture books, fiction and nonfiction titles. Carolrhoda Books is the home to authors that include Sally M. Walker, Vaunda Micheaux Nelson, and Laurie Friedman.

Freelance Potential: Publishes 20–25 titles annually.

Fiction: Story picture books, middle-grade, YA. Genres: contemporary, historical, multicultural, mystery, real life/problems.

Nonfiction: Early readers, chapter books, middle-grade. Topics: history, biography, contemporary.

Titles: *Picture Perfect*, by Elaine Marie Alphn (grades 5–12). *Rabbits on Mars*, by Jan Wahl (grades K–4).

Submissions and Payment: Guidelines and catalogue available at website. Does not accept unsolicited submissions. Does seek targeted submissions at specific reading levels and for certain subject areas. Also puts out periodic calls for submissions that it posts on its website and blog (http://carolrhoda.blogspot.com). Response time, publication period, and payment policy vary.

Parents, Divisions, Imprints

Carolrhoda Lab, See page 95
Lerner Publishing Group, See page 277

Carolrhoda Lab

Lerner Publishing Group, 1251 Washington Ave N, Minneapolis, MN 55401. www.carolrhodalab.com

Editorial Director: Andrew Karre

This young adult imprint of Lerner Publishing Group is dedicated to distinctive, provocative, boundry-pushing fiction for teens. The books from this imprint of Lerner probes and examines the teenage condition one novel at a time.

Freelance Potential: Publishes 6–8 titles annually.

Fiction: YA. Genres: contemporary, realistic, coming-of-age, paranormal.

Titles: *Savannah Grey,* by Cliff McNish (grades 7–12). *The Sin-Eater's Confession,* by Ilsa J. Blick (grades 9–12).

Submissions and Payment: Guidelines and catalogue available at website. Editorial Director Andrew Karre opens the imprint to solicited submissions from unagented authors periodically; check the blog (http://carolrhoda.blogspot.com) for updates. Email manuscript with brief cover letter to carolrhodasubmissions@lernerbooks.com. (Put "Query" in subject line; RTF attachments.) Other than occasional submission calls, accepts through agents and by author referral only. Accepts simultaneous submissions. Responds in 6 months. Publication period varies. Royalty; advance.

Parents, Divisions, Imprints

Carolrhoda Books, See page 94
Lerner Publishing Group, See page 277

Cartwheel Books

Scholastic Inc., 557 Broadway, New York, NY 10012 www.scholastic.com

Editor: Jeff Salane

This imprint from Scholastic Trade Divsion features innovative books for children up to the age 8. It only accepts submissions from agents.

Freelance Potential: Publishes 100+ titles annually: 1–10% by authors who are new to the publishing house. Receives about 100 queries monthly.

Fiction: Toddler books, concept books, picture books, early readers, story picture books, chapter books. Genres: humor, contemporary, friendship, family, animals, multicultural.

Nonfiction: Concept books, toddler books, picture books, early readers, story picture books. Topics: science, mathematics.

Titles: *Listening to Whales Sing*, by Faith McNulty and Lena Shiffman (ages 8–12). *The Easter Ribbit*, by Bernice Chardiet (ages 3–6).

Submissions and Payment: Accepts submissions from agents and previously published authors only. Responds in 3–6 months. Publication period and payment policy vary.

Parents, Divisions, Imprints

Scholastic Inc., See page 204

Charlesbridge Publishing

85 Main Street, Watertown, MA 02472
www.charlesbridge.com

Submissions Editor

Charlesbridge publishes high-quality books for children, with a goal of creating lifelong readers and lifelong learners. Our books encourage reading and discovery in the classroom, library and home. Our children's books offer accurate information, promote a positive worldview, and embrace a child's innate sense of wonder and truth.

Freelance Potential: Publishes about 45 titles annually: 1–10% developed from unsolicited submissions; 5% by agented authors. Receives 15 queries, 200–300 unsolicited manuscripts monthly.

Fiction: Toddler books, early picture books, early readers, middle-grade. Genres: contemporary, folktales, nature, bedtime stories, multicultural, the arts, poetry.

Nonfiction: Concept books, toddler books, early picture books, easy readers, story picture books, chapter books, middle-grade.

Topics: nature, history, social studies, science, math, multicultural themes.

Titles: *A Crow of His Own*, by Megan Dowd Lambert (ages 3–6). *A Path of Stars,* by Anne Sibley O'Brien (ages (6–10).

Submissions and Payment: Guidelines and catalogue available at website. Send cover letter and complete manuscript for picture books and shorter "bridge" books. For fiction longer than 30 manuscript pages, send a detailed synopsis, chapter outline, and 3 chapters. For nonfiction longer than 30 manuscript pages, send a detailed proposal, chapter outline, and 1–3 chapters. Accepts hard copy only. No simultaneous submissions (must write "Exclusive Submission" on envelope and cover letter). Responds in 3 months only if interested. Publication in 2-5 years. Royalty.

Chicago Review Press

814 North Franklin Street, Chicago, IL 60610
www.chicagoreviewpress.com

Senior Editor: Lisa Reardon

This independent publishing company was founded in 1973. It publishes general nonfiction on a wide range of topics inlcuding music, history, science, travel, and craft books, as well as an award-winning line of children's activity books and young adult biographies.

Freelance Potential: Publishes 60 titles annually. Receives 125 queries monthly.

Nonfiction: Early picture books, story picture books, middle-grade, YA. Topics: art, architecture, math, science, history, biography, geography, engineering, multicultural and ethnic issues, outdoor activities. Also publishes parenting books.

Titles: *101 Kid-Friendly Plants*, by Cindy Krezel (ages 5–10). *Abraham Lincoln for Kids,* by Janies Hebert (ages 8–12).

Submissions and Payment: Guidelines and catalogue available at website. Send cover letter describing your book and credentials, a table of contents, 1–2 sample chapters, market analysis, estimated word count, and projected date of completion. Accepts hard copy. Accepts simultaneous submissions, if identified. SASE. Responds in 8–10 weeks. Publication in 18 months. Royalty, 7–10%; advance, $1,500–$5,000.

Chicken Soup for the Soul

P.O. Box 700, Cos Cob, CT 06807-0700
www.chickensoup.com

Editor

Chicken Soup for the Soul is one of the world's most favorite recognized storytellers. It has sold more that 250 titles in 40 languages. Among its inspirational and humorous titles, it has also started to print books targeting middle grade and young adult readers with inspirational true stories and poetry.

Freelance Potential: Publishes about 15 titles annually.

Nonfiction: Middle-grade, YA, adult. Topics: inspirational, poetry.

Titles: *The Joy of Adoption*, by Amy Newmark and LeAnn Thieman (Parents). *Be the Best You Can Be*, by Amy Newmark and Dr. Milton Boniuk (ages 10–16).

Submissions and Payment: Catalogue and guidelines available at website. Send stories or poetry up to 1,200 words. Accepts email submissions through the website only. Responds if interested. Publication period, up to 3–4 years. Pays $200 per story on publication.

Children's Book Press

95 Madison Avenue, Suite #1205, New York, NY 10016
www.leeandlow.com

Executive Editor: Dana Goldberg

Children's Book Press was the first independent press in the U.S. to focus solely on publishing children's literature by and about people of color. Its titles promote the shared expereinces of cultures that have been historically underrepresented or misrepresented in literature for children.

Freelance Potential: Publishes 5 titles annually. Receives 100 unsolicited manuscripts monthly.

Fiction: Board books, story picture books. Genres: contemporary, ethnic, multicultural, humor.

Titles: *The Woman Who Outshone the Sun*, by Aleandro Martinez (grades 3–4). *In My Family*, by Carmen Lomas Garza (grades 4–5).

Submissions and Payment: Guidelines and catalogue available at website. Send complete manuscript with cover letter that includes brief author biography and publishing history; note whether manuscript is an exclusive or simultaneous submission. Accepts hard copy. Responds in 6 months if interested. Materials not returned. Publication in 2–3 years. Royalty; advance.

Parents, Divisions, Imprints

Lee & Low Books, See page 156

Chronicle Books

Children's Division, 680 Second Street, San Francisco, CA 94107
www.chroniclebooks.com

Children's Division Editor

Chronicle Books offers an exciting range of books, stationery kits, calendars and novelty items. Its list includes children's books and interactive formats, young adult books, cookbooks, and books on fashion, spirituality, pop culture, and relationships.

Freelance Potential: Publishes 170 titles annually. Receives 20 queries, 1,000 unsolicited manuscripts monthly.

Fiction: Toddler books, board books, early picture books, easy readers, story picture books, chapter books, middle-grade, YA. Genres: contemporary, historical, science fiction, adventure, humor.

Nonfiction: Concept books, toddler books, board books, early picture books, early readers, story picture books, chapter books, middle-grade, YA. Topics: art, crafts, nature, geography, history.

Titles: *I Can Dance*, by Betsy Snyder (ages 0–3). *House Arrest,* by K. A. Holt (ages 8–12).

Submissions and Payment: Guidelines and catalogue available at website. Send complete manuscript for toddler books and picture books. For books for older children, query with synopsis and 3 sample chapters. Accepts hard copy and simultaneous submissions, if identified. Responds in 6 months only if interested; materials are not returned. Publication in 2 years. Payment policy varies.

Clarion Books

Houghton Mifflin Harcourt, 215 Park Avenue South, New York, NY 10003. www.hmhbooks.com/kids

Vice President/Publisher: Dinah Stevenson

Changing people's lives by fostering passionate, curious learners is the mission of Clarion Books, a division of Houghton Mifflin Harcourt. Clarion creates engaging, dynamic, and effective educational content and experiences from early childhood to K–12, and beyond the classroom.

Freelance Potential: Publishes 35 titles annually: 8% developed from unsolicited submissions; 70% by agented authors; 30% by authors who are new to the publishing house; 8% by previously unpublished writers. Receives 40 queries, 300 unsolicited manuscripts monthly.

Fiction: Toddler books, early picture books, early readers, story picture books, chapter books, middle-grade, YA. Genres: fantasy, adventure, folklore, fairy tales, historical, multicultural, science fiction.

Nonfiction: Early readers, story picture books, chapter books, middle-grade, YA. Topics: animals, nature, science, history, holidays, biography, multicultural and ethnic issues.

Titles: *Mustache Baby Meets His Match*, by Bridget Heos (grades PreK–3). *Dragons at Crumbling Castle* (grades 5–7).

Submissions and Payment: Guidelines and catalogue available at website. Send complete manuscript for fiction. Query with synopsis and sample chapters for nonfiction. Accepts hard copy. Responds in 12 weeks only if interested; materials are not returned. Publication in 2 years. Royalty.

Parents, Divisions, Imprints

Houghton Mifflin Harcourt, See page 145

Clean Reads

www.cleanreads.com

Owner: Stephanie Taylor

Clean Reads offers wholesome reading without compromise. None of its titles feature profanity, sex or violence to catch a reader's attention. Instead, its stories are rich and vibrant with life, enticing readers in most fiction genres. Along with its adult titles, it also publishes romance, thriller, paranormal and mystery for young adults.

Freelance Potential: Publishes 40+ titles annually.

Fiction: Middle grade, YA, adult. Genres: contemporary, historical, fantasy, mystery/suspense, paranormal, all with a romance slant.

Titles: *The Stone of Kings*, by Shea McIntosh Ford (YA). *The Black Mage: Apprentice* (YA).

Submissions and Payment: Guidelines and catalogue available at website. Submit complete ms (15,000–100,00 words) with cover letter and 2–4 page synopsis. Accepts email to submissions@cleanreads.com (RTF attachments) and submissions through the website. Publication period, unknown. Royalty; 50% on its sales site, 40% on third party sites.

The Collaborative

Alloy Entertainment/Warner Brothers Television Group
http://alloyentertainment.com

Submissions Editor

A division of Alloy Entertainment, The Collaborative is a unique entity that is actively seeking chapter books, middle-grade, and YA fiction manuscripts appealing to the teen market. It collaborates with authors to prepare books for publication and helps place them with the appropriate publishers, but retains the rights to produce the properties in film, television, and new media. Alloy, which was acquired by Warner Brothers Television Group last year, is the developer of Pretty Little Liars, Gossip Girl, and Vampire Diaries.

Freelance Potential: Publishes up to 12 titles annually.

Fiction: Chapter books, middle-grade, YA. Genres: fantasy, contemporary, mystery, romance.

Titles: *Everything, Everything*, by Nicola Yoon (YA). *Firefly Hollow*, by Alison McGhee (8-10).

Submissions and Payment: Guidelines and catalogue available at website. Is only interested in manuscripts that have not been previously submitted to other publishing houses. For non-agented submissions, send query with brief overview of the premise of the book, short description of writing background, and the first 5 pages of the manuscript. Accepts email only to thecollaborative@alloyentertainment.com. Responds in 6–8 weeks. Publication period and payment policy vary.

Contemporary Drama Service

885 Elkton Drive, Colorado Springs, CO 80907
www.contemporarydrama.com

Editor

Contemporary Drama Service has become one of the nation's leading publishers of theatre and drama resources. Religious plays for churches should avoid denominational slants.

Freelance Potential: Publishes 1–5 titles annually: 50–75% developed from unsolicited submissions; 25–50% assigned. Receives 10 queries monthly.

Fiction: Middle-grade, YA. Genres: drama, musicals, folktales, farce, fantasy, novelty plays, skits, adaptations, parody, social commentary, prevention plays, Christian dramas.

Nonfiction: Middle-grade, YA. Topics: public speaking, acting, improvisation, auditioning, stage lighting, directing, theater arts.

Titles: *Around the World in 80 Minutes,* by Gary Peterson. *Ali Baba and the Arabian Nights,* by Craig Sodaro.

Submissions and Payment: Guidelines and catalogue available at website. Send complete manuscript for plays and musicals with cast list, costume information, and set specifications. Query with outline/synopsis, publishing credits/experience, and sample chapters for nonfiction. Accepts hard copy. General queries may be emailed to editor@meriwether.com (no attachments). SASE. Responds in 4–6 weeks. Publication in 6 months. Royalty. Flat fee.

Parents, Divisions, Imprints

Meriwether Publishing, See page 168

Coteau Books

2517 Victoria Avenue, Regina, Saskatchewan S4P 0T2 Canada
www.coteaubooks.com

Managing Editor: Nik L. Burton

Coteau Books publishes and promotes some of the best young
readers' fiction, poetry, and drama written in Canada. It is dedicated to presenting new voices and to helping develop the talent
of new writers. It also publishes educational resources to go
along with its books, when appropriate.

Freelance Potential: Publishes 10–20 titles annually: 75–100%
developed from unsolicited submissions; 10–25% by authors who
are new to the publishing house; 10–25% by previously unpublished writers. Receives 10–25 unsolicited manuscripts monthly.

Fiction: Chapter books, middle-grade, YA. Genres: contemporary, regional, historical, multicultural, realistic, sports, nature,
coming-of-age, fantasy, humor, folktales, poetry.

Nonfiction: Middle-grade, YA. Topics: Canada, current events,
social issues.

Titles: *Cave Beneath the Sea*, by Edward Willett (YA). *Day of the
Cyclone*, by Penny Draper (YA).

Submissions and Payment: Canadian authors only. Guidelines
and catalogue available at website. Send plot summary or table
of contents and 3-4 chapters (no more than 20 pages), with query
letter that includes author bio and publishing credits. Accepts
hard copy. No simultaneous submissions. SAE/IRC. Responds in
3–4 months. Publication in 18–24 months. No advance, royalty
only.

Creston Books

P.O.Box 9369, Berkeley, CA 94709
www.crestonbooks.co/books.html

Publisher: Marissa Moss

Creston Books values strong writing and powerful illustration
combined into picture books. Its books promote a love of reading, a curiosity about the world we live in, and inspire imaginative fiction.

Freelance Potential: Publishes 8 titles annually.

Fiction: Picture books, middle-grade, YA. Genres: animals, holidays, inspirational, concept.

Nonfiction: Picture books, middle-grade, YA. Topics: science, nature, social issues, social skills.
Titles: *Ada Byron Lovelace and the Thinking Machine*, by Laurie Wallmark (YA). *The Little Tree*, by Muon Van (ages 3–6).

Submissions and Payment: Guidelines and catalogue available at website. Send digital submissions (no more than one project per month) to submissions@crestonbooks.co (not attachments). Accepts multiple submissions.

Cuento de Luz

Urb. Monteclaro, Claveles 10, Pozuelo de Alarcón, Madrid 28223 Spain http://ecuentodelux.com

Founder, Chief Editor: Ana Eulate

Cuento de Luz publishes stories full of light that bring out the inner child within all of us. Stories that take the imagination on a journey and help care for our planet, respect differences, eliminate borders and promote peace. Based in Madrid, Spain, the company has an international outlook and specializes in children's literature.

Freelance Potential: Publishes 8 books annually: 40% by authors who are new to the publishing house, 20% by previously unpublished authors. Receives 500 queries, 200 unsolicited mss yearly.

Fiction: Picture books, early readers, middle-grade. Genres: animals, nature, humor, rhyme, adventure, magic.

Nonfiction: Picture books, early readers, middle-grade. Topics: nature, pirates, haunted houses.

Titles: *The Adventures of Kubi,* by Erik Speyer (ages 5–7). *The Winter Train*, by Susanna Isern (ages 5–7).

Submissions and Payment: At this time the publisher is not accepting submissions. Check website for changes in this policy.

Darby Creek Publishing

1251 Washington Avenue North, Minneapolis, MN 55401
www.lernerbooks.com

Editorial Director: Andrew Karre

Darby Creek publishes series fiction for emerging, striving, and reluctant readers ages 7 to 18. From beginning chapter books to intermediate fiction and page-turning YA, its books engage their readers with strong characters and formats. Publishes some titles as ebooks.

Freelance Potential: Publishes 10–15 titles annually.

Fiction: Early readers, chapter books, middle-grade, YA. Genres: contemporary, fantasy, science fiction, high-interest subjects.

Titles: *Mike & Riel Mysteries*, by Norah McClintock (grades 6–12). *Agent Amelia: Zombie Cows,* by Michael Broad (grade 2–5).

Submissions and Payment: Accepts agented submissions only. Puts out occasional calls for submissions on website; check website for changes to this policy. Publication period and payment policy vary.

Parents, Divisions, Imprints

Lerner Publishing Group, See page 276

Dawn Publications

12402 Bitney Springs Road, Nevada City, CA 95959
www.dawnpub.com

Editor: Glenn Hovemann

Dawn Publications is dedicated to inspiring in children a deeper understanding and appreciation for all life on Earth. It strives to help parents and teachers encourage children to bond with the Earth in a relationship of love, respect, and cooperation through its books and materials.

Freelance Potential: Publishes about 6 titles annually: most developed from unsolicited submissions; about 50% by authors who are new to the publishing house; about 30% by previously unpublished writers. Receives about 170 unsolicited manuscripts monthly.

Nonfiction: Early readers, story picture books, middle-grade. Topics: the environment, conservation, ecology, rainforests, animal habitats, the water cycle, seasons, family relationships, personal awareness, multicultural and ethnic issues.

Titles: *Around One Cactus*, by Anthony Fredericks (ages 6–10). *How We Know What We Know About Our Changing Climate*, by Lynne Cherry.

Submissions and Payment: Guidelines available at website. Send complete manuscript with cover letter describing yourself, your vision for the book, and other books you have published, if any. Accepts email submissions (put "Manuscript Submission" followed by the title of your manuscript in subject line) to submission@dawnpub.com (Word or PDF attachments), and hard copy. SASE. Responds in 2 months. Publication in 18–24 months. Royalty; advance.

Dial Books for Young Readers

Penguin Young Readers Group, 375 Hudson Street, New York, NY 10014-3657. www.penguin.com

Publisher: Lauri Hornik

This imprint of Penguin Group publishes a variety of high-quality, engaging fiction and nonfiction hardcover titles for readers of many ages, from preschoolers to young adults.

Freelance Potential: Publishes 75 titles annually: 75% by agented authors; 25% by authors who are new to the publishing house; 10% by previously unpublished writers. Receives 100 queries, 100 unsolicited manuscripts monthly.

Fiction: Board books, concept books, early picture books, early readers, story picture books, chapter books, middle-grade, YA. Genres: contemporary, historical, science fiction.

Nonfiction: Concept books, toddler books, early picture books, early readers, story picture books, middle-grade, YA. Topics: animals, science, social issues.

Titles: *The Boys in the Boat*, by Daniel James Brown (YA). *Three Cups of Tea: Young Readers Edition,* by Greg Mortenson and David Oliver Relin (YA).

Submissions and Payment: Guidelines and catalogue available at website. Mailed submissions only; no electronic submissions. Send complete manuscript for picture books. Query with synopsis, 10 manuscript pages, and publishing credits for longer works. Materials are not returned. Responds in 4 months if interested. Publication period and payment policy vary.

Parents, Divisions, Imprints

Penguin Group (USA), See page 184

Disney-Hyperion

44 South Broadway, #10, White Plains, NY 10601
http://disney.go.com/books/index

Submissions Editor

This is an imprint of Disney Publishing Worldwide. It publishes quality fiction for middle-grade and young adult readers in a variety of genres. Books for younger readers are published under the Disney Press imprint. The Jump at the Sun imprint celebrates diversity and specializes in books for African American children.

Freelance Potential: Publishes 100 titles annually: all by agented authors.

Fiction: Middle-grade, YA. Genres: contemporary, fantasy, science fiction, mystery, multicultural, suspense.

Titles: *Benjamin Frankling: Huge Pain in my...*, by Adam Mansbach and Alan Zweibel (ages 9–12). T*he Story of Diva and Flea*, by Mo Willems and Tony DiTerlizzi (ages 6–8).

Submissions and Payment: Agented authors only. Does not accept unsolicited submissions.

Diversion Press

P.O. Box 3930, Clarksville, TN 37043. www.diversionpress.com

Acquisitions Editor

In business since 2008, this small publisher offers books for children, young adults, and adults. Diversion Press is open to working with new writers but is not interested in erotica or violence. It also does not publish Westerns, romance or science fiction.

Freelance Potential: Publishes 5–10 titles annually: 75–100% developed from unsolicited submissions; 75–100% by authors who are new to the publishing house; 75–100% by previously unpublished writers. Receives 125 queries monthly.

Fiction: Middle-grade, YA. Genres: historical, contemporary, adventure, humor, mystery, coming-of-age, animal stories, poetry.

Nonfiction: Story picture books, chapter books, activity books, middle-grade, YA. Topics: history, animals, the arts, biography, careers, crafts, current events, geography, humor, real life/ problems, social issues, social skills.

Titles: *Brooksticks*, by Sean McHug and Katie McHugh Parker (ages 8–12). *If You Don't Like Worms, Keep Your Mouth Shut,* by Linda Leogel (YA-A).

Submissions and Payment: Guidelines and catalogue available at website. Query with author bio and market analysis (up to 500 words). Accepts email to diversionpress@yahoo.com (no attachments). No simultaneous submissions. Responds in 4–6 weeks. Publication in 2 years. Payment varies.

DK Publishing

375 Hudson Street, New York, NY 10014
www.dk.com

Assistant Managing Editor: Allison Singer

DK Pulishing offers highly visual, photographic nonfiction for children and adults. The publisher looks to inform, enrich, and entertain readers of all ages.

Freelance Potential: Publishes 200+ children's titles annually: all by agented authors. Receives about 75 submissions monthly.

Nonfiction: Concept books, board books, toddler books, early readers, middle-grade, YA. Topics: animals, cars, trucks, numbers, letters, potty training, bedtime, families, cooking, nature, human body, religion, history, geography, science, reference, activities, crafts.

Titles: *Greatful Dead,* by Maurice Waite (YA). *Eyewitness Explorer: Bird Watcher* (ages 8–12).

Submissions and Payment: Guidelines and catalogue available at website. Queries and questions about submissions should be made in writing. Prefers agented submissions. Responds in 6 months. Publication in 2 years. Flat fee, rates vary.

Parents, Divisions, Imprints

Penguin Group (USA), See page 184

Doubleday Children's Books

Random House Children's Books UK, 61-63 Uxbridge Road, London W5 5SA, England. www.randomhouse.co.uk

Submissions

Doubleday Children's is an imprint of Random House Children's Publishers UK. Its list features hardcover fiction titles from a wide range of best-selling authors. This publisher only accepts submissions from literary agents.

Freelance Potential: Publishes 10–20 titles annually: Receives numerous queries monthly.

Fiction: Board books, picture books, early readers, chapter books, middle-grade, YA. Genres: contemporary, adventure, mystery, social issues, historical, fantasy, humor.

Titles: *What If...?,* by Anthony Browne (ages 5–8). *Itch Rocks,* by Simon Mayo (ages 12+).

Submissions and Payment: Guidelines and catalogue available at website. Only accepts agented submissions. Response time, publication period, and payment policy vary.

Dover Publications

31 East 2nd Street, Mineola, NY 11501-3582
www.doverpublications.com

Editorial Department

Founded in 1941, Dover Publications built its reputaton by offering remarkable products. Many of its titles are coloring and activity books that include hands-on projects for a wide variety of topics including science, nature, history, art, world cultures, crafts, and holidays. Dover welcomes nonfiction submissions but it is not open to fiction submissions, although it includes classic fiction on its list.

Freelance Potential: Publishes 500 titles annually: 3%–4% by authors who are new to the publishing house. Receives about 100 submissions monthly.

Nonfiction: Middle-grade, YA. Topics: science, natural history, wildlife, environment, history, biology, hobbies, crafts, activities.

Titles: *The Adventures of Bob White*, by Thornton W. Burgess (ages 6–10). *The Adventures of Pinocchio,* by Carlo Collodi, (ages 6–10).

Submissions and Payment: Guidelines and catalogue available at website. Query with outline, table of contents, sample chapter, and art sample if available. Accepts hard copy. Responds only if interested; materials are not returned. Publication period and payment policy vary.

Dramatic Publishing

311 Washington Street, Woodstock, IL 60098
www.dramaticpublishing.com

Submissions Editor: Linda Habjan

Dramatic Publishing offers musicals and one-act and full-length plays for professional, stock, community, school, and children's theater groups. It also publishes resource materials and reference texts about theater arts. It has an open submissions policy and is interested in receiving new plays.

Freelance Potential: Publishes about 40 titles annually: about 30% by authors who are new to the publishing house. Receives about 40 unsolicited manuscripts monthly.

Fiction: Full-length and one-act plays, monologues, and anthologies. Genres: drama, humor, fairy tales, musicals.

Nonfiction: YA. Topics: stagecraft, stage dialects, playwriting, production techniques, audition presentations, teaching theater arts.

Titles: *The Adventures of Peter Rabbit and His Friends*, by Joseph Robinette (ages 8–12). *Aesop's Fable-ous Barnyard Bash*, by Michael Gravois (ages 6+).

Submissions and Payment: Guidelines and catalogue available at website. Send complete manuscript with résumé, synopsis, production history, reviews, cast list, and set and technical requirements; include CD or audio cassette for musicals. Accepts hard copy. SASE for response only; material not returned. Responds in 4–6 months. Publication in 18 months. Payment policy varies.

Dundurn

3 Church Street, Suite 500, Toronto, Ontario M5E 1M2 Canada
www.dundurn.com

Acquisitions Editor

Dundurn's long, successful publishing program began in 1972 with fewer than five employees. With more than 2,500 books in print and 1,700 ebooks online, Dundurn offers a full line of chapter books, middle grade books, as well as YA and adult titles.

Freelance Potential: Publishes 100–120 titles annually: 5–15% developed from unsolicited submissions; 5–10% assigned; 10–25% by agented authors; 10–25% by authors who are new to the publishing house; 10–20% by previously unpublished writers. Receives 20–30 queries, 40–50 unsolicited manuscripts monthly.

Fiction: Chapter books, middle-grade, YA. Genres: multicultural, contemporary, historical, regional, fantasy, mystery, suspense, humor, animals, nature, environment, coming-of-age.

Nonfiction: Hi-lo, reluctant readers, middle-grade, YA. Topics: biography, current events, history, humor, social issues, nature, environment, the arts, Canada.

Titles: *A Miracle for Maggie,* by Stephen Eaton Hue (ages 13+). *A Hole in My Heart*, by Rie Charles (ages 8–12).

Submissions and Payment: Guidelines and catalogue available at website. Canadian authors only. Query with a cover letter, résumé with past publishing experience, synopsis (include table of contents for nonfiction), 3 sample chapters (first 3 for fiction), word count of complete manuscript, and marketing plan. Accepts hard copy and simultaneous submissions. Responds in 6 months if interested. Materials not returned. Publication in 12–24 months. Payment policy varies.

Dutton Children's Books

Penguin Young Readers Group, 345 Hudson Street, New York, NY 10014. http://us.penguingroup.com

Queries Editor

One of the oldest publishers in the U.S., Dutton is now an imprint of the Penguin Young Readers Group. It publishes fiction and nonfiction for children of all ages, and has a stated mission to create high-quality books that will transport young readers.

Freelance Potential: Publishes 50 titles annually: 2% by previously unpublished writers. Receives 85+ queries monthly.

Fiction: Concept books, early picture books, early readers, story picture books, middle-grade, YA. Genres: contemporary, adventure, mystery, fantasy, humor.

Nonfiction: Toddler books, picture books, YA. Topics: animals, history, nature, science.

Titles: *Looking for Alaska*, by John Green (YA). *Sophomores and Other Oxymorons,* by David Lubar (YA).

Submissions and Payment: Catalogue, guidelines, and editor list with specific genres they seek, available at website. Send 1-page query letter only; include brief synopsis of manuscript and author publishing credits (if any). Accepts hard copy. SASE required. Responds in 4 months if interested. Publication in 1+ years. Royalty; advance.

Parents, Divisions, Imprints

Penguin Group (USA), See page 184

Eifrig Publishing

P.O. Box 66, 701 Berry Street, Lemont, PA 16851
www.eifrigpublishing.com

This company's slogan is "good for our kids, good for the earth, and our communities." It has an additional focus on educational books with innovative ideas. Many of its titles promote healthy self-esteem, positive body image, and environmentally conscious behavior.

Freelance Potential: Publishes 15–20 titles annually: 70% by authors who are new to the publishing house, 70% by previously unpublished authors. Receives 60 queries yearly.

Fiction: Story picture books, early readers, chapter books, middle-grade, YA. Genres: contemporary, literary, historical, mystery, religious, social issues.

Nonfiction: Adult. Topics: Parenting, social issues, community.

Titles: *A Happy Day Keeps the Grouches Away,* by Sandy Cameli (ages ages 4–8). *Big and Strong, I Belong!,* by Bonnie Morris (ages 4–8).

Submissions and Payment: Guidelines and catalogue available at website. Submit a proposal (3–7 pages) that includes working title, summary, target audience, market and competition analysis, outline, and project status; along with sample chapters and author bio or résumé. Accepts electronic submissions through website and email queries to submissions@eifrigpublishing.com. Response time, publication period, and payment policy, unavailable.

Eldridge Plays and Musicals

P.O. Box 14367, Tallahassee, FL 32317
www.histage.com, www.95church.com

New Plays Editor: Susan Shore

Eldridge publishes full-length plays, one-act plays, melodrama, holiday and religious plays, children's theater plays, and musicals of all kinds. Plays must be suitabe for perfrmance by a community theatre, It is strongly recommended that your script is workshopped, read, or performed before submitting.

Freelance Potential: Publishes 35 titles annually: 85% developed from unsolicited submissions; 15% by authors who are new to the publishing house. Receives 40 unsolicited manuscripts monthly.

Fiction: Full-length plays, skits, musicals for grades 6–12 to perform. Genres: classical, contemporary, humor, folktales, melodrama, Westerns, religious themes. Also publishes plays and musicals for adults.

Titles: *Just Another Show,* by Bryan Starchman (ages 8+). *Frumpled Fairytales,* by Bill Springer (ages 4+).

Submissions and Payment: Guidelines and catalogue available at website. Send complete manuscript with cover letter briefly describing the work, its running time, performance history, and author background/writing experience. If submitting a musical, include CD of at least several songs and sample pages from score. Accepts simultaneous submissions, hard copy, and email to NewWorks@histage.com (cover letter in body of email, play in Word or PDF attachment). SASE. Responds in 2 months. Publication in 6–12 months. Royalty, 50% performances, 10% copy sales. Flat fee for religious plays.

Electric Monkey

239 High Street, Kensington, London W8 6SA United Kingdom
www.electricmonkeybooks.co.uk

Electric Monkey is the teen/YA imprint of Egmont UK. The corporation's goal is to feature a wide range of genres that will have broad appeal across ages and interests of teen readers. Titles from its first list include thrillers, historical, contemporary, and fantasy works.

Freelance Potential: Published 10–20 books its first year.

Fiction: YA. Genres: fantasy, contemporary, historical, multicultural, science fiction, romance.

Titles: *Shift*, by Em Bailey (YA). *Fat Boy Swim*, by Catherine Forde (YA).

Submissions and Payment: Guidelines and catalogue available at website. Accepts agented submissions only. Response time, publication period, and payment policy vary.

Entangled Publishing

www.entangledpublishing.com

Submissions Editor

This company publishes young adult romances of all varieties from "dark and angsty" to "fun and sassy" in standard and digital formats. It is currently interested in YA books for all levels (ages 13 to 19) and in particular for the following genres: historical, thrillers, science fiction, contemporary, paranormal, fantasy, and urban fantasy. All manuscripts must have strong romantic elements. It accepts agented and unagented submissions. Interested in publishing fresh voices and unique plot twists.

Freelance Potential: Publishes approximatley 24 print and 360 digital titles annually: 60% by agented authors, 40% by authors who are new to the publishing house, 50% by previously unpublished writers. Receives 2,000 queries yearly.

Fiction: YA. Genres: fantasy, contemporary, historical, science fiction, thriller, paranormal, fantasy and urban fantasy, all with romantic themes.

Titles: *Jane Unwrapped*, by Leah & Kate Rooper (YA). *Touching Fate,* by Brenda Drake (YA).

Submissions and Payment: Guidelines and catalogue available at website. YA novels, 20,000–60,000 words. Send 1-page query with genre, word count, brief synopsis, writing credentials, links to your website, and first 5 manuscript pages or complete manuscript. Accepts submissions via centralized system at website. Responds in 30 days. Publication period and payment policy vary.

Parents, Divisions, Imprints

Teen Crave, See page 224
Teen Crush, See page 225

Epic Reads Impulse

10 East 53rd Street, New York, NY 10022
www.harperteen.com

Editorial Department

This digital imprint from HarperCollins focuses on short stories and novellas for young adults. It publishes work from both new and established authors. It offers new titles each month. Epic Reads Impulse accepts submissions from literary agents only.

Freelance Potential: Publishes 60 titles annually.

Fiction: YA. Genres: contemporary, fantasy, science fiction, humor, mystery, romance.

Titles: *The Map to the Stars*, by Jen Malone (YA). *The Seventh Miss Hatfield*, by Anna Caltabiano (YA).

Submissions and Payment: Catalogue available at website. Accepts submissions through literary agents only. Publication in 18–36 months. Royalty; advance. HarperCollins also features an online community, Figment, which connects authors, agents, editors, publishers, and readers and allows writers to get feedback on works in progress.

Parents, Divisions, Imprints

HarperCollins, See page 137

Fantagraphic Books

7563 Lake City Way NE, Seattle, WA 98115
www.fantagraphics.com

Submission Editor

Fantagraphic Books has been a leading proponent of comics as a legitimate form of art and literature since it began publishing the critical trade magazine, The Comics Journal in 1976. Fantagraphics quickly established a reputation as an advocacy publisher that specilized in seeking out and publishing the kind of innovative work that traditional comics corporations wouldn't touch.

Freelance Potential: Publishes 10–20 titles yearly.

Fiction: YA. Genres: fantasy, contemporary, science fiction, thriller, paranormal, fantasy and urban fantasy.

Nonfiction: YA. Topics: biography, travel, horror, real life.

Titles: *Mox Nox*, by Joan Cornella (YA-A). *Ghosts and Ruins*, by Ben Catmull (YA).

Submissions and Payment: Guidelines and catalogue available at website. Submit a minimum of 5 pages of completed art and text, synopsis, and projected final page count. Accepts hard copy only. Responds if interested. Publication period and payment policy, unknown.

Farrar, Straus and Giroux Books for Young Readers

175 Fifth Avenue, New York, NY 10010
http://us.macmillan.com/fsgyoungreaders.aspx

Children's Editorial Department

This imprint from Macmillan as established in 1953. It is committed to publishing books of the highest literary quality for children and teenagers. It is know for its award-winning list of children's fiction, nonfiction, and picture books.

Freelance Potential: Publishes about 80 titles annually: all by agented authors.

Fiction: Toddler books, early picture books, picture books, early readers, story picture books, chapter books, middle-grade, YA. Genres: contemporary, adventure, fairy tales, fantasy, horror, humor, mystery, suspense, science fiction, graphic novels.

Nonfiction: Concept books, toddler books, picture books, middle-grade. Topics: biography, families, early learning concepts, science, history, nature.

Titles: *If Animals Kissed Goodnight*, by Ann Whitford Paul (ages 3–6). *The Not Very Merry Pout-Pout Fish* *A Pout-Pout Fish Adventure* (ages 2–6).

Submissions and Payment: Accepts submissions through agents only. Response time, publication period, and payment policy vary.

Parents, Divisions, Imprints

Margaret Ferguson Books, See page 118
Macmillan, See page 163

Feiwel & Friends

175 Fifth Avenue, New York, NY 10010
http://us.macmillan.com/FeiwelAndFriends.aspx

Editor

Part of Macmillan Children's Publishing Group, the Feiwel & Friends imprint looks for books that combine quality with substance and commercial appeal. Its catalogue features an eclectic mix of fiction and nonfiction titles for children from birth to age 16. It accepts manuscripts through literary agents only.

Freelance Potential: Publishes 40 titles annually: all by agented authors.

Fiction: Story picture books, chapter books, middle-grade, YA. Genres: contemporary, humor, fantasy, thrillers, historical, animal stories.

Nonfiction: Middle-grade. Topics: humor.

Titles: *Escape the Ordinary*, by various authors (ages 8–12). *Crenshaw*, by Katherine Applegate (ages 8–12).

Submissions and Payment: Agented authors only. Catalogue and guidelines available at website. Response time, publication period, and payment policy vary.

Parents, Divisions, Imprints

Macmillan, See page 163

Margaret Ferguson Books

Farrar, Straus and Giroux Books for Young Readers, 175 Fifth Avenue, New York, NY 10010
http://us.macmillan.com/fsgyoungreaders.aspx

Editorial Director: Margaret Ferguson

After 30 years at FSG in various capacities, including editorial director of FSG Books for Young Readers, Margaret Ferguson returned to her editorial roots with this eponymous imprint. It features fiction for all ages, from picture books to young adult novels, and a small number of nonfiction books. Ferguson focuses on developing books with authors who have worked with her for years, as well as adding new talent to her list.

Freelance Potential: Publishes 10–12 titles annually.

Fiction: Picture books, middle-grade, YA. Genres: contemporary, historical, mystery, realistic, graphic novels.

Nonfiction: Concept books, picture books. Topics: early learning topics, biography.

Titles: *Nelly May Has Her Say*, by Cynthia DeFelice and Henry Cole (ages 4–8). *Pug: And Other Animal Poems*, by Valerie Worth and Steve Jenkins (ages 4–9).

Submissions and Payment: Send complete manuscript for picture books. Send query letter for novels. Publication period and payment policy vary.

Parents, Divisions, Imprints

Farrar, Straus and Giroux, See page 117
Macmillan, See page 163

David Fickling Books

Random House Group, 31 Beaumont Street, Oxford OX1 2NP United Kingdom. www.davidficklingbooks.co.uk

Submissions: Matilda Johnson

A small imprint of Random House Group UK, David Fickling Books features fiction for toddlers through young adults across a variety of genres. Its editors choose books based on whether or not they will move a child—to laugh, cry, or just continue reading to the end. This publisher also offers a yearly contest that is open for submissions. Visit the website for more details.

Freelance Potential: Publishes 12–20 titles annually: 1–10% by authors who are new to the publishing house. Receives 40+ queries monthly.

Fiction: Toddler books, story picture books, chapter books, middle-grade, YA. Genres: contemporary, historical, science fiction, adventure, fairy tales, fantasy, humor, romance, poetry.

Titles: *Vikings in the Supermarket*, by Nick Sharratt (ages 6-10). *The Nest,* by Kenneth Oppel (YA).

Submissions and Payment: Guidelines and catalogue available at website. Accepts submissions from agents only. Publication in 1–2 years. Royalty; advance.

Fire and Ice

www.fireandiceya.com

Editor: Denise Meinstad

This is a young adult imprint of Melange Books. It publishes ebooks in all genres, including romance, humor, contemporary, fantasy, as novels and novellas. It seeks well-written stories with strong characters and plots that have a good balance between the characters' inner and outer journeys. Main characters should be 15–18 years old. No sex, foul language, violence, drugs, alcohol, or smoking by main characters. Fire and Ice will put out submission calls for specific topic; check the website for current needs.

Freelance Potential: Publishes 25–35 titles annually.

Fiction: YA. Genres: historical, romance, paranormal, western, contemporary.

Titles: *Swimming Alone*, by Nina Mansfield (YA). *Orphan's Inn,* by Martha Deeringer (YA).

Submissions and Payment: Guidelines and catalogue available at website. Send complete manuscript, minimum 40,000 words; maximum, 100,000 words. Accepts email to submissions-denise@ fireandiceya.com (doc or docx format). Responds in 10–18 weeks. Publication period varies. Royalty, 40% net royalties on digital; 20% on print.

Fitzhenry & Whiteside

195 Allstate Parkway, Markham, Ontario L3R 4T8 Canada
www.fitzhenry.ca

Children's Book Editor: Christie Harken

Fitzhenry & Whiteside is a family-owned corportation with deep roots in the North American publishing community. The house specializes in history, biography, children's fiction and nonfiction, young adult fiction and nonfiction, and books for mid-level readers. Fitzhenry & Whiteside also owns independent publishers Red Deer Press and Fifth House Publishers. Preference given to Canadian authors.

Freelance Potential: Publishes 15-20 titles annually: 30% by agented authors. Receives 80+ unsolicited manuscripts monthly.

Fiction: Early picture books, story picture books, chapter books, middle-grade, YA. Genres: contemporary, historical, multicultural, mystery, suspense, adventure, coming-of-age, humor, poetry.

Nonfiction: Early picture books, story picture books, middle-grade, YA. Topics: global citizenship, animals, history, biography, nature, the environment, educational.

Titles: *Gabby Drama Queen*, by Joyce Grant (ages 4–8). *Pay It Forward Kids: Small Acts, Big Change*, by Nancy Runstadler (ages 12+).

Submissions and Payment: Guidelines and catalogue available at website. Send cover letter and synopsis/proposal plus 3 sample chapters for nonfiction and novels; complete manuscript for picture books. Accepts hard copy only. SASE. No simultaneous submissions. Responds in 4–6 months. Publication in 1-2 years. Royalty; advance.

Parents, Divisions, Imprints

Red Deer Press, See page 198

Flashlight Press

527 Empire Boulevard, Brooklyn, NY 11225
www.flashlightpress.com

Editor: Shari Dash Greenspan

Offering books for children ages 4 through 8, this publisher looks to explore and illuminate the touching and humorous moments of family situations and social interactions through captivating writing and outstanding illustrations. It publishes picture books that are under 1,000 words.

Freelance Potential: Publishes 2–4 titles annually: 100% developed from unsolicited submissions by previously unpublished writers. Receives 100+ queries monthly.

Fiction: Story picture books. Genres: contemporary fiction with themes of family and social situations.

Titles: *When A Dragon Moves in Again*, by Jodi Moore (ages 4–8). *Maddi's Fridge* (ages 4–8).

Submissions and Payment: Guidelines and catalogue available at website. Email query with description of story, word count, and target audience to submissions@flashlightpress.com (no attachments). If interested, the manuscript will be requested. No hard copy submissions. Responds in 1 month, if interested. Publication period and payment policy vary.

Floris Books

15 Harrison Gardens, Edinburgh EH11 1SH Scotland
www.florisbooks.co.uk

Commissioning Editors: Sally Polson and Eleanor Collins

Floris produces Scottish-themed picture books, storybooks, and children's fiction for its popular Young Kelpies and Picture Kelpies imprints. Floris runs the Kelpies Prize annually for new writers of middle-grade fiction set in Scotland. Deadline for entry is the end of February. It also publishes children's books related to Steiner-Waldorf education.

Freelance Potential: Publishes 60 titles annually: 5% developed from unsolicited submissions; 20% by agented authors; 10% by authors who are new to the publishing house; 10% by previously unpublished writers. Receives 50 unsolicited manuscripts monthly.

Fiction: Board books, picture books, chapter books, middle-grade, YA. Genres: contemporary, fantasy, adventure, real-life issues, historical, all with Scottish characters or themes, or set in Scotland.

Titles: *Pippa and Pelle*, by Daniela Drescher (ages 2-4). *Pyrate's Boy*, by E. B. Colin (ages 8–12).

Submissions and Payment: Guidelines and catalogue available at website. Send synopsis, biography, and 3 sample chapters. Accepts hard copy only. SAE/IRC. Responds in about 3 months. Royalty.

Flux

Llewellyn Worldwide, 2143 Wooddale Drive, Woodbury, MN 55125–2989. www.fluxnow.com

Acquisitions Editor: Brian Farrey

This imprint of Llewellyn Worldwide is dedicated to producing high-quality fiction for teens. Its books relate to the issues and challenges teens encounter and present a teen's point of view whether a story is comic, tragic, or a journey of discovery. It accepts electronic submissions from agents only.

Freelance Potential: Publishes about 25 titles annually: about 60% by authors who are new to the publishing house; about 50% by previously unpublished writers. Receives about 60 queries, 40 unsolicited manuscripts monthly.

Fiction: YA. Genres: contemporary, realistic, coming-of-age, fantasy, thrillers.

Titles: *If You Wrong Us,* by Dawn Klehr (YA). *The Boy Meets Girl Massacre* (YA).

Submissions and Payment: Guidelines and catalogue available at website. Agented submissions via email only. Publication in 18-24 months. Royalty; advance.

Flying Eye Books

62 Great Eastern Street, London EC2A 3QR, England
www.flyingeyebooks.com

Submissions

This children's imprint of the award-winning visual publishing house Nobrow, was established in 2013. Flying Eye Books promise to take your child on a journey of wonder. It publishes both original titles and translations.

Freelance Potential: Unavailable.

Fiction: Activity books, picture books, story picture books, chapter books, graphic novels, middle-grade, YA. Genres: contemporary, fantasy, adventure, real-life issues, animals.

Nonfiction: Picture books, story picture books. Topics: animals, myths, science.

Titles: *Pablo & Jane*, by Jose Domingo (ages 4–8). *Whatever Happened to My Sister*, by Simona Ciraolo (ages 7–11).

Submissions and Payment: Guidelines and catalogue available at website. Accepts email queries to nobrowsubs@gmail or subs@nobrow.com. Payment policy varies.

Formac Publishing

5502 Atlantic Street, Halifax, Nova Scotia B3H 1G4 Canada
www.formac.ca

Acquisitions Editor

Formac Publishing offers books about Canada's Maritime provinces or titles by Maritime Canadian authors. Formac is open to new book proposals and is looking for beginner chapter novels that offer realistic and funny stories on themes like teasing, friendship, diversity, and bullying. The protagonists are ages 6 to 9; the length is about 4,000 words. Its regional fiction and nonfiction focuses on the Maritimes. Formac Lorimer distributes books for Formac and for James Lorimer & Company.

Freelance Potential: Publishes about 70 titles annually.

Fiction: Early readers, chapter books, middle-grade, YA. Genres: adventure, humor, regional, social issues.

Nonfiction: Middle-grade, YA. Topics: history, regional, multicultural, the environment.

Titles: *Explosion Newsie*, by Jacqueline Halsey (ages 3–9). *Healing the Bruises*, by Lori Morgan (ages 7–10).

Submissions and Payment: Canadian authors only. Guidelines and catalogue available online. Query with cover letter describing book idea, a brief outline, writing sample, schedule for completion, estimated final word count, and résumé. Accepts hard copy. Responds only if interested. Publication in 1–2 years. Royalty.

4RV Publishing

P.O. Box 6482, Edmond, OK 73083
www.4rvpublishing.com

Editor in Chief: Harry E. Gilleland, Jr., Ph.D.

4RV publishes children's, tween, and teen books, and adult books. It offers fiction and nonfiction in a broad range of categories and is currently accepting submissions for tween and teen novels. It is not currently looking for books for young children, but it is actively seeking books for tweens and teens.

Freelance Potential: Publishes about 20 titles annually.

Fiction: Picture books, early readers, chapter books, middle-grade, YA. Genres: fantasy, contemporary, historical, science fiction, social issues, social skills.

Nonfiction: Middle-grade, YA. Topics: history, animals, social issues.

Titles: *Tales from Mike's World,* by Mike McNair (YA). *Boo's Bad Day,* by Penny Lockwood (ages 4–8).

Submissions and Payment: Guidelines and catalogue available at website. Does not expect to open submissions for picture books until 2015. For all other categories, send cover letter indicating genre, audience age, content level, marketing/promotion plans, and if an artist is needed (2-page limit); synopsis of book (4-page limit); and first 3 chapters of manuscript. Accepts electronic submissions only with each component as a separate Word attachment to editor-chief@4rvpublishingllc.com, with a copy to vp_operations@4rvpublishingllc.com and President@4rvpublishingllc.com. Responds in 3 months if interested. Publication period varies. Royalty.

Free Spirit Publishing

6325 Sandburg Road, Suite 100, Golden Valley, MN 55427
www.freespirit.com

Acquisitions Editor

Based in Minnesota, Free Spirit Publishing is known for its unqiue understanding of what kids want and need to navigate life successfully. It is a leading publisher of self-help books for children and teens and also offers learning materials that are practical, positive, and solution-focused.

Freelance Potential: Publishes 15–20 titles annually.

Nonfiction: Board books, toddler books, early picture books, early readers, story picture books, middle-grade, YA. Topics: social skills, stress management, conflict resolution, character building, relationships, self-esteem. Also publishes adult titles about teaching methods, behavior issues, bullying prevention, learning differences, service learning, child development, special education, gifted education, and parenting book related to specific youth development issues.

Titles: *Building Everyday Leadership in All Teens*, by Mariam G. MacGergor (YA–A). *Penelope Perfect*, by Shannon Anderson (ages 5–9).

Submissions and Payment: Guidelines and catalogue available at website. Does not accept unsolicited queries. Accepts complete manuscript submissions and proposals that include a cover letter, at least two sample chapters (or entire text for picture book submissions, market analysis, and author résumé. See additional details in submission guidelines on the website. Responds in 2–6 months. Publication in 1–3 years. Royalty.

Samuel French

45 West 25th Street, 2nd Floor, New York, NY 10010–2751
www.samuelfrench.com

Literary Manager: Amy Rose Marsh

Our core value at Samuel French is "making theatre happen." No matter how large or small the audience, this publisher celebrates the ability to bring a group of people together to see a show.

Freelance Potential: Publishes 45–60 titles annually: 1–10% developed from unsolicited submissions; 50–100% by agented authors. Receives 25–75 queries, 16 manuscripts monthly.

Fiction: Full-length and one-act plays for both amateur and professional theater groups. Samuel French also reviews TYA and children's plays. Genres: musicals, drama, comedy, farce, mystery.

Titles: *The 39 Steps*, by Patrick Barlow and John Buchan (ages 11+). *The Amish Project*, by Jessica Dickey (ages 11+).

Submissions and Payment: Guidelines and catalogue available at website. Website contains most current closed areas and submission requirements. Check for updates. Accepts queries only to publications@samuelfrench.com (put "Query Submission and title of play" in the subject line. Attach PDF document with the following: title of play, contact info, one-page synopsis, casting requirements, genre, plot, list of upcoming productions, author bio and 10-page sample of the play or musical. Responds in 4–6 months, if interested. Payment policy varies.

Parents, Divisions, Imprints

Baker Publishing Group, Page 384

Fulcrum Publishing

4690 Table Mountain Drive, Suite 100, Golden, CO 80403
www.fulcrum-books.com

Submission Editor

For more than 20 years, Fulcrum has published an array of storybooks, novels, and nonfiction books for children ages 4 through young adult, as well as books for adult readers. It is not currently seeking fiction, but it is still reviewing nonfiction queries—particularly in the areas of history, Native American culture, nature, and the environment.

Freelance Potential: Publishes 16–20 titles annually: 10% by agented authors, 15% by authors who are new to the publishing house; 30% by previously unpublished authors. Receives 25 queries monthly.

Fiction: Early readers, middle-grade, YA. Genres: adventure, contemporary, historical, folktales.

Nonfiction: Early readers, middle-grade, YA. Topics: ecology, natural history, Native American culture, outdoor recreation, the American West.

Titles: *The Perfect Pumpkin*, by Gloria Evangelista (ages 4–8). *Musings: Tales of Truth and Wisdom*, by Linda Ford (ages 8–12).

Submissions and Payment: Guidelines and catalogue available at website. Query with synopsis, 2–3 sample chapters, author biography, intended audience, competition analysis, and marketing suggestions. Accepts email queries only to acquisitions@fulcrumbooks.com. Responds in 3 months, if interested. Publication in 18–24 months. Royalty; advance.

Gibbs Smith, Publisher

P.O. Box 667, Layton, UT 84041. www.gibbs-smith.com

Editorial Assistant: Debbie Uribe

The books from Gibbs Smith focus on lifestyle topics, popular culture, arts and crafts, and gift books for adults. For children, it offers fiction and nonfiction picture books, and activity books. Its subjects range from offbeat fiction to crafts and educational topics. It is currently reviewing children's activity book submissions only; no picture books will be accepted. Refer to the company's submission guidelines for updates to this policy.

Freelance Potential: Publishes about 60 titles annually: 1–10% by authors who are new to the publishing house; 1–10% by previously unpublished writers. Receives 85 queries monthly.

Fiction: Story picture books. Genres: adventure, Westerns, fantasy, folktales, humor, animal stories, nature, the environment.

Nonfiction: Activity books. Topics: drawing, crafts, the outdoors, holidays, science.

Titles: *A Young Scientist's Guide to Faulty Freaks of Nature*, by James Doyle (ages 8–12). *A Christmas Carol: A BabyLit Colors Primer,* by Aison Oliver (ages 4–8).

Submissions and Payment: Guidelines and catalogue available at website. Query with detailed outline and writing sample for activity books. Accepts email submissions only to DUribe@gibbs-sm. Responds in 3 months if interested. Publication in 1–2 years. Royalty; advance.

David R. Godine, Publisher

15 Court Square, Suite 320, Boston, MA 02108-2536
www.godine.com

Editorial Department

This small publishing house, located in Boston, Massachusetts, aims to identify and produce the best work possible. A number of its children's books have become classics including *A Farmer's Alphabet* and *The Secret Garden*.

Freelance Potential: Publishes 20–30 titles annually: all by agented authors; 25% by authors who are new to the publishing house. Receives about 85 queries monthly.

Fiction: Story picture books, chapter books. Genres: mystery, Westerns, historical, nature, animal stories.

Nonfiction: Story picture books, chapter books, YA. Topics: study skills, camping, crafts, activities, history, biography.

Titles: *The Lonely Typewriter*, by Peter Ackerman and Max Dillon (ages 6–10). *The Tyger Voyage*, by Richard Adams (ages 6-10).

Submissions and Payment: Guidelines and catalogue available at website. Query through literary agent. For consideration for freelance work in copyediting, proofreading, or indexing, send cover letter and résumé. Response time, publication period, and payment policy vary.

Goosebottom Books

543 Trinidad Lane, Foster City, CA 94404
www.goosebottombooks.com

Editor: Shirin Yim Bridges

Shirin Yim Bridges founded Goosebottom Books with her own series of middle-grade books, Thinking Girl's Treasury of Real Princesses, to reach girls and help them be determined and creative, but not confrontational. That series was followed by Thinking Girl's Treasury of Dastardly Dames, with books written by Mary Fisk Pack, Gretchen Maurer, Janie Havemeyer, Liz Hockinson, and Natasha Yim. Goosebottom Books wants to inspire girls with the stories of real women. It continues to expand slowly with new topics and authors.The company reviews writing samples from new authors but does not accept manuscript submissions. Selected authors are invited to write a book on a topic decided in-house.

Freelance Potential: Publishes 6 books annually: 60% by authors who are new to the publishing house, 30% by previously unpublished writers. Receives 300 queries annually.

Nonfiction: Middle-grade. Topics: women, history.

Titles: *The Lost Celt,* by Katherine Applegate (ages 8–12). *Call Me Ixchel—Mayan Goddess of the Moon*, by Janie Havenmeyer (ages 8–12).

Submissions and Payment: Catalogue and guidelines available at website. Email writing samples with expression of interest to submissions@goosebottombooks.com. Does not accept hard copy. Inquiries may be sent to mail@goosebottombooks.com.

Graphia

Houghton Mifflin Harcourt, 222 Berkeley Street, Boston, MA 02116. www.graphiabooks.com

Submissions: Julie Richardson

Today's teens are sophisticated, funny, confused, smart, scared and hopeful. Graphia offers books that reflect their lives that include relatable characters, and familiar situations and dilemmas that today's teens face.

Freelance Potential: Publishes 10–15 titles annually: 20–30% by authors who are new to the publishing house. Receives up to 50 queries, 85 unsolicited manuscripts monthly.

Fiction: YA. Genres: contemporary, historical, science fiction, mystery, suspense, humor, graphic novels.

Nonfiction: YA. Topics: history, multicultural issues.

Titles: *The Candy Darlings*, by Christine Wade (YA). *What Your Mama Never Told You*, by Tara Roberts (YA).

Submissions and Payment: Guidelines and catalogue available at website. Send complete manuscript for fiction. Query with synopsis and sample chapters for nonfiction. Accepts hard copy only. No SASE; materials not returned. Responds in 3 months, if interested. Publication period varies. Royalty; advance.

Parents, Divisions, Imprints

Houghton Mifflin Harcourt, See page 145

Greene Bark Press

P.O. Box 1108, Bridgeport, CT 06601-1108
www.greenebarkpress.com

Editor

A small Connecticut publisher, Greene Bark Press publishes colorful, imaginative picture books that enhance the growing and learning processes of young readers. Although it has not added to its list for two years, Greene Bark is again considering new titles. Fiction that tackles bullying and celebrates diversity is of special interest.

Freelance Potential: Publishes about 1 title annually: 75–100% by previously unpublished writers. Receives 25–50 unsolicited manuscripts monthly.

Fiction: Board books, early picture books, early readers, picture books, story picture books. Genres: contemporary, animal stories, social issues, social skills.

Titles: *Noses Are Not for Picking*, by Elizabeth Verdick (ages 0–4). *The Delmarva Conspiracy,* by Sharon Miner (ages 6+).

Submissions and Payment: No agented authors. Guidelines available. Catalogue available at website. Send complete manuscript. Availability of artwork improves chance of acceptance. Accepts hard copy. Accepts simultaneous submissions if identified. SASE. Responds in 6–12 months. Publication in 18 months. Royalty, 10%.

Greenwillow Books

HarperCollins Children's Books, 10 East 53rd Street, New York, NY 10022. www.harpercollinschildrens.com

Editorial Department

Stories for children of every age, created by authors and artists whose work is full of honesty, emotion, and depth is the mission of this imprint of HarperCollins Children's Books. Like all HarperCollins imprints, Greenwillow does not accept unsolicited submissions. It works through literary agents only.

Freelance Potential: Publishes 40 titles annually.

Fiction: Picture books, early readers, story picture books, chapter books, middle-grade, YA. Genres: contemporary, fantasy, science fiction, mystery.

Nonfiction: Picture books, early readers, story picture books. Topics: nature, animals, science, holidays, seasons.

Titles: *The Unquiet*, by Mikaela Everett (ages 12+). *A Riddle in Ruby*, by Kent Davis (ages 8–12).

Submissions and Payment: Guidelines and catalogue available at website. Accepts agented submissions only. Payment rates and policy varies.

Parents, Divisions, Imprints

HarperCollins, See page 137

Grosset & Dunlap

Penguin Young Readers Group, 345 Hudson Street, New York, NY 10014. http://us.penguingroup.com

Editorial Department

Grosset & Dunlap, an imprint of the Penguin Group, creates high-quality books at afforadble prices. The imprint targets children ages 0 to 12 and offers original series, leveled readers, nonfiction, and licensed books.

Freelance Potential: Publishes about 200 titles annually.

Fiction: Early readers, chapter books, middle-grade. Genres: contemporary, humor, mystery, fantasy, adventure.

Nonfiction: Early readers, chapter books, middle–grade. Topics: biography, holidays.

Titles: *George Brown Vlass Clown: A Royal Pain in the Burp #15,* by Nancy Krulik, (ages 6–8). *Curious About Zoo Vets*, by Gina Shaw (ages 6–8).

Submissions and Payment: Catalogue and guidelines available at website. Not accepting picture books at this time. Query with summary and first 1–2 chapters for all other works. Accepts hard copy. No SASE; materials not returned. Responds in 4 months if interested. Publication in 18–36 months. Royalty; advance.

Penguin Group (USA), See page 184

Groundwood Books

110 Spadina Avenue, Suite 801, Toronto, Ontario M5V 2K4
Canada. www.houseofanansi.com

Editorial Assistant: Suzanne Sutherland

Established in 1978, Groundwood Books is dedicated to the production of children's books of the highest possible quality for all
ages, including fiction, picture books, and nonfiction. It's primary
focus is to publish works by Canadian authors, though it sometimes publishes outstanding books from other countries.

Freelance Potential: Publishes 20–25 titles annually: 1–10%
developed from unsolicited submissions; 10–25% by agented
authors; 10–25% by authors who are new to the publishing
house; 1–10% by previously unpublished writers. Receives 15–40
queries monthly.

Fiction: Board books, picture books, middle-grade, YA. Genres: contemporary, bilingual, coming-of-age, historical, realistic, multicultural,
adventure, humor, folktales, nature, graphic novels, poetry.

Nonfiction: Board books, chapter books, middle-grade, YA. Topics: the arts, biography, Canada, history, current events, real life/
problems, religion, social issues, social studies, sports, technology.

Titles: *The Coyote Columbus Story*, by Thomas King (ages 5–8). *A
Simple Case of Angels*, by Caroline Adderson (grades 3–6).

Submissions and Payment: Guidelines and catalogue available
at website. Not currently accepting unsolicited submissions for
picture books. For longer works, query with synopsis and several
sample chapters. Accepts hard copy. Accepts simultaneous submissions if identified. SAE/IRC. Responds in 6 months. Publication in 2 years. Royalty.

Guardian Angel Publishing

12430 Tesson Ferry Road, #186, St. Louis, MO 63128
www.guardianangelpublishing.com

Publisher: Lynda S. Burch

Guardian Angel Publishing believes it can change the world by investing in children, one child at a time. It hopes the seeds of influence from its books live on and on.

Freelance Potential: Publishes 50–75 titles annually: 10–25% developed from unsolicited submissions; 1–10% by agented authors; 10–25% by authors who are new to the publishing house; 50–75% by previously unpublished writers.

Fiction: Toddler books, early picture books, early readers, picture books, story picture books, chapter books, middle-grade. Genres: adventure, contemporary, historical, regional, inspirational, bilingual, multicultural, fairy tales, sports, humor, nature, poetry.

Nonfiction: Concept books, toddler books, picture books, reluctant readers, hi/lo. Topics: animals, nature, holidays, seasons, recreation, science, social skills, social studies, math, language arts, health and fitness.

Titles: *Hockey Agony*, by Donna McDine (ages 6+). *Rainbow of Friendship*, by Joni Klein-Higger (6+).

Submissions and Payment: Guidelines and catalogue available at website. Send complete manuscript with cover letter containing genre and approximate word/page count between May 1 and September 1. Accepts email submissions only to editorial_staff@ guardianangelpublishing.com (.doc, RTF, or .wpd attachments only). Responds in 2–3 months. Publication in 12–18 months. Royalty, 30%.

Hachette Book Group

237 Park Avenue, New York, NY 10017
www.hachettebookgroup.com

CEO: Michael Pietsch

This international publishing company is part of the France-based Lagardère, with an American division. Hachette Book Group is part of the second largest publisher in the world. Its divisions and imprints include Little, Brown and Company and its imprints LB-Kids, LB-Teens, and Poppy, which publishes for teen girls; Orbit Books, a science fiction and fantasy imprint; and Yen Press.

Freelance Potential: Publishes 200+ children's titles, 800+ adult titles annually.

Fiction: Toddler books, concept books, novelty books, picture books, early readers, chapter books, YA. Genres: adventure, fantasy, contemporary, multicultural, holiday stories, sports, humor, graphic novels, manga.

Nonfiction: Concept books, story picture books, middle-grade, YA. Topics: sports, biography, animals, history, families, nature/environment, science, art, activities.

Titles: *Danger Is Everywhere*, by Davud O'Doherty (ages 8–12). *Guys and Me*, by Keith Richards (YA).

Submissions and Payment: Guidelines and catalogue available at website. Accepts agented submissions only.

Parents, Divisions, Imprints

Little, Brown and Company, See page 158
Orbit Books, See page 451
Yen Press, See page 244

Harcourt Children's Books

Houghton Mifflin Harcourt, 215 Park Avenue South, New York, NY 10003. www.hmhbooks.com/kids

Submissions Editor

Fiction and nonfiction picture books and contemporary and historical fiction for early readers up through young adult are all featured in the catalogue from Harcourt Children's Books. It has been publishing for more than 90 years and has established a reputation for producing fine literature for children. It is home to many well-known children's books, authors, and illustrators. Harcourt accepts unsolicited submissions, but due to the volume of submissions received it only responds if interested.

Freelance Potential: Publishes 30–60 titles annually: by agented and non-agented authors.

Fiction: Board books, toddler books, early picture books, early readers, story picture books, chapter books, middle-grade, YA. Genres: contemporary, historical, multicultural, mystery, fantasy, suspense, sports stories, poetry.

Nonfiction: Picture books. Topics: nature, the environment, biography, animals, world cultures.

Titles: *The Giver*, by Los Lowry (YA). *A Long Walk to the Water*, Linda Sue Park (YA).

Submissions and Payment: Guidelines and catalogue available at website. Send complete manuscript for picture books and novels. Accepts hard copy; materials not returned. Responds in 12 weeks only if interested. Royalty; advance.

Parents, Divisions, Imprints

Houghton Mifflin Harcourt, See page 145

Harlequin Teen

233 Broadway, Suite 1001, New York, NY 10279
www.harlequinteen.com

Executive Editor: Natashya Wilson
Associate Editors: T. S. Ferguson and Annie Stone

Harlequin Teen is the young adult romance imprint from Harlequin, the worldwide publisher of romantic fiction for women. Harlequin Teen focuses on fresh, authentic teen fiction featuring extraordinary characters and extraordinary stories set in contemporary, paranormal, fantasy, science fiction, and historical worlds. Part of the imprint, Kimani Tru, targets African American teens. It's looking for commercial, high-concept stories that capture the teen experience. Most of its titles include a romantic element. Harlequin Teen accepts submissions through literary agents only.

Freelance Potential: Harlequin publishes 100s of titles annually

Fiction: YA. Genres: contemporary, historical, fantasy, science fiction, coming-of-age, paranormal.

Titles: *The Iron Traitor*, by Julie Kagawa (YA). *A Mad Zombie Party*, by Gena Showalter (YA).

Submissions and Payment: Guidelines and catalogue available at website. Agented authors only. Agents may submit a partial or complete manuscript with full synopsis. Accepts email to Natashya_Wilson@harlequin.ca or TS_Ferguson@harlequin.ca or Annie_Stone@harlequin.ca (Word attachments). Response time, publication period, and payment policy vary.

HarperCollins

10 East 53rd Street, New York, NY 10022.
www.harpercollins.com

Editorial Departments

HarperCollins has many specialized divisions and imprints ranging from commercial and literary to academic, business, and religious. Its imprints for children and teens include Balzer + Bray, Amistad, Greenwillow Books, HarperFestival, and HarperCollins Children's Books.

Freelance Potential: Publishes thousands of titles annually: most by agented authors.

Fiction: Children, teens, and adults, across all genres.

Nonfiction: Children, teens, and adults, across all genres.
Titles: *The Perfect Season*, by Tim Green (YA). *Walking with Dinosaurs: The Winter Ground*, by Catherine Hapka (ages 4–8).

Submissions and Payment: Guidelines and catalogues for the various divisions and imprints available at website. Agented authors only. HarperCollins does feature an online writing community, Authonomy, which offers tips and opportunities for authors who want to get books published.

Parents, Divisions, Imprints

Amistad, See page 73
Balzer & Bray, See page 79
Greenwillow Books, See page 131
HarperCollins Children's Books, See page 137
HarperFestival, See page 138
HarperTeen, See page 139
HarperTrophy, See page 140

HarperCollins Children's Books

10 East 53rd Street, New York, NY 10022
www.harpercollinschildrens.com

Associate Editor: Alyson Day

This children's book imprint from HarperCollins brings readers some of the classics of children's literature, including Where the Wild Things Are, Goodnight Moon, and the Fancy Nancy series. Its list includes high-quality fiction and nonfiction for children from preschool through high school. HarperCollins Children's Books, like all of its sister imprints, works with agented authors only.

Freelance Potential: Publishes 500 titles annually: all by agented authors. Receives 85+ queries monthly.

Fiction: Story picture books, early readers, chapter books, middle-grade, YA. Genres: contemporary, historical, multicultural, science fiction, adventure, drama, humor, fantasy, folktales, mystery, horror, suspense, Westerns.

Nonfiction: Story picture books, early readers, chapter books, middle-grade, YA. Topics: animals, science, history, geography, social studies, biography.

Titles: *The Castle Behind Thorns*, by Merrie Haskell (ages 8–12). *Bedtime for Chickies,* by Janee Trasler (ages 0–3).

Submissions and Payment: Guidelines and catalogue available at website. Agented authors only. Royalty; advance.

Parents, Divisions, Imprints

HarperCollins, See page 137

HarperFestival

10 East 53rd Street, New York, NY 10022
www.harpercollinschildrens.com

Editorial Department

HarperFestival is home to books, novelties, and merchandise for the very young—children ages 0–6. Its list is comprised of board books, picture books, and character-based programs like the Biscuit, Little Critter and Berenstain Bears series. Consistent with the policy of all imprints of HarperCollins, HarperFestival reviews submissions from agented authors only.

Freelance Potential: Publishes 120 titles annually.

Fiction: Toddler books, novelty books, picture books, story picture books, early readers. Genres: contemporary, family, friends, animal stories.

Titles: *The Mouse and the Motorcyle,* by Beverly Cleary (ages 4–8). *Frog and Toad Are Friends,* by Arnold Lobel.

Submissions and Payment: Guidelines and catalogue available at website. Accepts queries through literary agents only. Royalty; advance.

Parents, Divisions, Imprints

HarperCollins, See page 137

HarperTeen

10 East 53rd Street, New York, NY 10022
www.harperteen.com

Editorial Department

The books from HarperTeen pull back the curtain on the fabulous lives of beautiful people. They go beneath the humdrum veneer of the girl next door, and offer a real glimpse into the lives of today's teens. The titles from this imprint of HarperCollins cover everyday realities, struggles and triumphs of teens. HarperTeen uses multiple media outlets to reach its audience, including social networks and e-newsletters.

Freelance Potential: Publishes 60 titles annually.

Fiction: YA. Genres: contemporary, fantasy, science fiction, humor, mystery, romance.

Titles: *Sideways Stories from Wayside School,* by Louis Sachar (ages 13+). *Julie of the Wolves,* by Jean Craighead George (ages 13+).

Submissions and Payment: Catalogue available at website. Accepts submissions through literary agents only. Publication in 18–36 months. Royalty; advance. HarperCollins also features an online community, Figment, which connects authors, agents, editors, publishers, and readers and allows writers to get feedback on works in progress.

HarperTrophy

10 East 53rd Street, New York, NY 10022
www.harpertcollinschildrens.com

Editorial Department

This premier imprint for children's books is part of HarperCollins.
Its list includes titles from award-winning authors like Laura Ingalls
Wilder, E. B. White, and Beverly Cleary. HarperTrophy offers a great
mix of old and new titles. In accordance with HarperCollins policies,
this imprint only accepts submissions from agents.

Freelance Potential: Publishes 60 titles annually.

Fiction: YA. Genres: contemporary, fantasy, science fiction,
humor, mystery, romance.

Titles: *Fancy Nancy Sees Stars*, by Jane O'Connor (ages 4–8).
Stolen Magic, by Gail Carson Levine (ages 8–12).

Submissions and Payment: Catalogue available at website.
Accepts submissions through literary agents only. Publication in
18–36 months. Royalty; advance. HarperCollins also features an
online community, Figment, which connects authors, agents, editors, publishers, and readers and allows writers to get feedback
on works in progress.

Parents, Divisions, Imprints

HarperCollins, See page 137

HCI Books

3201 SW 15th Street, Deerfield Beach, FL 33442
www.hcibooks.com

Editorial Committee

Dedicated to bringing readers quality books, HCI makes its distinction in the marketplace by not just publishing books, but "publishing people." The company carefully selects its authors, who inspire readers to achieve their dreams, live lives of abundance, and experience consolation when needed.

Freelance Potential: Publishes 60 titles annually: 1–10% developed from unsolicited submissions; 90% by agented authors; 15% by authors who are new to the publishing house; 1–10% by previously unpublished writers. Receives 40 queries monthly.

Fiction: YA. Genres: contemporary, fantasy.

Nonfiction: YA. Topics: teen issues, health, fitness, relationships. Also publishes parenting titles.

Titles: *Dark Territory*, by J. Gabriel Gates and Charlene Keel (YA). *Teen Love: A Journal on Relationships,* by Kimberly Kirberger and Colin Mortensen (YA).

Submissions and Payment: Guidelines and catalogue available at website. Send proposal with author information, including professional credentials and publishing credits; detailed marketing data that includes target audience and promotion ideas; book summary and purpose; its unique content and characteristics; competing titles and sales figures; specific information that is not provided by comparable titles; a detailed outline; table of contents; introduction; and 2 sample chapters. Accepts hard copy and email to Editorial@hcibooks.com. SASE. Responds in 6 months. Publication in 6–12 months. Payment policy varies.

Heuer Publishing

P.O. Box 248, Cedar Rapids, IA 52406. www.hitplays.com

Editor: Geri Albrecht

Heuer is one of the oldest U.S. publishing houses serving the educational and community theater markets. For the middle-grade and young adult set, it publishes short, full-length, and 10-minute plays and monologues, as well as musicals. Its current needs include classic, 10-minute, social, family, interactive, and dinner theater. It no longer publishes theater resources or texts.

Freelance Potential: Publishes 30–40 titles annually: 50–75% developed from unsolicited submissions; 1–10% by agented authors; 10–25% by authors who are new to the publishing house; 1–10% by previously unpublished writers. Receives more than 200 unsolicited manuscripts monthly.

Fiction: Middle-grade, YA. Genres: dramas, plays, monologues, musicals.

Titles: *Beatrice the Butterfly*, by Matt Thompson and Linda Sherry Thompson (youth play). *Chasing Charming*, by Alaska Reece Vance (youth play).

Submissions and Payment: Guidelines and catalogue available at website. Send complete manuscript with production history, synopsis, cast list, running time, and set requirements. Accepts submissions through the website only (Word, Adobe, or RTF formats). Responds in 4–6 months (10–12 months for plays without production history). Publication in 3–6 months. Payment policy varies.

Holiday House

425 Madison Avenue, New York, NY 10017
www.holidayhouse.com

Acquisitions Editor

Holiday House is an independent publisher of children's books. It specializes in quality hardcovers, from picture books to young adult fiction and nonfiction. Its books target children ages four and up. Most of its titles are also aligned with Common Core standards.

Freelance Potential: Publishes 70 titles annually: most by agented authors; 1–10% by authors who are new to the publishing house; 1–10% by previously unpublished writers. Receives 100 unsolicited manuscripts monthly.

Fiction: Early picture books, early readers, story picture books, chapter books, middle-grade, YA. Genres: contemporary, historical, multicultural, humor, mystery, fantasy.

Nonfiction: Early picture books, early readers, story picture books, middle-grade, YA. Topics: history, social issues, biography, science.

Titles: *Ah!*, by Geraldine Collet (ages 2–5). *Always Twins*, by Teri Weidner (ages 2–5).

Submissions and Payment: Guidelines and catalogue available at website. Send complete manuscript. Though not necessary, include copies of artwork if available. Accepts hard copy. No

SASE; materials not returned. Responds in 4 months, if interested. Publication period varies. Royalty; advance.

Henry Holt Books for Young Readers

Macmillan, 175 Fifth Avenue, New York, NY 10010
http://us.macmillan.com/holtyoungreaders.aspx

Submissions Editor

Founded in 1866, this imprint of Macmillan, is known for publishing high-quality picture books, chapter books, novels, and nonfiction for children from preschool through high school. Although the genres and subjects it publishes are diverse, the common denominators are quality writing and engaging story lines. Henry Holt accepts submissions through literary agents only.

Freelance Potential: Publishes about 40 titles annually. Receives 1,000 queries monthly.

Fiction: Toddler books, early picture books, early readers, story picture books, chapter books, middle-grade, YA. Genres: contemporary, historical, multicultural, ethnic, adventure, drama, fantasy, poetry.

Nonfiction: Story picture books, chapter books, middle-grade. Topics: biography, history, ethnic issues, mythology.

Titles: *Wonder Horse,* by Emily Arnold McCully (ages 8–12). *Los Gatos Black on Halloween*, by Marisa Montes and Yuyi Morales (ages 5–8).

Submissions and Payment: Guidelines and catalogue available at website. Accepts submissions through literary agents only. Publication period and payment policy vary.

Parents, Divisions, Imprints

Macmillan, See page 163

Honolulu Theatre for Youth

1149 Bethel Street, Suite 700, Honolulu, HI 96813
www.htyweb.org/education/workshops-for-professional-artists

Artistic Director: Eric Johnson

This publisher is committed to developing new theatrical works for children that focus on the geographic and cultural identity of Hawaii. It supports local writers, however national and international collaboration is acceptable as long as the work appeals to its target audiences. It seeks scripts for all age levels, and of all types, including musicals, classics, and Asian-influenced works.

Freelance Potential: Produces 6–10 new plays annually.

Fiction: Plays. Age ranges: PreK, K–3, 4–6, middle and high school. Genres: musicals, classics, multicultural.

Titles: *Rudolf's Reindeer Games* (ages 5+). *Mud Pies and Magic*, by Lee Cataluna (ages 5+).

Submissions and Payment: Guidelines and past plays available at website. Submission must be for one of the target grade groups, run under an hour, with no more than 5 cast members. Send inquiry letter by email to artistic@HTYweb.org or by regular mail. Response time varies.

Hot Key Books

80-81 Wimpole Street, W1G 9RE, London, England
www.hotkeybooks.com

Acquisitions Editor

Hot Key Books is a division of Boonier Publishing that targets books for children ages 9 to 19. Its catalogue is filled with standout fiction that people like to talk about. The company focuses on top-notch author care and connecting with readers who love books as much as they do.

Freelance Potential: Publishes 10–20 books annually

Fiction: Middle-grade, YA. Genres: contemporary, historical, , humor, mystery, fantasy, realistic, futuristic.

Titles: *100 Days of April-May*, by Edyth Bulbring (ages 11–14). *Clockwise to Titan,* by Elon Dann (YA).

Submissions and Payment: Guidelines and catalogue available at website. Send cover letter with author info and complete manuscript along with a full synopsis to enquiries@hotkeybooks.com (prefers Word or PDF attachments). Accepts email only. Responds in 3 months. Publication period and payment policy unknown.

Houghton Mifflin Books for Children

Houghton Mifflin Harcourt, 222 Berkeley Street, Boston, MA 02116-3764. http://hmhbooks.com/kids

Submissions Coordinator

Houghton Mifflin's trade division has published some of the world's more renowned novels, nonfiction, children's books and reference books. It is interested in works of the highest caliber only, whether they are fiction or nonfiction, for toddlers or young adults. It is interested in increasing the number of titles available electronically and eventually acquiring original e-content.

Freelance Potential: Publishes 60 titles annually: most by agented authors. Receives 100 queries, 1,700 unsolicited manuscripts monthly.

Fiction: Toddler books, early picture books, early readers, story picture books, middle-grade, YA. Genres: contemporary, historical, multicultural, adventure, animal stories.

Nonfiction: Middle-grade, YA. Topics: history, science, nature, the environment, biography.

Titles: *Boo Boo: A Small Gosling with a Big Appetite* (ages 0–3). *Talkin' Guitar: A Story of Young Doc Watson* (ages 4–8).

Submissions and Payment: Guidelines and catalogue available at website. Send complete manuscript for fiction. Query with synopsis and sample chapters for nonfiction. Accepts hard copy. No SASE; materials not returned. Responds in 12 weeks if interested. Publication period varies. Royalty; advance.

Parents, Divisions, Imprints

Houghton Mifflin Harcourt, See page 145

Houghton Mifflin Harcourt

Houghton Mifflin Harcourt, 222 Berkeley St., Boston, MA 02116
www.hmhco.com

Submissions Coordinator

Described as a "global learning company," Houghton Mifflin Harcourt publishes educational materials under its School Division, and trade books for adults and children. Houghton Mifflin Harcourt Children's Book Group includes the imprints Clarion Books, Houghton Mifflin Books for Children, Harcourt Children's Books, and the paperback lines Graphia and Sandpiper. It also publishes the American Heritage Dictionaries and Petersen Field Guides.

Freelance Potential: Publishes hundreds of titles annually across its divisions.

Fiction: Children, teens, and adults, across most genres.

Nonfiction: Children, teens, and adults, across most genres.

Titles: *What About Us!*, by Karen Beaumont (ages 4–8). *Penny and Jelly: The School Show*, by Maria Gianferrari (ages 4–8).

Submissions and Payment: Accepts unsolicited submissions by mail for the children's division, but only responds if interested. Royalty; advance.

Parents, Divisions, Imprints

Clarion Books See page tk.
Graphia, See page 130
Houghton Mifflin Books for Children, See page 100

Hungry Tomato

1251 Washington Avenue North, Minneapolis, MN 55401
www.lernerbooks.com

Editorial Director: Andrew Karre

This imprint of Lerner Books offers high-interest nonfiction for ages 8–12. Its titles combine gripping text and eye-catching images that engage even the most reluctant readers. The books from this imprint begin at the fifth grade level.

Freelance Potential: Publishes 10–15 titles annually.

Nonfiction: Middle-grade, YA. Topics: animals, history, the environment, and nature.

Titles: *Plan B*, by Charman Simon (grades 6–12). *Recruited*, by Suzanne Weyn grades 6–12).

Submissions and Payment: Accepts agented submissions only. Puts out occasional calls for submissions on website; check website for changes to this policy. Publication period and payment policy vary.

Parents, Divisions, Imprints

Lerner Publishing Group, See page 277

Illumination Arts

808 6th Street South, Suite 200, Kirkland, WA 98033
www.illumin.com

President: John Thompson
The mission of this children's publisher is to "inspire the mind, touch the heart, and uplift the spirit." The company is currently for sale and is closed to submissions. Check its website for updates.

Freelance Potential: Publishes 1 title annually: usually developed from an unsolicited submission by a previously unpublished writer.

Fiction: Toddler books, early picture books, story picture books, middle-grade. Genres: contemporary; religious; multicultural; stories about faith, love, and grief.

Titles: *One Voice,* by Cindy McKinley (ages 4-12). *Wings Within,* by Franklin Hill, Ph.D. (ages 4–8).

Submissions and Payment: Guidelines and catalogue available at website. Not accepting queries or manuscripts at this time. Check the website for updates to this policy.

Imajin

2111 Horizon Drice, West Kelowna, BC, Canada V1Z 3Y5
www.imajinbooks.com

Publisher: Cheryl Tardif

Imajin is an epublisher of fiction of all genres. It does publish some titles as traditional books as well. It publishes middle grade and YA novels (as well as adult titles). It is currently looking for mystery/suspense/thriller, horror, fantasy/paranormal (but no vampires, werewolves, or erotica). Requests ebook rights for a minimum of 5 years.

Freelance Potential: Publishes 8–12 titles annually; 10% by agented authors, 25% by authors who are new to the publishing house, 25% by previously unpublished authors. Receives 15–20 queries each year. Prefers writers to have at least 1 novel published traditionally or self-published.

Fiction: Middle-grade, YA. Genres: fantasy, mystery, paranormal, horror, adventure, chick lit, historical, literary, romance, religious, science fiction, and westerns.

Titles: *Metatron: The Angel Has Risen,* by Laurence St. John (ages 8–12). *The Traz,* by Elleen Schuh (YA).

Submissions and Payment: Guidelines and catalogue available at website. Query with author bio (include publishing history and social networking), genre, 3-sentence description of the novel, 5-paragraph synopsis, and first 5 chapters. Accepts email only to Cheryl Tardif at: imajinbooks@shaw.ca. Accepts multiple submissions. Responds in 4 weeks. Publication period varies. Royalty, 50%.

Imprint

175 Fifth Avenue, New York, NY 10010
http://us.macmillan.com/publishers/imprint

Publisher: Erin Stein

This new imprint from Macmillan was started by Erin Stein, after stints at HarperCollins and TokyoPop. The imprint features commercial branded books for early, middle grade, and young adult readers. It accepts manuscripts through literary agents only.

Freelance Potential: Unavailable.

Fiction: Picture books, chapter books, middle-grade, YA. Genres: commercial material, humor, coming-of-age, action adventure.

Titles: *The Lovely Reckless*, by Kami Garcia (YA). *Babies Ruin Everything*, by Matthew Swanson and Robbi Behr (ages 4–8).

Submissions and Payment: Agented authors only. Catalogue and guidelines available at website. Response time, publication period, and payment policy vary.

Parents, Divisions, Imprints

Macmillan, See page 163

Interlink Publishing Group

46 Crosby Street, Northampton, MA 01060-1084
www.interlinkbooks.com

Editorial Director

Interlink Publishing was established in 1987, specializing in world travel, art, wolrd history, and children's books from around the world. Authors should familiarize themselves with the books currently in Interlink's catalogue prior to submitting material. At this time, Interlink is closed to children's book submissions. Check website for updates to this policy.

Freelance Potential: Publishes 50 titles annually: about 35% by authors who are new to the publishing house; 15% by previously unpublished writers. Receives 150 queries monthly.

Fiction: Toddler books, early picture books, story picture books. Genres: multicultural, contemporary, myths, folktales, stories from other countries.

Nonfiction: Concept books, toddler books, early picture books, story picture books. Topics: nature, animals, cultures of the world.

Titles: *The Wee Book O Fairy Tales*, by James Robertson and Matthew Fitt (ages 4–8). *Constantine,* by Nancy Rogers Yaeger (ages 4–8).

Submissions and Payment: Guidelines and catalogue available at website. Publication in 18–24 months. Royalty, 6–7% of retail; small advance.

Jabberwocky

Sourcebooks, 1935 Brookdale Road, Suite 139, Naperville, IL 60563. www.sourcebooks.com

Editor: Rebecca Frazer

This children's imprint of Sourcebooks features engaging stories and characters for children in preschool through the middle grades. Young adult fiction is accepted by its sister imprint, Fire. At ths time, Jabberwocky is only accepting submissions through agents.

Freelance Potential: Sourcebooks publishes 300+ titles annually: 1–10% developed from unsolicited submissions; 1–10% assigned; 50–75% by agented authors; 50–75% by authors who are new to the publishing house; 10–25% by previously unpublished writers. Receives 200+ queries monthly.

Fiction: Toddler books, early picture books, early readers, story picture books, chapter books, middle-grade. Genres: contemporary, humor, historical, mystery, adventure.

Nonfiction: Chapter books, middle-grade. Topics: history, biography.

Titles: *If I Coud Keep You Little...*, by Marianne Richmond (ages 0–4). *My Name Is Not Isabella*, by Jennifer Fosberry (ages 4–8).

Submissions and Payment: Guidelines and catalogue available at website. Accepts submissions through literary agents only. Responds in 8–12 weeks. Publication in 1 year. Royalty; advance.

Parents, Divisions, Imprints

Sourcebooks, See page 214

Jolly Fish Press

P.O. Box 1773, Provot, UT 84603-1773. www.jollyfishpress.com

Editor: Ellen Larson

Based out of Provo, Utah, Jolly Fish Press publishes trade fiction and select nonfiction books in the national and international market. Its catalogue includes literary fiction, fantasy, romance for the adult market, as well as several titles for the YA audience.

Freelance Potential: Publishes 10–15 titles annually: 30% by agented authors, 50% by authors who are new to the publishing house; 60% by previously unpublished writers. Receives 50–100 mss monthly.

Nonfiction: YA. Topics: Biography, self-help, real life.

Fiction: YA. Genres: mystery, fantasy, action adventure, science fiction, romance.

Titles: *One Boy No Water*, by Lehua Parker (YA). *Up In the Air*, by Anne Marie Meyers (YA)

Submissions and Payment: Guidelines and catalogue available at website. Query with one page synopsis and first three chapters for fiction. Query with book proposal for nonfiction. Accepts email submissions to submit@jollyfishpress.com. Responds in 4–6 weeks. Publication period and payment rates vary.

Just Us Books

P.O. Box 5306, East Orange, NJ 07017. www.justusbooks.com

Submissions Manager

Children's books that reflect the diversity of Black history, heritage, and experiences comprise the catalogue from Just Us Books. Its catalogue includes fiction, nonfiction, and biographies for young children through young adults, but currently it is accepting only young adult submissions. Its new imprint, Marimba, publishes multicultural children's titles.

Freelance Potential: Publishes 4–6 titles annually. Receives 85+ queries monthly.

Fiction: Concept books, picture books, early readers, story picture books, chapter books, middle-grade, YA. Genres: contemporary, historical, multicultural, ethnic, adventure, mystery—all featuring African American characters or themes.

Nonfiction: Middle-grade. Topics: African-American history, culture, social issues, biography.

Titles: *My Friend Maya Loves to Dance*, by Cheryl Willis Hudson (ages 4–8). *Brown Eyes, Brown Skin*, by Cheryl Willis Hudson and Bernette Ford (ages 4–8).

Submissions and Payment: Guidelines and catalogue available at website. Currently open to YA fiction only. Query with 1-2 page synopsis, 3–5 sample pages, and author biography that includes publishing credits. Accepts hard copy. Send SASE for response. Responds in 6 months. Publication period varies. Royalty.

Kane Miller

10302 E. 55th Place, Yulsa, OK 74146. www.kanemiller.com

Editorial Department

Kane Miller offers the most-exciting, engaging, and educational books on the market today. Its titles are high-quality, innovative, and lavishly-illustrated. Its titles come from all over the world to bring a different feel, culture, or just a silly story that kids everywhere can enjoy.

Freelance Potential: Publishes about 45 titles annually: 1–10% developed from unsolicited submissions; 1–10% by agented authors; 45% by authors who are new to the publishing house; 10% by previously unpublished writers. Receives 100+ unsolicited manuscripts monthly.

Fiction: Concept books, toddler books, early picture books, story picture books, chapter books, middle-grade, YA. Genres: contemporary, historical, multicultural, adventure, humor, mystery, animal stories.

Titles: *Billy Goat's Big Breakfast*, by Jez Alborough (age 3+). *A Garden for Pig*, by Kathryn Thursman (ages 4–8).

Submissions and Payment: Guidelines and catalogue available at website. Send complete manuscript or query with synopsis and 2 sample chapters. Authors from other countries may send published book with a summary and outline in English. Accepts hard copy and email to submissions@kanemiller.com. SASE. Responds in 3 months. Publication in 1–2 years. Royalty; advance.

Kensington Publishing

119 West 40th Street, New York, NY 10018
www.kensingtonbooks.com

Editorial Director: Alicia Condon

Founded un 1974, Kensington Publishing is a full-range, independent publisher. It has two YA imprints. Dafina Books publishes African American and multicultural titles. Kensington Teen (KTeen) launched about a year ago, and seeks general YA submissions that reflect "emotionally authentic teen experiences." The goal is to feature unique voices and imaginative storytelling, all with the underlying theme of self-discovery. Both Dafina and KTeen publish series and stand-alone titles. Other Kensington imprints are Zebra (romance, especially historical); Pinnacle (thrillers, true crime); and Citadel (nonfiction).

Freelance Potential: Kensington publishes about 600 books a year; the new Teen imprint publishes about 12 titles annually.

Fiction: YA. Genres: urban fantasy, contemporary, historical, romantic, multicultural, social issues.

Titles: *Dreaming of Antigone,* Robin Bridges (YA). *Any Other Girl,* Rebecca Phillips (YA).

Submissions and Payment: Guidelines and catalogue available at website. Send cover letter, first 3 chapters, and a synopsis of no more than 5 pages to one editor (see list on website for current needs). Accepts hard copy. SASE. Will accept queries only by email to acondon@kensingtonbooks.com, no manuscripts or attachments. Responds in 3 months if interested. Publication period and payment policy vary.

Kids Can Press

Corus Quay, 25 Dockside Drive, Toronto, Ontario M5A 0B5 Canada. www.kidscanpress.com

Acquisitions Editor

The largest Canadian children's book publisher, this company produces a variety of high-quality fiction and nonfiction books for children in preschool through high school. Its titles include picture books, poetry, and science books. It prefers books that promote a world view, and works with Canadian writers only.

Freelance Potential: Publishes about 30 titles annually. Receives 300+ queries and unsolicited manuscripts monthly.

Fiction: Toddler books, early readers, story picture books, chapter books, middle-grade, YA. Genres: contemporary, historical, folklore, mystery, suspense, animal stories.

Nonfiction: Early readers, middle-grade. Topics: animals, crafts, hobbies, nature, history, biography, science.

Titles: *Aaron's Awful Allergies,* by Troon Harrison (ages 5–8). *At Grandpa's Sugar Bush,* by Margaret Carney (6–10).

Submissions and Payment: Canadian authors only. Guidelines and catalogue available at website. Currently not seeking YA fiction. Send complete manuscript for picture books. Query with synopsis and 3 sample chapters for all other books. Accepts hard copy. Accepts simultaneous submissions, if identified. No SASE; materials are not returned. Responds in 6 months, if interested. Publication period varies. Royalty; advance.

Alfred A. Knopf Books for Young Readers 🔑

Random House, 1745 Broadway, 8th Floor, New York, NY 10019
www.randomhouse.com/kids

Submissions Editor

This imprint of Random House Children's Books, publishes fiction and nonfiction for toddlers through young adults. Known for the caliber of its authors and artists, it publishes books intended to entertain, inspire, and endure. Its original middle-grade and YA novels are reprinted as paperbacks through Yearling, Ember, Bluefire, and Knopf Trade Paperbacks.

Freelance Potential: Publishes 60–75 titles annually: 1–10% developed from unsolicited submissions; 50% by agented authors; 1–10% by authors who are new to the publishing house.

Fiction: Toddler books, picture books, chapter books, middle-grade, YA. Genres: contemporary, adventure, fantasy, suspense, mystery, science fiction, animal stories.

Nonfiction: Story picture books, chapter books, middle-grade, YA. Topics: biography, history, real life issues.

Titles: *The Killer's Tears*, by Anne-Laure Bondoux (ages 12+). *The Book of the Maidservant,* by Rebecca Barnhouse (ages 8–12).

Submissions and Payment: Catalogue available at website. Like most Penguin Random House imprints, submissions are accepted through a literary agent. Responds in 6 months if interested. Publication period and payment policy vary.

Parents, Divisions, Imprints

Penguin/Random House Children's Books, See page 184

Wendy Lamb Books

Random House, 1745 Broadway, 10th Floor, New York, NY 10019
www.randomhouse.com/kids

Editor: Wendy Lamb

This first eponymous imprint of Random House Children's Books
publishes middle-grade and young adult fiction. While this
imprint will review queries from unagented authors, it recommends that writers go through a literary agent.

Freelance Potential: Publishes about a dozen titles annually:
most by agented authors. Receives 200 queries monthly.

Fiction: Middle-grade, YA. Genres: contemporary, historical,
multicultural, mystery, adventure, humor.

Titles: *The Chamber of Five*, by Michael Harmon (ages 14+). *The
Golden Christmas Tree Book*, by Jan Wahl (ages 3–7).

Submissions and Payment: Guidelines and catalogue available
at website. Query with up to 10 sample pages and a cover letter
explaining the book, the intended age group, and author's
publishing credits, if any. Accepts hard copy. SASE for reply only.
Materials not returned. Responds in 6 weeks. Publication period
and payment policy vary.

Parents, Divisions, Imprints

Penguin/Random House Children's Books, See page 184

Leap Books

P.O. Box 63, Otego, NY 13825. http://leapbks.net/

Editor

Leap Books focuses on fiction for tweens, teens, and reluctant
readers. Its Surge imprint publishes contemporary, inspirational,
paranormal, and mystery novels for young adults. The Frolic
imprint, for ages 10 to 14, focuses on the same categories, but
with a lighter tone appropriate for the age group. Leap Books is
looking to add fantasy, historical, and multicultural fiction to both
lines. It accepts submissions only from agents or from attendees

at conferences at which its editors speak. All submissions are evaluated by a teen panel.

Freelance Potential: Publishes between 12–20 titles annually: 75% by agented authors; 90% by authors who are new to the publishing house; 25–25% by previously unpublished writers. Receives 10–15 queries monthly.

Fiction: Hi/lo, reluctant readers, middle-grade, YA. Genres: adventure, contemporary, coming-of-age, realistic, fantasy, humor, historical, inspirational, multicultural, mystery/thriller, regional, religious, romance, and nature stories.

Titles: *Never Been Texted,* by Linda Joy Singleton (YA). *Half-Life,* by Tina Ferraro (YA).

Submissions and Payment: Guidelines and catalogue available at website. Primarily accepts submissions from literary agents, or from attendees at conferences at which the editors speak but does occasionally have open calls for unagented submissions; see website for current calls. Send email queries to submissions@leapbks.com for SHINE YA novella submissions; leapbks@gmail.com for SURGE YA novel submissions; and kellyhashway.leap-books@gmail.com for middle grade novel submissions. Include cover letter and query materials in body of email or with Word or RTF attachments. No simultaneous submissions. Responds in 3–6 months. Publication in 18 months. Royalty.

Lee & Low Books

95 Madison Avenue, Suite 1205, New York, NY 10016
www.leeandlow.com

Associate Editor: Emily Hazel

Lee & Low Books is the largest multicultural children's book publisher in the country. The publisher and its imprints Tu Books and BeBop Books, has a special interest in realistic and historical fiction, and in nonfiction with a distinct voice or unique approach. It is not interested in folklore or animal stories.

Freelance Potential: Publishes about a dozen titles annually: 15–25% developed from unsolicited submissions; 15% by agented authors; about 40% by authors who are new to the publishing house; 25% by previously unpublished writers. Receives 85 unsolicited manuscripts monthly.

Fiction: Story picture books, chapter books, middle-grade, YA. Genres: realistic, historical, contemporary, multicultural, ethnic.

Nonfiction: Story picture books, middle-grade, YA. Topics: multicultural and ethnic issues and traditions, biography.

Titles: *Piecing Earth & Sky Together*, by Nancy Raines Day (ages 8–12). *Lakas and the Makibaka Hotel*, by Anthony Robles (grades 3–6).

Submissions and Payment: Guidelines and catalogue available at website. See website for details and updates of current needs. It is seeking middle grade and YA submissions but is not looking for picture books or chapter books at this time. For middle-grade manuscripts of more than 10,000 words, query with story synopsis, chapter outline, and first 3 chapters. Include cover letter with brief author biography and publishing history; note whether manuscript is an exclusive or simultaneous submission. Accepts hard copy. Responds in 6 months if interested. Materials not returned. Publication in 2–3 years. Royalty; advance.

Parents, Divisions, Imprints

Children's Book Press, See page 98
Tu Books, See page 232

Arthur A. Levine Books

Scholastic, 557 Broadway, New York, NY 10012
www.arthuralevinebooks.com

Publisher: Arthur A. Levine

Founded in 1996, this imprint of Scholastic is interested in high-quality titles for children of all ages, from the very young to young adults. Embracing an array of genres and topics, Arthur A. Levine puts an emphasis on engaging characters and literary writing. It works with writers in various stages of their careers, from newcomers to award-winners.

Freelance Potential: Publishes 15–20 titles annually: most by agented authors. Receives 200+ queries, 30+ unsolicited manuscripts monthly.

Fiction: Story picture books, chapter books, middle-grade, YA. Genres: contemporary, multicultural, fantasy, poetry.

Nonfiction: Story picture books, middle-grade, YA. Topics: nature, animals, biography.

Titles: *The 14 Fibs of Gregory K.*, Greg Pincus (ages 8–12). *Abslutely, Positively Not*, by David LaRochelle (YA).

Submissions and Payment: Guidelines and catalogue available at website. For picture books, send query letter and full text. For novels, send query letter, first 2 chapters, and synopsis. For nonfiction and poetry, send query letter and 5 sample pages. All queries should describe the book, its strengths, and what makes it memorable or attention-getting. Accepts submissions through the website at www.arthuralevinebooks.submittable.com/submit. Responds in 6–8 weeks. Publication in 18–24 months. Payment policy varies.

Parents, Divisions, Imprints

Scholastic Inc., See page 204

Little, Brown and Company Books for Young Readers 🔑

Hachette Book Group, 237 Park Avenue, New York, NY 10017
www.lb-kids.com, www.lb-teens.com

Publisher: Megan Tingley

The children's division of Little, Brown and Company develops and markets picture books, chapter books, and teen titles through its LB Kids, LB Teen, and Poppy lines. Its extensive catalogue includes everything from alphabet books for toddlers to novels with cutting-edge themes for adolescents. It only reviews submissions that are made through literary agents.

Freelance Potential: Publishes 135 titles annually: all by agented authors.

Fiction: Toddler books, concept books, novelty books, picture books, early readers, chapter books, YA. Genres: adventure, fantasy, contemporary, multicultural, holiday stories, sports, humor, graphic novels, manga.

Nonfiction: Concept books, story picture books, middle-grade, YA. Topics: sports, biography, animals, history, families, nature/environment, science, art, and activities.

Titles: *The Peace Book,* by Todd Parr (ages 3–6). *Arthur Rocks with Binky,* by Marc Brown (ages 4–6).

Submissions and Payment: Guidelines and catalogue available at website. Accepts submissions from agented authors only. Publication period varies. Royalty; advance.

Parents, Divisions, Imprints

Hachette Book Group, See page 134

Little Creek Books

P.O. Box 701, Johnson City, TN 37605
www.jancarolpublishing.com

Submission Editor

Little Creek Books strives to continue to offer publishing for a diverse selection of authors from a wide variety of genres including children's fiction, romance, historical fiction and mystery. The imprint is part of Jan-Carol Publishing.

Freelance Potential: Publishes 35 titles annually: 0.5% by agented authors, 50% by authors who are new to the publishing house; 80% by previously unpublished authors. Receives 25 queries monthly.

Fiction: Early readers, middle-grade, YA. Genres: adventure, contemporary, historical, folktales.

Nonfiction: Early readers, middle-grade, YA. Topics: recreation, social issues.

Titles: *The Tale of Two Sisters (Book 3): Moving Out and Moving On,* by Rebecca Williams Spindler and Madelyn Spindler (YA). *Book 1 of Forever,* Marty Series: Marty Matters, by Jessica Hayworth (YA).

Submissions and Payment: Guidelines and catalogue available at website. Query with synopsis, author bio, and possible marketing ideas. Accepts email queries to submissions@jancarolpublishing.com. Accepts simultaneous submissions. Responds in 3 months, if interested. Publication in 1 month. Royalty; advance.

Little Devil Books

www.littledevilbooks.webs.com

Editor in Chief: Amy Alspach

Little Devil Books has renewed its vision to publish modern excellence for children and teens in the genres of mystery, suspense, scary stories, fantasy and science fiction. Little devil publishes print and ebooks. While it does work with new authors, this publisher has different windows of time where they accept submissions. Check the website for details.

Freelance Potential: Publishes 2–3 titles annually.

Fiction: Chapter books, middle-grade, YA. Genres: mystery, suspense, horror, fantasy, science fiction.

Titles: *Krystal Bull Rain Dancer,* by Shirley Harber (ages 10+). *Emma Tremendous,* by A. D. Goodman (ages 8–12).

Submissions and Payment: Guidelines and catalogue available at website. Query with synopsis and sample including first chapter of ms. See website for detailed guidelines, including age-group word lengths, which vary from 30,000 to 100,000 words. Accepts email to amy@littledevilbooks.com. Response time, publication period vary. Payment policy varies; no advance.

Little Simon

Simon & Schuster Children's Publishing, 1230 Avenue of the Americas, New York, NY 10020
http://imprints.simonandschuster.biz/little-simon

Submissions

The very youngest readers and pre-readers are the target audience of this imprint from Simon & Schuster. It engages young children with colorful picture books, board books, pop-up and lift-the-flap books, and other novelty formats. Its goal is to make reading fun for both young children and their parents. Due to the volume of submissions received, it is unable to review any submissions that do not come through literary agents.

Freelance Potential: Publishes 65 titles annually: 100% by agented authors. Receives about 20 queries monthly.

Fiction: Concept books, board books, novelty books, toddler books, picture books. Genres: animal stories, holidays, trucks, automobiles, families, friendship.

Titles: *I'm a Little Vampire*, by Sonali Fry (ages 2–4). *The Happy Little Yellow Box*, by David A. Carter (ages 4+).

Submissions and Payment: Accepts queries through literary agents only. Publication in 2 years. Royalty; advance. Flat fee.

Parents, Divisions, Imprints

Simon & Schuster, See page 207

Little Tiger Press

1 The Coda Centre, 189 Munster Road, London SW6 6AW United Kingdom. www.littletigerpress.com

Submissions Editor: Mara Alperin

Picture books and novelty books for children up to age 7 are the specialty of Little Tiger Press. It features a diverse list of award-winning books. Its brightly illustrated titles share exciting stories and inspiring messages with young readers as they develop and grow in confidence. At this time it is not accepting manuscripts. Check website for updates to this policy.

Freelance Potential: Publishes 60+ titles annually: 1–10% by authors who are new to the publishing house; 1–10% by previously unpublished writers. Receives 300 unsolicited manuscripts monthly.

Fiction: Concept books, board books, early picture books, story picture books. Genres: contemporary, classical.

Titles: *When Granny Saved Christmas*, by Julia Hubery (ages 3–5). *One Snowy Rescue*, by M. Christina Butler (ages 3–5).

Submissions and Payment: Guidelines and catalogue available at website. Not currently accepting submissions. Publication period and payment policy vary.

Lonely Planet Kids

150 Linden Street, Oakland, CA 94607
www.lonelyplanet.com

Lonely Planet Kids produces books that kick start the travel bug
and open the eyes and minds of children to the world around
them. Its books share the love of travel, a sense of humor, and a
continual fascination with what makes the world a diverse place.

Freelance Potential: Publishes about 6 titles annually.

Nonfiction: Middle-grade. Topics: travel.

Titles: *How to Be an International Spy*, by Andy Briggs (ages 10+).
How to Be a Dinosaur Hunter, by Scott Forbes (ages 9–11).

Submissions and Payment: Lonely Planet posts freelance
author, editor, and photographer opportunities on its website.
Check regularly for current needs. At press time the company
was not accepting book proposals. Response time, publication
period, and payment policy vary.

James Lorimer & Company

317 Adelaide Street West, Suite 1002, Toronto, Ontario M5V 1P9
Canada. www.lorimer.ca

Children's Book Acquisitions: Robin Studniberg

James Lorimer & Company publishes quality children's books
that reflect contemporary Canadian society. It is best-known for
its sports-themed fiction series (Sports Stories) for ages 10 to 13,
and its edgy, issue-based teen fiction series (SideStreets). Lorimer
also publishes nonfiction, self-help, and stand-alone fiction titles
for kids and teens. Lorimer does not publish speculative fiction,
picture books, or holiday books. Lorimer works only with Canadian authors on books that have a Canadian theme or subject.

Freelance Potential: Publishes 30 titles annually: 50% developed from unsolicited submissions; 25% by agented authors; 50%
by authors who are new to the publishing house; 20% by previously unpublished writers. Receives 5+ queries monthly.

Fiction: Chapter books, middle-grade, YA. Genres: contemporary, realistic, sports, social issues.

Nonfiction: Middle-grade. Topics: sports biographies, Canadian history, self-help, social issues.

Titles: *Gone Wild*, by Jodi Lundgren (ages 13–18). *Crack Coach*, by Steven Sandor, (ages 9–12).

Submissions and Payment: Canadian authors only. Guidelines and catalogue available at website. Send complete manuscript with cover letter, author biography with a list of previously published works, word count, and plot synopsis that includes setting and characters. Accepts hard copy only. SAE/IRC. Responds in 3–4 months if interested. Publication in 1–2 years. Royalty.

Macmillan

175 Fifth Avenue, New York, NY 10010. http://us.macmillan.com

Editor

Macmillan is a global publisher that has many divisions and imprints. The parent company is now the German-based Holtzbrinck Group. In the U.S., the companies of most import, especially to children's and YA writers, are Farrar Straus and Giroux, First Second, Henry Holt, Roaring Brook Press, Square Fish, and Tor/Forge Books. Note that Macmillan/ McGraw-Hill and Gale's Macmillan Reference are not part of the same company; they are divisions of an earlier company sold to other corporations.

Freelance Potential: Publishes hundreds of books annually.

Fiction: All ages and genres across a variety of imprints.

Nonfiction: All ages and genres across a variety of imprints.

Titles: *Amazing Agent Luna: Vol. 11*, by Nunzio DeFilippis (ages 10+). *My Life as a Gamer*, Janet Tashjian (ages 8–12).

Submissions and Payment: Submission policies vary by division or imprint, although most acquisitions are via agents.

Parents, Divisions, Imprints

Farrar, Straus and Giroux, See page 117
Feiwel & Friends, See page 117
Margaret Ferguson Books, See page 118
Henry Holt Books for Young Readers, See page 143

Marimba Books

P.O. Box 5306, East Orange, NJ 07017. http://justusbooks.com

Submissions

Marimba Books is a multicultural children's book imprint from Just Us Books. It features board books, picture books, and chapter books for middle-grade readers. At this time, it is only accepting queries for middle-grade chapter books. Check the website for updates to this policy.

Freelance Potential: Publishes 2–3 titles annually.

Fiction: Board books, early picture books, story picture books, chapter books, reluctant readers, middle-grade. Genres: contemporary, historical, multicultural, social issues, social skills, religious.

Titles: *I Told You I Can Play!*, by Brian Jordan (ages 4–8). *It's Church Going Time*, by Wade Hudson (ages 4–8).

Submissions and Payment: Guidelines and catalogue available at website. Currently accepting queries for chapter books only. Query with 1- to 2-page synopsis, 3–5 sample pages, and author biography that includes publishing credits. Accepts hard copy. Send SASE for response. Responds in 4–6 months. Publication period varies. Royalty.

Parents, Divisions, Imprints

Just Us Books See page 154.

Mayhaven Publishing

803 Buckthorn Circle, P.O. Box 557, Mahomet, IL 61853
www.mayhavenpublishing.com

Editor/Publisher: Doris Replogle Wenzel

The catalogue from Mayhave Pubishing offers books for children, young adult, and adults that includes both fiction and nonfiction titles.

Freelance Potential: Publishes 2–5 children's titles annually: 95% developed from unsolicited submissions; 1–5% by agented authors; 60% by authors who are new to the publishing house; 40% by previously unpublished writers. Receives 70 queries, 45 unsolicited manuscripts monthly.

Fiction: Early reader books, picture books, story picture books, chapter books, middle-grade, YA. Genres: contemporary, multicultural, historical, realistic, science fiction, romance, fairy tales, humor, mystery, adventure, sports, animals.

Nonfiction: Early readers, picture books, story picture books, chapter books, middle-grade, YA. Topics: biography, educational, history, pop culture, reference, travel, contemporary issues, poetry. Also publishes books on parenting and crossover titles of interest to both children and adults.

Titles: *The Petticoat Soldier*, by Nancy Polette (YA). *No Baseball in Fairview*, by Lynn Swango (ages 6+).

Submissions and Payment: Catalogue available at website. Query or send complete manuscript. Accepts hard copy and email submissions to mayhavenpublishing@mchsi.com (Word or PDF attachments). SASE. Response time varies. Publication period varies. Royalty.

Margaret K. McElderry Books

Simon & Schuster, 1230 Avenue of the Americas, New York, NY 10020
http://imprints.simonandschusterbiz/margaret-k-mcelderry-books

Submissions Editor

Founded by legendary editor Margaret K. McElderry, this boutique imprint from Simon & Schuster's Children's Division specializes in high-quality literary fantasy, contemporary and historical fiction, as well as nonfiction for early readers through teens. It accepts submissions through literary agents only.

Freelance Potential: Publishes 50 titles annually: all by agented authors.

Fiction: Picture books, story picture books, middle-grade, YA. Genres: contemporary, historical, fantasy, poetry, animal and nature stories.

Nonfiction: Middle-grade, YA. Topics: history, nature, natural history, mythology.

Titles: *The Key & The Flame*, by Claire M. Caterer (ages 8–12). *Clockwork Princess*, by Cassandra Clare (ages 14+).

Submissions and Payment: Agented authors only. Publication in 2–4 years. Royalty; advance.

Parents, Divisions, Imprints

Simon & Schuster, See page 207

McSweeney's McMullens

849 Valencia Street, San Francisco, CA 94110
www.mcsweeneys.net

Publisher: Dave Eggers
Editor and Art Director: Brian McMullen

McSweeney's is a publishing company based in San Francisco that offers a daily humor website, and publishes a quarterly book of stories, as well as an ever-growing selection of books.

Freelance Potential: Publishes 10 books annually.

Fiction: Picture books, middle grade. Genres: adventure, mystery, family, social skills.

Titles: *A Million Heavens*, by John Brandon (YA-A). *Morning in Serra Mattu: A Nubian Ode*, by Arif Gamal (YA-A).

Submissions and Payment: Guidelines and catalogue available at website. McSweeney's McMullens is open to book submissions from new and established authors, agented and unagented. Accepts submissions with cover letter that includes a brief synopsis; submit through submishmash at mcsweeneysbooksubmissions.submishmash.com/submit. Response time, publication period, and payment policy vary.

Medallion Press

4222 Meridian Pkwy, Suite 110, Aurora, IL 60504
www.medallionpress.com

Executive Editor: Helen Rich

Medallion Press offers a catalogue full of fiction and nonfiction for and young adults. It is also actively seeking young adult fiction written by young adults.

Freelance Potential: Publishes 12 titles annually: 33% developed from unsolicited submissions; 33% by agented authors; 33% by authors who are new to the publishing house. Receives 100 queries monthly.

Fiction: YA. Genres: mainstream, historical, mystery, thriller, suspense, romance, horror, science fiction, fantasy, literary, Christian.

Titles: *The Blue Woods*, by Nicole Maggi (YA). *Zombies Don't Surrender*, by Rusty Fischer (YA).

Submissions and Payment: Guidelines and catalogue available at website. Accepts email submission to emily@medallionpress.com. The email subject should include book title, genre, and word count. Send a 2- to 5-page synopsis and first 3 consecutive chapters. Accepts simultaneous submissions if identified. Responds in 2–3 months. Publication in 24-36 months. Royalty; advance.

MeeGenius

www.meegenius.com

MeeGenius, now a part of Houghton Mifflin Harcourt offers more than 700 interactive books for children. The books have digital features, such as highlighting, professional narration, and read-along technology. It is open to submissions from authors of works to be published in this manner.

Freelance Potential: Publishes 50 titles yearly.

Fiction: Picture books, story picture books, toddlers, early readers. Genres: animals, real life, adventure, social skills.

Nonfiction: Picture books, story picture books, toddlers, early readers. Topics: animals, weather, real life, social skills, inspirational, holiday.

Titles: *Mr. Wuffles,* by David Wiesner (ages 4–8). *Nighty-Night, Cooper,* by Laura Numeroff and Lynn Munsinger (ages (3–6).

Submissions and Payment: Guidelines and catalogue available at website. Query or send complete ms with author bio. Accepts email to: publish@meegenius.com. Responds in 2 weeks. Publication period, unknown. Payment policy, varies.

Merit Press Books

Adams Media Corportion, 57 Littlefield Street, Avon, MA 02322
www.fwcommunity.com

Editor in Chief: Jacquelyn Mitchard

Enduring, exciting, intensely readable young adult stories about young people facing an all-too-challenging contemporary world. Merit Press titles feature plot twists with a mix of extraordinary, heartbreaking, and seemingly magical events.

Freelance Potential: Publishes about 14 titles annually; 60% by agented authors, 90% by authors who are new to the publishing house, 75% by previously unpublished authors. Receives 200 queries, 500 mss yearly.

Fiction: YA. Genres: contemporary, mystery, fantasy, real life.

Titles: *Screwed*, by Laurie Plissner (YA). *The After Girls,* by Leah Konen (YA).

Submissions and Payment: Guidelines and catalogue available at website. Send queries, partial or complete manuscripts. Accepts email only to jacquelyn.mitchard@fwcommunity.com. Response time, publication period, and payment policy vary.

Meriwether Publishing

P.O. Box 4267, Englewood, CO 80155
www.meriwether.com

Submission Editor

Recently acquired by Pioneer Drama Service, Meriwether features how-to books on acting, directing, playwriting, and stagecraft for young performers are featured in this publisher's catalogue. It also publishes scene books, theater anthologies, and resources for theater arts educators.

Freelance Potential: Publishes 5–10 titles annually: 10–20% developed from unsolicited submissions; 70% by authors who are new to the publishing house; about 20% by previously unpublished writers. Receives 16 queries, 15 unsolicited manuscripts monthly.

Nonfiction: Middle-grade, YA. Topics: acting, directing, auditioning, improvisation, public speaking, interpersonal communication, debate, mime, clowning, storytelling, costuming, stage lighting, sound effects. Also publishes collections of monologues and scenes.

Titles: *Let's Put on a Show*, by Adrea Gibbs (ages 8+). *Self-Supporting Scenery for Children's Theatre...and Grown Ups, Too* (YA–A).

Submissions and Payment: Guidelines and catalogue available at website. Query with a synopsis, outline, sample chapters, market analysis, publishing credits, and payment expectations. Accepts hard copy and email to editor@meriwether.com (no attachments). Accepts simultaneous submissions if identified. SASE. Responds in 4–6 weeks. Publication in 6 months. Royalty.

Parents, Divisions, Imprints

Contemporary Drama Service, See page 102

Mighty Media Press

Mighty Media, 1201 Currie Avenue, Minneapolis, MN 55403
www.mightymediapress.com

Submissions Editor

Mighty Media Press delivers captivating books and media that ignite a child's curiosity, imagination, social awareness, and sense of adventure. Its titles target early readers with colorful picture books and piques the interest of middle grade readers with its selection of fiction and nonfiction titles.

Freelance Potential: Publishes between 30-60 titles annually.

Fiction: Picture books, early reader, middle-grade. Genres: adventure, real life issues, humor, and mystery.

Nonfiction: Middle grade. Topics: food and nutrition.

Titles: *Garden to Table*, by Katherine Hengel (8-12). *Monster Needs His Help*, by Paul Czajak (4-6).

Submissions and Payment: Guidelines and catalogue available at website. Submit cover letter with synopsis and no more than 30 pages of the ms. Accepts hard copy, submissions through the website and email submissions to media@mightymedia.com. Response time varies. Publication period and payment policy vary.

Milet Publishing

814 North Franklin Street, Chicago, IL 60610
www.milet.com

Editorial Director

Milet Publishing has expanded the scope of bilingual and multi-cultural titles for children and adults, combining artistic innovation with linguistic excellence.

Freelance Potential: Publishes about 10 titles annually: 10% by agented authors; 20% by authors who are new to the publishing house.

Fiction: Board books, picture books, middle-grade. Genres: multicultural, fantasy.

Nonfiction: Board books, picture books, middle-grade. Topics: world cultures, language.

Titles: *Zarife*, by Deniz Kavukcuoglu (YA). *Bella Balistica and the Itza Warriors*, by Adam Gullain (YA).

Submissions and Payment: Guidelines and catalogue available at website. Query with cover letter that includes author credentials, brief description of the work, target audience, and competing titles; synopsis of the work (one page or less); and sample text or chapters. Accepts email to info@milet.com. Responds in 3 months, if interested. Publication period and payment policy vary.

Milkweed Editions

1011 Washington Avenue South, Open Book, Suite 300, Minneapolis, MN 55415–1246. www.milkweed.org

Young Readers Editor

Founded in 1980, this independent publisher's mission is to identify, nurture, and publish transformative literature, and build an engaged community around it. It does not publish picture books or children's nonfiction. It is currently closed for submissions; check the website for changes in this policy.

Freelance Potential: Publishes 15–20 titles annually: about 5% developed from unsolicited submissions; 25% by agented authors; 30% by authors who are new to the publishing house; 15% by previously unpublished writers. Receives 250 unsolicited manuscripts monthly.

Fiction: Middle-grade, YA. Genres: contemporary, historical, multicultural, ethnic, nature stories.

Titles: *Waiting for the Queen: A Novel of Early America*, by Joanna Higgins (ages 8+). *I Will Not Leave You Comfortless: A Memoir*, by Jeremy Jackson (YA).

Submissions and Payment: Guidelines and catalogue available at website. Query from January to March, and July to September only, with the first 3 chapters. Prefers submissions through the website's Submissions Manager. Accepts hard copy. Responds in 4–6 months during reading periods. Publication in 2 years. Royalty, 6% of list price; advance, varies.

Moonbot Books

2031 Kings Hwy, Suite 102, Shreveport, LA 71103
www.moonbotstudios.com

Editor

Moonbot Studios is a place where outstanding individual talents combine to create extraordinary entertainment to an array of media platforms. It produces books, films, apps, and games.

Freelance Potential: Publishes about 3 titles annually.

Fiction: Picture books, chapter books, middle grade, YA. Genres: fantasy, contemporary, science fiction, fantasy.

Titles: *Billy's Booger*, A Memoir, by William Joyce (5–8). *The Numberlys Picture Book*, by William Joyce (ages 5–8).

Submissions and Payment: Guidelines and catalogue available at website. Accepts email submissions to info@moonbotstudios. com. Publication period and payment policy, unknown.

Move Books

P.O. Box 183, Beacon Falls, CT 06403. www.move-books.com

Editor: Eileen Robinson

Move Books stands behind the fact that boys do read when presented with materials that interest them. The key is finding that potential. Books with mystery, suspense, plot and action encourage boys to get hooked on reading. It is particulary open to middle-grade fiction.

Freelance Potential: Publishes 2–6 titles annually.

Fiction: Chapter books, middle grade. Genres: fantasy, contemporary, historical, humor, adventure.

Titles: *Salamaine's Curse*, by V. L. Burgess (ages 8–12). *Surviving Bear Island,* by Paul Greci (ages 8–12).

Submissions and Payment: Guidelines available at website. Query with synopsis and the first 25 pages of your manuscript. Accepts hard copy. Responds if interested. Publication period and payment policy varies.

MuseItUp Publishing

14878 James, Pierrefonds, Quebec H9H 1P5 Canada
www.museituppublishing.com

Acquisition Editor: Lea Schizas

This epublisher specializes in fiction for middle-graders and young adults as well as adults. It welcomes new writers in many genres, but is especially interested in young adult romance, middle-grade historical fiction, and stories for boys. It now has imprints specifically for children and young adults titled MuseIt Kids and MuseIt YA.

Freelance Potential: Publishes 150–200 titles annually: 50–70% developed from unsolicited submissions; 1–10% by agented authors; 25–50% by previously unpublished writers. Receives approximately 100 unsolicited manuscripts monthly.

Fiction: Middle-grade, YA. Genres: contemporary, fantasy, historical, inspirational, adventure, sports, mystery, romance, paranormal, Western.

Titles: *Palace of the Twleve Pillars*, by Christina Weigand (YA). *Isosceles*, By Scott R. Caseley (YA)

Submissions and Payment: Guidelines and catalogue available at website. Send complete manuscript with synopsis and cover letter that includes brief author bio, title, genre, and word count during open submission periods (check website for dates). Accepts email submissions to musesubs@gmail.com (Word or RTF attachments). Accepts simultaneous submissions, if identified. Responds in 3–4 months. Publication in 1 year. Royalty, 40%.

Namelos

www.namelos.com

Publisher: Stephen Roxburgh

Namelos publishes children's and young adult books and also helps authors develop their projects. It publishes both fiction and nonfiction work and publishes titles simultaneously in hardcover, paperback, and ebook formats. Unsolicited submissions require an evaluation fee. Each submission will receive a written evaluation and a phone or email follow-up with the goal of preparing a manuscript for submission to an agent or editor. All work is also considered for publication by namelos, and if a manuscript is accepted, the evaluation fee is refunded.

Freelance Potential: Publishes 6–10 titles annually. Receives 20 queries and 15 unsolicited manuscripts monthly.

Nonfiction: Middle-grade, YA. Topics: social issues, culture, history, poetry.

Fiction: Middle-grade, YA. Genres: historical, social issues, fantasy, Westerns, mystery, contemporary.

Titles: *Apple Island,* by Douglas Evans (ages 9–11). *The Ballad of Jesse Pearl,* by Shannn Hitchcock (ages 12+).

Submissions and Payment: Catalogue and guidelines available at website. Send a cover letter with author bio, up to 10,000 words of a manuscript, and $250 fee to info@namelos.com (Word attachments). Responds in 2 weeks. Publication period and payment policy vary.

National Geographic Society

National Geographic Children's Books, 1145 17th Street NW, 6th Floor, Washington, DC 20036-4688. www.ngchildrensbooks.org

Associate Editor: Kate Olesin

A division of the National Geographic Society, this publisher is dedicated to producing books that promote the mission of the organization: to inspire people to learn about, and care about, our planet. For children, it publishes nonfiction books for pre-schoolers through young adults. At this time it is not accepting submissions from authors.

Freelance Potential: Publishes 70 titles annually: 5% by authors who are new to the publishing house. Receives 20 queries monthly.

Nonfiction: Early readers, story picture books, activity books, chapter books, middle-grade, YA. Topics: the sciences, American and world cultures, myth, history, animals, multicultural issues, geography, biography.

Titles: *Alexander Graham Bell Invents*, by Anita Garmon (grade 2–4). *All About Ants,* by Sue Whtiting (grades 2–4).

Submissions and Payment: Guidelines and catalogue available at website. Not currently accepting submissions, Check website for changes to this policy.

Tommy Nelson Kids

501 Nelson Place, P.O. Box 141000, Nashville, TN 37214
www.tommynelson.com

Acquisitions Editor

Tommy Nelson is the children's division of Thomas Nelson, Inc. It publishes a wide variety of high-quality products that are consistent with the teachings found in the Bible. The products from Tommy Nelson are designed to expland children's imaginations and nurture their faith while pointing them to a personal relationship with God.

Freelance Potential: Publishes 50–75 titles annually: 100% by agented authors. Receives 20 queries monthly.

Fiction: Board books, concept books, toddler books, early picture books, early readers, story picture books, middle-grade. Genres: religious, real life/problems, contemporary, inspirational, adventure, fantasy, humor, science fiction, dystopian, mystery, of interest to girls.

Nonfiction: Concept books, early readers, story picture books, middle-grade, YA, devotionals. Topics: the Bible, Christianity, inspirational, biography.

Titles: *I Love You Even When*, by Allison Edgson and Donna Keith (ages 0–5). *Heaven Is for Real,* by Sonja Burpo (ages 3-5).

Submissions and Payment: Catalogue available at website. Accepts proposals through literary agents only. Also recommends christianmanuscriptsubmissions.com. Response time and publication period vary. Royalty; advance.

Parents, Divisions, Imprints

Thomas Nelson, See page 413

NorthSouth Books

600 Third Avenue, 2nd Floor, New York, NY 10016
http://northsouthbooks.com

Editor: Beth Terrill

Offering fresh, original, fiction and nonfiction picture books, NorthSouth targets readers ages 3–8. Submissions are currently being accepted from US-based authors and illustrators.

Freelance Potential: Publishes 30 titles annually: 95% by agented authors, 30% by authors who are new to the publishing house, 3% by previously unpublished writers.

Fiction: Board books, novelty books, toddler books, early picture books, early readers, story picture books, chapter books. Genres: contemporary, multicultural, adventure, drama, fairy tales, folklore, humor, nature stories.

Nonfiction: Concept books, early picture books, chapter books. Topics: early learning, holidays, animals, hobbies, crafts, humor, nature, religion, science, technology, social issues, sports, multicultural and ethnic issues.

Titles: *Five Little Ducklings Go to School*, by Carol Roth (ages 3–8). *Nugget on the Top of the World,* by Hans de Beer (ages 4–8).

Submissions and Payment: Catalogue available at website. Fiction and nonfiction, to 1,000 words. Prefers complete ms. Accepts email submissions to submissionsnsb@gmail.com Publication period and payment policy vary.

Nosy Crow

The Crow's Nest, 10a Lant Street, London SE1 1QR United Kingdom. http://nosycrow.com

Editorial Director: Camilla Reid
Head of Picture Books: Louise Bolongaro
U.S. Editor, Candlewick Press: Joan Powers

Nosy Crow is a small, award-winning independent company that publishes fiction and nonfiction for children ages 0 to 14. It's list is comprised of work from both new and well-known authors. In the US, the Nosy Crow imprint publishes under the umbrella of Candlewick Press.

Freelance Potential: Publishes 25 books and apps annually.

Fiction: Preschool, board books, novelty books, picture books, middle-grade, young YA, apps. Genres: adventure, humor, fairy tales, contemporary, historical, mystery.

Nonfiction: Preschool, board books, novelty books, picture books. Topics: animals, transportation, work.

Titles: *A Lullaby for Little One,* by Dawn Casey (ages 0–3). *The Fairiest Fairy,* by Anne Booth (ages 3–6).

Submissions and Payment: Guidelines available at website. For board, novelty, or picture books/apps, send full text and any supporting visual material (not original artwork). For longer fiction or nonfiction, send a cover letter with relevant information about you and the work, a short synopsis, and first chapter. Prefers email to submissions@nosycrow.com Word or PDF files). Put "Submission to Nosy Crow" in the subject line. Accepts hard copy. SASE. Responds in 3+ months.

Parents, Divisions, Imprints

Candlewick Press, See page 93

OnStage Publishing

190 Lime Quarry Road, Suite 106, Madison, AL 35758
www.onstagepublishing.com

Senior Editor: Dianne Hamilton

This small independent publishing house specializes in children's literature. Its list is comprised of chapter books, middle-grade novels and YA titles in both print and ebook formats. OnStage is always open to working with new authors and great storytellers.

Freelance Potential: Publishes 1–5 titles annually: 10–25% developed from unsolicited submissions; 10–25% by authors who are new to the company; 25–50% by previously unpublished writers. Receives 50–75 queries, 50–75 unsolicited manuscripts yearly.

Fiction: Chapter books, middle-grade, YA. Genres: adventure, drama, fantasy, horror, mystery, suspense, contemporary, historical, humor, science fiction.

Titles: *Missions Shanghai: A Nick Grant Adventure* (ages 8–12). *Heroes: A Gander Cove Mystery,* by Mary Ann Taylor (ages 8–12).

Submissions and Payment: Guidelines and catalogue available at website. Send a cover letter with a synopsis and the intended audience of your book and complete manuscript for works less than 100 pages; 3 sample chapters and plot summary for longer works. Accepts email queries to submissions@onstagepublishing.com (no attachments) and hard copy. SASE for response only; materials not returned. Accepts simultaneous submissions if identified. Responds in 3–6 months. Publication in 1–2 years. Royalty; advance.

Open Road Integrated Media

345 Hudson Street, Suite 6C, New York, NY 10014
www.openroadmedia.com

Director of Children's Acquisitions: Timothy Travaglini

Open Road Integrated Media is a digital publisher that markets its books through a proprietary online platform that uses video content and social media. It has recently hired a Director of Children's Acquisitions and has several titles in the works to be released in ebook format. While much of the company's focus is currently on publishing existing classics in digital formal, it is cautiously moving into publishing "E-riginal" projects.

Freelance Potential: Publishes about 12 titles annually.

Fiction: Picture books, middle grade, YA. Genres: historical, fantasy, mystery, contemporary.

Titles: *Dig Those Dinosaurs*, by Lori Haskins Houran (ages 3–6). *Sugar Hill: Harlem's Historic Neighborhood*, by Carole B Weatherford (ages 6–8).

Submissions and Payment: Catalogue available at website. Only accepts submissions from agented authors. Response time, publication period, and payment policy vary.

Orca Book Publishers

P.O. Box 5626, Station B, Victoria, British Columbia V8R 6S4 Canada. www.orcabook.com

Editor

Founded in 1984, Orca Book Publishers is an independently owned Canadian children's book publisher, with more than 700 titles in print. Accepting work from Canadian authors only, it publishes books for young children, juvenile and teen fiction, and a limited number of nonfiction titles. Its titles are sorted into divisions, each serving a specific type of reader or content.

Freelance Potential: Publishes 65+ titles annually: 50% developed from unsolicited submissions; 50% by agented authors; 55% by authors who are new to the publishing house; 20% by previ ously unpublished writers. Receives 166 queries, 42 unsolicited manuscripts monthly.

Fiction: Board books, toddler books, early picture books, early readers, story picture books, chapter books, reluctant readers, graphic novels, middle-grade, YA. Genres: regional, historical, contemporary, mystery, fantasy, adventure, sports stories.

Nonfiction: Middle-grade, YA. Topics: nature, history.

Titles: *A Sack Full of Feathers*, by Debby Waldman (ages 5–8). *Above All Else*, by Jeff Ross (YA).

Submissions and Payment: Canadian authors only. Guidelines and catalogue available at website. Send cover letter and complete manuscript for picture books, historical fiction, and graphic novels. Query for all others. (Refer to guidelines for submission details and current needs for each division.) Accepts hard copy. SASE. Responds in 4 months if interested. Publication in 18–24 months. Royalty, 10% split; advance.

Orchard Books

Scholastic, 557 Broadway, New York, NY 10012-3999
www.scholastic.com

Editorial Director: Ken Geist

This trade imprint from Scholastic focuses on increasing literacy and comprehension through high-quality, engaging stories and subjects. While its catalogue is filled with books for children of all ages, its current focus is on picture books. Like all Scholastic imprints, it accepts submissions through literary agents only.

Freelance Potential: Publishes 15–20 titles annually: all by agented authors; 10–25% by authors who are new to the publishing house; 5–25% by previously unpublished writers. Receives 17–30 queries monthly.

Fiction: Concept books, toddler books, early picture books, early readers, story picture books. Genres: historical; contemporary; multicultural; fairy tales; folktales; fantasy; humor; sports, animal, and nature stories.

Titles: *One Brown Bunny*, by Marion Dane Bauer (grades PreK-K). *Griffin's Castle*, by Jenny Nimmo (grades 4–7).

Submissions and Payment: Agented authors only. Publication period varies. Royalty; advance.

Parents, Divisions, Imprints

Scholastic Inc., See page 204

Owlkids Books

10 Lower Spadina Avenue, Suite 400, Toronto, Ontario M5V 2Z2 Canada. www.owlkidsbooks.com

Submissions Editor

Owlkids publishes entertaing, uniquue, high-quality books and magazines that nurture the potential of children and instill in them a love of reading and learning. It's titles focus not only on children, but also the world around them. Activity books, picture books, graphic novels, and early readers are also part of its list.

Freelance Potential: Publishes 10–12 titles annually.

Fiction: Toddler books, early picture books, early readers, story picture books, chapter books, graphic novels, middle-grade, YA. Genres: historical, contemporary, mystery, fantasy, adventure, humor.

Nonfiction: Toddler books, early picture books, early readers, story picture books, chapter books, graphic novels, middle-grade, YA. Topics: nature, history, science sports, animals, regional.

Titles: *Koala Hospital*, by Suzi Eszterhas (grades 4–6). *West Meadows Detectives: The Case of the Snack Snatcher*, by Liam O'Donnell (grades 3–5).

Submissions and Payment: Guidelines and catalogue available at website. Send query and complete manuscript for picture books and short works. For longer manuscripts, query with a few sample pages. For all submissions, include cover letter with author bio and publication credits. for inquiries regarding submissions email: submissions@owlkids.com. Accepts hard copy. SAE/IRE. Responds in 3–4 months. Publication period and payment policy, unknown.

PageSpring Publishing

P.O. Box 21133, Columbus, OH 43221
www.pagespringpublishing.com

Submissions Editor

This independent publisher specializes in high-quality novels for adults and younger readers. Its Lucky Marble imprint features middle grade and young adult fiction. It also offers women's fiction through its Cup of Tea Books imprint.

Freelance Potential: Publishes 4–5 titles annually: 100% by authors who are new to the publishing house; 75% by previously unpublished writers. Receives 50 queries monthly.

Fiction: Middle-grade, YA. Genres: historical, contemporary, science fiction, adventure, fantasy, folklore, folktales, romance, Westerns, horror.

Titles: *Washashore*, by Suzanne Goldsmith (YA). *Tent City Press,* by Lynn Anns (YA).

Submissions and Payment: Guidelines and catalogue available at website. Query with synopsis and the first 30 pages of the ms. Write "Young Adult Submission" in the subject line of the email. Response time varies. Payment policies varies.

Pajama Press

469 Richmond Street East, Toronto, Ontario M5A 0R1 Canada
www.pajamapress.ca

Publisher: Gail Winskill
Editor: Ann Featherstone

Pajama Press is a small literary publisher with big ideas. It offers books of exceptional quality that receive wide critical acclaim and awards. It produces books in all formats across a broad range of genres including board books, middle-grade and young adult novels.

Freelance Potential: Publishes 10–12 titles annually.

Fiction: Picture books, middle-grade, YA. Genres: contemporary, historical, humor.

Nonfiction: Picture books, middle-grade. Topics: history, current events, animals.

Titles: *A Brush Full of Color*, by Katherine Gibson and Margaret Ruurs (ages 3–7). *Bear on the Homefront*, by Harry Endrulat and Stephanie Inness (ages 5+).

Submissions and Payment: Guidelines and catalogue available at website. For permission to send manuscript, email query with a brief summary of the book and 1–2 sample pages of the finished book to info@pajamapress.ca. Also include link to online published writings. No hard copy. Simultaneous submissions discouraged. Response time, publication period, and payment policy vary.

Pavilion Children's Books

10 Southcombe Street, London W14 0RA United Kingdom
www.pavilionbooks.com

Submissions Editor

Formerly listed as Anova Books, the list from Pavilion Children's Books includes books for babies, picture books, early fiction and illustrated classics.

Freelance Potential: Publishes 200 titles annually. Receives about 20 queries monthly.

Fiction: Board books, picture books, middle-grade. Genres: contemporary, fairy tales, fantasy, humor.

Nonfiction: Concept books, picture books, middle-grade. Topics: animals, nature, science, humor.

Titles: *Grumpy Gertie*, by Sam Lloyd (ages 2–6). *The Saga of Erik the Viking*, by Micahel Foreman and Terry Jones (ages 8–12).

Submissions and Payment: Guidelines and catalogue available at website. Query with cover letter and outline of chapters, and sample chapter. Accepts hard copy. SAE/IRC. Responds in 2 months. Publication in 15 months. Royalty; advance. Flat fee.

Peachtree Publishers

1700 Chattahoochee Avenue, Atlanta, GA 30318-2112
www.peachtree-online.com

Acquisitions Editor: Helen Harriss

Peachtree is an independently owned trade book publisher specializing in quality children's books. From picture books to young adult fiction and nonfiction, to consumer references in health, education, and parenting, you can find it all in the catalogue from Peachtree.

Freelance Potential: Publishes 25 titles annually: 5% developed from unsolicited submissions; 15% by authors who are new to the publishing house. Receives 1,600 manuscripts monthly.

Fiction: Early picture books, early readers, story picture books, chapter books, middle-grade, YA. Genres: contemporary, regional, historical, multicultural.

Nonfiction: Early picture books, story picture books, middle-grade. Topics: nature, sports, biography, the outdoors.

Titles: *The Amazing Flight of Darius Frobisher*, by Bill Harley (ages 8–12). *About Amphibians*, by Cathryn Sill (ages 3–8).

Submissions and Payment: Guidelines and catalogue available at website. Send complete ms for picture books. For all others, send complete manuscript or query with table of contents and 3 sample chapters. For all submissions, include author biography and publishing credits. Accepts hard copy only. SASE. Responds in 6–9 months. Publication period and payment policy vary.

Penguin Random House UK Children's Books

20 Vauxhall Bridge Road, London SW1V 2SA United Kingdom
www.randomhouse.co.uk/browse/children

Picture Books: Hannah Featherstone
Fiction: Naomi Wood

Random House Group Ltd. is based in the UK and comprises five publishing companies: Cornerstone, Ebury Publishing, Transworld Publishers, Vintage and Random House Childrens's Publishers. It is a Penguin Random House Company. Juvenile divisions for both Penguin and Random House publish everything board books and picture books to novels and series. Most imprints accept submissions from agented authors only.

Freelance Potential: Publishes 200+ titles annually: all by agented authors. Receives 250 queries monthly.

Fiction: Toddler books, early picture books, early readers, picture books, story picture books, chapter books, middle-grade. Genres: contemporary, multicultural, historical, fantasy.

Titles: *Dixie O'Day and the Haunted House*, by Shirley Hughes (ages 5–7). *Jed's Really Useful Poem*, by Ragnhild Scamell (ages 5–7).

Submissions and Payment: Catalogue and guidelines available at website. Accepts submissions from agented authors only. Publication in 1–2 years. Royalty; advance.

Parents, Divisions, Imprints

David Fickling Books, See page 119

Penguin Random House Chidlren's Books USA

1745 Broadway, New York, NY 10019
www.penguinrandomhouse.com

Editor

Penguin Random House is the international home to nearly 250 editorially and creatively independent publishing imprints. It is committed to expanding its role as a cultural institution that serves society not only with the books it publishes, but also by making investments in new ideas and diverse voices.

Freelance Potential: Publishes hundreds of books annually.

Fiction: All ages and genres across a variety of imprints.

Nonfiction: All ages and genres across a variety of imprints.

Titles: *Rabbit Who Wants to Fall Asleep*, by Carl Jordan Forsssen Ehrlin (ages 3–7). *Shadow of the Shark* (part of the Magic Treehouse series) by, Mary Pope Osborne (ages 7–10).

Submissions and Payment: Guidelines and catalogue available at website. Submission policies vary by division or imprint, although many acquisitions are made via agents. For details, see http://us.penguingroup.com/static/pages/aboutus/pyrg-sub-guides.html.

Parents, Divisions, Imprints

Dial Books for Young Readers, See page 106
DK Publishing, See page 108
Dutton Children's Books, See page 112
Grosset & Dunlap, See page 132
Philomel Books, See page 187
Puffin Books, See page 192
G. P. Putnam's Sons, See page 193
Viking Children's Books, See page235

Persea Books

277 Broadway, Suite 708, New York, NY 10007
www.perseabooks.com

Fiction Editor/Nonfiction Editor

Persea Books is an independent, literary publishing house founded in 1975 by Michael and Karen Braziller. It offers books on a wide range of themes, styles, and genres. It also continues to expand its young adult selections.

Freelance Potential: Publishes 16 - 20 titles annually: 30% by authors who are new to the publishing house; 25% by previously unpublished writers. Receives 50+ queries monthly.

Fiction: YA, adult. Genres: literary, real-life, contemporary, multicultural, adventure, mystery.

Nonfiction: YA, adult. Topics: social issues, multicultural, real life issues.

Titles: *The Heart Knows Something Different: Teenage Voices from the Foster Care System*, by Al Desetta (YA). *The Girl in the Mirror: A Novel in Poems and Journal Entries*, by Meg Kearney (YA).

Submissions and Payment: Guidelines and catalogue available at website. Query with cover letter that includes author background and publication history, detailed synopsis, and a sample chapter or send complete ms. Accepts hard copy and electronic submissions to Fiction or Nonfiction Editor. Accepts email to info@perseabooks.com or hard copy. SASE. Accepts simultaneous submissions if identified. Responds in 8–10 weeks. Publication period and payment policy vary.

Peter Pauper Press

202 Mamaroneck Avenue, Suite 400, White Plains, NY 10601-5376. www.peterpauper.com

Children's Editor

Peter Pauper Press is one of America's leading publishers of fine gift books, humorbooks, travel guides and innovative children's activity books.

Freelance Potential: Publishes 30 titles annually: 15% developed from unsolicited submissions, 10% by agented authors, 10% by authors who are new to the pubishing house, 5% by previously unpublished writers. Receives 120 mss yearly.

Fiction: Story picture books, story-based activity books. Genres: humor, fantasy, adventure.

Nonfiction: Story-based activity books, puzzle books. Topics: biography, history, nature, science.

Titles: *The Big Circus Mystery*, by Karen Orloff (ages 4–9). *Hank Finds an Egg*, by Rebecca Dudley (3–5).

Submissions and Payment: Guidelines and catalogue available at website. Query with cover letter (describing the work as a whole, the intended market, and how the project differs from the competition); author credentials; and 2 sample chapters and artwork samples, if applicable, or the complete manuscript. Accepts electronic submissions through the website and hard copy. SASE. Responds in 3 months. Publication period varies. Fee varies.

Phaidon Press

Regent's Wharf, All Saints Street, London N1 9PA United Kingdom. www.phaidon.com

Editorial Submissions

Phaidon Press offers books for adults on art, architecture, music, theater, film, and the performing arts. It also includes some illustrated storybooks and arts and crafts titles for younger readers. Though it has offices in New York, editorial submissions are accepted through the London office.

Freelance Potential: Publishes 20+ titles annually: 50% developed from unsolicited submissions. Receives 10–20 queries monthly.

Fiction: Early picture books, board books, early readers, story picture books. Genres: contemporary, multicultural, social skills.

Nonfiction: Early picture books, story picture books. Topics: cooking, the arts, crafts, games.

Titles: *The Finger Travel Game*, by Hervé Tullet (ages 1–6). *The Game of Shapes,* by Herve Tullet (ages 1–6).

Submissions and Payment: Guidelines and catalogue available at website. Query with resume and a short synopsis. Accepts email only to submissions@phaidon.com. Responds in 3 months if interested. Publication period varies. Royalty; advance.

Philomel Books

Penguin Group, 345 Hudson Street, New York, NY 10014
http://us.penguingroup.com

Editorial Assistant

Philomel produces high-quality picture books for young readers as well as books for middle grade books and young adult titles. This publisher takes pride in its ability to reach the reluctant reader. Philomel strives to foster a love of reading in children and young adults. Philomel accepts submissions from agents only.

Freelance Potential: Publishes 40–50 titles annually: 1-10% developed from unsolicited submissions; 90% by agented authors. Receives 50 queries monthly.

Fiction: Early picture books, story picture books, chapter books, reluctant readers, middle-grade, YA. Genres: fantasy, contemporary, historical, multicultural, science fiction.

Nonfiction: Story picture books, YA. Topics: biography and first-person narratives.

Titles: *It's Your World*, by Chelsea Clinton (ages 10+). *Henry's Starts*, by David Elliot (ages 5–8).

Submissions and Payment: Guidelines and catalogue available at website. Prefers submissions from literary agents. Responds in 4 months if interested. Publication in 1–2 years. Royalty.

Parents, Divisions, Imprints

Penguin Group (USA), See page 184

Piccadilly Press

5 Castle Road, London, NW1 8PR, England
http://www.piccadillypress.co.uk

Submissions Editor

Piccadilly publishes family-friendly stories for young readers, engaging novels for teens, and nonfiction books for young adults.

Freelance Potential: Publishes about 25 titles annually.

Fiction: Toddler books, early picture books, early readers, story picture books, chapter books, middle-grade, YA. Genres: historical, contemporary, mystery, fantasy, adventure, humor.

Nonfiction: Story picture books, middle-grade, YA. Topics: real life, social issues.

Titles: *Beasts of Olympus, Dragon Healer*, by Lucy Coats (ages 8–12). *Suzy P, Forever Me* (ages 8–12).

Submissions and Payment: Guidelines and catalogue available at website. Send cover letter and complete manuscript for picture books. For longer manuscripts, include a cover letter, synopsis, and a few sample pages. Accepts email submissions only to books@piccadillypress.com. Responds in 6 weeks. Publication period and payment policy, unknown.

Pinata Books

Arte Público Press, University of Houston, 4902 Gulf Freeway, Building 19, Rm 100, Houston, TX 77204-2004 www.artepublicopress.com

Submissions

The children's imprint from Arte Publico Press, Pinata Books is dedicated to the realistic and authentic portrayal of themes, languages, chracters, and customs of Hispanic culture in the United States.

Freelance Potential: Publishes about 20–25 titles annually.

Fiction: Picture books, middle-grade, YA. Genres: contemporary, historical, multicultural.

Nonfiction: Picture books, middle-grade, YA. Topics: biography, social issues, self-help.

Titles: *A Good Long Way*, by Rene Saldana, Jr. (YA). *A So-Called Vacation*, by Genaro Gonzalez.

Submissions and Payment: Guidelines and catalogue available at website. Query with sample chapters or send complete manuscript in English or Spanish. Accepts electronic submissions through form at website (Word or RTF files only). Responds in 2–6 months. Publication period and payment policy vary.

Pioneer Drama Service

P.O. Box 4267, Englewood, CO 80155-4267
www.pioneerdrama.com

Submissions Editor: Lori Conary

Publishing scripts for middle school, high school, and community theater, Pioneer Drama Services looks to touch lives through theater. It prefers titles that are family-friendly and suitable for audiences of all ages with a running time of 20 to 90 minutes. All submitted plays must be unpublished and should be accompanied by proof of production. Submissions from authors not previously published by Pioneer Drama will be automatically entered into the Shubert Fendrich Memorial Playwriting Contest.

Freelance Potential: Publishes 10–20 titles annually: 75–100% developed from unsolicited submissions; 1–10% by authors who are new to the publishing house; 1–10% by previously unpublished writers. Receives 50–75 queries, 25–50 unsolicited manuscripts monthly.

Fiction: Middle-grade, YA play scripts and musicals. Genres: comedy, mystery, fantasy, adventure, folktales.

Titles: *Charming!*, by Judy Wickland. *Cinderella and the Candy Kingdom*, by Kelly Lazenby.

Submissions and Payment: Guidelines and catalogue available at website. Query through website. or send complete manuscript with cover letter and/or résumé, synopsis, cast list, age of intended audience, running time, and technical requirements. Accepts hard copy and email to submissions@pioneerdrama. com (Word, PDF, and text attachments). Accepts simultaneous submissions if identified. SASE. Responds to queries in 1 week, to manuscripts in 2–4 months. Publication period varies. Royalty paid annually.

Playwrights Canada Press

202–269 Richmond Street West, Toronto, Ontario M5V 1X1 Canada. www.playwrightscanada.com

Submissions Editor

Catering to drama production and theater groups by offering plays of all types, as well as books on topics such as stage management and acting technique, Playwrights Canada Press publishes plays from Candian authors only. It also publishes plays for young audiences. Announcements regarding the occasional call for material for anthologies and drama festivals will be posted on the website.

Freelance Potential: Publishes 30 titles annually: 1-10% developed from unsolicited submissions. Receives 8–10 queries monthly.

Fiction: Dramatic plays for elementary, middle school, and high school students.

Nonfiction: Middle-grade, YA. Topics: acting, play production. Also publishes theater resources for drama teachers.
Titles: *A Foster Christmas*, by Norm Foster (ages 5–adult). *Danny, King of the Basement*, by David S. Craig (ages 12–18).

Submissions and Payment: Canadian authors only. Guidelines and catalogue available at website. Send complete manuscript. Plays must include first production information, including cast and crew. Accepts email to submissions@playwrightscanada.com (Word or PDF attachments) and hard copy. SASE. Responds in

6–8 months. Publication in 5 months. Royalty.

The Poisoned Pencil

6962 E. First Avenue, Suite 103, Scottsdale, AZ 85251
www.thepoisonedpencil.com

Editor: Ellen Larson

This young adult mystery publisher is committed to publishing original, high-quality mystery books for teens. It is an imprint of Poisoned Pen Press, one of the largest publishers of myseries in the country.

Freelance Potential: Publishes 4–6 titles annually: 15% by agented authors, 100% by authors who are new to the publishing house; 80% by previously unpublished writers. Receives 20 mss monthly.

Fiction: YA. Genres: mystery.

Titles: *Jesus Jackson*, by Ellen Larson (YA). *Disconnected*, by Lisa M. Cronkhite (YA).

Submissions and Payment: Guidelines and catalogue available at website. Send complete ms with a detailed synopsis. Responds in 4–6 weeks. Publication period varies. Advance, $1,000.

Price Stern Sloan

Penguin Young Readers Group, 345 Hudson Street, New York, NY 10014. http://us.penguingroup.com

Editorial Department

This imprint of Penguin Young Readers Group produces innovative, fun, and engaging books in a variety of formats, including board books, doodle books, activity books, and some novelty titles, as originals and for licensed properties, for children up to age 12. It offers both fiction and nonfiction. Well-known characters and licenses include Mad Libs, Adventure Time, and Mr. Men Little Miss. It is accepting submissions in all book formats except picture books and Mad Libs.

Freelance Potential: Publishes about 70 titles annually.

Fiction: Board books, activity and doodle books, middle-grade. Genres: contemporary, humor, horror.

Nonfiction: Activity and doodle books. Topics: humor, holidays, crafts.

Titles: *Build a Boyfriend* (ages 10+). *The Thanksgiving Activity Book*, by Karl Jones (ages 8–12).

Submissions and Payment: Catalogue and guidelines available at website. Not accepting picture books at this time. Query with summary and first 1–2 chapters for all other works. Accepts hard copy. No SASE; materials not returned. Responds in 4 months if interested. Publication in 18–36 months. Flat fee, advance, royalty.

Parents, Divisions, Imprints

Penguin Group (USA), See page 184

Puffin Books

Penguin Group, 345 Hudson Street, New York, NY 10014
http://us.penguingroup.com

Manuscript Submissions

This imprint of Penguin Young Readers Group is one of the most prestigious children's publishers in the U.S. It publishes everything from picture books to groundbreaking middle-grade and teen fiction. The best way to put your idea in front of this publisher is through a literary agent, but a truly great proposal will be noticed whether you are agented or not. Writers should note that Puffin is not currently accepting picture book submissions.

Freelance Potential: Publishes 225 titles annually. Receives 40+ queries monthly.

Fiction: Novelty books, early picture books, early readers, story picture books, chapter books, middle-grade, YA. Genres: contemporary, historical, science fiction, mystery, sports, adventure, romance.

Titles: *The Life of Ty* (ages 6–9). *Curiosity*, by Gary Blackwood (ages 9–12).

Submissions and Payment: Guidelines and catalogue available at website. Not accepting submissions for picture books. Query with a maximum of 30 sample pages for longer works and novels. Accepts hard copy. Novel submissions must include SASE.

Responds in 4 months if interested. Publication in 12–18 months. Royalty, 2–6%.

Parents, Divisions, Imprints

Penguin Group (USA), See page 184

Push

Scholastic Inc., 557 Broadway, New York, NY 10012
www.thisispush.com, www.scholastic.com

Editor: David Levithan

Push is about discovering the voices of here and now. It is about telling stories that feel real, even if they are not. An imprint of Scholastic, the books from Push show vulnerability and the roots of identity.

Freelance Potential: Publishes 5 titles annually: 40% by authors who are new to the publishing house.

Fiction: Middle-grade, YA. Genres: contemporary, multicultural, realistic, coming-of-age.

Titles: *Tyrell,* by Cee Booth (YA). *Hail Caesar,* by ThuHuong Ha (YA)

Submissions and Payment: Guidelines and catalogue available at website. Accepts submissions from agented authors only. Young writers may submit to the PUSH contest. Publication period and payment policy vary.

Parents, Divisions, Imprints

Scholastic Inc., See page 204

G. P. Putnam's Sons Books for Young Readers

Penguin Group, 345 Hudson Street, New York, NY 10014
http://us.penguingroup.com

Manuscript Editor

For more than two decades, G. P. Putnam's Sons has led the publishing industry with more hardcover *New York Times* bestsellers than any other imprint. Among its distingushed authors are Dave Barry, Tom Clancy, and Robin Cook.

Freelance Potential: Publishes 50 titles annually: 1-10% developed from an unsolicited submission; 50-60% by agented authors; 30% by authors who are new to the publishing house; 1-10% by previously unpublished writers. Receives 125 queries, 600 unsolicited manuscripts monthly.

Fiction: Toddler books, early picture books, early readers, story picture books, chapter books, middle-grade, YA. Genres: contemporary, multicultural, fantasy, mystery, humor.

Titles: *Black Glass*, by Karen Joy Fowler (YA-A). *Lionheart*, by Sharon Kay Penman (Adult).

Submissions and Payment: Guidelines and catalogue available at website. Send complete manuscript for picture books. For longer works, query with a maximum of 10 pages from the opening chapter(s) of the manuscript and a cover letter briefly describing the plot, genre, intended age group, and author's publishing credits, if any. Accepts hard copy. No SASE; materials not returned. Responds in 4 months if interested. Publication period varies. Royalty; advance.

Parents, Divisions, Imprints

Penguin Group (USA), See page 184

Pyr Books

59 John Glenn Drive, Amherst, NY 14228-2197
www.pyrsf.com

Editor

Pyr is an imprint from Prometheus Books, a leader in publishing books for the scientific, professional, library, educational, and popular consumer markets. Pyr publishes in many areas of speculative fiction including steampunk, epic fantasy, sci-fi blends, and near future thrillers.

Freelance Potential: Publishes 30 titles (6 juvenile) annually.

Fiction: YA, adult. Genres: science fiction; fantasy; subgenres of speculative fiction including epic fantasy, sword and sorcery, contemporary/urban fantasy.

Titles: *Apollo's Outcasts*, by Allen Steele (YA). *Fair Coin*, by E. C. Coin (YA).

Submissions and Payment: Guidelines and catalogue available at website. Send complete manuscript with 1- to 3-paragraph synopsis. Accepts email to rsears@prometheusbooks.com (Word or RTF attachments). For agented submissions send query to landers@prometheusbooks.com. Response time, publication period, and payment policy vary.

Parents, Divisions, Imprints

Prometheus Books, See page 289

QED

6 Blundell Street, N7 9BH, United Kingdom
www.qed-publishing.co.uk

Associate Publisher: Maxime Boucknooghe

The mission of QED Publishing is simple—to create fresh, informative, high-quality books that appeal to children, parents, and teachers alike. Its diverse range of titles cover everything from entertaining, innovative facts for classrooms, to beautifully illustrated fiction.

Freelance Potential: Publishes 80 titles annually: 1-10% by authors who are new to the publishing house; 20% by previously unpublished writers. Receives 4–8 queries monthly.

Fiction: Toddler books, early picture books, early readers, picture books, chapter books, middle-grade. Genres: contemporary.

Nonfiction: Concept books, toddler books, early readers, picture books, story picture books, middle-grade. Topics: early learning, animals, science, nature, games, geography, history, math, religion, technology.

Titles: *Albert and Sarah Jane*, by Malachy Doyle (ages 4+). *Hens*

Don't Crow!, by A. H. Benjamin and Rebecca Elliott (ages 3–6).

Submissions and Payment: Catalogue available at website. Query with clips. Accepts hard copy and email queries to amandaa@quarto.com. Availability of artwork improves chance of acceptance. SAE/IRC. Response time and publication period vary. Royalty. Flat fee.

Quirk Books

215 Church Street, Philadelphia, PA 19106. http://quirkbooks.com

Associate Publisher/Creative Director: Jason Rekulak

Quirk Books feature unique angles and irreverent treatments of topics. The company is best known as the creator of the Worst-Case Scenario Survival Handbook series and Pride and Prejudice and Zombies, but it publishes titles on a broad range of nonfiction topics, from parenting to history to crafts, as well as horror, science fiction, and mysteries for adults and children.

Freelance Potential: Publishes 25 titles annually.

Fiction: Picture books, middle-grade, YA. Genres: fantasy, contemporary, science fiction, humor, horror.

Nonfiction: Picture books, middle-grade, YA. Topics: cooking, humor, family.

Titles: *Kid Athletes,* by David Staber and Doogie Horner (7–10). *Lovecraft Middle School: Substitute Creature* (ages 8–12).

Submissions and Payment: Guidelines and catalogue available at website. Send 1-page query describing the project and 1–2 sample chapters. See guidelines for specific editors and interests. For most YA and middle grade submission, email jason@quirkbooks.com. Also accepts hard copy. SASE. Response time, publication period, and payment policy vary.

Ramsey & Todd

445 Park Avenue, 9th Floor, New York, NY 10022
www.turnerpublishing.com

Acquisitions

Ramsey & Todd is the children's imprint from Turner Publishing. Headquartered in New York, Turner publishes more than 3,000 titles yearly. Its books are currently sold in more than 55 countries and continues to grow.

Freelance Potential: Publishes about 10–12 annually: most are developed from unsolicited submissions. Receives 20 queries monthly.

Fiction: Early readers, middle grade, YA; Genres: Real life problems.

Nonfiction: Middle grade, YA, adults. Topics: self-help, social skills, health, and entertainment.

Titles: *Leopold*, by Ruth K. Westheimer (ages 6–8). *101 Dialogues, Sketches and Skits: Instant Theatre for Teens and Tweens* (ages 11–16).

Submissions and Payment: Guidelines and catalogue available at website. Query with proposal containing an overview, chapter-by-chapter outline, approximate length, illustrations and other features, author biography, and market analysis. Accepts hard copy, or email to submissions@turnerpublishing.com. Accepts simultaneous submissions if identified. SASE. Responds in 3–4 months. Publication in 1–2 years. Royalty.

Raven Productions

P.O. Box 188, Ely, MN 55731. www.ravenwords.com

Editor: Johnna Hyde

Publishing children's books about nature and natural places is the focus of Raven Productions. Its catalogue includes both fiction and nonfiction, as well as titles for adults. At this time it is not open to submissions. Check the website for changes to this policy.

Freelance Potential: Publishes 5–10 titles annually: 75–100% developed from unsolicited submissions; 75–100% by authors who are new to the publishing house; 25–50% by previously unpublished writers. Receives 1–10 unsolicited manuscripts monthly.

Fiction: Early picture books, picture books, early readers, story picture books, chapter books, middle-grade, YA. Genres: adventure, coming-of-age, contemporary, folktales, historical, seasonal, regional, stories about nature.

Nonfiction: Early picture books, early readers, picture books, story picture books, YA. Topics: animals, nature, activities, history, holidays/seasons, the outdoors, recreation, science.

Titles: *A Bird On My Hand*, by Mary Bevis (ages 6+). *The Best Part of a Sauna*, Sheryl Petersen (ages 7+).

Submissions and Payment: Guidelines and catalogue available at website. Not currently accepting submissions.

Raven Tree Press

6213 Factory Rd, Suite B, Crystal Lake, IL 60050–7030
www.raventreepress.com

Acquisitions Editor

Raven Tree Press specializes in award-winning children's picture books in English, Spanish, and bilingual editions. Its books are used for language develoment and they provide a place where a child's imagination can soar.

Freelance Potential: Publishes 15 titles annually: 13% by agented authors; 66% by authors who are new to the publishing house; 20% by previously unpublished writers. Receives 42 unsolicited manuscripts monthly.

Fiction: Picture books, early readers, story picture books. Genres: contemporary, historical, multicultural, folktales, adventure, family stories.

Titles: *Marc Flamingo/Marco Flamenco*, by Sheila Jarkins (grades 12). *Pedro the Pirate*, by Tim Hoppey (grade 2).

Submissions and Payment: Guidelines and catalogue available at website. At press time submissions were closed; check website for updates. Publication in 1 year. Royalty, 10%; advance, varies.

Red Deer Press

195 Allstate Parkway, Markham, Ontario L3R 4T8 Canada
www.reddeerpress.com

Children's Editor: Peter Carver

Upscale children's books, young adult titles, and adult fiction and nonfiction written by Canadian authors can be found in the catalogue from Red Deer Press. Red Deer is focusing less on picture books and more on middle-grade and young adult fiction. It is owned by Fitzhenry & Whiteside.

Freelance Potential: Publishes 14–18 titles annually: 25% by authors who are new to the publishing house; 12% by previously unpublished writers. Receives 165+ unsolicited manuscripts monthly.

Fiction: Story picture books, middle-grade, YA. Genres: regional, contemporary, adventure, fantasy, mystery, suspense, science fiction.

Nonfiction: Middle-grade, YA. Topics: activities, field guides, biography, Canadian nature, wildlife, First Nations, history, sports.

Titles: *From the Lands of Night,* by Tololwa M. Mollel (ages 6–9). *Carbon Rush*, by Amy Miller (ages 12+).

Submissions and Payment: Canadian authors only. Guidelines and catalogue available at website. Submit via mail or email to rdp@reddeerpress.com. Send complete manuscript for picture books. For fiction, send query letter or 3 sample chapters; for nonfiction, submit query letter or sample chapter with outline. SASE. Accepts multiple submissions. Responds in 4-6 months.

Parents, Divisions, Imprints

Fitzhenry & Whiteside, See page 120

Red Rock Press

331 West 57th Street, Suite 175, New York, NY 10019
www.redrockpress.com

Creative Director: Ilene Barth

This independent book publisher produces beautiful and entertaining gift books for aduts and children. It prefers manuscripts from agents, but will look at unsolicited proposals.

Freelance Potential: Publishes 6 titles annually: 2 developed from unsolicited submissions; 1 by a previously unpublished writer. Receives 67 unsolicited manuscripts monthly.

Fiction: Picture books, story picture books. Genres: contemporary, adventure, historical, multicultural.

Titles: *Pop, You Rock Because...*, by Tomow Sasaki Farley (ages 6–10). *Amazing Menorah,* by Joy Fate and Harold Dresner (ages 5–10).

Submissions and Payment: Guidelines and catalogue available at website. Prefers agented submissions. Send complete manuscript with marketing plan. Accepts hard copy. SASE. Responds in 2–4 months. Publication in 18 months. Royalty; advance. Flat fee.

Regnery Publishing

300 New Jersey Ave NW, Suite 500, Washington, DC 20001
www.regnery.com

Editor

Regnery Publishing is one of the country's leading publisher of conservative books. Its children's imprint Regnery Kids, provides charming stories combined with beautiful illustrations while teachig children about history, science, and culture. Its publishing program also includes Little Patriot Press, a series of educational books for young readers.

Freelance Potential: Publishes 6–8 titles annually.

Fiction: Picture books, story picture books. Genres: contemporary, adventure, historical.

Nonfiction: Picture books, story picture books. Topics: history, biography, science, animals, patriotism.

Titles: *Christmas in America*, by Callista Gingrich and Susan Arciero (ages 5+). *The Ten Commandments*, by Dennis Prager (ages 8–12).

Submissions and Payment: Catalogue available at website. Accepts only agented submissions. Publication period and payment policy, unknown.

Ripple Grove Press

P.O. Box 86740, Portland, OR 97286. www.ripplegrovepress.com

Submissions Editor

This small press has a passion for well-written and beautifully illustrated children's picture books. Each story selected has been read dozens of times, then slept on, then walked away from, then talked about again and again. Its mission is to surround itself with great writers and talented illustrators to make the best and most beautiful book possible.

Freelance Potential: Publishes 3 titles annually: about 80% by authors who are new to the publishing house; 100% by previously unpublished writers.

Fiction: Picture books, dinosaurs, vehicles, families. Also publishes parenting books.

Titles: *Mae and the Moon*, by Jami Gigot (ages 2–8). *The Peddler's Bed*, by Lauri Fortino (ages 2-8).

Submissions and Payment: Guidelines and catalogue available at website. Send complete manuscript only. Accepts hard copy and email submissions to submit@ripplegrovepress.com. Responds in 5 months. Standard contract.

Roaring Brook Press

Macmillan, 175 Fifth Avenue, New York, NY 10010
http://us.macmillan.com/RoaringBrook.aspx

Editor: David Langva

Roaring Brook Press is a publisher of high-quality literature for young readers, from toddlers to teens. Since its first list was published in 2002, many of its titles have received pretigious awards, including The Caldecott Medal and Newbery Honor award.

Freelance Potential: Publishes about 40 titles annually.

Fiction: Picture books, early readers, middle-grade, YA. Genres: adventure, contemporary, fantasy, history, humor, multicultural, nature/environment, poetry, religion, science fiction, sports, suspense/mystery, graphic novels.

Nonfiction: Picture books, early readers, middle-grade, YA. Topics: history, politics, biography, social issues, sports, reference, geography, culture.

Titles: *A Boy, A Ball and A Dog*, by Gianna Marino (ages 4–8). *Fish*, by Liam Francis Walsh (ages 3-8).

Submissions and Payment: Guidelines and catalogue available at website. Agented submissions only.

Macmillan, See page 163

Running Press Kids

2300 Chestnut Street, Suite 200, Philadelphia, PA 19103-4399
www.runningpress.com

Submissions Editor

Running Press,has been providing consumers with an innovative
list of quaity books and book related kits since 1972. Its imprints
Running Press Kids and Running Press Teens feature exciting and
thought-provoking titles for children of all ages.

Freelance Potential: Publishes 80 titles annually: 4% by authors
who are new to the publishing house; 10% by previously unpublished writers.

Fiction: Board books, novelty books, early picture books, early readers, picture books, chapter books, middle-grade, YA. Genres: contemporary, multicultural, mystery, coming-of-age, animal stories.

Nonfiction: Board books, picture books, story picture books,
middle-grade. Topics: history, nature, biography, activities.

Titles: *Butterfly Park*, by Elly MacKay (ages 5–9). *Secret Side of
Empty*, by Maria E. Andreu (YA).

Submissions and Payment: Guidelines and catalogue available
at website. Currently only accepting submissions from agents.
Check webste for changes to this policy.

Salina Bookshelf

3120 North Caden Court, Suite 4, Flagstaff, AZ 86011
www.salinabookshelf.com

Editor: LaFrenda Frank

This publisher features picture books, chapter books, informational texts, and electronic media that offer authentic depictions
of Navajo life, both contemporary and traditional. Though its

children's list is comprised mostly of picture books, it is open to submissions of middle-grade and young adult fiction. It is currently seeking Navajo/English bilingual manuscripts suitable for picture books for students in grades preK to 6 as well as chapter books for readers in grades 4 to 6.

Freelance Potential: Publishes 10 titles annually: 50% developed from unsolicited submissions; 60% by authors who are new to the publishing house; 20% by previously unpublished writers. Receives 10–12 unsolicited manuscripts monthly.

Fiction: Toddler books, early picture books, early readers, story picture books. Genres: folklore, folktales, multicultural and ethnic fiction, and stories about nature and the environment.

Nonfiction: Middle-grade, YA. Topics: Navajo history and culture, biography.

Titles: *Ashkii's Journey*, by Verna Clinton (ages 8–12). *Beauty Beside Me, Stories of My Grandmother's Skirts,* by Stephanie Yazzie (ages 8+).

Submissions and Payment: Guidelines and catalogue available at website. Query with sample chapter or send complete manuscript. Accepts hard copy. SASE. Responds in 6 months. Publication in 1 year. Royalty, varies; advance, varies.

Scarlet Voyage

29 East 21st Street, New York, NY 10010.
www.scarletvoyage.com

Acquisitions Editor: Ben Rosenthal

Scarlet Voyage is a young adult fiction imprint, dedicated to providing original stories with a strong vice and an independent spirit. Its mission is to create books that take readers on a voyage and will leave them burning for more.

Freelance Potential: Plans to publishes 2–4 titles annually.

Fiction: YA. Genres: fantasy, science fiction, thriller/mystery, contemporary, real-life, dypstopia, paranormal romance.

Titles: *In the River Darkness,* by Marlene Roder (YA). *Paint Me a Monster*, by Janie Baskin (YA)

Submissions and Payment: Guidelines available at website. Send query or complete ms with résumé and/or list of published works, and synopsis of ms. Accepts electronic submissions only through the website. Response time, publication period, and payment policy vary.

Parents, Divisions, Imprints

Enslow Publishers, See page 263

Scholastic Children's Books UK

Euston House, 24 Eversholt Street, London NW1 1DB
United Kingdom. www.scholastic.co.uk

Editorial Department

Scholastic Children's Books UK is dedicated to developing reading and literacy in children and supporting parents and teachers, this children's publisher creates books that educate, entertain, and motivate children of all ages.

Freelance Potential: Publishes 200 titles annually: most by agented authors. Receives 30–33 unsolicited manuscripts monthly.

Fiction: Concept books, toddler books, early picture books, early readers, chapter books, middle-grade, YA. Genres: contemporary, historical, adventure, mystery, suspense, drama, fantasy.

Nonfiction: Chapter books. Topics: geography, history, math, sports.

Titles: *Ten Flying Brooms*, by Jaqueline WIlson (ages 7+). *Stick Man,* by Julia Donaldson (ages 4–7).

Submissions and Payment: Guidelines and catalogue available at website. Send cover letter and first 3 chapters for trade books. For educational projects, send query with the idea and sample activities or sections to the Education Division. No electronic submissions. SAE/IRC. Responds in 6 months. Publication period and payment policy vary.

Scholastic Inc.

557 Broadway, New York, NY 10012. www.scholastic.com

Senior Editor: Jennifer Rees

Scholastic is the largest children's book and magazine publisher and distributor in the world. Its divisions encompass trade and educational publishing, licensing, and media. Its trade division includes a variety of imprints that market hardcover and paperback books in many genres for the very youngest readers through young adults. Scholastic only accepts queries from agented authors and writers who have worked with the company in the past.

Freelance Potential: Publishes 600+ titles annually: all by agented authors. Receives 200+ queries monthly.

Fiction: Toddler books, early picture books, story picture books, chapter books, middle-grade, YA. Genres: contemporary, science fiction, adventure, fantasy, humor, and mystery.

Nonfiction: Story picture books, chapter books, middle-grade, YA. Topics: history, nature, biography, humor, the environment, multicultural subjects.

Titles: *Stay Alive: Crash*, by Joseph Monninger (ages 8–12). *Ranger in Time #2: Danger in Ancient Rome*, by Kate Messner (ages 7–10).

Submissions and Payment: Guidelines and catalogue available at website. Accepts queries from agented authors only. Will accept submissions from educators for its professional books; see website for guidelines. Publication in 1–2 years. Royalty; advance.

Parents, Divisions, Imprints

Blue Sky Press, See page 89
Cartwheel Books, See page95
Children's Press, See page 258
Arthur A. Levine Books, See page 157
PUSH, See page 193

Seven Stories Press

140 Watts Street, New York, NY 10013. www.sevenstories.com

Acquisitions

Founded in 1995, this publisher is named for the seven authors who committed to a home with a fiercely independent spirit. It is widely known for its books on politics, human rights, and social justice, but also publishes books for children and young adults.

Freelance Potential: Publishes 20–30 titles annually; 4–8 juvenile.

Fiction: Story picture books, early readers, middle grade, YA. Genres: contemporary, realistic, coming-of-age, historical, graphic novels.

Nonfiction: Picture books, early readers, middle grade, YA. Topics: history, the women's movement, human rights, social justice, gender equality, science, the environment, social issues.

Titles: *Sex Is a Funny Word: A Book About Bodies, Feelings, and YOU,* by Cory Silverberg and Fiona Smyth (ages 8–10). *Counting on Community,* by Innosanto Nagara (ages 7–10).

Submissions and Payment: Guidelines and catalogue available at website. Query only with cover letter and no more than 2 sample chapters. Accepts hard copy. SASE. Responds in 2–4 months. Publication in 18 months. Royalty.

Shadow Mountain

P.O. Box 30178, Salt Lake City, UT 84130–0178
www.shadowmountain.com

Editor: Lisa Magnum

Shadow Mountain appeals to a values-based, general market that specializes in non-religious books. An imprint of Deseret Book, Shadow Mountain publishes and promotes a variety of books, all of which reflect the values espoused by The Church of Latter-day Saints.

Freelance Potential: Publishes 2-5 YA titles annually, parent company publishes 150 titles annually: 12 developed from unsolicited submissions; 5 by agented authors. Receives 200 queries monthly.

Fiction: Picture books, middle-grade, YA. Genres: romance, social issues, contemporary, fantasy, thriller, science fiction.

Titles: *Curse of the Broomstaff (Janitors),* by Tyler Whitesides (ages 9–12). *Cragbridge Hall, Book 1: The Inventor's Secret,* by Chad Morris (ages 9–12).

Submissions and Payment: Guidelines and catalogue available at website. Send query with outline or table of contents and two or three sample chapters or complete manuscript. Accepts email submissions to submissions@shadowmountain.com or online at http://submissions.shadowmountain.com. Responds in approximately 2 months. Publication in 6–12 months. Payment policy varies.

Shen's Books

95 Madion Avene, Suite 1205, New York, NY 10016
www.shens.com

Owner: Renee Ting

In 2013 Shen's Books was acquired by multicultural books publisher, Lee & Low Books. The imprint publishes books emphasizing cultural diversity and tolerance, with a focus on introducing children to the cultures of Asia.

Freelance Potential: Publishes 2 titles annually: 100% developed from unsolicited submissions; 50% by authors who are new to the publishing house; 50% by previously unpublished writers. Receives 50 unsolicited manuscripts monthly.

Fiction: Story picture books. Genres: fairy tales, folklore, historical, multicultural fiction about Asia and its people.

Nonfiction: Story picture books, middle-grade. Topics: world cultures and immigrants, Asian Americans, Asian culture.

Titles: *Selvakmar Knew Better*, by Virginia Kroll (Grades PreK-3). *Grandfather's Story Cloth*, by Linda Gerderner Langford (grades 1–4).

Submissions and Payment: Guidelines and catalogue available at website. Accepts hard copy. SASE. Publication in 18–24 months. Payment policy varies.

Simon & Schuster

Simon & Schuster Children's Publishing, 1230 Avenue of the Americas, New York, NY 10020. www.simonandschuster.com

Submissions Editor

Simon & Schuster comprises many famous "publishing units"

including Pocket, Scribner, and the Simon & Schuster imprint for adults. The Children's Division is made up of Aladdin, Atheneum Books for Young Readers, Beach Lane Books, Little Simon, Margaret K. McElderry Books, Simon & Schuster Books for Young Readers, Simon Pulse, Simon Spotlight, and Paula Wiseman Books.

Freelance Potential: Publishes hundreds of titles annually.

Fiction: Children, teens, adults, across all genres.

Nonfiction: Children, teens, adults, across all categories.

Titles: *Brooklyn,* by Colm Toibin (YA-A). *Spooksville: The Deadly Past,* by Christopher Pike (ages 8–12).

Submissions and Payment: Guidelines and catalogues available at website. Most imprints accept submissions through literary agents only.

Parents, Divisions, Imprints

Simon & Schuster Books for Young Readers 🔑

Simon & Schuster Children's Publishing, 1230 Avenue of the Americas, New York, NY 10020
http://imprints.simonandschuster.biz/BFYR

Submissions Editor

Simon & Schuster Books for Young Readers is the flagship imprint of the Simon & Schuster Children's Division. It publishes a wide array of picture books, chapter books, and novels for teens and tweens in a variety of genres, while also offering nonfiction, biographies, and anthologies. It accepts submissions from agented authors only.

Freelance Potential: Publishes 90 titles annually: most by agented authors. Receives 830 queries monthly.

Fiction: Novelty books, board books, toddler books, early picture books, early readers, story picture books, chapter books, middle-grade, YA. Genres: contemporary, historical, multicultural, mystery, fantasy, folklore, fairy tales.

Nonfiction: Story picture books, middle-grade, YA. Topics: social issues, science, nature, math, history, biography.

Titles: *Revenge of the Bully*, by Scott Starkey (ages 9–11). *A Shiloh Christmas*, by Phyllis Reynolds Naylor.

Submissions and Payment: Guidelines and catalogue available at website. Accepts submissions through literary agents only. Responds in 2 months. Publication in 2–4 years. Royalty; advance.

Parents, Divisions, Imprints

Simon & Schuster, See page 207

Simon Pulse

Simon & Schuster Children's Publishing, 1230 Avenue of the Americas, New York, NY 10020
http://imprints.simonandschuster.biz/simon-pulse

Submissions Editor

Simon Pulse delivers fresh, bold voices that inspire compulsive reading for teens and beyond. With a focus on high-concept commercial fiction, this imprint of Simon & Schuster is known for pushing boundaries. It publishes single titles and series, and select nonfiction. Publisher Bethany Buck heads Simon Pulse and Annette Pollert is Editor. They and other members of the editorial team reveal the kinds of books they look for at http://imprints.simonandschuster.biz/simon-pulse.

Freelance Potential: Publishes 100+ titles annually: 10% by authors who are new to the publishing house.

Fiction: YA. Genres: contemporary, inspirational, ethnic, multicultural, historical, mystery, myth, romance, suspense, science fiction, fantasy, dystopian, horror.

Nonfiction: YA. Topics: Social issues, relationships.

Titles: *Beauty of the Broken*, by Tawni Waters (ages 14+). *Magnolia*, by Kristi Cook (ages 14+).

Submissions and Payment: Catalogue available at website. Accepts agented submissions only. Response time, publication period, and payment policy vary.

Parents, Divisions, Imprints

Simon & Schuster, See page 207

Simply Read

501-5525 West Boulevard, Vancouver, British Columbia V6M 3W6, Canada. www.simplyreadbooks.com

Submissions

The approach that Simply Read Books takes to producing its children's books, follows the finest publishing tradition and spirit with inspired content, extraordinary artwork, and outstanding graphic design. It is currently seeking manuscripts for picture books, early readers, chapter books, middle grade fiction and graphic novels.

Freelance Potential: Unavailable.

Fiction: Board books, story picture books, toddler, early readers, chapter books, middle grade, YA. Genres: fantasy, contemporary, classics, folktales, fairy tales, social issues, real life, nature.

Titles: *The Good Night Books,* by Lori Joy Smith (ages 4+). *Jayde the Jaybird,* by Brandee Buble (ages 5–8).

Submissions and Payment: Guidelines and catalogue available at website. Query or send complete manuscript with a cover letter that includes a short synopsis and author information. Accepts hard copy only. SASE. Responds if interested in 5 months. Publication period, and payment policy vary.

Skyhorse Publishing

307 West 36th Street, 11th Floor, New York, NY 10018
www.skyhorsepublishing.com

Editor: Sky Pony Press: Julie Matysik

The core cateogories of Skyhorse Publishing include outdoor sports, adventure, team sports, nature, along with politics and military history. It consists of several imprints Arcade Publishing, Talos Press, Sports Publishing, and its children's imprint Sky Pony Press.

Freelance Potential: Publishes 250 books (15–20 juvenile) annually.

Fiction: Picture books, early readers, middle grade, YA. Genres: contemporary, social issues, animals, coming-of-age, special needs.

Nonfiction: Middle-grade. Topics: sports, activities, outdoors, nature/environment, horses, art, autism. For adults, travel, home, health, history, games and gambling, horses, pets and animals, nature, science, food and wine, aviation, true crime, current events.

Titles: *Green Bay Packers: Where Have You Gone?*, by Chuck Carlson (YA-A). *Cheating Is Encouraged: A Hard-nosed History of the 1970s Raiders*, by Mike Siana and Kristine Clark (YA-A).

Submissions and Payment: Guidelines available at website. Query or send complete manuscript with author bio, publishing credits, and qualifications to write in the subject area of your submission. Accepts email to for each imprint. Visit the website for complete information. Response time, publication period, and payment policy vary.

Sky Pony Press

307 West 36th Street, 11th Floor, New York, NY 10018
www.skyhorsepublishing.com

Editor, Sky Pony Press: Julie Matysik

An imprint of Sky Horse Press, Sky Pony's goal is to provide books for readers with a wide variety of interests. Its lists continues to grow and includes fiction, picture books, educational titles, and novelty books. It views its readers as individual children, rather than by age group in order to celebrate their specific talents and needs.

Freelance Potential: Publishes 15–20 juvenile annually.

Fiction: Picture books, early readers, middle grade, YA. Genres: contemporary, social issues, animals, coming-of-age.

Nonfiction: Middle-grade. Topics: sports, activities, outdoors, nature/environment, horses, art, autism.

Titles: *The Peanut Pickle,* by Jessica Jacobs (ages 4-10). *Baby Farm Animals*, by Sandra Grimm (ages 4–8).

Submissions and Payment: Guidelines and catalogue available at website. Query or send complete manuscript with author bio, publishing credits, and qualifications to write in the subject area of your submission. Accepts email submissions to skyponysubmissions@skyhorsepublishing.com. Visit the website for complete information. Response time, publication period, and payment policy vary.

Skyscape

P.O. Box 81226, Seattle, WA 98108-1226. www.apub.com

Editor

This imprint is part of Amazon Publishing, which is a full service publisher that develops original titles in print, e-book, audio, and other formats. It produces young adult titles only. It currently does not accept unsolicited submissions.

Freelance Potential: Unavailable.

Fiction: YA. Genres: contemporary, historical, graphic novels, adventure, mystery/suspense.

Nonfiction: YA. Topics: science, activities, biography, sports, reference, real-life.

Titles: *The Consequence of Loving Cotton*, by Rachel Van Dyken (YA). *Girls on a Wire*, by Gwenda Bond (YA).

Submissions and Payment: Catalogue available at website.

Does not accept unsolicited submissions. Publication period varies. Monthly royalty payments.

Smart Pop Books

10300 North Central Expressway, Suite 530, Dallas, TX 75231
www.smartpopbooks.com

Editor in Chief: Leah Wilson

This publisher specializes in books about pop culture and entertainment. On its list are titles about the authors and characters in popular books, essays on favorite novels and authors, as well as topics related to movies and TV shows. The books cover pop culture icons that appeal to tweens, teens and adults.

Freelance Potential: Publishes 8–10 titles annually, large anthologies of 12–15 essays each.

Nonfiction: Middle grade, YA, adult. Topics: biography, pop-culture, books, movies, television shows, cooking.

Titles: *Unhomely Places*, by Kate Milford (YA). *My Dragon, Myself,* by Kelly McClymer (YA).

Submissions and Payment: Guidelines and catalogue available at website. Email proposal or query or writing sample and author bio to be considered for essay writing for anthologies to leah@benbellabooks.com. Response time, publication period, and payment policy vary.

Soho Teen

853 Broadway, New York, NY 10003. www.sohopress.com

Editorial Director: Daniel Ehrenhaft

Soho Teen focuses on titles that "put mystery front and center." It is interested in a broad range of categories, including dystopian and paranormal. All books feature a 14–17 year old protagonist with stories and characters that reflect the entire spectrum of the teen experience. It is not currently accepting unsolicited manuscripts but check th website for updates to this policy.

Freelance Potential: Publishes 12 titles annually: 70% by authors who are new to the publishing house; 80% by agented authors; 25% by previously unpublished writers. Receives 30 queries monthly.

Fiction: YA mystery. Genres: adventure, thriller, dystopian, paranormal, contemporary.

Titles: *More Happy than Not*, by Adam Silvera (YA). *The Devil and Winnie Flynn*, by Micol and David Ostow (YA).

Submissions and Payment: Guidelines and catalogue available at website. Even though not currently accepting unagented submissions; (check website for updates to this policy), the following guidelines are available. Query with cover letter, a paragraph pitch, 2–3 page synopsis (including the ending), and the first 50 pages of the book. Not currently interested in acquiring series but if a stand-alone title has series potential, include future plots in the synopsis. Accepts email to rkowal@sohopress.com (Word attachments). Publication period, and payment policy vary.

Sourcebooks

1935 Brookdale Road, Suite 139, Naperville, IL 60563
www.sourcebooks.com

Editorial Submissions

Sourcebooks believes in authorship. It works with authors to develop great books that find and inspire a wide audience. It's children's imprint Jabberwocky publishes titles for all age ranges. It accepts submissions from agents only.

Freelance Potential: Publishes 300+ titles annually: 1–10% developed from unsolicited submissions; 1–10% are assigned; 50–75% within house; 10–25% by previously unpublished writers. Receives 200+ queries, 200+ manuscripts monthly.

Fiction: Early picture books, early readers, story picture books, chapter books, middle-grade, YA. Genres: contemporary, historical, adventure, romance, mystery, fantasy, science fiction, coming-of-age, realistic, humor, horror.

Nonfiction: Chapter books, middle-grade, YA. Topics: history, biography, humor. Also publishes titles on parenting, college, careers.

Titles: *The Girl Who Never Makes Mistakes*, by Gary Rubenstein (ages 4–8). *Dream Big, Little Pig*, by Kristi Yamaguchi (ages 4–8).

Submissions and Payment: Guidelines available at website. Accepts submissions from agents only. Responds in 8–12 weeks. Publication in 1 year. Royalty; advance.

Parents, Divisions, Imprints

Sourcebooks Fire, See page 215
Jabberwocky, See page 149

Sourcebooks Fire

Sourcebooks, 232 Madison Avenue, #1100, New York, NY 10016
www.sourcebooks.com

Submissions: Aubrey Poole

Young adult fiction is the focus of this imprint from Sourcebooks. Its titles feature voices with a fresh premise and a lively pace for the teen audience. It is actively seeking strong writers who are excited about promoting and building their community of readers, and whose books have something fresh to offer the ever-growing young adult audience. At this time it is only accepting submissions through agents.

Freelance Potential: Sourcebooks publishes 300+ titles annually: 1–10% developed from unsolicited submissions; 1–10% assigned; 50–75% by agented authors; 50–75% by authors who are new to the publishing house; 10–25% by previously unpublished writers. Receives 200+ queries monthly.

Fiction: YA. Genres: contemporary, historical, coming-of-age, realistic, fantasy, mystery, romance, science fiction.

Titles: *Dreaming Anastasia*, by Joy Preble (YA). *A Bad Day for Voodoo*, by Jeff Strand (YA).

Submissions and Payment: Guidelines and catalogue available at website. Accepts submissions through agents only. Responds in 8–12 weeks. Publication in 1 year. Royalty; advance.

Parents, Divisions, Imprints

Sourcebooks, See page 214

Speeding Star

29 East 21st Street, New ork, NY 10010. www.speedingstar.com

Acquisitions Editor

This imprint of Enslow Publishing, produces books that will "keep boys reading." It seeks easy-to-read, engaging fiction and informational nonfiction geared to boys from third grade to high school. Writing should be on a fourth-grade level. It prefers male protagonists for fiction, and strong secondary characters. Each book will be either 48, 64, or 96 pages and available in print and digital formats.

Freelance Potential: Publishes about 15 titles annually.

Fiction: Middle grade, YA. Genres: fantasy, science fiction, thriller/mystery, adventure, sports.

Nonfiction: Middle grade, YA. Topics: Sports, cars, topics of interest to boys.

Titles: *Zombie Camp*, by Nadia Higgins (grades 3–6). *Cal Ripken, Jr.: Hall of Fame Baseball Superstar*, by Glen Macnow (YA).

Submissions and Payment: Guidelines and catalogue available at website. For nonfiction, send query, résumé, and a sample chapter or other writing sample. For fiction, send complete ms (between 5,000 and 12,000 words), along with résumé or list of published works. Accepts electronic submissions only through the website. Response time, publication period, and payment policy vary.

Parents, Divisions, Imprints

Enslow Publishers, See page 263

Spencer Hill Press

P.O. Box 247, Contoocook, NH 03229. www.spencerhillpress.com

Lead Editor: Patricia Riley

This publisher specializes in science fiction, urban fantasy, and paranormal romance for young adult readers. It prides itself on publishing books that have that "I couldn't put it down!" quality. It imprints include Spencer Hill Contemporary and Tulip Romance, targeted at teens. The small independent press is also interested in middle-grade and New Adult fiction "with a strong and interesting voice." While it mainly accepts submissions from literary agents, it does offer periods throughout the year for open submissions.

Freelance Potential: Publishes about 25 titles annually:

Fiction: Middle-grade, YA. Genres: science fiction, historical, contemporary, mystery, fantasy, paranormal, romance.

Titles: *Amarok*, by Angela Townsend (YA). *Finn Finnegan*, by Darby Karchut (YA).

Submissions and Payment: Guidelines and catalogue available at website. Accepts agented queries at all times, and also has open submission periods for unsolicited works. See website for submission periods. Send query and first 10 pages of ms. Accepts email only (not attachments) to: Patricia Riley at submissions@spencerhillpress.com. Response time varies. Publication period and payment policy, unknown.

Splashdown Books

www.splashdownbooks.com

Founder: Grace Bridges

Found in 2009, Splashdown, is a speculative fiction indie press based out of New Zealand. Its catalogue features stories that refresh, surprise you, and energize you. It offers both family-friendly and mature material.

Freelance Potential: Publishes about 8 titles annually.

Fiction: YA. Genres: fantasy, science fiction, supernatural, paranormal.

Titles: *Tales of the Dim Knight*, by Adam and Andrea Graham (YA-A). *The Crystal Portal*, by Travis Perry and Mike Lynch (YA–A).

Submissions and Payment: Guidelines and catalogue available at website. Submit brief description, author bio, and first 500 words electronically through form on the website. Response time and publication period vary. Royalty.

Splinter Books

Sterling Publishing Co., Inc., 387 Park Avenue South, New York, NY 10016. www.sterlingpublishing.com

Editorial Director

This children's imprint from Sterling Publishing offers books for children of all ages. Its titles are innovative and promote a love of reading. Picture books, early readers, chapter books and young adult titles can all be found in its catalogue.

Freelance Potential: Publishes about 6 titles annually.

Fiction: Early picture books, early readers, middle grade, YA. Genres: fantasy, contemporary, historical, romance, mystery, thriller, classics.

Titles: *Goodnight Songs*, by Margaret Wise Brown (ages (3–6). *Monster Trouble*, by Lane Fredrickson (ages 4–8).

Submissions and Payment: Guidelines and catalogue available at website. Send complete manuscript with author's biography, special qualifications in the subject area, and publishing history. Accepts hard copy. Accepts simultaneous submissions if identified. SASE. Response time varies. Publication in 1 year. Royalty; advance.

Parents, Divisions, Imprints

Sterling Publishing, See page 221

Star Bright Books

13 Landsdowne Street, Cambridge, MA 02139
www.starbrightbooks.org

Editor: Lola Bush

Offering children's books in over 24 different languages, the catalogue from Star Bright Books reveals its focus on diversity and multiethnic views, with books featuring subjects and characters of varying cultural backgrounds and physical and mental abilities. Star Bright is particularly interested in nonfiction books for toddlers to preteens, in the areas of science, biographies, natural world, animal life, and how things work. Many of its books are bilingual or translated into several languages.

Freelance Potential: Publishes 15-20 titles annually: 25–50% developed from unsolicited submissions; 1–5% by agented authors; 25–50% by authors who are new to the publishing house; 25–50% by previously unpublished writers. Receives 1–10 queries, 50–75 unsolicited manuscripts monthly.

Fiction: Toddler books, early picture books, early readers, story picture books. Genres: contemporary, multicultural, bilingual, educational, folktales, stories about animals and children with disabilities.

Nonfiction: Concept books, board books, toddler books, early picture books, chapter books. Topics: biography, families, animals, history, holidays, mathematics, science, seasons.

Titles: *Alicia's Happy Day*, by Meg Starr (ages 4–8). *A Garden for a Groundhog*, by Lorna Balian (ages 3–8).

Submissions and Payment: Guidelines and catalogue available at website. Query or send complete manuscript. Accepts hard copy. SASE. Responds in 6 months only if interested. Publication in 1–2 years. Payment policy varies.

Starscape

Tom Doherty Associates, 175 Fifth Avenue, New York, NY 10010
www.tor-forge.com

Acquisitions Editor, Children's/YA

Science fiction and fantasy for middle grade readers ages 10 and up are the mainstay of Starscape. It is an imprint of Tor Books, a publisher within Macmillan. All titles are age- and theme-appropriate. Its sister imprint, Tor Teen, publishes similar books for young adults.

Freelance Potential: Publishes 30 titles annually. Receives thousands of submissions monthly.

Fiction: Middle grade, YA. Genres: fantasy, science fiction, horror.

Titles: *Hidden Talents*, by David Lubar (ages 10+). *Dragon and Thief*, by Timothy Zahn (ages 10+).

Submissions and Payment: Guidelines and catalogue available

at website. Send a proposal that includes first 3 chapters (up to 60 pages); 3- to 10-page synopsis; and dated cover letter with contact information, title of submitted work, its genre, any author qualifications that pertain to book, and publishing credits, if any. Do not send query letter. SASE for reply only; materials not returned. Responds in 4–6 months. Publication in 18–24 months. Royalty; advance.

Parents, Divisions, Imprints

Macmillan, See page 163
Tor Books, See page 229

Stemmer House Publishers

4 White Brook Road, P.O. Box 89, Gilsum, NH 03448
www.stemmer.com

Editor: Becky Dalzell

Stemmer House is interested in both fiction and nonfiction for preschool, elementary, and middle-grade readers. Its fiction list features "timeless" stories, poetry, and nature tales. Encyclopedia books on nature and science topics comprise its nonfiction list.

Freelance Potential: Publishes 3 titles annually: 65% developed from unsolicited submissions; 65% by authors who are new to the publishing house; 35% by previously unpublished writers. Receives 15 queries, 20 unsolicited manuscripts monthly.

Fiction: Picture books, early readers, story picture books. Genres: contemporary, historical, multicultural fiction, nature stories.

Nonfiction: Early readers, picture books, story picture books, chapter books, middle-grade. Topics: nature, animals, science, natural history, art, music, geography.

Titles: *The AnimAlphabet Encyclopedia Coloring Book*, by Keith McConnel (ages 4–8). *Ask Me If I'm a Frog,* by Ann Milton (ages 4–10).

Submissions and Payment: Guidelines available. Catalogue available at website. Send complete manuscript for picture books. Query with outline, synopsis, and 2 sample chapters for longer works. Accepts hard copy. Accepts simultaneous submissions if identified. SASE. Responds in 2 weeks. Publication in 1–3 years. Royalty; advance.

Sterling Children's Books

387 Park Avenue South, New York, NY 10016-8810
www.sterlingpublishing.com/kids

Children's Book Editor

Sterling Publishing is an innovatve and forward-thinking publishing company committed to creating books that inspire and entertain. It's children's imprint, Sterling Children's Books features stories for all ages, along with educational resources and self-help books.

Freelance Potential: Publishes 160 titles annually: 15% developed from unsolicited submissions; 15% by agented authors. Receives 100–150 unsolicited manuscripts monthly.

Fiction: Toddler books, early picture books, early readers, story picture books. Genres: contemporary, fairy tales, fantasy, ghost stories, animal stories, myth.

Nonfiction: Toddler books, early picture books, early readers, middle-grade, YA. Topics include history, biography, early learning, animals, nature, science, holidays, seasons, crafts, activities, games.

Titles: *Lady Pancake & Sir French Toast,* by Josh Funk (ages 4–8). *A Dozen Cousins*, by Lori Haskins Houran (ages 5–9).

Submissions and Payment: Guidelines and catalogue available at website. Send complete manuscript with author's biography, special qualifications in the subject area, and publishing history. Accepts hard copy. Accepts simultaneous submissions if identified. SASE. Response time varies. Publication in 1 year. Royalty; advance.

Parents, Divisions, Imprints

Splinter Books, See page 218

Storey Publishing

#210 MASS MoCA Way, North Adams, MA 01247
www.storey.com

Editorial Director: Deborah Balmuth

This publisher of books features books filled with practical information on subjects that include animals, gardening, crafts such as sewing and woodworking, health and well-being, food, and the home also published children's books until about 10 years ago. It is now beginning again, with 5 books in the first year. Many of the practical titles aimed at children will still be ageless, and appeal to the entire family.

Freelance Potential: Publishes 5 juvenile books annually.

Nonfiction: Board books, early readers, middle-grade. Topics: animals, activities, games and puzzles, crafts, gardening, sewing, farming, equestrian, cooking.

Titles: *Excavate! Dinosaurs*, by Jonathan Tennant (age 7+). *Candy Construction*, by Sharon Parrish Bowers (ages 7+).

Submissions and Payment: Guidelines and catalogue available at website. Send a proposal consisting of a letter of introduction, 1-paragraph description of the book, why the book is needed and who the readers are, a list of competitive titles and why your book is different, a 1-paragraph author bio with credentials, table of contents with chapter descriptions, proposed book length and possible art, writing sample, and sample chapter from the proposed book. Accepts hard copy. SASE. Response time, publication period, and payment policy vary.

Stripes Publishing

1 The Coda Centre, 189 Munster Road, London SW6 6AW United Kingdom. www.littletigerpress.co.uk

Submissions Editor: Mara Alperin

This imprint from Little Tiger Press specializes in series for children and young teens.

Freelance Potential: Publishes 60+ titles annually: 1–10% by authors who are new to the publishing house; 1–10% by previously unpublished writers. Receives 300 unsolicited manuscripts monthly.

Fiction: Concept books, board books, early picture books, story picture books. Genres: contemporary, classical.

Titles: *When Granny Saved Christmas*, by Julia Hubery (ages 3–5). *One Snowy Rescue,* by M. Christina Butler (ages 3–5).

Submissions and Payment: Guidelines and catalogue available at website. Query with first three chapters, and a cover letter with an author bio. Accepts hard copy. Publication period and payment policy vary.

SynergEbooks

948 New Highway 7, Columbia, TN 38401
www.synergebooks.com

Editor: Debra Staples

SynergEbooks publishes both fiction and nonfiction for adults, as well as books for young adults and a line of children's ebooks. This digital publisher accepts submissions in all genre and age ranges, but at the time of press was currently seeking nonfiction, self-help, paranormal, New Age, and spirituality.

Freelance Potential: Publishes about 24–36 titles annually: 50% by authors who are new to the publishing house; 60–75% by previously unpublished writers. Receives 50 unsolicited manuscripts annually.

Fiction: Middle grade, YA. Genres: fantasy, mystery, paranormal, horror, adventure, nature, animals.

Nonfiction: Middle grade, YA Topics: self help, spirituality.

Titles: *Adora the Albino Alligator,* by Rhonda Edwards (ages 8–10). *The Bear and The Bull,* by Harvey Mendez (YA).

Submissions and Payment: Guidelines and catalogue available at website. Check website for open submission periods. Query with brief synopsis (up to 300 words), genre, brief author bio that includes writing credits (up to 300 words), and why you think your book is a good fit for SynergEbooks, all contained in the body of the email. Attach first 3 chapters (Word only) in one attachment. Ms should be complete at time of query. Email to: synergebooks@aol.com or synergedeb@yahoo.com. Accepts hard copy but will only respond via email. Responds in 60 days. Publication in 6–12 months. Royalty, percentages vary by genre and format; see website for specifics.

Tanglewood Press 🔒

P.O. Box 3009, Terre Haute, IN 47803
www.tanglewoodbooks.com

Acquisitions Editor: Peggy Tierney

This small, independent publisher has a large catalogue of fiction for children. Its list includes books for kids of all ages, on all kid-centric topics. Due to an overwhelming number of submissions, this publisher is temporarily closed. Check website for updates.

Freelance Potential: Publishes 5–10 titles annually: 75–100% developed from unsolicited submissions; 1–10% by agented authors; 50–75% by authors who are new to the publishing house; 25–50% by previously unpublished writers.

Fiction: Early picture books, story picture books, middle-grade, YA. Genres: fantasy, coming-of-age, historical, real life/problems.

Nonfiction: Middle-grade, YA. Topics: biography, history.

Titles: *Blackbeard and the Sandstone Pillar*, by Audrey Penn (ages 8-12). *Ashen Winter,* by Mike Mullin (ages 14+).

Submissions and Payment: Guidelines available at website. Currently closed to submissions. Check website for updates. Responds in 3–6 months. Publication in 2 years. Royalty; advance.

Teen Crave

www.entangledpublishing.com

Submissions Editor

An imprint of Entangled Publishing, Teen Crave offers print and digital romance novels featuring characters ages 16 to 18. It is seeking sci-fi, paranormal, fantasy, dystopian, and cyberpunk romances. It prefers novels in third person point of view, with light or dark tones.

Freelance Potential: Publishes approximately 50 titles annually: 60% by agented authors, 40% by authors who are new to the publishing house, 50% by previously unpublished writers. Receives 300 queries yearly.

Fiction: YA. Genres: fantasy, contemporary, historical, science fiction, thriller, fantasy and paranormal, all with romantic themes.

Titles: *Consumed by You*, by Lauren Blakely (YA). *His Lover to Protect*, by Katee Robert (YA).

Submissions and Payment: Guidelines and catalogue available at website. YA novels, 45,000–60,000 words. Send 1-page query with genre, word count, brief synopsis, writing credentials, links to your website, and first 5 manuscript pages or complete manuscript. Accepts submissions via centralized system at website. Responds in 30 days. Publication period and payment policy vary.

Parents, Divisions, Imprints

Entangled Publishing, See page 114

Teen Crush

www.entangledpublishing.com

Submissions Editor

Teen Crush is one of Entangled Publishing's first teen category romance imprints. It specializes in heart-stopping feelings and never-ending drama, ranging from funny to emotional and from flirty to dark. All of its titles feature engaging, irresistible first-love stories with teen characters ages 16 to 18.

Freelance Potential: Publishes approximatley 50 titles annually: 60% by agented authors, 40% by authors who are new to the publishing house, 50% by previously unpublished writers. Receives 300 queries yearly.

Fiction: YA. Genres: fantasy, contemporary, historical, science fiction, thriller, fantasy and paranormal, all with romantic themes.

Titles: *Anya and the Shy Guy*, by Suze Wubegardner (YA). *Daisy and the Front Man,* by Rebecca L. Purdy (YA).

Submissions and Payment: Guidelines and catalogue available at website. YA novels, 45,000–60,000 words. Send 1-page query with genre, word count, brief synopsis, writing credentials, links to your website, and first 5 manuscript pages or complete manuscript. Accepts submissions via centralized system at website. Responds in 30 days. Publication period and payment policy vary.

Parents, Divisions, Imprints

Entangled Publishing, See page 114

Templar Publishing

107-109 The Plaza, 535 Kings Road, Chelsea Harbor, London SW10 0SZ United Kingdom. www.templarco.co.uk

Submissions Editor

Templar Publishing is a leading UK children's publisher. Templar focuses on illustrated children's fiction, novelty, and picture books and offers titles in over 25 different languages.

Freelance Potential: Publishes 60 titles annually: 2% developed from unsolicited submissions; 20% by agented authors; 20% by authors who are new to the publishing house; 10% by previously unpublished writers. Receives 34 unsolicited manuscripts monthly.

Fiction: Board books, baby books, novelty books, picture books, story picture books, middle-grade. Genres: contemporary, fantasy, animal stories.

Nonfiction: Story picture books, middle-grade. Topics: science, animals, natural history, nature.

Titles: *Calm Down Boris!*, by Sam Lloyd (ages 4–8). *Greenling*, by Levi Pinfold (ages 5–10).

Submissions and Payment: Guidelines and catalogue available at website. Send complete manuscript. Accepts hard copy. SAE/IRC. Responds in 3–4 months. Publication period and payment policy vary.

Theytus Books

Green Mountain Road, Lot 45, RR 2, Site 50, Comp. 8, Penticton, British Columbia V2A 6J7 Canada. www.theytus.com

Submissions: Anita Large

Theytus Books is a leading North American publisher of Indigenous voices. It is recognized and respected internationally for its contributions to Aboriginal literature. Its catalogue includes books for children in grades K through 12, as well as books for use in universities and colleges.

Freelance Potential: Publishes 10 titles annually: 33% by authors who are new to the publishing house; 10–20% by previously unpublished writers. Receives 2 queries, 3–5 unsolicited manuscripts monthly.

Fiction: Story picture books, middle grade, YA. Genres: contemporary, historical, literary fiction, folktales, adventure, drama, humor, poetry.

Nonfiction: YA. Topics: Aboriginal history, policy, and social issues.

Titles: *Healthy Choices, Healthy Lives,* by Karen W. Olson (ages 3–5). *Jenneli's Dance,* by Elizabeth Denny (ages 6–7).

Submissions and Payment: Canadian Aboriginal authors only. Guidelines and catalogue available at website. For children's books, send complete manuscript with synopsis and intended age group. For young adult books, query with synopsis, intended age group, and 4 sample chapters. All submissions must be accompanied by a cover letter and author biography that includes tribal affiliation and previously published works. Accepts hard copy. No simultaneous submissions. SASE. Responds in 6–8 months. Publication in 1–2 years. Royalty, 10%.

Thistledown Press

118-20th Street West, Saskatoon, Saskatchewan S7M 0W6 Canada. www.thistledownpress.com

Publisher: Allan Forrie

This Canadian publisher offers fiction for juvenile and young adult readers. It works with Canadian authors only. It also publishes literary fiction, nonfiction, and poetry for adults. At this time it is not accepting juvenile fiction submissions but is still seeking YA novels.

Freelance Potential: Publishes 18 titles annually: 55% by authors who are new to the publishing house; 39% by previously unpublished writers. Receives 50 queries monthly.

Fiction: Chapter books, middle-grade, YA. Genres: contemporary, multicultural, fantasy, mystery.

Titles: *Yuletide Blues,* by R. P. MacIntyre (YA). *Barnabas Bigfoot - A Hairy Tangle,* by Marty Chan (ages 8–11).

Submissions and Payment: Canadian authors only. Guidelines and catalogue available at website. Not accepting juvenile fiction submissions at this time. Query for YA fiction from October 1–January 1 with cover letter, first chapter or significant representative sampling, and biographical note about relevant writing experience or significant recent publications. Accepts hard copy. SASE. No simultaneous submissions. Responds in minimum of 4 months. Publication in 1 year. Royalty.

Toon Books

RAW Junior, 27 Greene Street, New York, NY 10013
www.toon-books.com

Editorial Director: Francoise Mouly

Books for early or emerging readers in comic form, for ages 4 and up are the focus of Toon Books, which is an imprint of Candlewick Press. In addition to the graphic novels themselves, TOON supports classroom use of the books with teacher guides and other materials. Titles are divided into 3 reading levels: First Comics for Brand-New Readers (K grade 1); Easy-to-Read for Emerging Readers (grades 1–2); and Chapter Book Comics for Advanced Beginners (grades 2–3). The books follow specific word length, vocabulary, and syntactical guidelines.

Freelance Potential: Publishes 6–10 books annually. Fiction: Early readers, chapter books, reluctant readers. Genres: graphic novels/comics.

Titles: *Benjamin Bear in Brain Storms,* by Philippe Coudray (ages 4+). *Flop to the Top!* by Eleanor Davis and Drew Weing (ages 5+).

Submissions and Payment: Toon Books accepts proposals fom agents only. Response time, publication and payment policy vary.

Parents, Divisions, Imprints

Candlewick Press, See page 93

Topaz Books

www.topazpublishingllc.com

Acquisitions: Marilyn L. Godfrey

This online publisher offers sweet, Christian, and inspirational romance, as well as titles for children, pre-teens, and young adults. Its books are designed to enhance positive behaviors.

Freelance Potential: Publishes 10–15 titles annually.

Fiction: Early readers, middle-grade, YA. Genres: contemporary, romance, adventure, fantasy.

Nonfiction: Early readers, middle-grade, YA. Topics: biography.

Titles: *First Place, Love*, by Annie Laura Smith (YA). *Roses for Jessi*, by Cassi Reed (YA).

Submissions and Payment: Guidelines and catalogue available at website. Query with brief synopsis of manuscript. Accepts email to topazpublishing@aol.com. Response time, publication period, and payment policy vary.

Tor Books

Tom Doherty Associates, 175 Fifth Avenue, New York, NY 10010
www.tor-forge.com

Acquisitions Editor, Children's/YA

Part of the Macmillan publishing family, Tor Books is a science fiction, fantasy, and horror publisher for adults and children. Its Starscape imprint publishes fiction for grades 5 and up, and Tor Teen produces science fiction and fantasy titles for young adults. Tor has an open submissions policy, and will review every submission it receives.

Freelance Potential: Publishes 30 titles annually. Receives thousands of submissions monthly.

Fiction: Chapter books, middle-grade, YA. Genres: fantasy, science fiction, thriller, suspense, mystery.

Titles: *A School for Unusual Girls*, by Kathleen Baldwin (YA). *The High Rocks and Stamping Ground*, by Loren D. Estleman (YA).

Submissions and Payment: Guidelines and catalogue available at website. Send a proposal that includes first 3 chapters (up to 60 pages); 3- to 10-page synopsis of entire book; and dated cover letter with contact information, title of submitted work, its genre, author qualifications that pertain to the book, and publishing credits, if any. Accepts hard copy. SASE for reply only; materials not returned. Responds in 4–6 months. Publication in 18–24 months. Royalty; advance.

Parents, Divisions, Imprints

Macmillan, See page 163
Starscape, See page 219
Tor Teen, See page 230

Tor Teen

Tom Doherty Associates, 175 Fifth Avenue, New York, NY 10010
www.torteencom

Acquisitions Editor, Children's/YA

This critically acclaimed science fiction and fantasy for young adult readers ages 13 and up in both hardcover and paperback. All titles are appropriate for the teen audience. Tor Teen is part of the MacMillan Publishing Group.

Freelance Potential: Publishes 30 titles annually. Receives thousands of submissions monthly.

Fiction: YA. Genres: fantasy, science fiction.

Titles: *Pirate Cinema,* by Cory Doctorow (YA). *Steeplejack*, by A. J. Hartley (YA).

Submissions and Payment: Guidelines available at website. Send a proposal that includes first 3 chapters; 3- to 10-page synopsis of entire book (up to 60 pages); and dated cover letter with contact information, title of submitted work, its genre, author qualifications that pertain to the book, and publishing credits, if any. Accepts hard copy. SASE for reply only; materials not returned. Responds in 4–6 months. Publication in 18–24 months. Royalty; advance.

Parents, Divisions, Imprints

Macmillan, See page 163
Tor Books, See page 229

Tradewind Books

202-1807 Maritime Mews, Vancouver, British Columbia V6H 3W7
Canada. www.tradewindbooks.com

Publisher

This small publishing house has been in the business of publishing
prize-winning picture books, novels, and poetry for children of all
ages. Its books are distributed through Fitzhenry & Whiteside Limited.

Freelance Potential: Publishes 7–8 titles annually: 10–25%
developed from unsolicited submissions; 10–25% by agented
authors; 10–25% by authors who are new to the publishing
house; 15% by previously unpublished writers. Receives 50–75
unsolicited manuscripts monthly.

Fiction: Picture books, early readers, chapter books, middle-grade, YA. Genres: contemporary, multicultural, mystery,
folktales, fairy tales, poetry.

Titles: *Where I Belong,* by Tara White (ages 12–14). *No-Matter-
What-Friend,* by Kari-Lynn Winters.

Submissions and Payment: Guidelines and catalogue available
at website. Send complete manuscript for picture books. Query
with first 3 chapters, a chapter outline, and plot summary for
longer works. For poetry, send book-length collection of poems.
With all submissions send a cover letter that shows you have
read at least 3 books published by Tradewind in the genre in
which you are submitting and also includes author bio and publishing credits. Accepts hard copy only. SAE/IRC. Responds in 3
months. Publication in 3 years. Royalty, 10%.

Treehouse Publishing Group

4168 Hartford St., St. Louis, MO 63116
www.amphoraepublishing.com

Editor

Treehouse Publishing Group offers high-quality picture books,
children's chapter books, as well as fiction and nonfiction for
middle grade students and young adults. It is particularly interested in historical fiction, contemporary stories, and science
fiction and fantasy featuring strong female characters. It also
welcomes multicultural submissions.

Freelance Potential: Publishes 15 titles annually.

Fiction: Early picture books, early readers, story picture books, middle-grade, YA. Genres: historical, contemporary, multicultral, fantasy, science fiction, steampunk.

Nonfiction: Story picture books, middle grade, YA. Topics: history, social studies, and social skills.

Titles: *Iron Horsemen*, by Brad R. Cook (ages 8–12). *Painting for Peace in Ferguson,* by Carol Swartout Klein (ages 8–12).

Submissions and Payment: Catalogue and guidelines available at website. Query or send complete manuscript. Accepts submissions through the online submission form at the website. Responds in 10–12 weeks. Publication period and payment policy varies.

Tu Books

Lee & Low Books, 95 Madison Avenue, Suite 1205, New York, NY 10026. www.leeandlow.com/p/tu.mhtml

Submissions Editor

Tu Books is an imprint from Lee & Low Books that is dedicated to publishing high-quality middle grade and young adult novels that spark imagination, move the spirit, and keep teens turning pages. This imprint is focused on adventure, fantasy, science fiction, and mystery.

Freelance Potential: Publishes 5 titles annually.

Fiction: Middle-grade, YA. Genres: fantasy, science fiction, mystery.

Titles: *Awakening* (Tankborn Trilogy), by Karen Sandler (YA). *Hammer of Witches*, by Shana Mlawski (YA).

Submissions and Payment: Guidelines and catalogue available at website. Tu Books is temporarily closed to submissions; check website to find out when they will re-open. Send cover letter that includes author biography and publishing credits, synopsis, and first 3 chapters. Accepts hard copy. Also accepts submissions electronically through the website. Accepts simultaneous submissions if identified. No SASE; materials not returned. Responds in 6 months if interested.

Tumblehome Learning

201 Newton Street, Weston, MA 02493
www.tumblehomelearning.com

Submissions

Tumblehome Learning helps kids imagine themselves as young scientists or engineers and encourages them to experience science through adventure and discovery. It offers exciting mystery and adventure tales as well as fun experiements carefully designed to engage students from ages 8 and up.

Freelance Potential: Publishes 3–6 titles annually.

Fiction: Story picture books, chapter books, middle-grade, YA. Genres: fantasy, contemporary, historical, adventure, mystery, science fiction.

Nonfiction: Story picture books, chapter books, middle-grade, YA. Topics: biography, science, social issues.

Titles: *The Perilous Case of Zombie Potion*, by Pendred Noyce (ages 8–12). *Kelvin McCloud and the Seaside Storm*, by Michael Erb (ages 8–12).

Submissions and Payment: Guidelines available. Catalogue available at website. Send query with cover letter detailing qualifications to write on the topic and previous publishing experience, synopsis of entire book, and first 3 chapters. Accepts electronic submissions only (Word or PDF attachments) with "Submission: [Title]" in the subject line to submissions@tumblehomelearning.com. No simultaneous submissions. Response time, publication period, and payment policy vary.

Turquoise Morning Press

P.O. Box 43958, Louisville, KY 40253
www.turquoisemorningpressbookstore.com

Senior Editor YA: Shelby C. Madison

This small, international publishing house offers both digital and print formats of romance novels for adults and teens. It is open to cross-genre titles such as romantic mystery and paranormal romance.

Freelance Potential: Publishes 25 titles annually.

Fiction: Adult, YA. Genres: romance, paranormal, fantasy, contemporary, real-life, mystery.

Titles: *Existence*, by Debbie Kump (YA). *Firecracker Queen*, by Cat Shaffer (YA).

Submissions and Payment: Guidelines and catalog available at website. Send complete ms or 2-5 page synopsis and 3 sample chapters along with a cover letter that includes author bio, online presence, and marketing plan. Accepts email to yasubmissions@turquoisemorning.com (Word or RTF attachments). Responds in 6 weeks. Publication period and payment policy, unknown.

Tuttle Publishing

364 Innovation Drive, North Clarendon, VT 05759-9436
www.tuttlepublishing.com

Acquisitions Editor: Brandy LaMotte

Established in 1948, Tuttle Publishing is built upon one objective: pioneering into the future while building upon the past. It's children's line centers Asian culture, crafts, and language.

Freelance Potential: Publishes 120 titles annually: 25–50% developed from unsolicited submissions; 1–10% assigned; 1–10% by agented authors; 25–50% by authors who are new to the publishing house; 75–100% by previously unpublished writers. Receives 10–25 queries, 10–25 unsolicited manuscripts monthly.

Fiction: Early readers, chapter books, middle grade, YA. Genres: multicultural, fantasy, fairy tales, folktales, graphic novels, poetry.

Nonfiction: Activity books, early readers, story picture books, chapter books. Topics: Asian topics, animals, the arts, crafts, holidays, humor, language arts, multicultural topics, reference.

Titles: *Young-Hee and the Pullocho*, by Mark James Russell (YA).

Samurai Awakening, by Benjamin Martin (YA).

Submissions and Payment: Guidelines and catalogue available at website. Send proposal with cover letter, annotated table of contents, 1 or 2 sample chapters, target audience, and competition and market report. Prefers email to submissions@tuttlepublishing.com (Word or PDF attachments); will accept hard copy. Accepts simultaneous submissions if identified. Availability of artwork improves chance of acceptance. SASE. Responds in 3 months. Publication in 1 year. Royalty.

Two Lions

P.O. Box 81226, Seattle, WA 98108-1226. www.apub.com

Editor

This imprint from Amazon Children's Publishing offers high-quality picture books, chapter books, and middle grade novels that delight and enterain children. It is not currently accepting submissions.

Freelance Potential: Unavailable.

Fiction: Picture books, chapter books, middle grade. Genres: animals, mystery, real-life problem, multicutural.

Titles: *Family Sabbatical*, by Carol Ryrie Brink and Nancy Pearl (ages 8–12). *Turkey Trick or Treat*, by Wendi Silvano and Lee Harper (ages 4–8).

Submissions and Payment: Catalogue available at website. Does not accept unsolicited submissions. Publication period, unknowns. Monthly royalty payments.

Parent/Imprints

See Skyscape, page 212

Viking Children's Books

Penguin Group, 345 Hudson Street, New York, NY 10014
http://us.penguingroup.com

Editorial Assistant: Joanna Cardenas

Founded in 1933, this imprint from the Penguin Young Readers Group, offers a wide variety of fiction and carefully chosen nonfiction titles, from picture books for young children to novels for teenagers. It has a rich backlist that includes many award-winning classics.

Freelance Potential: Publishes about 60 titles annually: most by agented authors.

Fiction: Picture books, chapter books, middle-grade, YA. Genres: contemporary, historical, realistic, multicultural, science fiction, adventure, mystery.

Nonfiction: Middle-grade, YA. Topics: nontraditional.

Titles: *Archie the Daredevil Penguin*, by Andy Rash (ages 4–8). *Stone Wall*, by Ann Bausum (ages 12+).

Submissions and Payment: Guidelines and catalogue available at website. Agented authors preferred. Query with complete or partial manuscript. Accepts hard copy. SASE. Responds in 4 months if interested. Publication period varies. Royalty, 5–10%; advance. Flat fee.

Parents, Divisions, Imprints

Penguin Group (USA), See page 184

Walden Pond Press

10 East 53rd Street, New York, NY 10022
www.harpercollinschildrens.com

Editor: Jordan Brown

Walden Pond Books is a collaboration between HarperCollins and Walden Media, the studio that produced the movie versions of *The Lion, The Witch and the Wardrobe* and *Holes*. It seeks fast-paced and engaging stories by veteran authors and new talent. Many of its titles are available in audio format.

Freelance Potential: Publishes about 22 titles annually. Open to new talent.

Fiction: Middle-grade. Genres: fantasy, contemporary, historical, science fiction, sports, mystery, humor.

Titles: *Guys Read: Other Worlds*, by Jon Scieszka (ages 8–12). *Disappearance at Hangman's Bluff*, by J. E. Thompson.

Submissions and Payment: Guidelines and catalogue available at website. Agented authors only. Royalty; advance.

Parents, Divisions, Imprints

HarperCollins Children's Books, See page 137

White Mane Kids

73 West Burd Street, P.O. Box 708, Shippensburg, PA 17257
www.whitemane.com

Acquisitions Department

White Mane Kids publishes historical based fiction for middle grade and young adult readers. Each of its books contains accurate historical information while captivating the readers with fascinating stories. Many of its titles are published with educational resource guides. 30% self-, subsidy-, co-venture, or co-op published material.

Freelance Potential: Publishes 3 titles annually: 35% developed from unsolicited submissions. Receives 8 queries monthly.

Fiction: Middle-grade, YA. Genres: historical fiction.

Titles: *A Rose at Bull Run: Romance and Realities at First Bull Run* (10+). *As the Crow Flies: Preface to Gettysburg-The Enemy Is Here!* (ages 8–12).

Submissions and Payment: Guidelines and catalogue available at website. Query with proposal form found at website, statement of purpose, marketing ideas, sample dust jacket paragraph, and general manuscript information (including page count, word count, and number of images). Accepts hard copy only, no digital submissions. SASE. Responds in 6–9 months. Publication period varies. Royalty.

Albert Whitman & Company

250 South Northwest Highway, Suite 320, Park Ridge, IL 60068
www.albertwhitman.com

Editorial Director: Kelly Barrales-Saylorf

Albert Whitman & Company is dedicated to treating their readers in a caring and respectful manner, helping them to grow intellectually and emotionally. Its catalogue features both fiction and nonfiction, and it has an extensive backlist that includes holiday books, concept books, and books in the classic Boxcar Children series. It also publishes books for parents.

Freelance Potential: Publishes 40 titles annually. Receives 25 queries, 375 unsolicited manuscripts monthly.

Fiction: Board books, early picture books, chapter books, middle-grade, YA. Genres: historical fiction, humor, mystery, contemporary.

Nonfiction: Concept books, early picture books, chapter books, middle-grade, YA. Topics: social, multicultural, ethnic, and family issues; history; biography.

Titles: *An Apple for Harriet Tubman*, Glennette Tilley Turner (grades PreK–3). *Daisy and the Girl Scouts*, by Fern Brown (grades 1–5).

Submissions and Payment: Guidelines and catalogue available at website. Query with cover letter and 3 sample chapters; or send complete manuscript. Accepts hard copy and simultaneous submissions if identified. No SASE; materials not returned. Responds in 4 months if interested. Publication in 18–24 months. Royalty; advance.

Parents, Divisions, Imprints

Albert Whitman Teen, See page 239

Albert Whitman Teen

250 South Northwest Highway, Suite 320, Park Ridge, IL 60068
www.albertwhitman.com

Editor: Wendy McClure

This YA imprint of Albert Whitman and Company aims to do for teens what its parent company does for younger children: publish books on issues that matter to its readers. It seeks titles that ask questions about the inner and outer worlds of teens. Stories should not just feature a teen protagonist, they should be about teen experiences and written for a teen audience. Editors are open to reality-bending, magic, or paranormal threads as long as they help the story not define it. Albert Whitman is currently only publishing fiction but does not rule out nonfiction for the future.

Freelance Potential: Publishes about 5 titles annually.

Fiction: YA. Genres: fantasy, contemporary, historical, multicultural, real life/problems, coming of age, social issues.

Titles: *Has to Be Love*, by Jolene Perry (YA). *Burn Girl*, by Mandy Mikulencak (YA).

Submissions and Payment: Guidelines and catalogue available at website. Query with cover letter and 3 sample chapters; or send complete manuscript. Accepts email submissions to Submissions@awhitmanco.com Accept simultaneous submissions if identified. No SASE; materials not returned. Responds in 4 months if interested. Publication in 18–24 months. Royalty; advance.

Parents, Divisions, Imprints

Albert Whitman and Company, See page 238

Wido Publishing

840 S. West Temple #1, Salt Lake City, UT 84101
www.widopublishing.com

Editor

Established in 2007, Wido Publishing is a family-owned small press. Its mission is to publish books that would stand out through excellent writing, careful editing, and artistic design. Its titles run the gamut from childhood memoirs, to middle grade fantasy, to YA paranormal.

Freelance Potential: Publishes about 12–15 titles annually: 50%

by authors who are new to the publishing house, 75% by previously unpblished writers. Receives 300 queries yearly.

Fiction: Middle grade, YA. Genres: action, fantasy, contemporary, historical, mystery, science fiction.

Titles: *Red-Tailed Rescue*, by John Irby (ages 8–12). *The Fourth Wall*, by Elizabeth Maria Naranjo (YA).

Submissions and Payment: Guidelines and catalogue available at website. Query with first three chapters of manuscript and author bio/résumé. Accepts email only to submissions@widopublishing.com with query in body of email and manuscript chapters as pdf or rtf attachment. Responds in 4–6 weeks. Publication period, and payment policy vary.

Wild Child Publishing

P.O. Box 4897, Culver City, CA 90231-4897
www.wildchildpublishing.com

Publisher: Marci G. Baun

The goal at Wild Child Publishing has been to offer high-quality, entertainig reading material. This publisher is willing to take a chance on material you can't find anywhere else. At this time it is only accepting submissions from its current authors.

Freelance Potential: Publishes 25–30 titles (2–5 juvenile) annually: 70% developed from unsolicited submissions; 10% by agented authors.

Fiction: Middle-grade, YA. Genres: contemporary, science fiction, fantasy, mystery, suspense, romance, animal stories.

Titles: *City of Thieves*, by Audrey Cuff, Ed.D. (YA). *The Blue Hills*, by Steve Shilstone (ages 9–12).

Submissions and Payment: Guidelines and catalogue available at website. Only accepting submissions from current authors at this time. Check websites for updates to this policy. Publication period varies. Royalty, 40% on ebooks, 10% on print books.

Windward Publishing

5995 149th Street West, Suite 105, Apple Valley, MN 55124
www.finneyco.com/windward.html

President: Alan E. Krysan

A division of Finney Company since 2001, Windward Publishing offers nature and children's books on popular subjects including sheels, fishing, mammals, and birds. Windward is the home to most of Finney Company's children's books.

Freelance Potential: Publishes 4–5 titles annually: 1–10% developed from unsolicited submissions; 1–10% by authors who are new to the publishing house; 1–10% by previously unpublished writers. Receives 15–20 queries monthly.

Fiction: Early readers, story picture books. Genres: nature stories.

Nonfiction: Early readers, story picture books, chapter books, middle-grade, YA. Topics: nature, flowers, birds, reptiles, amphibians, animals, fishing, seashells, sea life, space.

Titles: *Alligators & Crocodiles of the World*, by Laurie Perrero (ages 6–10). *By the Light of the Moon*, by Judie Olsson Kenagy (ages 3–7).

Submissions and Payment: Guidelines and catalogue available at website. Query with letter explaining manuscript and author background/qualifications, 1-page overview, table of contents, introduction, at least 3 sample chapters, and a short description of proposed market. Accepts hard copy. Accepts simultaneous submissions if identified. SASE. Responds in 10–12 weeks. Publication in 6–8 months. Royalty, 10% of net.

Paula Wiseman Books

Simon & Schuster, 1230 Avenue of the Americas, New York, NY 10020
http://imprints.simonandschuster.biz/paula-wiseman-books

Editors: Paula Wiseman and Alexandra Penfold
Associate Editor: Sylvie Frank

This imprint of Simon & Schuster Children's Publishing offers picture books, novelty books, and novels. It has the works of today's most beloved talents including Diane Goode, Kate Feiffer, and Meghan McCarthy. It is interested in receiving submissions from new and published authors through agents and SCBWI conferences only.

Freelance Potential: Publishes 20–30 titles annually: 20% by authors who are new to the publishing house; 8% by previously unpublished authors.

Fiction: Novelty books, toddler books, early picture books, early readers, chapter books, middle-grade, YA. Genres: contemporary, multicultural, adventure, coming-of-age, historical, humor.

Nonfiction: Board books, early readers, story picture books. Topics: animals, nature, sports, biography.

Titles: *Cat,* by Matthew Van Fleet (ages 2–7). *Ghost Ship*, by Mary Higgins Clark (ages 6–10).

Submissions and Payment: Guidelines and catalogue available at website. Accepts submissions through literary agents or at conferences. Response time varies. Publication in 18–24 months. Royalty; advance.

Parents, Divisions, Imprints

Simon & Schuster, See page 207

Wordsong

Boyds Mills Press, 815 Church Street, Honesdale, PA 18431
www.wordsongpoetry.com

Manuscript Submissions

Wordsong is the poetry imprint of Boyds Mills Press., dedicated solely to poetry for children. Wordplay, imagery, lyricism, and humor are among the important qualities of its books, which range from the serious to the lighthearted. It publishes poetry for the very young as well as poetry collections designed for older children. Rebecca Davis was recently named Senior Editor for this imprint.

Freelance Potential: Publishes 9 titles annually. Receives 25–30 unsolicited manuscripts monthly.

Fiction: Story picture books, poetry collections. Genres: contemporary, multicultural, folktales, humor.

Titles: *Another Jar of Tiny Stars*, by various authors (ages 4–6). *Cat Poems*, by Dave Crawley (grades 2–7).

Submissions and Payment: Guidelines and catalogue available at website. Send complete, book-length collection of poems with cover letter of relevant information, including author's publishing experience. Accepts hard copy. SASE. Responds in 3 months. Publication period varies. Royalty; advance. Flat fee.

Parents, Divisions, Imprints

Boyds Mills Press, See page 90

Workman Publishing

225 Varick Street, New York, NY 10014–4381
www.workman.com

Children's Department

Home of the popular Scanimation series for children, including the best-selling Gallop, Workman publishes fun and educational children's nonfiction in addition to its best-selling adult nonfiction titles. It does not publish picture books or middle-grade/young adult fiction.

Freelance Potential: Publishes 40 titles annually: 15% by agented authors. Receives 25 unsolicited manuscripts monthly.

Nonfiction: Novelty books, concept books, baby books, chapter books, activity books, puzzle books. Topics: science, nature, animals, humor, hobbies, crafts.

Titles: *The Amazing Adventures of Supercat!*, by Kate McMullan (ages 2–7). *10 Button Book*, by William Accorsi (ages 5–7).

Submissions and Payment: Guidelines and catalogue available at website. Query with outline and as much of the project as possible; or send complete manuscript. Prefers electronic submissions to submissions@workman.com (Word or PDF attachments). Accepts hard copy. SASE. Response time varies, usually 6 months or more. Publication period varies. Royalty; advance.

Algonquin, See page 70
Black Dog and Leventhal, See page 84
Storey Publishing, See page 221

Yen Press

237 Park Avenue, New York, NY 10017. www.yenpress.com

Submissions

Yen Press publishes graphic novels and manga, including adaptations of popular novel series such as Twilight and Maximum Ride; English versions of Japanese, Korean, and other foreign works; and original titles. The books target many ages, from early readers to teens and adults. Yen Press is open to project submissions from artists or writer/artist teams. It is not currently seeking pitches from writers who are not already working with an illustrator.

Freelance Potential: Publishes 80–90 books annually.

Fiction: Early readers, middle-grade, YA, adult. Genres: adventure, fantasy, thrillers, historical fiction, humor, fairy tales.

Titles: *Rust Blaster*, by Vana Tobo (ages 10+). *Homura Tamura*, by Puella Magi (ages 8–12).

Submissions and Payment: Guidelines and catalogue available at website. Send project summary, intended audience, plot outline with character descriptions, initial concept designs and a minimum of 5–10 pages of sequential art. Accepts email to yenpress@hbgusa.com and hard copy. Responds only if interested. Publication period and payment policy varies.

Parents, Divisions, Imprints

Hachette Book Group See page tk.

Bettie Youngs Books

www.bettieyoungsbooks.com

Submissions

With a reputation of excellence in publishing, Bettie Youngs Books focuses on memoirs of people who have lived interesting lives and have had incredible life journeys. They are meant to inspire, show the indomitability of the human spirit, and reawaken in their readers a passion for life. It publishes a children's imprint, Kendhal House Press and one for teens called Teen Town Press.

Freelance Potential: Publishes 4–6 titles yearly.

Nonfiction: Memoirs. Early readers, middle grade, YA, adult.

Titles: *Toby, the Pet Therapy Dog, Says Be a Buddy, NOT a Bully,* by Charmaine Hammond (ages 4–8). *I have a Restaurant,* by Ryan Afromsky (ages 4–8).

Submissions and Payment: Guidelines and catalogue available at website. Send a cover letter and proposal that includes target audience, promotion suggestions, summary and purpose, competition analysis, detailed outline, table of contents, introduction, two sample chapters, author credentials. Accepts email to info@bettieyoungsbooks.com. Publication period and payment policy varies.

Zest Books

35 Stillman Street, Suite 121, San Francisco, CA 94107
http://zestbooks.net
Editorial Director: Daniel Harmon

Zest Books is a leader in young adult nonfiction, publishing books on entertainment, history, science, health, fashion, and more. Zest relies on a Teen Advisory Board for research and feedback.

Freelance Potential: Publishes about 8–12 titles annually.

Nonfiction: YA. Topics: biography, how-to, pop-culture, health, careers, relationships, fashion, entertainment.

Titles: *Plotted*, by Andrew DeGraff (YA). *A Girl's Guide to Fitting in Fitness,* by Erin Whitehead and Jennifer Walters (YA).

Submissions and Payment: Guidelines and catalogue available at website. Send brief description of the book, table of contents, 1–5 sample pages, competition research, résumé, and 3–5 published writing samples. To be considered for author pool for in-house projects, send a cover letter stating interest and expertise in young adult nonfiction, résumé, and 3–5 writing samples. Accepts email to dan@zestbooks.net and hard copy. SASE. For graphic novels, the editors are looking for smart, edgy, compelling, and funny stories that are teen-friendly and different. Send a 3- to 5-page synopsis, including possible titles, character descriptions, and the story arc; a 5-page sample with finished panel art and text; a résumé; and an SASE. Accepts hard copy or email to info@zestbooks.net, with "Graphic Novel Submission" in the subject line. Response time, publication period, and payment policy vary.

Zumaya Publications

3209 South Interstate 35, #1086, Austin, TX 78741-6905
www.zumayapublications.com

Acquisitions Editor: Rie Sheridan Rose

This innovative publishing company strives to bring the best of fiction to the public. It's philosophy is simple, if it's a great, well-written story, they'll publish it. Zumaya's production is completely electronic, including an online editing process. It asks that its authors either have a knowledge or willingness to learn to use utilities such as google drive and Skype.

Freelance Potential: Publishes 35 titles annually: 50% developed from unsolicited submissions; 20% by authors who are new to the publishing house; 15% by previously unpublished writers. Receives 70 queries monthly.

Fiction: Middle-grade, YA. Genres: historical, contemporary, science fiction, adventure, fantasy, folklore, folktales, romance, Westerns, horror.

Titles: *Ebenezer*, by JoSelle Vanderhooft (YA). *Calico*, by Dorien Grey (YA).

Submissions and Payment: Guidelines and catalogue available at website. Query with cover letter and brief (to 500 words) synopsis. Accepts submissions through the website and by email to production@zumayapublications. com. Put "Query: [Title of Book]" in subject line. No simultaneous submissions. Responds in 2 weeks. Publication period varies. Royalty, 20% of publisher's net for print books; 50% for ebooks.

Classroom Publishing for Children

Approaching educational publishers, and developing working arrangements with them, can be quite different than approaching trade publishers. Companies that target schools and libraries—institutional markets—often publish in series, especially in non-fiction. They often look for particular expertise in subject matter, and may even give weight to writers with classroom experience. Rather than pay royalties, educational publishers may use the work of freelancers on a per-project or work-for-hire basis, meaning they use *contract writers* or work *on assignment* only. What editors of classroom books look for reflects these arrangements. Some want full-blown proposals, including bibliographies, market analyses, and so on. Others prefer to receive author résumés and other information to help them evaluate whether writers are a good match for their company, and might be brought into the *freelance stable* for assignments.

Classroom—school and library—markets, are a strong choice for writers looking to create a career. A writer who can meet the needs of an editor in this part of the publishing industry, write to spec, and be creative too can establish a long-lasting editorial relationship and a writing portfolio to carry on to other publishers.

ABDO Publishing Company

8000 West 78th Street, Edina, MN 55439
www.abdopublishing.com

Submissions Committee

For more than 30 years, ABDO has been publishing exceptional children's PreK-12 educational titles for libraries and schools. When it began, it specialized in nonfiction but the company has expanded to include fiction, and now is comprised of four divisions: ABDO Publishing, Magic Wagon, Spotlight, and ABDO Digital. Each book is leveled using grade-appropriate language, and designed to be of high interest. ABDO Publishing Company works with contract writers only, and accepts résumés and clips; it does not accept unsolicited manuscripts.

Freelance Potential: Publishes 600 titles annually: less than 10% developed from unsolicited submissions; less than 10% by authors who are new to the publishing house. Receives 30 queries monthly.

Fiction: Early picture books, early readers, story picture books, chapter books, middle-grade, YA. Genres: adventure, animals, folklore, mythology, science fiction, seasonal, contemporary.

Nonfiction: Early picture books, early readers, story picture books, chapter books, middle-grade, YA. Topics: animals, nature, travel, geography, sciences, social studies, sports, history, biography, leisure, multicultural/ethnic.

Titles: *Airy Fairy Magic Music!,* by Margaret Ryan (grades 1–3). *Ancient Civilizations: Egypt*, by L. J. Amstutz (grade 7–8).

Submissions & Payment: Catalogue available at website. Guidelines provided to writers under contract only. To be considered for writing assignments, send résumé with cover letter, area of expertise, and publishing credits. Accepts email to submissions@abdopublishing.com. Response time varies. Publication period varies. Flat fee.

Parents, Divisions, Imprints

Magic Wagon, See page 278
Spotlight, See page 298

Amicus Publishing

P.O. Box 1329, Mankato, MN 56002
www.amicuspublishing.us

Associate Publisher: Rebecca Glaser

Amicus Publishing is made up of three book lines: Amicus Readers (leveled nonfiction for kindergarten to grade 2); Amicus Illustrated (fiction and nonfiction for preK to grade 6); and Amicus High Interest (informational books with a high-interest presentation, grades 2 to 6). All of Amicus's books promote critical thinking.

Freelance Potential: Publishes 100 titles annually.

Fiction: Picture books. Genres: contemporary, mysteries, all curriculum subject areas.

Nonfiction: Early readers, elementary. Topics: animals, science, social studies, health, careers, math, holidays, community, geography, sports, biology, technology, current events, social issues, nature/environment, economy.

Titles: *Manners at School* (ages 4–8). *Inside My Body: Brains* (ages 6–10).

Submissions and Payment: Catalogue available at website. Does not accept unsolicited manuscripts. Projects are work-for-hire. To be considered, send cover letter, resume, and two unedited writing samples. Accepts email to info@amicuspublishing.us and hard copy.

August House

3500 Piedmont Road NE, Suite 310, Atlanta, GA 30305
www.augusthouse.com

Editorial Department

August House is a highly acclaimed multimedia publisher of children's stories, folktale anthologies, and resource books. Its editorial mission focuses on the art and uses of storytelling and world folktales. The company's materials are used by teachers, parents, and camp counselors. It is in the process of adapting and licensing titles across multiple channels, including television, the internet, ebooks, mobile devices, and film.

Freelance Potential: Publishes 5–10 titles annually.

Fiction: Picture books, story picture books, early readers, middle-grade. Genres: folktales, animal fables, multicultural, social issues, ethics.

Titles: *Adventures of High John the Conqueror,* by Steve Sanfield (ages 8–14). *Anansi And Turtle Go to Dinner,* by Bobby Norfolk and Sherry Norfolk (grades PreK-3).

Submissions and Payment: Guidelines and catalogue available at website. Query or send manuscript with author biography and publishing history. For multi-chapter or multi-story books, send query or proposal with sample chapters (at least 40 pages) rather than complete manuscript; descriptive outline or table of contents; estimate of final manuscript pages or word count; and completion date. Give sources for folktales. Accepts hard copy only. Accepts simultaneous submissions. SASE for manuscript receipt. Responds in 5 months if interested. Publication period and payment policy vary.

Barron's Educational Series

250 Wireless Boulevard, Hauppauge, NY 11788
www.barronseduc.com

Acquisitions Manager: Wayne Barr

With more than 2,000 titles, this publisher is known for its reference and educational series, including school and study guides and test preparation books. It also publishes in many other categories and offers a large list of children's fiction and nonfiction, foreign language titles, and family and health books.

Freelance Potential: Publishes 150–200 titles (60-85 juvenile) annually: 1–10% developed from unsolicited submissions; 1–10% assigned; 1–10% by agented authors. Receives 150-200 queries, 25–50 unsolicited manuscripts monthly; 200+ manuscripts yearly.

Fiction: Concept books, board books, toddler books, early picture books, early readers, story picture books, chapter books, middle-grade, YA. Genres: fairy tales, fantasy, adventure, retold stories, graphic novels, animals.

Nonfiction: Toddler books, early readers, story picture books, middle-grade, YA. Topics: art, activities, biography, concepts, prehistory, history, self-help, magic, bugs, cooking, pet memoirs, test prep guides, Spanish language.

Titles: *My Mommy Is Magic,* by Dawn Richards (ages 2–5). *Mariella Mystery Investigates,* by Kate Pankhurst (ages 7+).

Submissions and Payment: Guidelines and catalogue available at website. Prefers query with author credentials. Send complete manuscript with résumé for fiction. Query with table of contents, 2 sample chapters, market overview (including intended audience), and résumé for nonfiction. Accepts hard copy. SASE. Accepts simultaneous submissions if identified. Also accepts queries for work-for-hire assignments. Responds in 8 months. Publication in 6 months. Royalty; advance.

Bellwether Media

5357 Penn Avenue South, Minneapolis, MN 55419
www.bellwethermedia.com

Founder: John Martin

Bellwether provides attractive, accessible and engaging books for libraries and classrooms. It strives to nurture early reading experiences as well as inspire reluctant readers toward higher achievement. All Bellwether books are designed in accordance with the 5 tenets of effective reading instruction: Phonics, Fluency, Comprehension, Phonemic Awareness, and Vocabulary.

Freelance Potential: Unavailable.

Nonfiction: Early readers, reluctant readers, high lo,chapter books. Topics: Science, technology, sports, miltary, vehicles, careers, animals, geography, cultures, biography.

Titles: *My First Sports: Football,* by Ray McClellan (grades K–3). *Abrams Tanks,* by Jack David (grades 2–4).

Submissions and Payment: Catalogue available at website. Works with freelancers on a work for hire basis. To be considered, send résumé and writing samples. Accepts hard copy and email to careers@bellwethermedia.com. Response time and payment policy, unknown.

A & C Black

50 Bedford Square, London WC1B 3DP United Kingdom
www.acblack.com/children

Submissions Editor

This company owned by Bloomsbury, publishes reference titles and teacher resources for all reading levels. Its diverse catalogue includes a broad range of topics.

Freelance Potential: Publishes 80 titles annually. Receives few queries monthly.

Fiction: Early readers, chapter books, middle-grade, YA. Genres: contemporary, historical, science fiction, adventure, fantasy, myths and legends, humor, drama, poetry.

Nonfiction: Early readers, chapter books, middle-grade, YA. Topics: art, design, technology, geography, history, music, physical education, sports, science, social issues, animals. Also publishes reference books and teacher resources.

Titles: *The Genealogist's Internet,* by Peter Christian (ages 12+). *Whitaker's Little Book of Knowledge* (ages 10+).

Submissions and Payment: Guidelines and catalogue available at website. Accepts agented submissions. Query or send complete manuscript with synopsis, intended market, comparison with current competition, and brief author bio with qualifications that pertain to the subject matter. Accepts email to enquiries@acblack.com with "Submission" in the subject line, or see website for specific topic editors. Responds in 2 months. Publication period and payment policy vary.

Black Rabbit Books

P.O. Box 3263, Mankato, MN 56002
www.blackrabbitbooks.com

Managing Editor: Ann Schwab

Black Rabbit Books was founded on the principle that quality books produce quality readers. Its list is divided between BRB Kids (kindergarten to grade 5) and BRB Teens (grades 6 to 12). Black Rabbit Books has multiple imprints: Arcturus Publishing (content-rich books for the upper grades); Brown Bear Books (high-interest books with primary sources); Cherrytree Books (nonfiction with unique features); New Forest Press (contemporary interests and strong photography); Sea-to-Sea Publications (specialty authors and classroom reading strategies); Smart Apple Media (nonfiction emphasizing point of view); Stargazer Books (creative takes on nonfiction, including stories); Walter Foster Library (drawing and craft books); and Zak Books (books by expert authors for classroom libraries).

Freelance Potential: Publishes hundreds of books annually.

Nonfiction: Beginning readers, early readers, middle-grade, YA. Topics: animals, nature, science, health, technology, the arts, language arts, geography, history, reference, social studies, sports, high-interest.

Titles: Emergency Vehicles series (grades 2+). New Technology series (grades 8+).

Submissions and Payment: Catalogue available at website. Does not accept unsolicited manuscripts. Does offer work-for-hire writing and editing. To be considered, send cover letter, resume, and writing samples. Accepts hard copy. Response time and payment policy vary.

Britannica Educational Publishing

Rosen Publishing, 29 East 21st Street, New York, NY 10010
www.rosenpublishing.com

Editorial Director

Britannica Educational Publishing, as part of Rosen Publishing, presents authoritative and engaging reference books to help primarily middle and high school students develop a comprehensive understanding of curriculum topics and current events. Its titles give accurate background information as well as analysis on a wide variety of academic subjects. All of its books are also available in ebook format.

Freelance Potential: Parent company Rosen Publishing publishes 700+ books annually over multiple imprints.

Nonfiction: YA. Topics: science, history, geography, current events, biography, literature, philosophy, math.

Titles: *Living Legends of Sports* series (grades 5–8). *Let's Find Out* series (grades 2–3).

Submissions and Payment: Catalogue available at website. Contact Customer Service team via website for information about submissions. Responds in 3 months. Publication in 9–18 months. Flat fee.

Parents, Divisions, Imprints

Rosen Publishing, See page 376

Butte Publications

P.O. Box 1328, Hillsboro, OR 97123-1328
www.buttepublications.com

Acquisitions Editor

Butte Publications is a specialty publisher that focuses on educating the deaf and hard of hearing. It also markets resource materials for professionals working in the fields of speech language pathology, special education, English as a Second Language, early childhood, and early intervention, as well as for parents.

Freelance Potential: Publishes about 5 titles (2 juvenile) annually. Receives 1–2 queries monthly.

Nonfiction: Publishes resources and educational books. Topics: signing, interpreting, vocabulary, reading, writing, language skills, lipreading, and mathematics. Also publishes titles for parents who are raising deaf and hard-of-hearing children.

Titles: *Happily Ever After: Using Storybooks in Preschool Settings,* by Kate Bannister, Katy Preston, and Julie Primozich. *Finding Abby,* by Virginia M. Scott.

Submissions and Payment: Guidelines and catalogue available at website. Send complete manuscript or query with table of contents and 1–2 sample chapters. Include cover letter with author credentials, audience, competition analysis, estimate of total number of pages, and completion date. Accepts hard copy. SASE. Responds in 6 months minimum. Publication in 1 year. Royalty.

Capstone

1710 Roe Crest Drive, North Mankato, MN 56003
www.capstonepub.com

Editorial Director

This large publishing house offers a wide variety of nonfiction and fiction for children in preK through middle school. It covers many curriculum areas. Its nonfiction Capstone Press imprint specializes in emergent and reluctant readers and high-interest topics. Other imprints include Compass Point Books, Heinemann-Raintree, Picture Window Books, and Stone Arch Books. Capstone has launched a new trade line called Capstone Young Readers (CYR).

Most Capstone titles are conceptually developed in-house and written on a work-for-hire basis.

Freelance Potential: Publishes 600+ titles annually: 1-10% developed from unsolicited submissions; 75-100% assigned; 1-10% by agented authors; 10-25% by authors who are new to the publishing house; 1-10% by previously unpublished writers. Receives 10-25 queries monthly.

Fiction: Early picture books, early readers, story picture books, chapter books, middle-grade, graphic novels. Genres: adventure, bilingual, fairy tales, historical, humor, multicultural, realistic, sports.

Nonfiction: Concept books, early picture books, early readers, chapter books, graphic nonfiction, middle-grade. Topics: animals, arts, activities, games, crafts, biography, bilingual, education and career, current events, entertainment, social studies, history, geography, health, science, math.

Titles: *Adventures in Space*, by Andrew Langley and Ben Hubbard (grades 4–6). *Autobiographies You Never Thought You'd Read!*, by Catherine Chambers ((grades 1–3).

Submissions and Payment: Guidelines and catalogue available at website. For nonfiction, query with cover letter, résumé, and 3 writing samples. Accepts hard copy only. For fiction, query with sample chapters, résumé, and list of publishing credits. Prefers email to author.sub@stonearchbooks.com. Responds in 6 months if interested. Publication period and payment policy vary.

Parents, Divisions, Imprints

Compass Point Books, See page 259
Heinemann-Raintree, See page 270
Picture Window Books, See page 286
Stone Arch Books, See page 300

Carson-Dellosa Publishing

P.O. Box 35665, Greensboro, NC 27425-5665
www.carsondellosa.com

Submissions Editor: Julie Killian

A leading provider of supplemental classroom material for more than 30 years, Carson-Dellosa offers a wide array of products to enhance children's learning potential. Most titles are written by teachers for teachers and parents in all academic subject areas for preK to grade 8. Carson-Dellosa is currently closed to manuscript submissions and book proposals, although its website does include a page listing freelance opportunities for independent contractors.

Freelance Potential: Publishes about 230 titles annually: all are assigned. Receives 10–15 queries monthly.

Nonfiction: Publishes supplementary educational material, activity books, resource guides, classroom material, and reproducibles, preK–grade 8. Topics: reading, language arts, mathematics, science, the arts, social studies, English Language Learners (ELL), early childhood, crafts. Also publishes Christian education titles.

Titles: *Multicultural Kids with Books with Straight Borders* (ages 4–11). *Step-by-Step Problem Solving* (grade 7).

Submissions and Payment: Guidelines and catalogue available at website. Does not currently accept unsolicited manuscripts or book proposals.

Cavendish Square

303 Park Avenue South, Suite 1247, New York, NY 10010
www.cavendishsq.com

Editor

This publisher offers a robust and diverse list of library-bound circulating nonfiction series and early readers that range in age level from kindergarten through college. Books are published in print, as ebooks and many also have digital platforms and databases.

Freelance Potential: Publishes 50 annually.

Nonfiction: Reference books, series, early readers. Topics: science, health, social studies.

Titles: *A Carpenter's Job*, by Erika de Nijs (grades K+). *America in the Fifties*, by Enzo George (grades 4+).

Submissions and Payment: Catalogue available at website. For submission information email csqedit@csqpub.com. Response time, publication period, and payment policy, unknown.

Cengage Learning

10650 Toebben Drive, Independence, KY 41051. www.cengage.com

Editor

Cengage Learning believes that engagement is the foundation of learning. An engaged learner is a successful one, and this leading publisher offers titles to support reading teachers and library professionals.

Freelance Potential: Publishes hundreds of titles over several imprints yearly.

Nonfiction: Middle-grade, YA. Topics: history, social studies, sports, business, politics, health and medicine, law, media, teen issues, culture and society, education, social issues, the arts, literature, the environment, reference.

Titles: *World Cultures and Geography,* by Andrew J. Milson (grades 6–9). *Classical Readings in Cultural Anthropology*, by Gary Ferraro (grades 9–12).

Submissions and Payment: See individual publishers for information on submissions.

Parents, Divisions, Imprints

Greenhaven Press, See page 268
Lucent Books, See page 278
U-X-L, See page 304

Chelsea House

132 West 31st Street, 17th Floor, New York, NY 10001
www.infobasepublishing.com

Managing Editor: Justine Ciovacco

For more than 30 years, Chelsea House has published curriculum-based nonfiction books for middle school and high school students in the core subject areas of science, health, and high-interest titles.

Freelance Potential: Publishes 300+ titles annually: less than 10% developed from unsolicited submissions; 10-25% by agented authors; 10-25% by authors who are new to the publishing house. Receives 50-75 queries, 100-150 unsolicited manuscripts monthly.

Nonfiction: Middle-grade, YA, reference. Topics: careers/college, geography, biography, government and law, health/fitness, the arts, history, math, religion, nature, science, social studies, technology.

Titles: *Legends of the Wild West: Annie Oakley*, by Rachel A. Koestler-Grack (grades 6–12). *Earth's Journey through Space*, by Trudy E. Bell (grades 5–8).

Submissions and Payment: Guidelines and catalogue available at website. Query with subject overview, intended audience, brief description of contents, sample chapter, competition and market analysis, and author bio. Accepts hard copy and email to editorial@factsonfile.com. Responds in 4 weeks. Publication period, 9 months–2 years. Payment policy varies.

Children's Press

Scholastic Library Publishing, Old 90 Sherman Turnpike, Danbury, CT 06816. www.scholastic.com

Editor in Chief

This imprint of Scholastic Library Publishing is well known for its popular book series and biographies for children in kindergarten through grade 8. Its titles guide rookie readers through stages of independent reading. It accepts agented submissions and manuscripts from educators only.

Freelance Potential: Publishes 250 titles annually. Receives 150–200 queries monthly.

Nonfiction: Concept books, early readers, story picture books, chapter books, middle-grade. Topics: animals, arts, culture, biography, economics, geography, history, the human body, military, science, social studies, sports, transportation.

Titles: *You Wouldn't Want to Be an American Colonist!*, by Jacqueline Morley and David Antram (grades 5–6). *The Superstorm Hurricane Sandy (True Books)*, by Josh Gregory (ages 8-10).

Submissions and Payment: Agented authors only. If you are a professional educator, send a brief description of the idea, targeted grade range, table of contents, sample chapter or activities, and author biography. Responds in 10–12 weeks. Publication in 1–2 years. Flat fee.

Parents, Divisions, Imprints

Scholastic Inc., See page 204

Compass Point Books

Capstone, 1710 Roe Crest Drive, North Mankato, MN 56003
www.capstonepub.com

Editorial Director: Nick Healy

Compass Point Books, an imprint of Capstone Press, publishes "smart nonfiction" that engages readers through thoughtful perspectives on topics such as history, science, biography, and careers. Its titles target grades 5 to 12.

Freelance Potential: Parent company Capstone publishes 700+ titles annually.

Nonfiction: Middle-grade, YA. Topics: science, social studies, geography, history, biography, careers, health, the environment, cooking.

Titles: *All About the Green: The Teens' Guide to Finding Work and Making Money*, by Kara McGuire (grades 6–7). *World War II: Why They Fought*, by Katie Marisco (grades 5–9).

Submissions and Payment: Guidelines and catalogue available at website. Query with cover letter, résumé, and 3 writing samples. Accepts hard copy only. Responds in 6 months if interested. Publication period and payment policy vary.

Parents, Divisions, Imprints

Capstone, See page 254

Continental Press

520 East Bainbridge Street, Elizabethtown, PA 17022
www.continentalpress.com

Managing Editor

Continental Press publishes educational materials for grades K–12, specializing in reading, mathematics, and test preparation. It publishes leveled readers for preK through second grade with its Seedling books. It seeks materials that have been classroom-tested and fit specific educational purposes.

Freelance Potential: Publishes 50+ titles (40 juvenile) annually: 10% developed from unsolicited submissions. Receives 20 queries, 20 unsolicited manuscripts monthly.

Fiction: Early readers, middle-grade, YA. Genres: animals, fantasy, adventure, social issues, education, counting, colors.

Nonfiction: Early readers, middle-grade, YA. Topics: math, science, social studies, language arts, ESL, Spanish, technology, test prep. Also publishes teacher resources.

Titles: *Reading for Comprehension* (grades 1–3). *Finish Line Reading,* (grades 1–8).

Submissions and Payment: Guidelines and catalogue available at website. For instructional manuscripts, send manuscript with program rationale; author biography; outline; and sample lesson, chapter, or unit. For Seedling fiction submissions, send manuscript. No queries. Accepts hard copy only. SASE. Responds in 6 months. Publication period and payment policy vary.

Creative Teaching Press

15362 Graham Street, Huntington Beach, CA 92649
www.creativeteaching.com

Idea Submissions

Creative Teaching Press is a family-owned and teacher-managed supplemental educational publisher for children ages 3–14. It is a recognized leader in the educational industry and offers a wide range of classroom learning decor and researched-based, teacher tested products.

Freelance Potential: Publishes 84 titles (48 juvenile) annually: 15% developed from unsolicited submissions; 5% by authors who are new to the publishing house; 5% by previously unpublished writers. Receives 20–25 queries, 10–20 unsolicited manuscripts monthly.

Fiction: Early readers. Genres: ethnic, multicultural, social issues, ethics and responsibility, fantasy.

Nonfiction: Early readers, chapter books. Topics: history, social issues, science, mathematics, writing. Also publishes supplemental resource books for teachers.

Titles: *Be a Friend,* by Reina Burch (grade 1). *How to Make a Mudpie,* by Rozanne Lanczak Williams (grade K–1).

Submissions and Payment: Guidelines and catalogue available at website. Prefers ideas from teachers that have been successfully used in classrooms. Send proposal or complete manuscript along with submission form at website, and a cover letter including: brief description of material (including grade level), synopsis of your background as an educator, audience and competition analysis, summary of material with table of contents, and at least 1 sample chapter. Accepts hard copy. Accepts simultaneous submissions. SASE. Response time varies. Publication period and payment policy vary.

Critical Thinking Company

1991 Sherman Avenue, Suite 200, North Bend, OR 97459
www.criticalthinking.com

President: Michael Baker

The Critical Thinking Co. is a publisher of educational products for parents, homeschoolers, and teachers. It publishes material for students in preschool through eighth grade. It is currently seeking activity-based products in reading, writing, math, science, and social studies that teach and develop critical thinking skills.

Freelance Potential: Publishes 5–30 titles annually: 20% by authors who are new to the publishing house; 30% by previously unpublished writers. Receives 10–20 queries, 20 unsolicited manuscripts yearly.

Fiction: Concept books. Genres: stories that promote development of critical thinking skills.

Nonfiction: Concept books, early picture books, early readers, chapter books. Topics: general thinking skills, grammar, spelling, vocabulary, reading, writing, mathematics, science, history. Also publishes activity books.

Titles: *Visual Perception Skill Building,* Book 1 (grade 1). *What Would You Do?* Book 1 (grade 2–5).

Submissions and Payment: Guidelines and catalogue available at website. Prefers complete manuscript or software program; accepts query with outline or table of contents and several sample pages. Send cover letter with description of material, target market, and synopsis of your background. Accepts hard copy. SASE. Responds in 6–9 months. Publication in 1–2 years. Royalty.

Edcon Publishing Group

30 Montauk Boulevard, Oakdale, NY 11769–1399
www.edconpublishing.com

Editor in Chief

Edcon produces learning materials for grades K–12, adult/special education, homeschooling, English as a second Language, and English language learners. Educators use the products from this publisher to improve basic reading and math skills.

Freelance Potential: Publishes 10 titles annually: 20% developed from unsolicited submissions; 10% by authors who are new to the publishing house; 20% by previously unpublished writers. Receives 10 unsolicited manuscripts monthly.

Fiction: Early readers, chapter books, middle-grade, YA. Genres: science fiction, adventure, multicultural and ethnic, fairy tales. Also publishes hi/lo fiction, 6–18 years.

Nonfiction: Chapter books, YA. Topics: reading comprehension, mathematics, science, technology, social issues, personal growth. Also publishes educational materials for homeschooling and activity books for ages 6–12.

Titles: *Leap in Lower Case Learning* (grades PreK–K). *Reading Comprehension Vocabulary* Series (grades 1–2).

Submissions and Payment: Guidelines available. Send complete manuscript. Accepts hard copy. Accepts simultaneous submissions if identified. Submissions are not returned. Responds in 1 month. Publication in 6 months. Flat fee, $300–$1,000.

Editorial Buenas Letras

Rosen Publishing, 29 East 21st Street, New York, NY 10010
www.rosenpublishing.com

Editorial Director

Editorial Buenas Letras is an imprint of Rosen Educational Publishing offering a wide variety of books in Spanish and bilingual formats for grades preK to 12. Its primary aim is to provide vocabulary-building and language-development tools, while demonstrating respect for the culture and heritage of Spanish-speaking students. This company seeks to satisfy biliteracy needs and foster a lifelong love of reading.

Freelance Potential: Parent company Rosen Publishing publishes 700+ titles annually.

Nonfiction: Story picture books, early readers, middle-grade, YA. Topics: biography, life skills, geography, culture, mythology, science, animals, nature, social issues, food, contemporary issues.

Titles: *Transporte Publico/Public Transportation* (grades 1–2). *Ovnis: El Caso Roswell (UFOs: The Roswell Incident)* (grades 2–3).

Submissions and Payment: Catalogue available at website. Contact Customer Service team via website for information about submissions. Responds in 3 months. Publication in 9–18 months. Flat fee.

Parents, Divisions, Imprints

Rosen Publishing, See page 291

Enslow Publishers, Inc.

101 West 23rd Street, #240, New York, NY 10011
www.enslow.com

Editor in Chief: Dorothy Goeller

This company specializes in curriculum-based nonfiction books. It produces high-interest titles for school-age children and young adults in a wide range of subjects, for placement in schools and libraries. Its aim is to make books that are informative and appealing even to the most reluctant reader. The company is expanding its list to include YA fiction.

Freelance Potential: Publishes 200 titles annually. Receives 20 queries monthly.

Fiction: Middle-grade, YA. Genres: Historical fiction, sports fiction.

Nonfiction: Early readers, middle-grade, YA. Topics: contemporary issues, health and drug education, history, government, holidays and customs, mathematics, science, technology, sports and recreation, biography.

Titles: *California Missions*, by Lynda Amez (grades 3–5). *Far-Out Guide to Icy Dwarf Planets*, by Mary Kay Carson (grade 4+).

Submissions and Payment: Catalogue available at website. Query with outline. Accepts hard copy. SASE. Responds in 1–6 months. Publication in 1 year. Royalty; advance. Flat fee.

Epic Press

8000 West 78th Street, Edina, MN 55439
www.abdopublishing.com/our-products/epic-press

Submissions Committee

This new division of ABDO Publishing focuses entirely on young adult fiction. It delivers content that young adult readers will love; fiction that's bold, edgy, and mature. While all of its titles connect with a YA audience, many of it's books are also hi/lo.

Freelance Potential: Publishes 20 titles annually. Receives 30 queries monthly.

Fiction: YA. Genres: social issues, sports, mystery, realistic fiction, science fiction, contemporary.

Titles: *Hoop City Chicago*, Sam Moussavi (YA). *Coming Out: Alex*, by Sylvia Aguilar-Zeleny (YA).

Submissions & Payment: Catalogue available at website. Guidelines provided to writers under contract only. To be considered for writing assignments, send résumé with cover letter, area of expertise, and publishing credits. Accepts email to submissions@abdopublishing.com. Response time varies. Publication period varies. Flat fee.

Parents, Divisions, Imprints

ABDO Publishing, See page 248

Facts On File

132 West 31st Street, 17th Floor, New York, NY 10001
www.infobasepublishing.com

Editorial Director: Laurie Likoff

This imprint of Infobase Publishing is an award-winning publisher of print, electronic, and online reference materials for the school and library market. It specializes in core subject areas such as history, literature, and geography. Facts on File also produces curriculum-based reference and news service databases.

Freelance Potential: Publishes 300+ titles annually: less than 10% developed from unsolicited submissions; 10-25% by agented authors; 10-25% by authors who are new to the publishing house. Receives 50-75 queries and 100-150 unsolicited manuscripts monthly.

Nonfiction: Middle-grade, YA. Topics: history, the arts, careers/college, biography, geography, health/fitness, social studies, current affairs, politics, government, multicultural subjects, math, science, the environment.

Titles: *African History Online Database. Genes and Diseases Online.*

Submissions and Payment: Guidelines and catalogue available at website. Query with subject overview, intended audience, brief description of contents, sample chapter, competition and market analysis, and author bio. Accepts hard copy and email to editorial@factsonfile.com. Responds in 4 weeks. Publication period, 12 months. Payment policy varies.

Ferguson Publishing

132 West 31st Street, 17th Floor, New York, NY 10001
www.infobasepublishing.com

Editor in Chief: James Chambers

Ferguson Publishing is a source of reference databases, ebooks, and some print books on careers, for middle schools, high schools, and libraries. Part of Infobase Publishing, its titles provide comprehensive, up-to-date information on a variety of fields, and guidance on essential career skills.

Freelance Potential: Publishes 10–20 books annually: less than 10% developed from unsolicited submissions; 10-25% by agented authors; 10-25% by authors who are new to the publishing house. Receives 10–20 queries, 5–10 unsolicited manuscripts monthly.

Nonfiction: Middle-grade, YA. Topics: college planning, career advice, career exploration and guidance, changing careers, job training.

Titles: *Gloria Estefan: Singer,* by James Robert Parish (grades 6–12). *Sally Ride: Astronaut,* by Joanne Mattern (grades 6–12).

Submissions and Payment: Guidelines and catalogue available online. Majority of books are assigned. Query or send manuscript proposal with an overview of the subject, intended audience, brief description of contents, sample chapter, competition analysis, brief author bio, completion timetable, and relevant experience. To be considered for assignments, send résumé. Accepts hard copy and email to editorial@factsonfile.com. SASE. Responds in 4 weeks. Publication in 12 months. Payment policy varies.

Goodheart-Willcox

18604 West Creek Drive, Tinley Park, IL 60477-6243
www.g-w.com

President: John F. Flanagan

Goodheart-Willcox specializes in textbooks in the categories of technical/trades/technology; family/consumer sciences; and business/marketing/career education for middle, high school and college students. Its books, supplements, and multimedia resources combine authoritative content, case studies, and engaging designs to help students learn important life skills. It also produces teacher resource guides, software, and professional training manuals.

Freelance Potential: Publishes 10 titles annually. Receives 10+ queries monthly.

Nonfiction: YA, adult. Publishes textbooks, instructor's guides, software, professional development books, and how-to titles. Topics: life management, personal development, family living, child care, child development, parenting, consumer education, nutrition, housing and interiors, technical trades, fashion, career education, business, marketing, computers, technology, visual arts.

Titles: *Introduction to Health Science,* by Dorothy Winger and Susan Blahnik (grades 9–12). *Professional Communication* (grades 9–12).

Submissions and Payment: Guidelines and catalogue available at website. Submit proposal with introductory letter, including targeted audience, résumé, book outline, and sample chapter. Accepts hard copy. SASE. Responds in 2 months. Publication in 2 years. Royalty.

Go Teach It!

c/o Design Spike, Inc., 522 West First Avenue, Spokane Valley, WA 99201. www.goteachit.com

Submissions Editor

Educators working in kindergarten through grade 12 classrooms are the target audience of this online publisher. It specializes in professionally edited, curriculum-based teaching units and lesson plans in downloadable formats. It prefers to publish curricula relating to established works in print, such as literary classics. Authors must have strong writing skills, understand cross-competency education, and be able to address a variety of learning styles.

Freelance Potential: Publishes many titles annually: all by authors who are new to the publishing house; 75% by previously unpublished writers. Receives 4–5 queries monthly.

Nonfiction: Publishes teacher curricula, grades K–12. Topics: computers, current events, geography, history, civics, language, wellness, math, science, technology, social issues, literature, vocabulary, reading comprehension. Also publishes activity packets, projects, and teaching aids.

Titles: *A Series of Unfortunate Events: The Bad Beginning Complete Teaching Unit,* by Fanny Hofer (grades 4–6). *A Week in the Woods Complete Teaching Unit,* by Ron Price (grades 4–6).

Submissions and Payment: Guidelines and catalogue available at website. Prospective authors are asked to contact company directly via mail, phone (509)252-5060, or email at goteachit@goteachit.com before submitting curriculum. Responds in one week to initial inquiry. Publication period varies. Royalty, 30%.

Greenhaven Press

27500 Drake Road, Farmington Hills, MI 48331-3535
www.solutions.cengage.com/greenhaven

Publisher

Freelance Potential: Publishes about 190 titles annually: 5–10% by authors who are new to the publishing house; few by previously unpublished writers. Receives 25–50 queries monthly.

Nonfiction: YA. Topics: contemporary social issues, biography, American and world history, geography, literature, multicultural, explorations of mysteries, religion, science, medicine and health, global issues.

Titles: *Exploring Science 2: Student Edition*, by Randy Bell, Malcolm Butler, Kathy Cabe Trundle, and Judith Lederman. *Reach for Reading,* by Nancy Frey, Lada Kratky, Nonie K. Lesaux.

Submissions and Payment: Catalogue available at website. Submit ideas for new publications via form on website. Qualifying submissions that result in a Gale publication are eligible for a $1,000 reward. Response time and publication period vary.

Parents, Divisions, Imprints

Cengage Learning, See page 257

Gryphon House

P.O. Box 10, 6848 Leon's Way, Lewisville, NC 27023
www.gryphonhouse.com

Editor in Chief: Kathy Charner

Established in 1981, Gryphon House has nearly 200 titles in print. The company strives to publish and distribute the highest-quality books for educators, parents, and caregivers. Its books help enrich the lives of children from birth to age 8.

Freelance Potential: Publishes 20 titles annually: 2 developed from unsolicited submissions; 6 reprint/licensed properties. Receives 20 queries monthly.

Nonfiction: Publishes books for parents and teachers working with children up to age 8. Topics: art, mathematics, science, literacy, language development, teaching strategies, conflict resolution, program development, games, lesson plans.

Titles: *Hands-On Science and Math*, by Beth Rosenthal Davis. *Bubbles, Rainbows, and Worms*, by Sam Ed Brown (PreK).

Submissions and Payment: Guidelines and catalogue available at website. Query with proposed title, purpose of the book, table of contents, introductory material, 20–40 sample pages, market and competition analysis, intended audience, author qualifications, and writing sample. Accepts hard copy. SASE. Responds in 3–4 months. Publication in 1–2 years. Payment policy varies.

Hayes School Publishing

321 Pennwood Avenue, Pittsburgh, PA 15221
www.hayespub.com

President: Clair Hayes

The catalogue from Hayes School Publishing features educational books and resources for preschool through grade 12. This company seeks reproducibles, workbooks, teacher planning guides, and support materials for all subjects and curricula. It is always seeking new material in all academic subject areas, especially testing and Spanish.

Freelance Potential: Publishes 20–30 titles annually: 8% by authors who are new to the publishing house; 15–20% by previously unpublished writers. Receives 30–45 queries monthly.

Nonfiction: Publishes educational resource materials, grades K–12. Topics: language arts, multicultural studies, math, computer literacy, foreign language, social studies, science, health, creative thinking, handwriting, geography, standardized testing.

Titles: *Teacher's Daily Plan Book* (teachers). *Standardized Testing Series* (grades 2–8).

Submissions and Payment: Catalogue available at website. Guidelines available via email to chayes@hayespub.com, or send SASE for hard copy. Responds in 2–3 weeks. Publication period varies. Flat fee.

Heinemann Raintree

1710 Roe Crest Drive, North Mankato, MN 56003
www.capstonepub.com

Editorial Director

Acquired in 2008 from Pearson, this imprint from Capstone publishes curriculum-driven nonfiction that encourages inquiry and satisfies curiosity for students in grades K through 8. Among its most recognized brands are Acorn, Heinemann Library First, and Raintree Perspectives

Freelance Potential: Publishes 600+ titles annually: 1-10% developed from unsolicited submissions; 75-100% assigned; 1-10% by agented authors; 10-25% by authors who are new to the publishing house; 1-10% by previously unpublished writers. Receives 10-25 queries monthly.

Fiction: Early picture books, early readers, story picture books, chapter books, middle-grade, graphic novels. Genres: adventure, bilingual, fairy tales, historical, humor, multicultural, realistic, sports.

Nonfiction: Concept books, early picture books, early readers, chapter books, graphic nonfiction, middle-grade. Topics: animals, arts, activities, games, crafts, biography, bilingual, education and career, current events, entertainment, social studies, history, geography, health, science, math.

Titles: *Amphibian Body Parts*, by Clare Lewis (grades PreK–12). *Bigfoot*, by Catherine Chambers (grades 1–3).

Submissions and Payment: Guidelines and catalogue available at website. For nonfiction, query with cover letter, résumé, and 3 writing samples. Accepts hard copy only. Responds in 6 months if interested. Publication period and payment policy vary.

Parents, Divisions, Imprints

Capstone Presss, See page 254

High Noon Books

20 Leveroni Court, Novato, CA 94949. www.highnoonbooks.com

Acquisitions Editor

Helping struggling readers succeed is the main goal of High Noon Books. An imprint of Academic Therapy, its titles provide a means to expose and reinforce the most common words in the English language for at-risk, ELL, struggling readers, and special education populations.

Freelance Potential: Publishes 20 titles annually.

Fiction: Early readers, phonics-based chapter books. Genres: adventure, historical, mystery, science fiction, graphic.

Nonfiction: Early readers, phonics-based chapter books. Topics: high-interest biography, history, social studies, math, science, sports, travel.

Titles: *Mystery at Bear Lake*, by Bob Wright (ages 9–14). *Juno's Twins*, by Michael Milone, Ph.D. (ages 9–14).

Submissions and Payment: Catalogue available at website. Email ideas for new products to sales@academictherapy.com. Response time and publication period vary. Flat fee.

Parents, Divisions, Imprints

Academic Therapy, See page 310

History Compass

25 Leslie Road, Auburndale, MA 02466
www.historycompass.com

CEO: Lisa Gianelly

History Compass is known for its primary source-based U.S. history books, guides, and historical fiction for elementary and secondary school students. Its goal is to provide information and stories that give insight into our nation's history. Its titles are well-researched and rely heavily on primary source documents that tell a compelling story.

Freelance Potential: Publishes about 8 titles annually: 35% by authors who are new to the publishing house; 12% by previously unpublished writers. Receives 4–5 queries monthly.

Fiction: Middle-grade, YA. Genre: historical.

Nonfiction: Early readers, chapter books, middle-grade, YA. Topic: American history. Also publishes biographies and guidebooks for adults.

Titles: *Forward Into Light: The Struggle for Woman's Suffrage,* by Madeleine Meyers (ages 8–12). *The Beat Generation,* by Juliet H. Mofford (ages 12+).

Submissions and Payment: Catalogue available at website. Guidelines available. Query with cover letter containing description of content, source material, intended audience, author biography, competition analysis, and marketing plan; table of contents or outline; and sample chapter. Accepts hard copy. Accepts simultaneous submissions if identified. SASE. Responds in 1 month. Publication in 2–8 months. Royalty.

Innovative Kids

50 Washington Street, Norwalk, CT 06854
www.innovativekids.com

Publisher: Shari Kaufman

Books, puzzles, games, and toys that offer both fun and learning are offered by this publisher, whose publishing program is based on the belief that "having fun leads to the best sort of learning." Its fiction and nonfiction titles are geared toward children up to age 12. It does not publish traditional picture books, but titles that lend themselves to interactive, educational formats, often with an added bonus: for example, book series with incentive stickers.

Freelance Potential: Publishes 50 titles annually: 40% by authors who are new to the publishing house. Receives 15–20 queries, 15–20 unsolicited manuscripts monthly.

Fiction: Concept books, board books, early readers, chapter books, graphic books. Genres: phonetics, animals, fantasy, adventure, real life.

Nonfiction: Concept books, early readers, chapter books, middle-grade. Topics: numbers, phonetics, animals, life skills, real life, jobs.

Titles: *An Elephant Eye Spy* (ages 3+). *Farm Faces* (ages Birth to 3).

Submissions and Payment: Guidelines and catalogue available at website. Query or send complete manuscript with dummy. Accepts hard copy and email to info@innovativekids.com. Responds in 6–12 months if interested. Publication period varies. Flat fee. Also considers writers for work-for-hire projects. Send writing sample and credentials.

JIST Publishing

875 Montreal Way, St. Paul, MN 55102. www.jist.com

Product Manager: Rebecca Wagner

The catalogue from JIST features workbooks, videos, and assessments on job searching, career exploration, occupational information, life skills, and character education. While most of its titles are directed toward adults, many are geared toward students in middle school or high school.

Freelance Potential: Publishes 20 titles annually. Receives 5–10 queries monthly.

Nonfiction: Middle-grade, YA. Topics: career exploration and assessment, occupations, job retention, job searching, character education, career development.

Titles: *Young Person's Character Education Handbook* (ages 7+). *Soft Skills in the Workplace* (YA–A).

Submissions and Payment: Guidelines and catalogue available at website. Query with 3- to 7-page proposal that includes working title, summary of book, target audience, target market, competitive analysis, sales and marketing analysis, outline, sample chapters, résumé, and project status. Prefers email to rwagner@ jist.com. Responds in 14–16 weeks. Publication in 6–9 months. Royalty, 8–10%.

Kaeden Books

P.O. Box 16190, Rocky River, OH 44116. www.kaeden.com

Editor: Lisa Stenger

Kaeden Books publishes leveled books in English and Spanish for early, emergent, and fluent readers in preschool through grade 2. It specializes in both fiction and nonfiction early literacy books and beginning chapter books that are designed to help teachers guide children through their first years of the reading experience.

Freelance Potential: Publishes 12–20 titles annually: all developed from unsolicited submissions. Receives 100+ unsolicited manuscripts monthly.

Fiction: Early readers, story picture books, chapter books. Genres: contemporary, animals, humor, life skills.

Nonfiction: Early readers, story picture books, chapter books. Topics: animals, science, nature, nutrition, biography, careers, recreation, social studies.

Titles: *Adventures of Sophie Bean: The Pond Hockey Challenge,* by Kathy Yevchak (grade 2). *Brave Knight Nicholas,* by Patty Haley (grade 2).

Submissions and Payment: Guidelines and catalogue available at website. Send complete manuscript with cover letter that includes author bio and manuscript title. Accepts hard copy only. Accepts simultaneous submissions. Responds only if interested. Response time, publication period, and payment policy vary.

Kane Press

350 Fifth Avenue, Suite 7206, New York, NY 10118
www.kanepress.com

Submissions Editor

This award-winning publisher offers illustrated titles for children ages 3 to 11. Its books feature authentic content and they relate that content to a child's everyday experiences.

Freelance Potential: Publishes 15+ titles annually.

Fiction: Story picture books, early readers, chapter books, middle-grade; primary series. Genres: contemporary, historical, multicultural, mystery, social skills, math, literature, science, social studies, animal stories.

Titles: *A Thousand Theos,* by Lori Haskins Houran (ages 6–8). *Make a Wish, Albert!,* by Lori Haskins Houran (ages 6–8).

Submissions and Payment: Catalogue available at website. Does not accept unsolicited submissions. Does seek targeted submissions for specific reading levels and subject areas. Check website for current needs. For questions, email info@kanepress.com. Response time, publication period, and payment policy vary.

Kingfisher

Macmillan, 175 Fifth Avenue, New York, NY 10010
www.us.macmillan.com/Kingfisher

Submissions Editor

This leading international publisher offers illustrated information books, with a readership ranging from preschool through young adults. Among the topics Kingfisher covers are natural history, science, geography, history, art and philosophy. Kingfisher is part of Macmillan Publishers.

Freelance Potential: Publishes 10+ titles annually.

Nonfiction: Pre-K. early readers, middle-grade, YA. Topics: natural history, science, geography, history, art, philosophy.

Titles: *Animal Babies in Rain Forests* (ages 3+). *Who's That? Roaring* (ages 3+).

Submissions and Payment: Catalogue available at website. Guidelines available. Response time, publication period, and payment policy vary.

Learning A-Z

1840 E. River Road, Suite 320, Tucson, AZ 85718
www.learninga-z.com

Vice President of Development: Katherine Burdick

Learning A-Z's award-winning PreK-6 teaching products provide leveled books, printable worksheets, projectable activities, and interactive tools designed to meet the needs of each unique learner. It also offers teacher resources online that seemlessly integrate with any school curriculum.

Freelance Potential: Publishes numerous print and digital products annually.

Fiction: Toddler books, early readers, middle-grade. Genres: contemporary, social issues, poetry.

Nonfiction: Early readers, middle-grade. Topics: science, reading, writing, history, sports, careers.

Titles: *The Woodsy Band Jam*, by Pam Bull (grades K–6). *Career Files: Food Science Technician*, (grades 5–6).

Submissions and Payment: Catalogue available at website. Submit writing samples that demonstrate an ability to write developmentally appropriate material for different level learners in grades preK–6. Response time, publication period, and payment policy vary.

Lerner Publications

241 First Avenue North, Minneapolis, MN 55401–1607
www.lernerbooks.com

Editorial Director: Patricia Stockland

This flagship imprint of Lerner Publishing Group specializes in curricular and high-interest nonfiction series for children in grades K through 8. Its educational titles offer photo-driven designs and features that help young readers understand, enjoy, and share information. This company does not accept unsolicited submissions but does put out calls for specific submissions via its website or in writers' newsletters.

Freelance Potential: Publishes 250 titles annually: most are developed in-house; 1–10% developed from unsolicited submissions; 20% by agented authors; 1–10% by authors who are new to the publishing house.

Nonfiction: Early readers, chapter books. Topics: ethnic and multicultural issues, nature, the environment, science, sports, history, biography.

Titles: *People and the Environment*, Jennifer Boothroyd (grades K–2). *Persians Are the Best!*, by Elaine Landau (grades 2–4)

Submissions and Payment: Guidelines and catalogue available at website. Does not accept unsolicited submissions. Does seek targeted submissions for specific reading levels and subject areas. Check website for current needs. Response time, publication period, and payment policy vary.

Lerner Publishing Group

241 First Avenue North, Minneapolis, MN 55401–1607
www.lernerbooks.com

Submissions Editor

Lerner Publishing group is a large, independent company focusing on fiction and nonfiction for preschoolers to young adults. It targets classrooms and libraries. Its imprints are Carolrhoda Books (picture books, chapter books); Carolrhoda Lab (YA fiction); Lerner Digital; Lerner Publications (photo-illustrated, high-interest nonfiction, grades K–8); Graphic Universe (graphic novels); Millbrook Press (nonfiction, grades K–5); Darby Creek (series fiction, grades 2–12); Kar-Ben (Jewish titles, preK to YA); Twenty-First Century Books (nonfiction, grades 6–12); LernerClassroom (classroom paperbacks, preK–grade 5); First Avenue Editions (fiction, nonfiction paperbacks); and ediciones Lerner (Spanish language editions, preK–grade 5).

Freelance Potential: Publishes hundreds of titles annually: most are developed in-house.

Fiction: PreK, picture books, early readers, chapter books, middle-grade, YA. Genres: adventure, mystery, animals, nature, folktales, myths, multicultural, history, sports.

Nonfiction: PreK, picture books, early readers, chapter books, middle-grade, YA. Topics: ethnic and multicultural issues, nature, the environment, science, sports, history, biography.

Titles: *Be an Explorer,* by Chris Oxlade (grades 3–6). *Anthony Davis,* by Jon M. Fishman (grades 2–5).

Submissions and Payment: Guidelines and catalogue available at website. Does not accept unsolicited submissions. Does seek targeted submissions at specific reading levels and subject areas. Check website for current needs. Response time, publication period, and payment policy vary.

Parents, Divisions, Imprints

Carolrhoda Books, See page 94

Lucent Books

27500 Drake Road, Farmington Hills, MI 48331-3535
www.gale.cengage.com/greenhaven/lucent

Administrative Assistant: Kristine Burns

Lucent Books publishes under the Gale banner to support a range of grades and reading levels. Its goal is to provide divergent points of view on controversial topics and to present complex ideas and events in a way that middle-school students will understand, but with depth and objectivity. Among its popular series are Technology 360, Crime Scene Investigations, and Hot Topics. All work is assigned.

Freelance Potential: Publishes 110 titles annually: 10% by authors who are new to the publishing house; 3% by previously unpublished writers. Receives 8–10 queries monthly.

Nonfiction: Middle-grade, YA. Topics: contemporary social issues, biography, history, geography, health, science, sports.

Titles: *Parasitic Diseases*, by Lizabeth Craig (grades 7–10). *Natural Disasters,* by Kevin Hillstrom (grades 7–10).

Submissions and Payment: Catalogue available at website. Submit ideas for new publications via form on website. Qualifying submissions that result in a Gale publication are eligible for a $1,000 reward. Response time and publication period vary.

Parents, Divisions, Imprints

Cengage Learning, See page 257

Magic Wagon

P.O. Box 398166, Minneapolis, MN 55439. www.abdopub.com

Editor in Chief: Paul Abdo

This imprint of Abdo Publishing offers titles for kids in PreK through grade 8 that blend imagination with original illustrations and story lines. Its focus is on picture books, illustrated chapter books and leveled readers, and graphic novels for preK to grade 8. It publishes nonfiction, original fiction, (usually in a 4–6 title series) and adaptations of classic fiction.

Freelance Potential: Parent company publishes 600 titles annually. All writing is done on assignment or a work-for-hire basis.

Fiction: Early picture books, early readers, story picture books, leveled readers, chapter books, middle-grade. Genres: humor, retold classics, graphic novels, animals.

Nonfiction: Early picture books, early readers, story picture books, chapter books, middle-grade. Topics: animals, nature, travel, geography, sciences, social studies, sports, history, biography, leisure, language arts, multicultural.

Titles: *Lightning Strikes Twice,* by Jan Fields (8–10). *Band Geeks: Snaring the Trumpet,* by Amy Cobb (ages 8+).

Submissions and Payment: Catalogue available at website. Guidelines provided to writers under contract only. To be considered for future writing assignments, send résumé with cover letter, area of expertise, and publishing credits. It is currently accepting submissions for picture book, beginning reader, and chapter book manuscripts with the potential to become a series (4–6 titles). Send a detailed outline of the manuscript and series, an introduction, and two sample chapters. Accepts email to submissions@abdopublishing.com. Responds in 6 months. Publication period varies. Flat fee.

Parents, Divisions, Imprints

Abdo Publishing Company, See page 248

Millbrook Press

Lerner Publishing, 241 First Avenue North, Minneapolis, MN 55401
www.lernerbooks.com

Editorial Director: Carol Hinz

This imprint of Lerner Publishing Group offers entertaining and informative nonfiction picture books and series as well as photo-driven titles to teach young minds. Its list focuses on curricular topics in the form of picture books, illustrated nonfiction, and photo-driven titles for kindergarten to grade 5. Many of its books are published in series. Nearly all are available as ebooks.

Freelance Potential: Publishes 40 titles annually.

Fiction: Picture books, chapter books, middle grade. Genres: historical, sports, math, language arts, mystery, adventure.

Nonfiction: Picture books, middle-grade. Topics: the arts, sports, social studies, history, language arts, math, science, biography, nature, the environment, crafts.

Titles: *Pitch and Throw, Grasp and Know,* by Brian P. Cleary (grades 2–5). *Play Ball, Jackie!,* by Joe Morse (grades 2–5).

Submissions and Payment: Guidelines and catalogue available at website. Does not accept unsolicited submissions. Does seek targeted submissions for specific reading levels and subject areas. Check website for current needs. Response time, publication period, and payment policy vary.

Parents, Divisions, Imprints

Lerner Publishing Group, See page 277

Mitchell Lane Publishers

P.O. Box 196, Hockessin, DE 19707. www.mitchelllane.com

Publisher: Barbara Mitchell

The books on this publisher's list target children who do not like to read. To capture the attention of these readers, Mitchell Lane publishes engaging nonfiction on high-interest topics. It works with established authors on a work-for-hire basis.

Freelance Potential: Publishes 75 titles annually: very few by authors who are new to the publishing house. Receives 30 queries monthly.

Nonfiction: Early readers, chapter books, middle-grade, YA. Topics: animals, natural disasters, biography, sports, mythology, art, history, poets, playwrights, science, music, health and fitness, multicultural, entertainment, pop culture, science, community service and volunteering, environmental topics, genealogy, and the Middle East.

Titles: *Bessie Smith (American Jazz)*, by Kathleen Tracy (grades 4–8). *The Amazon River (Rivers of the World)*, by Kevin Gillman (grades 3–6).

Submissions and Payment: Guidelines and catalogue available at website. Work-for-hire only. Query with cover letter, unedited writing sample, comprehensive résumé, and publishing credits. Accepts hard copy. Material is not returned. Responds if interested and when a suitable assignment becomes available. Publication period varies. Flat fee.

Morgan Reynolds

620 South Elm Street, Suite 223, Greensboro, NC 27406
www.morganreynolds.com

Associate Editor

This publisher has one simple goal—to publish high quality nonfiction for young adult readers. Each title captures the life story and details of a historical figure or event that impacted the world.

Freelance Potential: Publishes 30 titles (10 juvenile) annually: 6–10% developed from unsolicited submissions; 10–15% by authors who are new to the publishing house; 10% by previously unpublished writers. Receives 10 queries, 5 unsolicited manuscripts monthly.

Nonfiction: YA. Topics: history, music, science, business, feminism, world events, biography, social studies, literature, music.

Titles: *Out in Front: Malala Yousafzai and the Girls of Pakistan,* by David Aretha (YA). *Asteroids and Comets,* by Don Nardo (YA).

Submissions and Payment: Catalogue available at website. Published authors, query with outline and sample chapter; unpublished authors, send complete manuscript. Accepts hard copy. SASE. Accepts simultaneous submissions if identified. Responds to queries in 1 month, to manuscripts in 1–3 months. Publication in 12–18 months. Payment policy varies.

Neal-Schuman Publishers

ALA Editions, 50 Huron Street, Chicago, IL 60611
www.neal-schuman.com

Marketing Assistant: Brett Beasley

Part of the American Library Association, Neal Schuman publishes books for school and public librarians. It focuses on curriculum, literacy, and information science titles.

Freelance Potential: Publishes 40 titles annually: 25% developed from unsolicited submissions; 30% by authors who are new to the publishing house; 80% by previously unpublished writers. Receives 20 queries monthly.

Nonfiction: Publishes resource materials for school media specialists and librarians. Topics: curriculum support, the Internet, technology, literacy skills, reading programs, collection development, reference needs, staff development, management, communication.

Titles: *The Student's Survival Guide to Research*, by Monty L. McAdoo. *Including Families of Children with Special Needs: A How-to Manual for Librarians,* by Carrie Scott Banks, Sandra Feinberg, Kathleen Deerr, and Michelle Langa (librarians).

Submissions and Payment: Guidelines and catalogue available at website. Query with proposal that includes: general description of book including audience and market; competitive analysis; table of contents; detailed outline; sample chapter or 6–10 sample pages; draft preface addressing topic, reasons for writing, how book is compiled and organized; projected completion date; software used; special considerations (e.g. illustrations, permissions, etc.); and résumé. Accepts hard copy and email queries with Word attachments to editionsmarketing@ala.org. Responds in 6–8 weeks. Publication in 10–12 months. Royalty.

Nelson Education

1120 Birchmount Road, Scarborough, Ontario M1K 5G4 Canada
www.nelson.com

Nelson Education is Canada's leading educational publisher, providing innovative products and solutions for learners of all ages. Nelson values and respects the lifelong learning continuum and dedicates its business efforts to the diverse learning needs of both students and educators.

Freelance Potential: Publishes 60 titles annually. Receives 8–10 queries monthly.

Fiction: Early readers, chapter books. Genres: social skills, sports, activities, relationships, adventure, language arts, graphic novels.

Nonfiction: Early readers, middle-grade, YA. Topics: writing, literacy, science, the arts, math, technology, business, social studies, French.

Titles: *Informative Assessment: When It's Not About a Grade*, by Robin J. Fogarty (educators). *Canada: Our Century, Our Story*, by John Fielding and Rosemary Evans (YA).

Submissions and Payment: Guidelines and catalogue available at website. Query with proposal that includes statement of purpose and intended market, market analysis, project description, detailed table of contents, project timeline, and competition review; and 1–2 sample chapters. Accepts hard copy and email to nelson.hededitorial@nelson.com. Responds in 6–12 months. Publication period and payment policy vary.

Nomad Press

2456 Christian Street, White River Junction, VT 05001
www.nomadpress.net

Acquisitions Editor

Passionate about sparking the interest of young readers, Nomad Press takes kids far beyond the words on a page, into a world of exploration and experiential education.

Freelance Potential: Publishes 10–12 titles annually: 60% by authors who are new to the publishing house; 25% by previously unpublished writers. Receives 2–3 queries monthly.

Nonfiction: Early readers, middle-grade. Topics: science, geology, the environment, energy, social studies, history, foreign countries, biography, math, astronomy, food.

Titles: *Human Migration: Investigate the Global Journey of Humankind*, by Judy Dodge Cummings (grade 7–9). *Renewable Energy: Discover the Fuel of the Future*, by Erin Twamley and Joshua Sneideman (grades 4–6).

Submissions and Payment: Guidelines and catalogue available at website. Does not accept unsolicited manuscripts. For work-for-hire, query with résumé and publishing credits. Prefers email to info@nomadpress.net. Accepts hard copy. Responds in 3–4 weeks. Publication in 6–18 months. Royalty. Flat fee.

Richard C. Owen Publishers

P.O. Box 585, Katonah, NY 10536
www.rcowen.com

Director of Children's Books: Phyllis Greenspan

Literacy education with an emphasis on reading and writing is the main focus at Richard C. Owen. It produces fiction and nonfiction on a variety of topics, as well as English/Spanish sets and teacher resource material geared to grades pre-K through 8.

Freelance Potential: Publishes 2 titles annually: all by authors who are new to the publishing house. Receives 80–90 unsolicited manuscripts monthly.

Fiction: Story picture books, early readers, chapter books. Genres: contemporary, mystery, humor, folktales, animals and nature, social issues, multicultural.

Nonfiction: Story picture books, early readers. Topics: current events, geography, music, history, careers, science, nature, the environment, biography. Also publishes professional books and resources for teachers.

Titles: *At the Horse Show*, by Phonda Cox (PreK–3). *Breakfast with John,* by Janice Boland (PreK–3).

Submissions and Payment: Catalogue available at website. Send manuscript. Accepts hard copy. SASE. Accepts simultaneous submissions if identified. Responds in 3–6 months. Publication period and payment policy vary.

Pacific Educational Press

Faculty of Education, University of British Columbia, 411–2389 Health Sciences Mall, Vancouver, British Columbia V6T 1Z3 Canada. www.pacificedpress.ca

Acquisitions Editor

Pacific Educational Press is a unit of the Faculty of Education at the University of British Columbia produces children's nonfiction books with teacher guides for classroom use. It also publishes professional resources for teachers and textbooks for teacher education programs at the college level.

Freelance Potential: Publishes about 4 titles annually: 50% by authors who are new to the publishing house; 50% by previously unpublished writers. Receives 5–10 queries monthly.

Nonfiction: Middle-grade, YA. Also publishes books for teachers. Topics: math, language arts, the sciences, social studies, multicultural education, critical thinking, the arts, home economics.

Titles: *Stepping into Drama*, by George Belliveau (educators). *Understanding Dyslexia and Other Learning Disabilities*, by Linda Siegel (educators).

Submissions and Payment: Guidelines and catalogue available at website. Prefers proposal with detailed chapter-by-chapter description of the book; relevant information about charts, illustrations, or photographs; copyrighted material you plan to include; 2 sample chapters or writing samples; résumé; a list of contributors and a brief biographical statement for each if the book is a collection; a completion schedule; a competition analysis; audience analysis; and course type and level for which the textbook will be used. Accepts hard copy and email to barbara.kuhne@ubc.ca for post-secondary market submissions or catherine.edwards@ubc.ca for school market submissions. Responds in 4–6 months. Publication in 18–24 months. Royalty, 10% of net.

Phoenix Learning Resources

P.O. Box 510, Honesdale, PA 18431
www.phoenixlearningresources.com

Supporting students of all ages, Phoenix Learning Resources offers skill-based and supplemental material for PreK through adults. Its catalogue is filled with a wide range of resources in all subject areas including special education, ESL and adult basic education.

Freelance Potential: Publishes 45 titles annually. Receives 2–3 queries monthly.

Nonfiction: Publishes textbooks and educational materials for preK–grade 12 and beyond. Also publishes books for special education and for gifted students, materials for use with ESL students, and reference books. Topics: biography, language skills, integrated language arts, reading comprehension, social studies, math, study skills, social skills.

Titles: *How to Be a Recycling Hero* (grades 3+). *Social Skills Simplified* (grades PreK–K).

Submissions and Payment: Catalogue available at website. Query with résumé. Accepts hard copy. SASE. Accepts simultaneous submissions if identified. Responds in 1–4 weeks. Publication in 1–15 months. Royalty. Flat fee.

Picture Window Books

Capstone, 1710 Roe Crest Drive, North Mankato, MN 56003
www.capstonepub.com

Editorial Director: Nick Healy

Founded in 2001, the mission of Picture Window Books is to create bright, wholesome books to delight and educate young readers. The imprint publishes illustrated fiction and nonfiction easy readers, picture books, and chapter books for grades preK–4.

Freelance Potential: Publishes 40 titles annually: 2% by agented authors; 20% by authors new to the publishing house; 5% by previously unpublished writers. Receives 30 queries monthly.

Fiction: Concept books, early picture books, story picture books, early readers, chapter books. Genres: realistic, adventure, humor, folklore, fantasy, mystery, life skills, contemporary, character values.

Nonfiction: Picture books, early readers, chapter books. Topics: science, geography, history, social sciences, language, folklore, mythology, the environment, arts and recreation.

Titles: *Adeline Porcupine*, by Charles Ghigna (grades PreK–2). *Animals: Can You Tell the Facts from the Fibs?*, by Kelly Milner Halls (grade K–3).

Submissions and Payment: Guidelines and catalogue available at website. For nonfiction, query with cover letter, résumé, and 3 writing samples. Accepts hard copy only. For fiction, query with sample chapters, résumé, and list of publishing credits. Responds in 6 months if interested. Publication period and payment policy vary.

Parents, Divisions, Imprints

Capstone, See page 254

Pieces of Learning

1990 Market Road, Marion, IL 62959. www.piecesoflearning.com

President: Kathy Balsamo

This cutting-edge publisher looks for innovative ideas and unique ways to present enrichment activities and thinking skills to students. It offers a broad range of books across all core subjects, including language arts, math, science, and social studies, that support standardized assessment criteria. It also offers titles geared to staff development.

Freelance Potential: Number of books and other products published annually is unavailable.

Nonfiction: Teachers of elementary, middle-grade, YA. Topics: differentiation, common core standards, assessment, science, social studies, reading, writing, research, gifted education.

Titles: *Comics in Your Curriculum*, by Richard Jenkins and Debra Detamore (grades 3–6). *Think Harder!*, by Pamela M. McAneny (grades 4–8).

Submissions and Payment: Catalogue and submission guidelines available at website. Query or send complete manuscript with a statement giving right of first refusal to the manuscript; anticipated length of book; grade levels of intended audience; 1-page description of the contents; 1-page answer to the question, "Who needs this book and why?"; 100-word description stating why a teacher would need the book; how the book complements other titles published by the company; and a résumé. Accepts email to kathy@piecesoflearning.com. Responds in 8 weeks. Publication period and payment policy vary.

PowerKids Press

Rosen Publishing, 29 East 21st Street, New York, NY 10010
www.rosenpublishing.com

Editorial Director: Rachel O'Connor

Since 1995, PowerKids Press has set the pace for providing rich and diverse material to support the needs of primary, emergent, and elementary students. It is an imprint of Rosen Publishing.

Freelance Potential: Publishes 200 titles annually: 8% by authors who are new to the publishing house, 8% by previously unpublished writers. Receives 40–45 queries monthly.

Nonfiction: Story picture books, early readers, middle-grade. Topics: art, social studies, science, geography, health, fitness, sports, math, Native Americans, ancient history, natural history, politics and government, multicultural and ethnic issues, biography. Also titles for special education and bilingual programs.

Titles: *A Trip to the Grocery Store*, by Josie Keogh (grades K–2). *Lions*, by Clara Reade (grades K–2).

Submissions and Payment: Catalogue available at website. Contact Customer Service team via website for information about submissions. Responds in 3 months. Publication in 9–18 months. Flat fee.

Parents, Divisions, Imprints

Rosen Publishing, See page 291

Pro-Ed

8700 Shoal Creek Boulevard, Austin, TX 78757
www.prodedinc.com

Executive Editor: Kathy Synatschk, Ph.D.

Formerly listed as PCI Education, this research-based publisher was acqured by Pro-Ed. It specializes in educational materials and curriculum. Its products are designed for students with special needs, including students with intellectual and developmental disabilities, students with learning disabilities, and English language learners.

Freelance Potential: Publishes about 5–10 titles annually: 1–10% developed from unsolicited submissions; 75–100% assigned.

Fiction: Elementary and secondary special education curriculum materials. Genres: reading, writing, literature.

Nonfiction: Elementary and secondary special education curriculum materials, supplemental materials. Topics: education, school-to-work transition, life skills, language arts, math, science, social studies, social skills.

Titles: *Conversation Basics and Beyond*, by Larry Irwin Kleiman and Paul F. Johnson (grades 6+). *AGS World Geography and Cultures-Student Text* (ages 6–12).

Submissions and Payment: Guidelines and catalogue available at website. Send prospectus containing title, overview, target audience, proposed length, comparison to competing materials, and 1–2 completed chapters. Accepts hard copy and email submissions to ksynatschk@proedinc.com. Responds in 9–12 months. Publication period varies. Payment policy varies.

Prometheus Books

59 John Glenn Drive, Amherst, NY 14228-2197
www.prometheusbooks.com

Editor in Chief: Steven L. Mitchell

This publisher has been a leader in books for the educational, scientific, professional, library, and consumer markets. Its children's titles focus on sciences, sexual education, and contemporary issues. Prometheus publishes science fiction under its Pyr imprint and mystery/thriller fiction under its Seventh Street Books.

Freelance Potential: Publishes 110 titles annually.

Nonfiction: Early readers, middle-grade, YA. Topics: social issues, health, sexuality, religion, politics, critical thinking, science, moral issues, emotional issues, decision-making.

Titles: *I Miss You!: A Military Kid's Book about Deployment,* by Beth Andrews (ages 4+). *What's Wrong with Grandma? A Family's Experience with Alzheimer's,* by Margaret Shawver (families).

Submissions and Payment: Guidelines and catalogue available at website. Query with topic, brief outline, competition analysis, potential market, completion schedule of the manuscript, tentative length, and résumé that includes publishing history. Accepts hard copy. Accepts simultaneous submissions if identified. SASE. Responds in 1–2 months. Publication in 12–18 months. Payment policy varies.

Renaissance House

465 Westview Avenue, Englewood, NJ 07631
www.renaissancehouse.net

Editorial Director: Raquel Benatar

Renaissance House is a book packager that provides editorial, translation, creative, and production services to publishers. It specializes in the development, translation, and illustration of educational materials in English and Spanish. Its focus on educational titles specifically includes bilingual children's books, multicultural books, legends, and biographies. The packager/editorial service company is "looking for opportunities in partnering with illustrators and authors [who] want to copublish their book projects."

Freelance Potential: Publishes 30 titles annually: 90% by authors who are new to the company; 75% by previously unpublished writers. Receives 10-25 queries, 75–100 manuscripts monthly.

Fiction: Middle-grade, YA. Genres: bilingual, multicultural, biography, folktales.

Nonfiction: Middle-grade, YA. Topics: biography, multicultural.

Titles: *Jose Carreras*, by Cesar Vidal (8–12). *Rigoberto Menchu*, by Raquel Benatar (8–12).

Submissions and Payment: Catalogue available at website. Send complete manuscript for fiction. Query with outline for nonfiction. Accepts email submissions to raquel@renaissancehouse. net (Word or PDF attachments). Responds in 3-6 weeks. Publication in 1 year. Flat fee.

Rosen Central

Rosen Publishing, 29 East 21st Street, New York, NY 10010
www.rosenpublishing.com

Editorial Director

Rosen Central, an imprint of Rosen Publishing, gives a comprehensive, thoughtful voice to the middle school experience. Its titles provide insight into the self and the events, issues, and conflicts of the world. Its books are written with an understanding that students in grades 5 through 8 have vastly diverse abilities in reading and comprehension as well as wide-ranging interests.

Freelance Potential: Parent company Rosen Publishing publishes 700+ titles annually.

Nonfiction: Chapter books, middle-grade. Topics: health, technology, study skills and research, sports, recreation, history, careers, contemporary issues, geography, science, ethics.

Titles: *Dracula and Other Vampires*, by Heather Moore Niver (grades 5–6). *King Kong and Other Monstrous Apes*, by Jennifer Way (grades 5–6).

Submissions and Payment: Catalogue available at website. Contact Customer Service team via website for information about submissions. Responds in 3 months. Publication in 9–18 months. Flat fee.

Parents, Divisions, Imprints

Rosen Publishing, See page 291

Rosen Publishing

29 East 21st Street, New York, NY 10010
www.rosenpublishing.com

Editorial Director, YA Division: Iris Rosoff

Rosen Pubishing provides information to schools and libraries. It has endured a tradition of addressing relevant topics and ensured the dissemination of information through library-bound editions of its titles. Rosen specializes in producing circulating reference material for school and public libraries. Many of its titles are part of series.

Freelance Potential: Publishes 700+ titles annually: very few by authors who are new to the publishing house. Receives 5–7 queries monthly.

Nonfiction: Concept books, board books, early readers, chapter books, middle-grade, YA. Topics: digital and information technology, health, reference, history, geography, science, life skills, guidance, careers, contemporary social issues.

Titles: *Top 101 Athletes,* by Jeanne Nagle (grades 7–12). *Maine Coon Cats,* by Jennifer Quasha (grade 3).

Submissions and Payment: Catalogue available at website. Contact Customer Service team via website for information about submissions. Responds in 3 months. Publication in 9–18 months. Flat fee.

Parents, Divisions, Imprints

Rosen Young Adult

Rosen Publishing, 29 East 21st Street, New York, NY 10010
www.rosenpublishing.com

Editorial Director

For more than 60 years, Rosen Young Adult has been a trusted go-to resource for teens, parents, librarians, counselors, and teachers seeking books that explore these situations, while speaking to the teen audience. Its titles tackle challenging and intriguing topics, supported with thought-provoking analytical activities.

Freelance Potential: Parent company Rosen Publishing publishes 700+ titles annually.

Nonfiction: Middle-grade, YA. Topics: health, technology, ethics, philosophy, economics, current events, history, careers, contemporary issues, geography, science.

Titles: *Juvenile Detention Centers* (grade 6). *I Have ADD/ADHD. Now What?*, by Nicki Peter Petrikowski (grades 6–7).

Submissions and Payment: Catalogue available at website. Contact Customer Service team via website for information about submissions. Responds in 3 months. Publication in 9–18 months. Flat fee.

Parents, Divisions, Imprints

Rourke Educational Media

P.O. Box 643328, Vero Beach, FL 32964
www.rourkeeducationalmedia.com

Editor in Chief: Luana Mitten

Since 1980, Rourke Educational Media has been publishing eye-catching, engaging nonfiction children's books that comply with national curriculum standards. It also offers cutting-edge software for science, social studies, and other classroom programs.

Freelance Potential: Publishes 150–200 titles annually: many by freelance or contract writers, and previously unpublished writers.

Nonfiction: Early readers, chapter books, middle-grade. Topics: science, social studies, reading adventures, sports, biography, reference.

Titles: *Sugar Glider,* by Karen Glider(grades 3–6). *Evan in the Middle,* by Kelli Hicks (grades K–3).

Submissions and Payment: Catalogue available at website. Query with résumé, indicating the topic and age you are interested in writing for. Accepts hard copy and email queries to luana@rourkepublishing.com. Guidelines are sent to writers with their contracts. Work-for-hire agreements, with a choice of 20% of payment when the manuscript is approved and 80% after proofs, or a single payment after proofs.

Rubicon Publishing

2040 Speers Rd, Oakville, Ontario L6L 2X8 Canada
www.rubiconpublishing.com

Associate Publisher: Amy Land

Founded in 1987, Rubicon Publishing is an award-winning publisher of K–12 educational resources for students and educators. The titles from this publisher combine innovative ideas with a strong foundation in education to create original and high-quality titles. All of its educational resource books are assigned.

Freelance Potential: Publishes 30+ titles annually: 100% are assigned; 2% by authors new to the publishing company; 5% by previously unpublished writers. Receives 5 queries monthly.

Fiction: Early picture books, early readers, story picture books, chapter books, middle-grade, YA. Genres: poetry, drama, graphic novels, fairy tales, fantasy, historical, multicultural, romance, science fiction, social issues, sports, westerns.

Nonfiction: Early picture books, early readers, story picture books, chapter books, middle-grade, YA, books for educators. Topics: current events, math, language arts, social studies, science, entertainment, humor, social issues, sports, multicultural and ethnic issues, technology. Also publishes teacher resources.

Titles: *Saving Cash,* (grade 4). *Spirit of the Mountain,* (grade 8).

Submissions and Payment: Catalogue available at website. All work is assigned. Query with clips. Accepts hard copy and email to submissions@rubiconpublishing.com. SASE. Response time varies. Publication in 1 year. Royalty.

Saddleback Educational Publishing

3120-A Pullman Street, Costa Mesa, CA 92626
www.sdlback.com

Editorial Director: Carol Pizer

Established in 1982, Saddleback publishes curriculum-based and reference books across all major disciplines, including math, science, language arts, social studies, special education, and life skills/careers. Most of its titles are geared toward middle and high school students, although it does offer a few elementary level reference books. It also publishes fiction and series for reluctant readers in middle and high school, as well as graphic novel- style nonfiction.

Freelance Potential: Publishes 10–20 titles yearly.

Fiction: Middle-grade, YA. Genres: the classics, contemporary, real life, hi-lo, reluctant reader.

Nonfiction: Elementary, Middle-grade, YA. Topics: science, language arts, math, social studies, career, lifestyle, technology, reference, teacher references.

Titles: *A Heart Like Ringo Star*, by Linda Oatman High (YA). *Great Spies of the World*, by John Ferritano (grades 3–8).

Submissions and Payment: Catalogue available at website. Query only; does not accept unsolicited manuscripts. Not currently seeking curriculum material but is always looking for fiction and urban fiction appropriate for grades 6–12. Response time, publication period, and payment policy, unknown.

School Zone Publishing

1819 Industrial Drive, P.O. Box 777, Grand Haven, MI 49417
www.schoolzone.com

Editor

School Zone Publishing has fast-emerged as a market leader in workbooks and flashcards for preschoolers through sixth grade students. It also offers books with research-based content, designed by educators and delivered across multiple learning platforms.

Freelance Potential: Publishes 5–6 titles annually. Receives 8–10 queries monthly.

Fiction: Story picture books, early readers. Themes: phonetics, animals, life skills, contemporary, jobs, social and character issues.

Nonfiction: Publishes workbooks, software, and flashcards for grades preK–6. Topics: reading, spelling, writing, mathematics, bilingual studies, music, arts, language arts, geography.

Titles: *My First Book of Opposites* (PreK). *The Giant Book of Jokes*, (ages 8+).

Submissions and Payment: Catalogue available at website. Query with résumé and writing samples. Response time and publication period vary. Flat fee.

Science, Naturally!

725 Eighth Street SE, Washington, DC 20003
http://sciencenaturally.com

President: Dia L. Michels

Publishing award winning STEM books and resources for elementary and middle grade kids, Science, Naturally makes curriculum fun. With a tagline of "Bridging the gap between the blackboard and the blacktop," this independent press is committed to increasing science and math literacy. Naturally! publishes books, ebooks, iPod/iPhone/iPad apps, and interactive whiteboard content for students in upper elementary and middle school, along with educational resources for teachers. Its titles are filled with interesting facts, important insights, and key connections with the goal of helping readers gain a better understanding of how science and math affect everyday life.

Freelance Potential: Publishes 4 titles annually: 50% developed from unsolicited submissions; 50% by authors who are new to the publishing house. Receives 10 queries monthly.

Fiction: Chapter books, middle-grade, YA. Themes: science, mathematics, mystery and adventure (with science/math theme).

Nonfiction: Chapter books, middle-grade, YA. Topics: science, mathematics.

Titles: *Leonardo da Vinci Gets A Do-Over*, by Mark P. Friedlander, Jr. (ages 10–14). *101 Things Everyone Should Know About Math*, by various authors (grades 5–9).

Submissions and Payment: Guidelines and catalogue available at website. Query. Accepts hard copy. Accepts simultaneous submissions if identified. SASE. Response time varies. Publication in 12–18 months. Royalty; no advance.

Scobre Press

2255 Calle Clara, La Jolla, CA 92037. www.scobre.com

Editor: Scott Blumenthal

Created by two 21-year-old college students, Scobre Press offers relevant and engaging elementary, middle grade, and young adult books that would have appealed to them as young readers. Its titles are available on two different reading levels.

Freelance Potential: Publishes about 6 titles annually: 65% by authors who are new to the publishing house; 35% by previously unpublished writers. Receives 1–2 queries monthly.

Fiction: Middle-grade, YA. Genres: sports, dance, music, popular culture, character issues, contemporary, real life/problems.

Nonfiction: Middle-grade, YA. Topics: sports, technology, music, popular culture, real life/problems, contemporary. Also publishes teacher resources.

Titles: *Being Sara,* by Chris Passudetti (grades 3–6). *Turning Green,* by Barbara Rudow (grades 4–6).

Submissions and Payment: Catalogue available at website. Guidelines available via email to info@scobre.com. Query. Accepts hard copy and email to info@scobre.com. SASE. Responds in 1 week. Publication in 6 months. Royalty, 12%.

Seedling Publications

520 East Bainbridge Street, Elizabethtown, PA 17022
www.continentalpress.com

Managing Editor: Megan Bergonzi

Part of Continental Press, Seedling offers a line of early literacy resources and parent involvement tools for grades K–2. Fiction must have a well-developed plot and a clear beginning, middle, and end. Nonfiction must include accurate facts and details. Seedling also publishes nonfiction resource books for parents and educators.

Freelance Potential: Publishes 50+ titles (40 juvenile) annually: 10% developed from unsolicited submissions. Receives 20 unsolicited manuscripts monthly.

Fiction: Early readers. Genres: fairy tales, adventure, humor, sports, nature, real life.

Nonfiction: Early readers. Topics: nature, science, technology, mathematics, animals, multicultural. Also publishes workbooks and test prep materials, as well as resources for parents and teachers.

Titles: *The Tall Baby Giraffe*, by Julie Blair Haggerty (grades K–2). *Chickens on Vacation*, by Deborah Hall Williams (grades K–2).

Submissions and Payment: Guidelines and catalogue available at website. Send complete manuscript. Manuscript should be an 8-, 12-, or 16-page format (including title page); 25–300 words. Does not accept poetry, full-length picture books, rhyming manuscripts, or religious books. Accepts hard copy only. Accepts simultaneous submissions if identified. SASE. Responds in 6 months. Publication in 1 year. Payment policy varies.

Parents, Divisions, Imprints

Continental Press, See page 259

Silver Moon Press

400 East 85th Street, New York, NY 10028
http://silvermoonpress.com

Submissions Editor

Silver Moon develops attractive, innovative early chapter books for the higher elementary grades. Its titles have an emphasis placed on the state assessments and adequate yearly progress. Its list includes historical novels suitable for guided reading, language arts, social studies, and mathematics.

Freelance Potential: Publishes 2 titles annually. Receives 4–12 queries monthly.

Fiction: Early readers, chapter books. Genre: historical.

Nonfiction: Early readers, middle–grade, YA. Topics: test preparation, study skills, language arts, math, social studies, history, biography.

Titles: *Leo Politi: Artist of the Angels,* by Ann Stalcup (ages 9+). *Ezra Jack Keats: A Biography with Illustrations,* by Dean, Freedman, and Florence Engel (ages 8+).

Submissions and Payment: Catalogue available at website. Does not accept unsolicited manuscripts. Query with résumé, table of contents, and first chapter. Accepts hard copy. Accepts simultaneous submissions if identified. SASE. Responds in 6 months. Publication period and payment policy vary.

Spotlight

P.O. Box 398166, Minneapolis, MN 55439. www.abdopub.com

Editor in Chief: Paul Abdo

PreK through grade 8 fiction comes to life exclusively in the titles from Spotlight. This division of Abdo publishing offers licensed character titles, graphic novels, and more.

Freelance Potential: Parent company publishes 600 titles annually. All writing is done on assignment or a work-for-hire basis.

Fiction: Early picture books, early readers, story picture books, chapter books, graphic novels, middle-grade. Genres: stories about licensed and popular characters.

Titles: *Amelia vs. the Sneeze Barf,* by Jimmy Gownley (ages 8–10). *Bear Wants More,* by Karma Wilson (ages 4–8).

Submissions and Payment: Catalogue available at website. Guidelines provided to writers under contract only. To be considered for future writing assignments, send résumé with cover letter, area of expertise, and publishing credits. Accepts email to submissions@abdopublishing.com. Response time varies. Publication period varies. Flat fee.

Parents, Divisions, Imprints

Abdo Publishing Company, See page 248

State Standards Publishing

1788 Quail Hollow, Hamilton, GA 31811
www.statestandardspublishing.com

President: Jill Ward

The founder of this company started it in response to the need for books to supplement curriculum for specific state studies. Titles are produced to meet state education requirements at specific grade levels and are determined by the publisher. The publisher prefers to hire writers from the state that each book is about.

Freelance Potential: Publishes 6–10 titles annually.

Nonfiction: Early readers, middle-grade, YA. Topics: state history, geography, regional, biographies, natural history and resources.

Titles: *George Washington Carver,* by Doraine Bennet (grades 4–6). *Henry Hudson,* by Moira Rose Donahue (grades 4–6).

Submissions and Payment: Catalogue available at website. Does not accept unsolicited manuscripts or queries. To be considered for work-for-hire, send résumé and nonfiction writing sample. Prefers authors living in title's state. Accepts hard copy and email to jward@statestandardspublishing.com and mchandler@statestandardspublishing.com. Response time, publication period, and payment policy vary.

Stone Arch Books

Capstone, 1710 Roe Crest Drive, North Mankato, MN 56003
www.capstonepub.com

Editorial Director: Michael Dahl

Stone Arch Books debuted its first list in 2006 with a focus on inspiring independent reading with compelling contemporary and appropriate fiction for readers in grades K–9.

Freelance Potential: Publishes 161 titles annually: 5–10% by agented authors; 15–20% reprint/licensed properties; 20% by authors who are new to the publishing house; 5% by previously unpublished writers. Receives 50 queries monthly.

Fiction: Early readers, chapter books, middle-grade, graphic novels. Genres: realistic, historical, war stories, adventure, fantasy, horror, science fiction, mystery, sports, humor, fairy tales, folklore.

Titles: *The Baking Life of Amelie Day*, by Vanessa Curtis (grades 4–8). *Blood Shark!*, by Michael Dahl (grades 1–3).

Submissions and Payment: Guidelines and catalogue available at website. For nonfiction, query with cover letter, résumé, and 3 writing samples. Accepts hard copy only. For fiction, query with sample chapters, résumé, and list of publishing credits. Prefers email to author.sub@stonearchbooks.com. Responds in 6 months if interested. Publication period and payment policy vary.

Parents, Divisions, Imprints

Capstone, See page 254

Teacher Created Resources

6421 Industry Way, Westminster, CA 92683
www.teachercreated.com

Editor in Chief: Karen Goldfluss

This educational publisher has an extensive inventory of quality and affordable materials, school supplies, lessons, and more. Teacher Created Resources is currently interested in acquiring

ELL titles for K–8 and books in the areas of language arts, reading, math, science, and social studies. Books should be based on successful classroom lessons. The majority of titles are created by teachers for teachers and parents.

Freelance Potential: Publishes 50–75 titles annually: 10–25% developed from unsolicited submissions; 50–75% assigned; 5% by authors who are new to the publishing house; 5% by previously unpublished writers.

Nonfiction: Publishes workbooks, activity books, teacher resources, and classroom aids, aimed at preK–grade 8. Topics include writing, reading, science, geography, history, technology, Christian education. Also publishes teacher materials on student testing, multiple intelligences, assessment, and classroom management.

Titles: *Comprehending Text Using Literal, Inferential, and Applied Questioning* (Grade 5). *U.S. History Little Books: Famous Events* (grades (K–3).

Submissions and Payment: Guidelines and catalogue available at website. Query with résumé, summary, intended audience, table of contents, and 10–12 manuscript pages. Accepts hard copy. SASE. Responds in 6 months. Publication in 3–12 months. Work-for-hire, flat fee.

Thompson Educational Publishers

20 Ripley Avenue, Toronto, Ontario M6S 3N9 Canada
www.thompsonbooks.com

Submissions: Faye Thompson

For more than 25 years, Thompson Education Publishing has offered educational resources for grades K through 12 and university classes are the focus of this publisher. It specializes in textbooks and scholarly titles in the fields of health, physical education, the social sciences, and the humanities. It is particularly interested in Canadian scholars and books that feature a uniquely Canadian perspective to the subject at hand.

Freelance Potential: Publishes 8 titles annually: 25% by authors who are new to the publishing house; 25% by previously unpublished writers. Receives 1–2 queries monthly.

Nonfiction: Middle-grade, YA, adult. Topics: social studies, sociology, social work, economics, communication, native studies, labor studies, sports, health, physical education, business, family, ethics, law, media, politics, aboriginal studies. Also publishes single-author monographs for use in undergraduate education, as well as books for educators.

Titles: *Kinesiology: An Introduction to Exercise Science*, by Ted Temertzoglou (grades 5+). *Healthy Active Living*, by Ted Temertzoglou (grade 9–10)

Submissions and Payment: Catalogue available at website. Query with outline and résumé. Accepts hard copy and email queries to faye@thompsonbooks.com. SAE/IRC. Response time, publication period, and payment policy vary.

Tilbury House, Publishers

103 Brunswick Avenue, Gardiner, ME 04345
www.tilburyhouse.com

Children's Books Editor: Audrey Maynard

The children's division of Tilbury House publishes award-winning children's picture books about cultural diversity, social justice, nature, and the environment. In response to the increasing classroom use of its books, it also began developing teacher guides for many of its titles.

Freelance Potential: Publishes 1–5 titles annually: 25–50% developed from unsolicited submissions; 25–50% by authors who are new to the publishing house; 25–50% by previously unpublished writers. Receives 75–100 unsolicited manuscripts monthly.

Fiction: Picture books, story picture books. Genres: realistic, contemporary, multicultural, nature and the environment.

Nonfiction: Picture books, story picture books. Topics: nature, the environment, real-life issues, social issues, social skills.

Titles: *Lailah's Lunchbox*, by Reem Faruqi (ages 8–12). *I Am Coyote,* by Geri Vistein (ages 10+).

Submissions and Payment: Guidelines and catalogue available at website. Send complete manuscript. Accepts hard copy and email submissions to audmaynard@tilburyhouse.com (no attachments). Accepts simultaneous submissions if identified. SASE. Responds in 1 month. Publication in 1–2 years. Royalty.

Toy Box Productions

CRT, Custom Products, Inc., 7532 Hickory Hills Court, Whites Creek, TN 37189. www.crttoybox.com

President: Cheryl J. Hutchinson

Dedicated to creating high-quality, entertaining, and educational children's books, Toy Box Productions began publishing in 1995. It offers series titles including Bible Stories for Kids and Time Traveler's Adventure as a way for children to learn about history and events from the Bible.

Freelance Potential: Publishes about 2 titles annually: 50% by authors who are new to the publishing house; 50% by previously unpublished writers. Receives 1–2 queries yearly.

Fiction: Story picture books, chapter books. Genres: historical, Western, multicultural, ethnic, religious.

Nonfiction: Story picture books, middle-grade. Topics: history, religion, multicultural and ethnic issues, the Bible.

Titles: *Rosa Parks: Not Giving In,* by James Collins (ages 6–8). *The Star of Bethlehem,* by Joy Loesch (ages 4–8).

Submissions and Payment: Catalogue available at website. All work is assigned. Query with résumé and clips. Accepts hard copy. SASE. Response time, publication period, and payment policy vary.

Twenty-First Century Books

241 First Avenue North, Minneapolis, MN 55401
www.lernerbooks.com

Editorial Director: Domenica Di Piazza

Twenty-First Century Books offers high-interest nonfiction titles that make curriculum-oriented subjects dynamic and accessible for young adult readers. The imprint of Lerner Books is committed to producing meaningful high-interest and curriculum-related nonfiction content across disciplines, cultures, and points of view for a young adult readership. The titles from this publisher are an excellent launching pad for stimulating in-depth research and supporting evidence-based coursework.

Freelance Potential: Publishes around 50 titles annually. Receives 8-10 queries monthly.

Nonfiction: Middle-grade, YA. Topics: human interest, history, social studies, contemporary issues, language arts, biography, sports, multicultural, current events, science, technology, health, medicine, government, politics.

Titles: *Peru in Pictures,* by Heron Marquez (grades 5-12). *Anxiety Disorders*, by Cherry Pedrick and Bruce Hyman (YA).

Submissions and Payment: Guidelines and catalogue available at website. Does not accept unsolicited submissions. Does seek targeted submissions for specific reading levels and subject areas on an as-needed basis. Check website for current needs. Response time, publication period, and payment policy vary.

Parents, Divisions, Imprints

Lerner Publishing Group, See page 277

U-X-L

27500 Drake Road, Farmington Hills, MI 48331-3535
www.gale.cengage.com/uxl

Publisher

Part of Cengage Learning, this publisher offers an extensive line of reference books for students in upper elementary through high school. Most titles are written at a seventh-grade reading level. Primary source volumes, encyclopedias, almanacs, chronologies, and biographies can all be found in its catalogue, which covers a broad range of academic subject areas.

Freelance Potential: Publishes 20 titles annually.

Nonfiction: Middle-grade, YA. Topics: science, medicine, history, social studies, current events, biographies, multicultural issues, the arts, sports, careers. Also publishes curriculum-based reference titles, encyclopedias.

Titles: *Doomed: The Science Behind Disasters*, K. Lee Lerner (grades 6-10). *Junior Worldmark Encyclopedia of the States,* (grades 4+).

Submissions and Payment: Catalogue available at website. Accepts some unsolicited material; most work is assigned on a work-for-hire basis. Query with résumé and writing samples. Accepts hard copy. Accepts simultaneous submissions if identified. SASE. Response time and publication period vary. Flat fee.

Parents, Divisions, Imprints

Cengage Learning, See page 257

Walch Education

40 Walch Drive, Portland, ME 04103–1286. http://walch.com

Submissions: Jill Rosenblum

Walch Education is a leading developer and publisher of Common Core Math I, II, and III resources. It also offers a variety of middle grade, high school, and adult education titles. The company has a large, in-house team of educators that creates most of its materials, but it does employ freelance writers on large projects and commissioned titles, and considers unsolicited manuscripts.

Freelance Potential: Publishes 50 titles annually: 2% developed from unsolicited submissions. Receives 2 queries monthly.

Nonfiction: Middle-grade, YA. Topics: reading, writing, vocabulary, grammar, geometry, algebra, critical thinking, world history, social studies, math, science, chemistry, physics, money management, careers, life skills, art, special education. Also publishes resource materials for teachers.

Titles: *Geometry Station Activities for Common Core Standards* (grades 9–12). *Expeditions in Your Classroom: English Language Arts for Common Core State Standards* (grades 9–12).

Submissions and Payment: Guidelines and catalogue available at website. Query with detailed proposal that includes author introduction; why you are writing this book; target audience, including subject area, teacher skill level, student grade level and ability; learning objectives, including No Child Left Behind requirements and state standards; marketing potential; table of contents; a sample chapter and supporting materials; and manuscript development timeline. Prefers email to ideas@walch.com (Word or PDF attachments). Accepts hard copy. SASE. Responds in 4–6 months. Publication period varies. Royalty. Flat fee.

Weigl Publishers

350 Fifth Avenue, 59th Floor, New York, NY 10118
www.weigl.com

Managing Editor: Heather Hudak

Weigl produces supplementary material for the school and library markets. Its titles have eye-catching visuals and well-researched content. All of its titles are written on assignment.

Freelance Potential: Publishes about 100 titles annually: 5% by authors who are new to the publishing house.

Nonfiction: Early readers, chapter books, middle-grade. Topics: global cultures, social and environmental issues, plant and animal life, biography, sports, science, social studies, language arts.

Titles: *Lady Gaga,* by Anita Yasuda (grades 4–6). *Deer,* by Christine Webster (grades 2–4).

Submissions and Payment: Catalogue available at website. All work is done on a work-for-hire basis. Send résumé, publishing history, and subject area of expertise only. No queries or unsolicited manuscripts. Accepts hard copy and email to linda@weigl.com. SASE. Responds in 6–12 months. Publication in 2 years. Flat fee.

Windmill Books

Rosen Publishing, 29 East 21st Street, New York, NY 10010
www.rosenpublishing.com

Editorial Director

From captivating concept books to thrilling historical fiction to photo-drive nonfiction, each book from Windmill is a celebration of its core tenet—to inspire a love of learning through reading.

Freelance Potential: Parent company Rosen Publishing publishes 700+ titles annually.

Fiction: Concept books, board books, story picture books, early readers, chapter books, middle-grade. Genres: real life/problem, multicultural, adventure, classics, historical, mystery, contemporary issues.

Nonfiction: Concept books, board books, story picture books, early readers, chapter books, middle-grade. Topics: math, history, biography, life skills, science, contemporary issues, real life problems, leisure.

Titles: *Stop that Stew,* by Margaret Mahy (grade 1). *Florence the Flamingo: A Tale of Pride,* by Felicia Law (grade 2).

Submissions and Payment: Catalogue available at website. Contact Customer Service team via website for information about submissions. Responds in 3 months. Publication in 9–18 months. Flat fee.

Parents, Divisions, Imprints

Rosen Publishing, See page 291

World Book

233 North Michigan Avenue, Suite 2000, Chicago, IL 60601
www.worldbook.com

Editor in Chief: Paul A. Kobasa

Reference books and nonfiction for all ages are the mainstay of World Book. It prides itself on accurate, objective, and reliable research materials in the form of encyclopedias, reference sources, and digital products for home and school use.

Freelance Potential: Publishes numerous titles each year.

Nonfiction: Early readers, middle-grade, YA, adult. Topics: animals, careers, concepts, geography, health, history, how-to, languages, multicultural, reference, science.

Titles: *Deserts and Scrublands. Mountain and Polar Regions. Rivers, Lakes and Wetlands.*

Submissions and Payment: Catalogue available at website. Query with outline/synopsis. Do not send manuscript. Accepts simultaneous submissions. Responds in 2 months. Publication in 18 months. Payment policy varies by product.

Zaner-Bloser Educational

1201 Dublin Road, Columbus, OH 43215–1026
www.zaner-bloser.com

Senior Vice President of Editorial: Marytherese Croarkin

Zaner-Bloser's mission is to create dynamic, appealing, and effective educational programs and services. Its focus is on distinctive programs that inspire all students to become engaged, literate participants in the global society. Both fiction and nonfiction titles are found in its catalogue. Spanish language books are also featured.

Freelance Potential: Publishes 200+ titles annually.

Fiction: Early readers, story picture books, middle-grade, YA. Genres: contemporary, life skills, animals, language arts, fantasy, historical, adventure.

Nonfiction: Early readers, story picture books, middle-grade, YA. Topics: language arts, phonics, vocabulary, reading, spelling, handwriting, math, science, social studies.

Titles: *Spelling Connections: Opportunities Beyond Words!,* by J. Richard Gentry, Ph.D. (grades 1–8). *Inquire* (grades 4–12).

Submissions and Payment: Catalogue available at website. Query with résumé and clips. Accepts hard copy. SASE. Response time and publication period vary. Flat fee.

Publishing for Educators & Caregivers

Children's writers may also be interested in writing books for those who educate and care for children and teens. These readers fill wide-ranging roles and often have an important place in the lives of young people.

The publishers listed in this section offer professional resources, classroom aids, and other materials in support of teachers, early childhood educators, librarians, principals, child psychiatrists, homeschoolers, those who work in gifted or special education, pediatric health, and many other areas. Some houses also publish books directed to children and teens themselves— books that educators, caregivers, and other adults might use with them.

While educational writers often have expertise or backgrounds in education, health, or other professional fields, they may also have personal experience that qualifies them to write books of this kind. Establishing a relationship with companies such as these can result in regular work, and a niche that extends a writing career.

ABC-CLIO

130 Cremona Drive, Suite C, Santa Barbara, CA 93117
www.abc-clio.com

Acquisitions Editor

An industry leader in the creation of innovative reference and professional development resources, ABC-CLIO is comprised off our imprints: ABC-CLIO/Greenwood, Praeger, Libraries Unlimited, and ABC-CLIO Solutions. It offers reference and educational titles that offer coverage of history, humanities, and general interest topics that complement secondary and higher education curriculum.

Freelance Potential: Publishes 12 titles annually: 25% by authors who are new to the publishing house. Receives 10 queries monthly.

Nonfiction: Middle grade, YA Topics: technology, history, humanities, social issues, culture, geography.

Titles: *Imperialism and Expansionism in American History,* by Chris J. Magoc and David Bernstein. *Ethnic Groups of North, East, and Central Asia: An Encyclopedia* (Ethnic Groups of the World), by James B. Minahan.

Submissions and Payment: Guidelines and catalogue available at website. Query with author qualifications. Accepts email (see website for appropriate acquisitions editor) and hard copy. SASE. If interested, publisher will ask for proposal with working title, scope and purpose of book, an outline, methodology and presentation, and competitive titles. Responds in 8–10 weeks. Publication in 10–12 months. Royalty. For magazine articles, send complete manuscript (1,200–3,000 words) via email to appropriate editor (see website). Response time varies.

Parents, Divisions, Imprints

Libraries Unlimited, See page 323

Academic Therapy

20 Leveroni Court, Novato, CA 94949
www.academictherapy.com

Acquisitions Editor

Academic Therapy Publications is a publisher and distributor of assessments for speech, language, occupational therapists, rehabilitation specialists, school psychologists, and special education teachers. It's High Noon imprint specializes in high/low reading material.

Freelance Potential: Publishes 15 titles annually: 10% developed from unsolicited submissions. Receives 50 queries monthly.

Nonfiction: Standardized tests and reference books, curriculum materials, teacher/parent references, and visual/perceptual training aids. Topics: speech/language, occupational therapy, rehabilitation, special education, school psychology.

Titles: *You Can Control Your Class*, by A. Gudmundsend, E. Williams, and R. B. Lybbery. *Sharing Books and Stories to Promote Language and Literacy*, by Anne van Kllek, Ph.D.

Submissions and Payment: Catalogue available at website. Query with synopsis and author biography. Accepts hard copy. SASE. Response time varies. Publication period varies. Flat fee.

Parents, Divisions, Imprints

High Noon Books, See page 271

ALA Editions

American Library Association, 50 East Huron Street, Chicago, IL 60611-2729. www.alaeditions.org

Acquisitions Editor: Rachel Chance

ALA Editions offers librarians the professional resources they need to serve their patrons and develop their careers is the mission of ALA Editions, the publishing arm of the American Library Association. Its materials cover topics ranging from children's programming to library management strategies. Many of its authors are library information professionals, but ALA Editions is open to working with writers from other disciplines, as long as the research is sound and the advice is practical.

Freelance Potential: Publishes 30–35 titles annually: nearly all by authors who have written for the publishing house before.

Receives 4–5 queries monthly.

Titles: *The Wiki Way of Learning: Creating Learning Experiences Using Collaborative Web Pages,* by Michele Notari, Rebecca Reynolds, Samul Kai Wah Chu, and Beat Dobeli Honegger.

Submissions and Payment: Guidelines and catalogue available at website. Query with outline, 300-word synopsis, table of contents, author biography, and writing sample. Will request proposal if interested. Accepts email to rchance@ala.org. Responds in 6–8 weeks. Publication in 7–10 months. Royalty.

Association for Childhood Education International

1101 16th Street, NW, Washington, DC 20036. www.acei.org

Director of Publications/Editor: Anne Bauer

This nonprofit organization provides resources that enhance childhood education programs throughout the world, and advocate for social reform. Its publishing arm offers books with innovative ideas and practices related to education, literacy, early childhood development, parenting, special education, and curricula-related subjects.

Freelance Potential: Publishes 3 titles annually. Receives 10 unsolicited manuscripts monthly.

Nonfiction: Professional resources for educators and parents of children from infancy through early adolescence. Topics: education theory, innovative practices, key research, global education issues.

Titles: *To Play or Not to Play: Is It Really a Question*, by Christine Jeandheur Ferguson and Ernest Dettore, Jr (educators). *The Earth Is Our Home: Children Caring for the Environment*, by James L. Hoot and Judit Szente (parents and educators).

Submissions and Payment: Guidelines available at website. Submit an initial inquiry on a unique, timely topic that includes an outline or table of contents, an explanation of the topic and audience, and a description of your writing tone (or writing samples). If interested, ACEI will request a proposal, and then a manuscript; details are in the guidelines. No simultaneous submissions. Accepts hard copy. SASE. Responds in 2 weeks. Publication in 1–3 years. No payment.

Alexander Graham Bell Association for the Deaf and Hard of Hearing

3417 Volta Place NW, Washington, DC 20007-2778
http://nc.agbell.org

Production/Editorial Manager

The Alexander Graham Bell Association for the Deaf and Hard of Hearing helps families, health care providers, and education professionals understand childhood hearing loss and the importance of early diagnosis and intervention.

Freelance Potential: Publishes about 6 titles annually. Receives 12–14 queries monthly.

Nonfiction: Books and educational resources. Topics: childhood hearing loss, early intervention, speech development, auditory-verbal therapy, educational management.

Titles: *Learn to Talk Around the Clock: A Professional's Early Intervention Toolbox. The Baby Is Listening.*

Submissions and Payment: Catalogue available at website. Query. Accepts hard copy. SASE. Responds in 3 months. Publication in 9–16 months. Royalty, to 10%.

Claire Publications

Tey Brook Craft Centre, Unit 8, Great Tey, Colchester, Essex CO6 1JE United Kingdom. www.clairepublications.com

Managing Editor: Noel Graham

Educational books and teaching resources for preschool through grade 12 comprise the catalogue of this international publisher. It offers books on all curriculum subjects, as well as titles on early childhood development, special and gifted education, and teaching at home. It seeks products and books that challenge children to think creatively. Although it continues to review submissions for all grade levels, its most pressing need is for kindergarten through grade 6 material.

Freelance Potential: Publishes 5 titles annually: all developed from unsolicited submissions; 40% by authors who are new to the publishing house; 40% by previously unpublished writers. Receives 5 queries, 2 unsolicited manuscripts monthly.

Nonfiction: Books and activity kits, preK–grade 12. Topics: mathematics, English, ESL, science, languages, design and technology, homeschooling, early education, special needs, gifted education.

Titles: *Challenges for Children*, by Sonia Hyams. *Circles: Activities for Children*, by Noel Graham.

Submissions and Payment: Catalogue available at website. Query with résumé and clips, or send complete manuscript. Accepts hard copy and email submissions to mail@clairepublications.com. SAE/IRC. Response time varies. Publication in 1 year. Royalty, 10%.

Collins

1350 Avenue of the Americas, New York, NY 10019
www.collins.co.uk

Known throughout the world for providing accessible and information content in print and digital formats, this imprint of HarperCollins UK is a pioneer in reference publishing. It publishes material for the UK and international school curriculums, as well as titles for home school learning.

Freelance Potential: HarperCollins publishes hundreds of titles annually.

Nonfiction: Early readers, middle grade, YA. Topics include history, language arts, math, science, homeschooling.

Titles: *Primary History Invades,* by Kevin Jane (YA). *Play Foundations - Rhymes and Stories*, by Jean Evans (ages 0–3).

Submissions and Payment: Guidelines and catalogue available at website. Accepts submissions through literary agents only. Publication in 18–36 months. Royalty; advance.

Parents, Divisions, Imprints

HarperCollins, See page 137

Corwin Press

2455 Teller Road, Thousand Oaks, CA 91320. www.corwin.com

Editorial Director: Lisa Shaw

Corwin has one objective: to help you do your important work better. It offers a host of integrated and independent professioanl learning options that conform with every budget.

Freelance Potential: Publishes 260 titles annually. Receives 80+ queries monthly.

Nonfiction: Resource books and manuals for educators, grades K–12. Topics: administration, assessment, evaluation, professional development, curriculum development, classroom practice and management, gifted and special education, bilingual learning, counseling, school health, educational technology.

Titles: *Advocating for English Learners,* by Diane Staehr Fenner. *Girls Without Limits,* by Lisa Hinkelman.

Submissions and Payment: Guidelines and catalogue available at website. Send prospectus with rationale, outline, target audience, competitive titles, length and completion schedule, sample chapters, and résumé. Accepts email (see website for appropriate editor). Response time varies. Publication in 7 months. Royalty.

Course Crafters

P.O. Boc 100, Amesbury, MA 01913
www.coursecrafters.com

CEO & Publisher: Lise Ragan

Course Crafters has specialized in the English language learner market, one of the fastest growing markets in education publishing. It offers books, professional development support and resources for ELLs in content classrooms.

Freelance Potential: Publishes 10–12 titles annually. Receives 1–2 queries monthly.

Nonfiction: Educational materials for English language teachers of grades K–12.

Titles: *Academic Language Notebooks: The Language of Math* (Grades 3–5). *English Language Learner* (ELL) Reference Center (Grades 5–12).

Submissions and Payment: Guidelines available at website. Send résumé and cover letter summarizing ELL experience. Accepts hard copy and email to jobs@coursecrafters.com. SASE. Responds in 1 month. Publication in 1–2 years. Flat fee.

The Creative Company

P.O. Box 227, Mankato, MN 56002
www.thecreativecompany.us

Editor: Aaron Frisch

The Creative Company publishes nonfiction children's book series on a wide variety of subjects. It looks for 4, 6, or 8 titles per series, written at a grade 7 reading level. It also publishes a small number of fiction picture books for young children. It also has imprints Creative Editions, Creative Education, Creative Paperbacks, and Creative Digital.

Freelance Potential: Publishes 100–150 titles annually: 1–10% developed from unsolicited submissions; 50–75% assigned. Receives 10–25 queries, 10–25 unsolicited manuscripts monthly.

Fiction: Early picture books, story picture books, early readers. Genres: adventure, fairy tales, poetry.

Nonfiction: Early picture books, story picture books, early readers, middle-grade. Topics: animals, nature, biography, computers, current events, politics, education, regional, social studies, sports, science, history, architecture, geography, the arts.

Titles: *I Met a Dinosaur*, by Jan Wahl (ages 4–8). *How to Draw with Your Funny Bone*, by Elwood H. Smith (ages 6–10).

Submissions and Payment: Guidelines available. Catalogue available at website. Query with proposal for nonfiction series including an outline of the whole series (4–8 titles) and sample pages. Send complete manuscript for picture books. Accepts hard copy. Accepts simultaneous submissions. SASE. Responds in 2–3 months. Publication period and payment policy vary.

Creative Learning Press

5926 Balcones Drive, Suite 220, Austin, TX 78731
www.creativelearningpress.com

Editor: Kay McDowall

Now a part of Prufrock Press, Creative Learning Press is dedicated to developing quality resources for educators and parents of gifted and talented children. The team at CLP is focused on supporting schools across the country that effectively serve gifted students. It also publishes a limited amount of titles for children and young adults.

Freelance Potential: Publishes 4 titles annually. Receives 8 queries, 8 unsolicited manuscripts monthly.

Nonfiction: Textbooks, educational materials, how-to books, teaching resources, and audio cassettes for grades K–12. Topics: science, mathematics, language arts, geography, history, research skills, business, fine arts, and leadership.

Titles: *101 Success Secrets for Gifted Kids: The Ultimate Handbook,* by Christine Fonseca (parents). *Smart Start: Let's Go to the Market,* by Barbara Dullghan, Nancy B. Hertzog, Ph.D., and Ellen Honeck, Ph.D.

Submissions and Payment: Guidelines and catalogue available at website. Send proposal that includes working title, general description, target audience, marketing and promotion suggestions, annotated table of contents, competition analysis, anticipated length and completion date, and résumé. Accepts hard copy. SASE. For questions, email editorial@prufrock.com. Response time, publication period, and payment policy varies.

Didax

395 Main Street, Rowley, MA 01969. www.didax.com

President: Brian Scarlett

For more than 30 years, Didax has specialized in helping educators to address individual learning styles and diverse student needs. All of its products come directly from teachers and it is open to considering new ideas, needs, or suggestions.
Freelance Potential: Publishes 25 titles annually: 1% by authors who are new to the publishing house.

Nonfiction: Reproducible activity books and teacher resources for preK–grade 8. Topics: math fundamentals, fractions, geometry, algebra, probability, problem-solving, the alphabet, pre-reading, phonics, word study, spelling, vocabulary, writing, reading comprehension, social studies, science, art, and character education.

Titles: *Bully in a Cyber World* (grades 6–8). *Success with Syllables*, by Tony Walsh (grades 2–4).

Submissions and Payment: Catalogue available at website. Query with résumé and outline. Accepts hard copy and email queries to brian@didax.com. Accepts simultaneous submissions if identified. SASE. Responds in 2 weeks. Publication in 1 year. Royalty; advance.

Edupress

P.O. Box 8610, Madison, WI 53708–8610
www.edupressinc.com

Product Development Manager: Liz Bowie

From classroom decor to test prep, Edupress has been providing teachers with quality educational materials for the past 30 years. Its mission is to help busy educators bring fun and excitement to the classroom.

Freelance Potential: Publishes 100+ titles annually: 1–10% by authors who are new to the publishing house. Receives 2+ queries monthly.

Nonfiction: Activity books and resource materials for educators, preK–grade 8. Topics: social studies, science, curriculum coordination, language arts, early learning, math, holidays, arts and crafts, classroom decor.

Titles: *Patterns with a Purpose* (grades K–1). *Hands-On Heritage* (grades 3+).

Submissions and Payment: Guidelines and catalogue available at website. Send proposal and cover letter with résumé, targeted grade range, outline, sample pages, relevant curriculum information, software and platform you use, potential illustrations, and a "Key Market Statement" describing why you wrote/designed the product and competitive products currently in the market. Accepts hard copy and email queries to lbowie@highsmith.com (with "Manuscript Submission" in subject line). SASE. Responds in 2–4 months. Publication in 1 year. Flat fee.

Great Potential Press

1650 North Kolb Road, #200, Tucson, AZ 85715
www.greatpotentialpress.com

Acquisitions Editor: Janet L. Gore, MA, MEd

This award-winning publishing company is devoted to informational resources for gifted adults and for parents, educators, and counselors of gifted children.

Freelance Potential: Publishes 4–8 titles (1–2 juvenile) annually: 75–100% developed from unsolicited submissions; 25–50% by authors who are new to the publishing house; 25–50% by previously unpublished writers. Receives 2+ queries monthly.

Nonfiction: Books and videos for gifted children of all ages, resources for parents and educators. Topics: gifted students, gifted education, academic, social, and emotional needs of gifted children and adults.

Titles: *Smart Girls in the 21st Century: Understanding Talented Girls and Women,* by Barbara A. Kerr, Ph.D. and Robin McKay, Ph.D. *From School to Homeschool: Should You Homeschool Your Gifted Child?,* by Suki Wessling.

Submissions and Payment: Guidelines and catalogue available at website. Query with introduction, market analysis, market statement, competitive titles, estimated length, table of contents, 2 sample chapters, and author biography. Accepts queries through form at website. Responds in 2 months. Publication period varies. Royalty.

Hazelden Publishing

Editorial Department RW 15, P.O. Box 176, Center City, MN 55012-0176. www.hazelden.org

Manuscript Coordinator

This publishing arm of the nonprofit organization Hazelden has an extensive line of prevention books and programs, created specifically for students in elementary through high school. Its mission is to provide products and services to help people recognize, understand, and overcome chemical dependency and closely related problems. Its books are written for professionals in the treatment field, criminal justice workers, prevention specialists, and individuals in or seeking recovery from addiction. Many of its titles target preteens and teens, but it is not interested in receiving submissions of children's books.

Freelance Potential: Publishes 50 titles annually. Receives 26 queries monthly.

Nonfiction: Books for young adults with alcohol and drug addictions, and for parents, teachers, and professionals who work with people suffering from addiction problems. Also publishes ebooks, multimedia products, training materials, and webinars. Topics: alcohol and substance abuse, health, fitness, social issues, mental health, family and relationships, spirituality.

Titles: *Cyber Bullying* (grades 6–12). *Drugs in Trial Marijuana* (YA).

Submissions and Payment: Guidelines and catalogue available at website. Send proposal with an overview and objective of your project, target audience, proposed market, competitive titles, table of contents, an introduction, detailed chapter outline, 2–3 sample chapters, and author biography. Accepts hard copy. SASE. Responds in 3 months. Publication in 12–18 months. Royalty. Flat fee.

Heinemann

361 Hanover Street, Portsmouth, NH 03801-3912
www.heinemann.com

Acquisitions Editor

Heinemann is a publisher of professional resources and a provider of educational services for teachers, kindergarten through college. It urges all prospective writers to review its publishing program at the website before deciding to submit a proposal.

Freelance Potential: Publishes 100 titles annually: 10% by agented authors; 10% by previously unpublished writers. Receives 100+ queries monthly.

Nonfiction: Educational resources and multimedia material for teachers and school administrators. Topics: math, science, social studies, art education, reading, writing, ESL, bilingual education, special and gifted education, early childhood development, school reform, curriculum development, creative arts.

Titles: *Amplify: Digital Teaching and Learning in the K–6 Classroom,* by Katie Muhtaris and Kristin Ziemke. *No More Teaching a Letter a Week*, by Rebecca McKay, William H. Teale.

Submissions and Payment: Guidelines and catalogue available at website. Send a proposal with cover letter, a statement describing your objectives and reasons for writing the book, table of contents with chapter summaries, sample chapters, and résumé. Accepts email to proposals@heinemann.com and hard copy. SASE. Discourages simultaneous submissions. Response time varies. Publication in 10–12 months. Payment policy varies.

Incentive Publications

233 North Michigan Avenue, Suite 2000, Chicago, IL 60601
www.incentivepublications.com

Director of Development & Production: Jill Norris

Incentive Publications, an imprint of World Book produces supplemental resources for student use and instruction. With more than 400 titles available, this company specializes in resources for middle grade students, as well as teaching strategies for grade K–12.

Freelance Potential: Publishes 30 titles annually. Receives 20+ queries monthly.

Nonfiction: Teaching strategy books for all grade levels, and reproducible student materials for grades 5–9. Topics: core curriculum subjects, art, study skills.

Titles: *202 Science Investigations,* by Marjorie Frank (grades K–6). *Because You Teach*, by Kathy Hint-Ullock, Monte Selby, Debbie Silver, and Rick Wormeli (educators).

Submissions and Payment: Guidelines and catalogue available at website. Query with cover letter, table of contents, and a sample chapter. Accepts hard copy. SASE. Responds in 6–8 weeks. Publication period varies. Royalty. Flat fee.

International Reading Association

800 Barksdale Road, P.O. Box 8139, Newark, DE 19714-8139
www.reading.org

Book proposals

Knowing that the ability to read, write, and communicate connects people and empowers them to achieve things they never thought possible, the publishing arm of the International Reading Association produces books for literacy professionals. Its list includes titles on professional development, teacher development, assessment, and all aspects of literacy development for all grade levels. It is especially interested in manuscripts connected to the Common Core State Standards, research-based best practice, and assessment.

Freelance Potential: Publishes 12 titles annually: 10–15% by authors who are new to the publishing house; 50% by previously unpublished writers. Receives 8+ queries monthly.

Nonfiction: Research-based educational titles for policymakers and teachers at all levels, including preservice, teacher educators, and literacy researchers. Topics: literacy programs, reading comprehension, reading research and practice, adolescent literacy, literacy coaching, differentiated literacy, learning/instruction, content-area literacy.

Titles: *Literacy Strong All Year Long: Powerful Lessons for K–2*, by Valerie A Ellery, Lori Oczkus, and Timonthy V. Rasinski.*The Writing Thief,* by Ruth Cullam (educators).

Submissions and Payment: Guidelines and catalogue available at website. Send proposal including: letter of intent containing abstract or overview, intended audience, research base, professional development extensions, and estimated completion date; table of contents, chapter-by-chapter outline, special features and/or supplementary materials, one sample chapter, and author bio. Accepts submissions via website to Manuscript Central. Response time, publication period, and payment policy vary.

Jossey-Bass

One Montgomery Street, Suite 1200, San Francisco, CA 94104
www.josseybass.com/WileyCDA

Editorial Assistant

Jossey-Bass publishes products and services to inform and inspire those interested in developing themselves, their organizations, and communities. Its catalogue includes print and digital books, subscription content, webinars, and online courses. Jossey-Bass is a part of John Wiley & Sons, Inc.

Freelance Potential: Publishes 250 titles annually.

Nonfiction: Adults. Topics: K–12 education, school counseling and psychology, curriculum tools, culture and gender, leadership and administration, assessment and research, teaching strategies, professional development, special education, and technology.

Titles: *Teach Like a Champion 2.0: 63 Techniques that Put Students on the Path to College*, by Doug Lemov.

Submissions and Payment: Accepts project proposals that include the purpose in developing the project, the audience, why the topic is important, what new information will be included, research background, author bio with your relevant experience, outline, chapter descriptions, sample chapters, format, estimated length, completion timetable, and competition information. Accepts hard copy to appropriate editor (see website). Accepts simultaneous submissions but wants the names of the publishers its been submitted to. Response time, publication period, and payment policy vary.

Parents, Divisions, Imprints

Wiley, See page 336

Libraries Unlimited

ABC-CLIO, 130 Cremona Drive, Suite C, Santa Barbara, CA 93117
www.abc-clio.com

Acquisitions Editor

Part of ABC-CLIO, Libraries Unlimited is committed to serving academic, public, school libraries by producing library science textbooks, reference works, practical handbooks, and professional guides of unparalleled quality.

Freelance Potential: Publishes 100 titles annually: 5-10% developed from unsolicited submissions; 50% by authors who are new to the publisher. Receives 35 queries monthly.

Nonfiction: Bibliographies, professional reference titles and materials, textbooks, handbooks, and manuals. Topics: library science, information science, professional development.

Titles: *The Organization of Information*, by Daniel N. Joudrey and Arlene G. Taylor. *Discovering Hidden Treasures in Government Documents: The Master Guide to Library of Congress and National Digital Collections.*

Submissions and Payment: Catalogue available at website. Query with author qualifications. Accepts email (see website for appropriate acquisitions editor) and hard copy. SASE. If interested, publisher will ask for proposal with working title, scope and purpose of book, an outline, methodology and presentation, and competitive titles. Responds in 8–10 weeks. Publication in 10–12 months. Royalty.

Parents, Divisions, Imprints

ABC-CLIO, See page 310

Lorenz Educational Press

P.O. Box 802, Dayton, OH 45401-0802
www.lorenzeducationalpress.com

Submissions

Every product created by Lorenz Educational Press is based on their committment to helping teachers provide a positive educational experience for students. We strive to produce products that embrace its mission to define learning areas vital to developing well-rounded students and empowering our future leaders.

Freelance Potential: Publishes 35 titles annually: 85% developed from unsolicited submissions; 17% by authors who are new to the publishing house; 8% by previously unpublished writers. Receives 100 unsolicited manuscripts monthly.

Nonfiction: Educational teacher resource materials and supplementary classroom materials for preK through grade 12, in print and electronic formats. Topics: arts and crafts, current events, language arts, mathematics, multicultural issues, science, social studies.

Titles: *100 Little Language Lessons*, by Margaret Brinton (grades 1–4). *101 Creative Writing Activities* (grades 3–6).

Submissions and Payment: Guidelines and catalogue available at website. Send complete manuscript with cover letter describing targeted grade level, page count, and content areas covered. Accepts hard copy. SASE. Response time varies. Publication in 1–3 years. Flat fee.

Maupin House

1710 Roe Crest Drive, North Mankato, MN 56003
www.capstonepub.com

Acquisitions Editor

Part of Capstone Professional, the Maupin House imprint provides a wide range of print and eBooks written by today's leading authors. Its authors are classroom practitioners with vast experiences in helping children of all levels and ability succeed academically.

Freelance Potential: Publishes 9 titles annually: 30% by authors who are new to the publishing house. Receives 25 manuscripts monthly.

Nonfiction: Professional educational resources for kindergarten through grade 12. Topics: literacy, writing, reading comprehension.

Titles: *Discovering Voice: Lessons to Teach Reading and Writing of Complex Text*, by Nancy Dean. *Formative Assessment in the New Balanced Classroom*, by Margaret Mary Policastro, Becky McTague, and Diane Mazeski.

Submissions and Payment: Guidelines and catalogue available at website. Send proposal with résumé, publishing credits, book overview, intended audience, research base, intended length, complete table of contents, detailed outline, summary of each chapter, 2 sample chapters, or complete manuscript. Accepts email submissions to proposals@capstonepd.com or hard copy. Response time varies. Publication in 12–18 months. Standard royalty rates.

Mondo Publishing

980 Avenue of the Americas, New York, NY 10018
www.mondopub.com

Editorial Director

Founded in 1986, Mondo Publishing specializes in professional learning. Its dedicated to modeling and supporting best practices in literacy instruction and leadership development. believing that all students can achieve high standards given sufficient time and support. It accepts submissions of both fiction and nonfiction material for emerging and reluctant readers. Work that can be included in any of its existing series is welcome, as are new, stand-alone books.

Freelance Potential: Publishes 30 titles annually.

Fiction: Easy-to-read books, story picture books, chapter books, middle-grade. Genres: contemporary and historical fiction, science fiction, fantasy, mystery, folktales, adventure, humor.

Nonfiction: Early picture books, story picture books, YA. Topics: science, nature, animals, the environment, history, music, crafts, hobbies, language arts.

Titles: *Now I Get it! K–5 Comprehension Strategies for Fiction and Nonfiction. Finding Out About Series: Engaging Animal Series for Grades K–6.*

Submissions and Payment: Catalogue available at website. Query. Accepts hard copy. SASE. Response time varies. Publication in 1–3 years. Royalty.

National Council of Teachers of English

The Books Program, 1111 West Kenyon Road, Urbana, IL 61801-1096. www.ncte.org

Senior Editor: Bonny Graham

The National Council of Teachers of English (NCTE) publishes professional development books and resources for teachers of kindergarten through college. Its books focus on current issues and challenges in teaching, research findings and their applications to classrooms, and ideas for teaching all aspects of English. It is not accepting proposals or manuscripts at this time.

Freelance Potential: Publishes 8–10 titles annually: less than 10% developed from unsolicited submissions.

Nonfiction: Books for English and language arts teachers. Topics: reading, writing, grammar, literature, poetry, rhetoric, censorship, media studies, technology, research, classroom practices, student assessment, professional issues.

Titles: *Connected Learning*, by Mary Ellen Dakin. *Beyond Standardized Truth: Improving Teaching and Learning through Inquiry-Based Reading Assessment*, by Scott Filkins.

Submissions and Payment: Not currently accepting unsolicited submissions for books; check the website for changes to this policy.

National Science Teachers Association Press

1840 Wilson Boulevard, Arlington, VA 22201
www.nsta.org/publications

Submissions

This publishing arm of the National Science Teachers Association produces titles that are of interest to science teachers of students in kindergarten through grade 12 and at the undergraduate college level. It accepts submissions that deal with science content, best teaching methods, and classroom activities; it is especially interested in works that link science with reading or math.

Freelance Potential: Publishes 15–20 titles annually.

Nonfiction: Textbooks, teacher manuals, activity books. Topics: science, teaching techniques.

Titles: *Picture-Perfect Science Lessons,* by Karen Ansberry and Emily Morgan (K–5). *Stop Fakin It! Finally Understanding Science So You Can Teach It*, by Bull Robertson (K–5).

Submissions and Payment: Guidelines and catalogue available at website. Send completed Book Proposal Form (at website), detailed outline or table of contents, curriculum vitae, introduction or preface, and 1 or 2 sample chapters. Accepts electronic submissions through website. For questions, email: nstapresseditorialof@nsta.org. Publication in 6 months. Royalty.

Pembroke Publishers

538 Hood Road, Markham, Ontario L3R 3K9 Canada
www.pembrokepublishers.com

President: Mary Macchiusi

Pembroke has produced top-quality, practical books for teaching and learning since 1985. Its products explore a wide range of topics, from reading and writing, to drama and speaking, to critical thinking and technology in the classroom.

Freelance Potential: Publishes 20 titles annually: 5% by authors who are new to the publishing house. Receives 4+ queries monthly.

Nonfiction: Chapter books, middle-grade. Topics: history, science, writing, notable Canadians. Also publishes titles for educators about reading, writing, literacy learning, drama, the arts, school leadership, discipline, and working with parents.

Titles: *Power Up: Making the Shift to 1:1 Teaching and Learning*, by Diane Neebe and Jen Roberts. *The Construction Zone: Building Scaffolds for Readers and Writers*, by Terry Thompson.

Submissions and Payment: Guidelines available. Catalogue available at website. Query with résumé, outline, and sample chapter. Accepts hard copy. SAE/IRC. Accepts simultaneous submissions if identified. Responds in 1 month. Publication in 6–24 months. Royalty.

Portage & Main Press

100-318 McDermot Avenue, Winnipeg, Manitoba R3A 0A2 Canada
www.portageandmainpress.com

Acquisitions Editor

This independent Canadian publisher offers a wide range of innovative and practical K–12 educational materials. It seeks to build dynamic learning communities by bringing together authors, educators, and students. Portage & Main is not currently accepting submissions. Check the website for updates to this policy.

Freelance Potential: Publishes 15 titles annually.

Nonfiction: Educational resource books for teachers, grades K–12. Topics: literacy, reading, writing, spelling, assessment, ESL/ELL, arts education, readers theater, conflict resolution, language arts, science, mathematics, social studies.

Titles: *Teaching to Diversity: The Three-Block Model of Universal Design for Learning*, by Jennifer Katz. *Hands On Mathematics*, (grades 1–4).

Submissions and Payment: Guidelines and catalogue available at website. It is currently closed to unsolicited submissions. Check website for changes to this policy. Publication in 6 months. Royalty, 8–12%.

Prufrock Press

5926 Balcones Drive, Suite 220, Austin, TX 78731
www.prufrock.com

Submissions Editor: Lacy Compton

Prufrock Press is the nation's leading publisher supporting the education of gifted and advanced learners. Its line of more than 500 titles offers teachers and parents exciting research-based ideas for gifted, advanced, and special needs learners. It is actively seeking quality material written by professionals and educators.

Freelance Potential: Publishes 45–50 titles annually: 30% by authors who are new to the publishing house.

Nonfiction: Supplemental classroom materials and talent development resources for gifted and advanced learners in grades K–12, professional development books for teachers, resources for children with special needs, primary and supplementary college textbooks, trade books, general education, children's and teens' nonfiction. Topics: math; science; social studies; language arts; thinking skills; problem-solving; research; presentation skills; differentiated instruction; teaching strategies; independent study; identifying, parenting, and counseling gifted children; enrichment.

Titles: *Advanced Reading Instruction in Middle School: A Novel Approach,* by Janice I. Robbins, PH.D. *Challenging Common Core Math Lessons: Activities and Extensions for Gifted and Advanced Learners in Grade 5,* by Margaret Jess McKowen Patti.

Submissions and Payment: Guidelines and catalogue available at website. Send prospectus with working title, general book description, target market, annotated table of contents, competitive titles, your book's unique qualities, length, anticipated completion date, marketing suggestions, and résumé. Accepts hard copy. SASE. No simultaneous submissions. Responds in 10–12 weeks. Publication period varies. Royalty; advance. To be considered for freelance projects, send résumé to editorial@prufrock.com.

Redleaf Press

10 Yorkton Court, St. Paul, MN 55117–1065
www.redleafpress.org

Acquisitions and Development Editor: Kyra Ostendorf

Established in 1973, Redleaf Press is a leading nonprofit publisher of exceptional curriculum, management, and business resources for early childhood professionals. Its products aim to improve the lives of children by strengthening and supporting the teachers, trainers, and families who care for them.

Freelance Potential: Publishes 20–30 titles annually: 10–25% developed from unsolicited submissions; 1–10% assigned; 10–25% by authors who are new to the publishing house; 50–75% by previously unpublished writers. Receives 1–10 queries monthly.

Nonfiction: Books for educators on social/emotional issues; curriculum, management, and business resources for early child care professionals. Topics: math, science, language, literacy, cultural diversity, music, movement, health, safety, nutrition, child development, special needs, and teacher training and assessment.

Titles: *Noah Chases the Wind*, by Michelle Worthington (ages 3–6). *When You Just Have to Roar!*, by Rachel Robertson (ages 3–6).

Submissions and Payment: Guidelines and catalogue available at website. Does not accept proposals for children's picture books. Query with cover letter that describes book idea, intended audience, competition analysis, and author's expertise; résumé or CV; outline; table of contents; and sample chapters. Accepts email queries to acquisitions@redleafpress.org with Word attachments, and hard copy. Responds in 6 weeks. Publication in 24 months. Royalty for authors; fee-based payment for freelancers.

Red Line Editorial

1686 East Cliff Road, Burnsville, MN 55337
http://reditorial.com

President: Bob Temple

This book packager specializes in producing high-quality books for educators. It recognizes the need to meet school curricula needs, contain features that librarians seek, and still be appealing to young readers. It offers writers work-for-hire assignments for texts. Topics are mostly nonfiction. Red Line also produces trade books and offers editorial services.

Freelance Potential: Unavailable.

Nonfiction: Story picture books, early readers, middle grade, YA. Topics: history, science, sports, health, political science.

Titles: *Bridget and Bo Build a Blog,* by Amanda St. John (grades 2–4). Technology Pioneers series, (grades 5–8).

Submissions and Payment: Guidelines available at website. Send résumé and list of publishing credits. Prefers email to jobs@redline-editorial.com. Work for hire.

Ruckus Media Group

372 Danbury Road, Wilton, CT 06897. www.ruckusmediagroup.com

President: Rick Richter

Ruckus Media Group creates interactive applications for mobile devices designed to entertain and educate children. The Ruckus app delights children with interactive storybooks featuring well-known characters and brands.

Freelance Potential: Publishes 40 digital titles annually. Actively looking for new content.

Fiction: Early picture books, story picture books, early readers. Genres: adventure, fantasy, contemporary, licensed characters.

Nonfiction: Story picture books, early readers. Topics: animals, biography.

Titles: *Sid the Science Kid: Sid the Weatherman* (ages 2–6). *SeaWorld Penguin Pals* (ages 3–6).

Submissions and Payment: Guidelines and catalogue available at website. Submissions accepted via form on website. Response time, publication period, and payment policy vary.

Scarecrow Press

4501 Forbes Boulevard, Suite 200, Lanham, MD 20706
www.scarecrowpress.com

Senior Editor: Stephen Ryan

Best known for publishing scholarly, general interest, and reference works for the patrons of public, school, and academic libraries, as well as professional books for the librarians that serve them. Among the many topics covered are religions, wars, ancient civilizations, and politics.

Freelance Potential: Publishes 180 titles annually: 65% developed from unsolicited submissions; 5% by agented authors. Receives 100 queries, 12 unsolicited manuscripts monthly.

Nonfiction: Handbooks, reference tools, bibliographies, historical dictionaries, library science monographs, and other scholarly and professional works. Topics: the humanities, history, geography, religion, social and multicultural issues, ancient civilizations, music, science, library and information science.

Titles: *The Strong Gray Line War-time Reflections from the West Point Class of 2004*, edited by Cory Wallace. *Pete Seeger Discography*, by David King Dunaway.

Submissions and Payment: Guidelines and catalogue available at website. Query with tentative title, scope and purpose of book, target audience and potential market, potential expert reviewers, competitive titles, table of contents, market analysis, length, completion date, plans for illustrations, at least 2 sample chapters, and brief author bio. Prefers email to appropriate editor (Word attachments), see website for information; accepts hard copy. SASE. Response time varies. Publication in 6–12 months. Royalty, 8–12.5%.

Shell Education

5301 Oceanus Drive, Huntington Beach, CA 92649
www.shelleducation.com

Editor in Chief

Shell Education creates supplemental educational resources including practical, classroom-tested ideas, and professional development resources to administrators and educators internationally. It presents classroom-tested, standards and research-based solution for all training needs.

Freelance Potential: Number of books and other materials published annually is unavailable. Open to submissions.

Nonfiction: Early readers, middle-grade, YA. Topics: differentiation, professional development, math, science, writing, language arts, social studies, technology.

Titles: *Rhythm and Rhyme Literacy Time Level K. Think It, Show It Science: Strategies for Demonstrating Knowledge*, (grades 3–8).

Submissions and Payment: Guidelines and catalogue available at website. Query with 10–12 sample pages; outline or table of contents; and 1-page summary describing intended audience, content, and objectives. Accepts hard copy only. SASE. Response time, publication period, and payment policy vary.

Smith & Kraus

P.O. Box 127, Lyme, NH 03768. www.smithandkraus.com

Editor: Carol Boynton

Smith and Kraus is the leading source for books about theater—from collections of monologues and scenes for use in class or at auditions, to contemporary and classic play collections, to acting technique and career resource titles.

Freelance Potential: Publishes 12–24 titles annually: 45–50% by authors new to the publishing house. Receives 8+ queries monthly.

Fiction: Collections of plays, scenes, and monologues, grades K–12. Also publishes anthologies, translations, and collections of works by contemporary playwrights.

Nonfiction: Instructional books for teachers, grades K–12. Topics: theater history, stage production, Shakespeare, movement, dramatizing literature.

Titles: *The Complete TIPS Ideas for Actors,* by Jon Jory (YA–A). *Plays from Fairy Tales: Grades K–3*, by L. E. McCullough (Adult).

Submissions and Payment: Guidelines and catalogue available at website. Query with synopsis and writing sample; include reviews/production information if querying about a play. Accepts hard copy and email queries to editor@smithandkraus.com. SASE. Accepts simultaneous submissions if identified. Responds in 1–2 months. Publication in 1 year. Royalty; advance. Flat fee.

Southern Early Childhood Association

P.O. Box 55930, Little Rock, AR 72215-5930
www.southernearlychildhood.org

Editor: Janet F. Brown

The Southern Early Childhood Association is committed to improving the quality of care and education for young children and their families through advocacy and professional development. Along with book proposals, it accepts article submissions for its refereed journal and newsletter. All of its publications support high-quality experiences for young children, their families, and educators by advancing the best practices in, and knowledge base of, early childhood education.

Freelance Potential: Publishes 2 titles annually. Receives fewer than 1 unsolicited manuscript monthly.

Nonfiction: Early childhood and professional resource books. Topics: emergent curriculum for children from birth to age 8, professional development strategies, effective classroom practices, program administration, relationships with families.

Titles: *Activities that Build the Young Child's Brain*, by Suzanne Gellens, M.S. *Behavior Guidance for Infant and Toddlers,* by Alice Honig.

Submissions and Payment: Guidelines and catalogue available at website. Send complete manuscript and prospectus with intent and purpose of book, audience, approach, abstract, annotated outline or list of chapters, special features, sample chapter, and author qualifications. Accepts email queries to editor@southernearlychildhood.org. Responds in 3 months. Publication period varies. Royalty, 10%.

Teacher Created Resources

6421 Industry Way, Westminster, CA 92683
www.teachercreated.com

Editor in Chief: Karen Goldfluss

This educational publisher has an extensive inventory of quality and affordable materials, school supplies, lessons, and more. Teacher Created Resources is currently interested in acquiring ELL titles for K–8 and books in the areas of language arts, reading, math, science, and social studies. Books should be based on successful classroom lessons. The majority of titles are created by teachers for teachers and parents.

Freelance Potential: Publishes 50–75 titles annually: 10–25% developed from unsolicited submissions; 50–75% assigned; 5% by authors who are new to the publishing house; 5% by previously unpublished writers.

Nonfiction: Publishes workbooks, activity books, teacher resources, and classroom aids, aimed at preK–grade 8. Topics include writing, reading, science, geography, history, technology, Christian education. Also publishes teacher materials on student testing, multiple intelligences, assessment, and classroom management.

Titles: *Comprehending Text Using Literal, Inferential, and Applied Questioning* (Grade 5). *U.S. History Little Books: Famous Events* (grades (K–3).

Submissions and Payment: Guidelines and catalogue available at website. Query with résumé, summary, intended audience, table of contents, and 10–12 manuscript pages. Accepts hard copy. SASE. Responds in 6 months. Publication in 3–12 months. Work-for-hire, flat fee.

Charles C. Thomas Publisher

2600 South First Street, Springfield, IL 62704
www.ccthomas.com

Editor: Michael P. Thomas

This publisher has been producing a strong list of specialty titles and textbooks in biomedical science since 1927. It has an active program in producing books for the behavioral sciences, education and special education, speech-language and hearing, as well as rehabilitation and long-term care. Charles C. Thomas is also one of the largest producers of books in all areas of criminal justice and law enforcement.

Freelance Potential: Publishes 60 titles annually: all developed from unsolicited submissions. Receives 50 queries and unsolicited manuscripts monthly.

Nonfiction: Titles for educators, preK–grade 12. Topics: early childhood, elementary, and higher education; reading; research and statistics; physical education and sports; special education; the learning disabled; teaching the blind and visually impaired; gifted and talented education; speech-language pathology. Also publishes parenting titles and professional development books for the science and criminal justice fields.

Titles: *Best Practice in Motivation and Management in the Classroom*, by Dennis G. Wiseman and Gilbert H. Hunt. *Decoding Challenging Classroom Behaviors: What Every Teacher and Paraeducator Shoud Know!*, by Ennio Cipani.

Submissions and Payment: Guidelines and catalogue available at website. Query with preface outlining scope, plan, and purpose of your manuscript (300 words or more); possible illustrations; tentative outline and contents; estimated size and completion schedule; curriculum vitae; and authors/editors marketing questionnaire (on website). Or send complete manuscript with accompanying disk (Word format). Each section of the manuscript should be saved as a separate file, i.e. title page, preface, table of contents, list of figures or tables, etc. Accepts hard copy with disk. SASE. Response time varies. Publication in 6+ months. Payment policy, unknown.

Wiley

111 River Street, Hoboken, NJ 07030-5774
www.wiley.com/WileyCDA

Editor

Wiley is a large reference and educational publisher that includes nonfiction for children and teens in its mix. Among its imprints and brands are CliffsNotes, the Dummies books, and Jossey-Bass. In addition to educational books for students, the company publishes books on parenting, reference, self-help, and technology, as well as books for educators and counselors of children and teens. It also offers products and services on the Internet, along with a platform for scientific, technical, medical, and professional content, now called Wiley Online Library.

Freelance Potential: Publishes hundreds of titles annually.

Nonfiction: Middle-grade, YA, adult. Topics: accounting, agriculture, arts, business, computers, culinary, economics, education, engineering, environment, languages, lifestyle, math, medicine, psychology, reference, science, social sciences.

Titles: *African American Millionaires,* by Otha Richard Sullivan (YA). *American Medical Association Boy's Guide to Becoming a Teen* (12+).

Submissions and Payment: Guidelines and catalogue available at website. See website for specific guidelines for each division. Response time, publication period, and payment policy vary.

Parents, Divisions, Imprints

Jossey-Bass, See page 322

Young Palmetto Books

University of South Carolina Press
1600 Hampton Street, 5th floor, Columbia, SC 29208
www.sc.edu/uscpress/microsites/ypbooks/index.html

Book Series Editor: Kim Shealy Jeffcoat

Young Palmetto Books, an educational children's and young adult book series, is a publishing partnership between the Universty of South Carolina Press and the South Carolina Center for Children's Books and Literacy. A series educational board identifies new projections with connections to South Carolina authors and subjects.

Freelance Potential: Unavailable.

Fiction: Story picture books, middle-grade, YA. Themes: historical, regional, mystery, contemporary.

Nonfiction: Story picture books, middle-grade, YA. Topics: history, food, biography, travel, all with a South Carolina focus.

Titles: *AIDS in the End Zone,* by Kendra S. Albright and Karen W. Gavigan (YA). *Katie's Cabbage*, by Michelle H. Martin (ages 8–12).

Submissions and Payment: Guidelines and catalogue available at website. Send cover letter that describes scope, purpose, and length of the work, representative samples of illustrations, author résumé and complete ms for picture books; table of contents and representative chapter for longer works. Accepts hard copy and email to specific editors by topic. Check website for editor details. Response time, publication period, and payment policy, unavailable.

YouthLight

P.O. Box 115, Chapin, SC 29036
www.youthlightbooks.com

Submission Editor

YouthLight develops useful educational materials to help counselors, educators, mental health professionals, and parents maximize their effectiveness with young people. Its wide array of titles deal with everything from bullying and anger management to self-esteem and conflict resolution.

Freelance Potential: Publishes 15–20 titles annually: 40% developed from unsolicited submissions; 10% by authors who are new to the publishing house; 5% by previously unpublished writers. Receives 4 queries monthly.

Fiction: Easy-to-read books, story picture books, middle-grade, YA. Themes: multicultural fiction and stories about children dealing with social pressures.

Nonfiction: Easy-to-read books, story picture books, middle-grade, YA. Topics: self-help, social issues. Also publishes titles for adults.

Titles: *Why Do I Hurt Myself?*, by Susan Bowman and Karen Dean (grades 3–6). *Social Skills Comics: Handling Anxiety in School,* by Michael Canavan and Lawrence Shapiro (grades 2–7).

Submissions and Payment: Guidelines and catalogue available at website. Query with type of work (book, CD, kit), title, outline, and sample pages, or send complete manuscript. Include résumé, target audience, and marketing plan with all submissions. Prefers online submissions through website. Accepts hard copy. Responds in 1–3 months. Publication in 6 months. Royalty, 10%.

Parenting Publishing

Personal experience may be the motivating factor in writing books directed at parents, as there are many struggles that need to find an answer. The combination of writing books for children and teens with writing books about young people can offer additional opportunities for those passionate about raising and supporting kids.

The publishing companies in this section devote some or all of their focus to parenting books. Some have an even more defined niche: adoption, autism and other disorders, military families, healthy pregnancy and child development, family travel, emotional health, family nutrition, relationships, dealing with life struggles, and, on the other end of the spectrum, books about creating a home, parties, and activities for children.

Some of these publishers offer titles that target parents primarily, and some have books for adults and books for children. They represent another potential realm of writing for those looking to expand their careers.

Active Parenting Publishers

1220 Kennestone Circle, Suite 130, Marietta, GA 30066-6022
www.activeparenting.com

Product Development Manager: Molly Davis

Active Parenting Publishers provides video-based parenting courses and programs as well as parenting books that give parents the skills to help children thrive in a changing world. Its titles cover child development issues from birth through the teen years. The company also offers video-based educational programs for parents, children, and teachers, as well as hospitals, social service organizations, churches, and even corporations. The material is largely based on the active parenting theories of Alfred Adler and Rudolf Dreikurs, and strives to provide resources to build responsibility, courage, cooperation, and respect.

Freelance potential: Publishes about 4 titles annually. Receives 8–10 queries, 8 unsolicited manuscripts monthly.

Nonfiction: Parenting and educational books and videos. Topics: gifted and special education, social issues, parenting, self-help, education, real life/problems.

Titles: *Cooperative Parenting and Divorced Parent's Guide,* by Susan Boyan and Ann Marie Termini. *Co-Parenitng with a Toxic Ex*, by Amy J. L. Baker, Ph.D. and Paul R. Fine LCSW.

Submissions and Payment: Catalogue available at website. Query or send complete manuscript. Accepts hard copy and email submissions to cservice@activeparenting.com. SASE. Response time and publication period vary. Royalty. Flat fee.

Autism Asperger Publishing Company

11209 Strang Line Rd, Lenexa, KS 66215
www.aapcpublishing.net

Submissions: Kirsten McBride

AAPC Publishing is dedicated to providing practical, research-based solutions and promoting autism awareness through books for individuals with autism spectrum and related disorders across the lifespan.

Freelance Potential: Publishes about 30 titles (15% juvenile) annually: 15% developed from unsolicited submissions; 85% by authors who are new to the publishing house; 85% by previously unpublished writers. Receives 20 queries monthly.

Fiction: Story picture books, early readers, chapter books, middle-grade, YA. Genres: mystery, fantasy, education, real life/problems.

Nonfiction: YA, adult. Topics: education, social skills, health, real life/problems.

Titles: *The Secret Rules of Social Networking*, by Barbara Klipper and Rhonda Shapiro-Rieser. *Stuck! Strategies: What to Do When Students Get STUCK*, by Janice Carroll abd Terry Ellis Izraelevitz.

Submissions and Payment: Guidelines available. Query with cover letter including concept statement, intended audience, and what makes your book unique; table of contents/outline; synopsis and approximate length of each chapter; 1–2 sample chapters; suggested illustrations; author profile establishing your credibility; and promotion suggestions. Accepts hard copy only. SASE. Responds in 3–6 months. Publication in 8 months. Royalty, 10%.

Da Capo Press

44 Farnsworth Street, 3rd Floor, Boston, MA 02210
www.dacapopress.com

Editorial Director

Part of the Perseus Book Group, Da Capo Press offers a wide-ranging list of mostly nonfiction titles in both hardcover and paperback. Its books focus on history, music, performing arts, sports, and popular culture.

Freelance Potential: Publishes about 70 titles annually: all by agented authors. Receives 12–15 queries monthly.

Fiction: Adult. Genres: historical, short stories, fantasy, social issues, contemporary, mystery.

Nonfiction: Adult. Topics: history, health, nature, current events, entertainment, parenting, pregnancy, science, social issues, multicultural issues, religion, sports, self-help, humor, biography, cooking, crafts, arts, animals.

Titles: *10 Days to a Less Defiant Child*, by Jeffrey Bernstein.

Parenting on the Go, by David Elkind.

Submissions and Payment: Catalogue available at website. Does not accept unsolicited proposals or manuscripts. Only accepts agented submissions. Publication in 1 year. Royalty; advance.

Elva Resa

8362 Tamarack Village, Suite 119-106, St. Paul, MN 55125
www.elvaresa.com

Acquisitions: Elizabeth Snow

The small, independent publisher has a mission to make a positive difference in people's lives. It publishes books, newsletters, and workshop materials for and about military families. The children's imprint, Alma Little, publishes general interest picture books and novels for children up to age 10. Elva Resa also features books that cover military life topics for teens.

Freelance Potential: Publishes about 5 titles annually: 10–25% developed from unsolicited submissions; 75–100% assigned; 25–50% by authors who are new to the publishing house; 10–25% by previously unpublished writers. Receives 100–150 queries,15+ manuscripts monthly.

Nonfiction: Families. Topics: self-help, current events/politics, how-to, activities, biography, inspirational, real life/problems, religious, reference, parenting, military resources.

Titles: *The Good Fire Helmet,* Tim Hoppey (ages8+). *The Deployment Journal for Kids,* by Rachel Robertson, (ages 6+).

Submissions and Payment: Guidelines and catalogue available at website. Accepts submissions during their annual open call only. Check website for more information. Email queries only (Word or PDF attachments), including target audience, market opportunity, how your book compares with others on the market, and a book outline to submissions@elvaresa.com. Also accepts queries and résumés for work-for-hire assignments. Responds in 3 weeks if interested. Publication in 12–24 months. Royalty; advance. Flat fee.

Parents, Divisions, Imprints

Alma Little, See page 72

Familius

P.O. Box 204, Huntsville, UT 84317-0204
www.familius.com

Acquisitions Editor: Michele Lynne Robbins

Familius is all about strengthening families. Collectively, its authors and staff have experienced a wide piece of the family-life spectrum. Its mission is to help families be happy by creating beautiful books that teach, inspire, and bring families together.

Freelance Potential: Plans to publish about 50 titles annually digitally and approximately 30 in print. Receives 20 queries monthly.

Fiction: Story picture books, early readers, chapter books. Genres: social skills, social issues, contemporary, historical.

Nonfiction: All ages. Topics: parenting, marriage, family fun, health and wellness, education, children.

Titles: *Has Hollywood Lost Its Mind? A Parent's Guide to Movie Ratings*, by Chris Hicks. *Dude to Dad,* by Hugh Weber.

Submissions and Payment: Guidelines and catalogue available at website. Submit book idea, outline, elevator pitch, marketing platforms, writing sample, and author bio through the submission form at the website. Response time varies. Publication period varies. Royalty, 30% on digital and 10–20% on print versions, paid monthly.

Globe Pequot Press

246 Goose Lane, P.O. Box 480, Guilford, CT 06437
www.globepequot.com

Submissions Editor

For more than 60 years, Globe Pequot has been at the forefront of the movement to save local history for future generations. Its books tell untold or little known stories from history, celebrate the unique or iconic characteristics of specific places, and tap into local pride.

Freelance Potential: Publishes 400+ titles annually: many developed from unsolicited submissions; some reprint/licensed properties; about 20% by authors who are new to the publishing house. Receives 20–30 queries monthly.

Fiction: Adult. Genres: regional, mystery, adventure, outdoors, history.

Nonfiction: Adult. Topics: outdoor life, camping, hiking, nature, animals, travel, recreation, sports, regional, pets, biography, cooking, current events, home and garden, self-help, inspirational.

Titles: *Haunted Philadelphia*, by Darcu Oordt. *A Love for the Beautiful: Discovering America's Hidden Art Museums*, by Susan Jaques.

Submissions and Payment: Guidelines and catalogue available at website. Globe is currently closed to unsolicited manuscript and proposal submissions but is still offering freelance work. To be considered, send résumé, writing credits, and 3 brief writing samples. Accepts hard copy. Responds in 3 months. Publication in 18 months. Royalty, 8–12%; advance, $500–$1,500.

Harvard Common Press

535 Albany Street, 5th Floor, Boston, MA 02118
www.harvardcommonpress.com

Senior Editor: Valerie Cimino

Based in Boston, Massachusetts, this trade publisher produces parenting and child care titles that are renowned for combining professional advice with nurturing support. It also publishes high-quality cookbooks.

Freelance Potential: Publishes about 10 titles annually: 50% by agented authors. Receives 20 queries monthly.

Nonfiction: Adults. Topics: cooking, parenting, child care, family, pregnancy and birth.

Titles: *25 Things Every Mother Should Know*, by Martha and William Sears. *Crying Baby, Sleepless Nights,* by Sandy Jones.

Submissions and Payment: Guidelines and catalogue available at website. Query or send proposal with résumé, chapter-by-chapter outline, introduction, 1–2 sample chapters (for cookbooks include recipe list and sample recipe), market analysis, and competition report. Accepts hard copy, or email queries to editorial@harvardcommonpress.com. Responds only if interested. Publication period and payment policy vary.

Hunter House

445 Park Avenue, 9th Floor, New York, NY 10022
www.hunterhouse.com

Acquisitions

This imprint from Turner Publishing publishes books on physical, mental, and emotional health. It also produces titles on parenting and family issues, child development, and specialized teaching and counseling resources. It aims to present comprehensive books that provide balanced information, often for a neglected audience. It looks for authors with credentials in their subject area.

Freelance Potential: Publishes about 12 titles (4 juvenile) annually: most are developed from unsolicited submissions. Receives 15–25 queries monthly.

Nonfiction: Workbooks for children, YA, adults. Topics: health, fitness, family, personal growth, relationships, sexuality, violence prevention and intervention, teaching and counseling materials, lesser-known illnesses.

Titles: *Hey, Gid? Yes, Charles: Conversations on Life, Loss and Love,* by Rebecca H. Cooper. *The Secret Language of Women*, by Nina Romano.

Submissions and Payment: Guidelines and catalogue available at website. Query with proposal containing an overview, chapter-by-chapter outline, approximate length, illustrations and other features, author biography, and market analysis. Accepts hard copy, or email to submissions@turnerpublishing.com. Accepts simultaneous submissions if identified. SASE. Responds in 3–4 months. Publication in 1–2 years. Royalty.

Impact Publishers

P.O. Box 6016, Atascadero, CA 93423-6016
www.impactpublishers.com

Acquisitions Editor: Freeman Porter

Impact Publishers has joined forces with New Harbinger Publications. At press time, the merger and transition was still underway. Check the website for updates and current needs.

Freelance Potential: Publishes 5–10 titles annually. Receives 60–70 queries monthly.

Nonfiction: Middle-grade, YA, adult. Topics: emotional development, self-esteem, self-expression, marriage, divorce, careers, social issues, parenting, child development and behavior, health and wellness, practical therapy on parenting, divorce recovery, stress, personal growth, and mental health.

Titles: *The Child Custody Book,* by Judge James W. Stewart. *Finding Meaning, Facing Fears: In the Autumn of Your Years (45-65),* by Jerrold Lee Shapiro.

Submissions and Payment: Guidelines and catalogue available at website. Writers must be licensed professionals. Review the website prior to submitting material as guidelines may change with the merger. Query with letter of introduction, book summary, intended audience, author credentials, market analysis, annotated table of contents, sample chapters, and résumé. Accepts hard copy or email queries to submissions@impactpublishers.com. SASE. Responds in 4–12 weeks. Publication in 1 year. Royalty, 10–15%; advance.

Love and Logic Press

2207 Jackson Street, Golden, CO 80401-2300
www.loveandlogic.com

The Love and Logic Institute is dedicated to making parenting and teaching fun and rewarding, instead of stressful and chaotic. We provide practical tools and techniques that help adults achieve respectful, healthy relationships with their children.

Freelance Potential: Publishes 8–10 titles annually: all are assigned.

Nonfiction: Adults. Topics: parenting, family, discipline, education, social issues.

Titles: *Love and Logic Magic for Early Childhood*, by Jim Fay and Charles Fay, Ph.D.

Submissions and Payment: Catalogue available at website. All work is assigned. Send résumé only. No queries or unsolicited manuscripts.

Magination Press

750 First Street NE, Washington, DC 20002-4242
www.maginationpress.com

Director: Kristine Enderle

This imprint of the American Psychological Association publishes books related to mental health and psychological concerns. It seeks respectful and insightful child-driven fiction and kid/teen-friendly self-help that addresses issues and reflects children's inner experiences and points of view. Prefers titles written by PhD or PsyD psychologists. It does not want instructional books or classroom tools. All titles must contain relevant and accurate psychological research and follow established principles of psychology.

Freelance Potential: Publishes 10–12 titles annually: 1–10% developed from unsolicited submissions; 75–80% assigned; 1–10% by authors who are new to the publishing house; 1–10% by previously unpublished writers. Receives 75-100 unsolicited manuscripts monthly.

Fiction: Story picture books, chapter books, middle-grade. Topics: real life, social issues, family issues, social skills, mental health.

Nonfiction: Middle-grade, YA. Topics: divorce, ADHD/ADD, learning disabilities, depression, death, anxieties, self-esteem, family matters, real life/problems, self-help, social issues, social skills, mental health, workbooks.

Titles: *How I Learn: A Kid's Guide to Learning Disability,* by Brenda S. Miles PhD and Colleen A. Patterson, MA. *Learning to Be Kind and Understand Differences: Empathy Skills for Kids with ADHD,* by Judith M. Glasser PhD and Jill Menkes Kushner, MA.

Submissions and Payment: Guidelines and catalogue available at website. Send complete manuscript with résumé, synopsis, market analysis, and intended audience. Accepts hard copy only. SASE. Responds if interested. Publication in 18–24 months. Royalty.

Meadowbrook Press

6110 Blue Circle Drive, Suite 237, Minnetonka, MN 55343
www.meadowbrookpress.com

Submissions Editor

Meadowbrook specializes in titles on pregnancy, baby care, child care, and party planning; it also publishes activity books and humorous poetry for children, and humorous yet practical nonfiction books for grandparents, parents-to-be, and parents of babies and young children. When submitting a proposal, explain why you think your book will sell and your qualifications for writing it.

Freelance Potential: Publishes 10 titles annually. Receives 8+ queries monthly.

Nonfiction: Concept books, middle-grade, adult. Topics: toilet training, school, party games, arts and crafts, pregnancy, childbirth, child care, breastfeeding, and parenting. Also publishes poetry, nursery rhymes, and activity books.

Titles: *Early Bird Gets the Worm*, by Bruce Lansky. (ages 5–8). *Laurie Bird Preston in Playing for Pride*, by Timothy Tocker (ages 8–12).

Submissions and Payment: Guidelines and catalogue available at website. Query with book description, plans for illustrations, market analysis, potential secondary distribution channels, competitive titles, your book's unique qualities, table of contents, sample chapter, and publishing credits. Accepts hard copy (send to the attention of "Submissions Editor"). Accepts simultaneous submissions if identified. No SASE. Responds in 4 months only if interested. Publication in 2 years. Royalty; advance.

New Harbinger Publications

5674 Shattuck Avenue, Oakland, CA 94609
www.newharbinger.com

Acquisitions Director: Catharine Sutker

The books from New Harbinger are grounded in science, careful research, and a tradition of empirically validated clinical practice. Its self-help books teach skills to use to significantly improve the quality of their lives.

Freelance Potential: Publishes 50 titles (7 juvenile) annually: about 60% developed from unsolicited submissions; 40% by agented authors; 10% reprint/licensed properties; 60% by authors who are new to the publishing house; 75% by previously unpublished writers. Receives 50 queries, 50 manuscripts monthly.

Nonfiction: Therapeutic workbooks for children and young adults. Topics: communication, divorce, adoption, pregnancy,

ADHD, autism, sensory processing disorder, depression, social anxiety, eating disorders, self-injury, self-control. Also publishes parenting titles.

Titles: *The Cognitive Behavioral Workbook for Depression*, by William J. Knauss.. *The Bullying Workbook for Teens* , by Raychelle Cassada Lohmann MS, LPC, Julia V. Taylor MA, and Haley Kilpatrick.

Submissions and Payment: Guidelines and catalogue available at website. Send 2- to 3-page prospectus only (no manuscripts) explaining your primary and secondary audiences, the precise problem the book addresses, new or breakthrough techniques it covers, and 3 key selling points, along with a table of contents, 1–3 chapters, analysis of the competition, estimated completion date, and résumé. Accepts hard copy (to the attention of the acquisitions department) and email to proposals@newharbinger. com. SASE. Responds in 2–3 months. Publication in 9 months. Royalty; advance. Flat fee.

New Horizon Press

P.O. Box 669, Far Hills, NJ 07931
www.newhorizonpressbooks.com

Submissions: Ms. P. Patty

The catalogue from New Horizon Press features self-help titles for children on contemporary social and emotional issues, and books for parents on family relationships. For adults and young adults, it publishes books on true crime, social issues, self-help subjects, and true stories of real heroes. It looks for submissions that fit its :60 Second series as well as targeted self-help topics and hard-hitting issues with news impact and publicity value.

Freelance Potential: Publishes 12 titles (1 juvenile) annually: about 40% developed from unsolicited submissions; 100% by authors who are new to the publishing house; 90% by previously unpublished writers. Receives 141 queries, 125 unsolicited manuscripts monthly.

Nonfiction: Publishes self-help titles for children and adults on family, parenting, and relationship issues.

Titles: *Losing Patience: The Problems, Alarms, and Psychological Issues of Shaken Baby Syndrome*, by James Peinkofer, LCSW. *Adopting Older Children*, by Stephanie Bosco-Ruggiero MA, Gloria Russo Wassell LMHC, and Victor Groza Ph.D.

Submissions and Payment: Guidelines and catalogue available at website. Query or send manuscript (partial manuscript acceptable for previously published nonfiction authors) with cover letter, title page, table of contents, overview, chapter-by-chapter outline, author photograph, author bio, marketing outlook, competitive titles, and promotion outlets. Accepts email for queries only to nhp@newhorizonpressbooks.com; include "Attn: Ms. P. Patty" in the subject line and hard copy. SASE. Response time, publication period, and payment policy vary.

Parents, Divisions, Imprints

Small Horizons, See page 355
Impact publishers, See page 345

New Society Publishers

P.O. Box 189, Gabriola Island, British Columbia V0R 1X0 Canada
www.newsociety.com

Editor: Ingrid Witvoet

For more than 30 years, New Harbinger has been publishing books to build a new society. It is an activist, solutions-oriented publisher focused on bringing tools for a world of change. It looks for cutting edge ideas, analyses that are hard to find, and books that offer inspiration for daily struggles.

Freelance Potential: Publishes 25 titles annually: 60% by authors who are new to the publishing house; 25% by previously unpublished writers. Receives 25 queries monthly.

Nonfiction: YA. Topics: the environment, conflict resolution, social responsibility, democratic behavior in young people. Also publishes parenting titles.

Titles: *The Big Book of Nature Activiies*, by Jacob Rodenbrg and Drew Monkman. *Seeing Red: An Anger Management and Anti-bullying Curriculum for Kids*, by Jennifer Simmonds.

Submissions and Payment: Guidelines and catalogue available at website. Query with an annotated table of contents; sample chapter; and a proposal detailing what the book is about, author credentials, competitive titles, unique qualities of your book, why you are choosing New Society Publishers, target audience, your plans for promotion, number of copies you plan to purchase, book length, and target completion date. Accepts email to editor@newsociety.com (Word or PDF attachments) and hard copy. SAE/IRC. Responds in 6–8 weeks. Publication in 1 year. Payment policy varies.

Parents, Divisions, Imprints

Douglas & McIntyre, See page 365

New World Library

14 Pamaron Way, Novato, CA 94949.
www.newworldlibrary.com

Submissions Editor: Jonathan Wichmann

New World Library publishes books and audio that inspire and challenge us to improve the quality of our lives and our world. The ultimate goal of the company is a sweeping one: personal and planetary transformation—awakening both individual consciousness and global social potential by publishing inspirational and practical materials in spirituality, personal growth, and other related areas.

Freelance Potential: Publishes 35 titles annually. Receives many queries monthly.

Nonfiction: Adult. Topics: spirituality, personal growth, women's issues, religion, sustainable business, human-animal relationships, Native American interests, the environment, parenting.

Titles: *Reset Your Child's Brain,* by Victoria L. Dunckley, MD. *A to Z Guide to Raising Happy, Confident Kids,* by Dr. Jenn Berman.

Submissions and Payment: Guidelines and catalogue available at website. Query with brief synopsis, outline or table of contents, 2–3 sample chapters including any introduction or preface, a market assessment including competing titles and unique qualities of your book, and author bio with a detailed statement of your credentials. Prefers email to submit@newworldlibrary.com (Word or PDF attachments). Accepts simultaneous submissions. Responds only if interested. Publication in 12–18 months. Payment policy varies.

Parenting Press

P.O. Box 75267, Seattle, WA 98175-0267
www.parentingpress.com

Acquisitions: Carolyn J. Threadgill

This publisher offers parenting guides written by professionals in the field, people who work daily with kids, people who are realistic about children's temperaments, emotional meltdowns, teaching kids, values, and setting limits. It does not publish fiction of any kind.

Freelance Potential: Publishes 6 titles annually: 35% developed from unsolicited submissions; 35% by authors who are new to the publishing house. Receives 70 queries monthly.

Nonfiction: Concept books, books for parents and professionals. Topics: parenting, child development, problem-solving, emotions, abuse prevention, parent desertion, sleep issues, toilet training, personal safety, children's independence and responsibility.

Titles: *STAR Parenting Tales and Tools,* by Elizabeth Crary, M.S. *What Angry Kids Need*, by Jennifer Anne Brown, MSW and Pam Provonsha Hopkins, MSW.

Submissions and Payment: Guidelines and catalogue available at website. Send query with outline, table of contents, introduction, and 2 chapters; or send complete manuscript along with a letter of inquiry detailing your qualifications and publishing history, your goal in publishing the material, promotion plan, primary and secondary audiences, usefulness of the book, and comparison to competitive titles. Accepts hard copy. SASE. Responds in 4 months. Publication in 18–24 months. Royalty, 4–8% of net; advance, negotiable.

Pinter & Martin

6 Effra Parade, London, SW2 1PS, United Kingdom
www.pinterandmartin.com

Publishing Manager: Zoe Blanc

Established in 1997 by filmmaker Martin Wagner and childbirth educator Maria Pinter, this publisher's main focus is on parenting titles, breastfeeding, health, and nutrition. It also publishes a limited number of titles for children, as well as general nonfiction for adults.

Freelance Potential: Publishes about 15–20 titles annually.

Nonfiction: Publishes parenting titles on pregnancy, childbirth, health, and yoga.

Titles: *A Baby Wants to Be Carried: Everything You Need to Know about Baby Carriers and the Benefits of Babywearing*, by Evelyn Kirkilonis (parents). *How You Were Born*, by Monica Calaf (ages 5+).

Submissions and Payment: Guidelines and catalogue available at website. Query with sample chapters, author credentials, and target audience. Only accepts children's books from a writer/illustrator team. Accepts email queries to submissions@pinterandmain.com. Responds in 4 weeks. Payment policy and rates vary.

Platypus Media

725 8th Street SE, Washington, DC 20003
www.platypusmedia.com

Submissions Editor

Platypus Media is an independent publisher dedicated to promoting family life by creating and distributing high-quality materials for children and families. It offers books, booklets, videos, CDs, DVDs, and other products. It also publishes many of its titles in Spanish. Its sister company is Science, Naturally!

Freelance Potential: Publishes 4 titles annually: 50% by agented authors; 50% by authors who are new to the publishing house; 50% by previously unpublished writers. Receives 16 queries monthly.

Fiction: Middle-grade. Topics: families, family diversity, animals.

Nonfiction: Concept books, toddler books, easy-to-read books, story picture books, chapter books, middle-grade, YA. Topics: family issues, animal life cycles, science, math. Also publishes activity books and parenting titles.

Titles: *If My Mom Were a Platypus*, by Dia Michels (ages 8–12). *A Quick Guide to Safely Sleeping with Your Baby*, by James J. McKenna PhD.

Submissions and Payment: Guidelines and catalogue available at website. Query or send complete manuscript with a cover letter explaining your interest in the topic, brief author bio, and marketing assessment detailing how your book will be different from similar titles. Accepts hard copy. Accepts simultaneous submissions if identified. SASE. Response time varies. Publication in 9–12 months. Royalty; no advance.

Rainbow Books

P.O. Box 430, Highland City, FL 33846-0430
www.rainbowbooksinc.com

Editorial Director: Betsy Lampe

Rainbow Books publishes how-to, parenting, self-help, and travel books, and a limited line of fiction. Its nonfiction list includes titles that help build self-esteem and improve coping mechanisms in school-age kids, and improve parenting and family relationships. All of its titles are also produced as ebooks.

Freelance Potential: Publishes about 10–20 titles (2–4 juvenile) annually: 75–100% developed from unsolicited submissions; 1–10% by agented authors; about 75% by authors who are new to the company; about 75% by previously unpublished writers. Receives 25–35 queries monthly.

Fiction: YA, adults. Topics: MANfiction (the opposite of Chick Lit), mysteries, New Age, historical works.

Nonfiction: YA, adults. Topics: how-to, parenting, family, relationships, self-esteem, self-help, travel.

Titles: *The Whipped Parent: Hope for Parents Raising an Out-of-Control Teen* (parents). *Teen Grief Relief*, by Heidi Horsley Psy. D (teens and parents).

Submissions and Payment: Guidelines available at website. Query with 1-page synopsis, up to 3 sample chapters, description of photos or illustrations, author bio including publishing credits, and approximate word count. Accepts hard copy only. SASE. Accepts email for queries to submissions@rainbowbooksinc.com (no attachments). Responds in 6 weeks. Publication in 1 year. Royalty on the retail price; small advance.

Small Horizons

P.O. Box 669, Far Hills, NJ 07931
www.newhorizonpressbooks.com

Acquisitions Editor: P. Patty

This imprint of New Horizon Press publishes a Let's Talk series that uses stories and interesting characters to teach children tolerance, service skills, and how to cope with crises. It also publishes books for parents and teachers. Most of its titles are written by mental health professionals or educators, therefore, it is important to convey your professional expertise in your query.

Freelance Potential: Publishes 2 titles annually. Receives 16 queries monthly.

Fiction: Story picture books. Topics: coping with anger, anxiety, divorce, grief, and violence; understanding ADHD; fostering tolerance.

Nonfiction: Story picture books, early readers. Topics: coping with anger, anxiety, divorce, grief, and violence; hyperactive and aggressive children; tolerance; services. Also publishes parenting books and books for adults who work with children.

Titles: *A Home for Ruby*, by P.J. Neer PhD (ages 5–8). *Cassandra Gets Her Smile Back*, by Sheri Alpert, DDS (ages 5–8).

Submissions and Payment: Guidelines and catalogue available at website. For previously unpublished nonfiction authors, send complete manuscript with title page, table of contents, overview, chapter-by-chapter outline, author photograph and bio, marketing outlook, competitive titles, and promotion outlets. For published nonfiction authors, partial manuscript is acceptable. Accepts hard copy and emails for queries only to nhp@newhorizonpressbooks.com, include "Attn: Ms. P. Patty" in subject line. SASE. Response time, publication period, and payment policy vary.

Parents, Divisions, Imprints

New Horizon Press, See page 349

Square One Publishers

115 Herricks Road, Garden City, NY 11040
www.squareonepublishers.com

Acquisitions Editor

Labeling itself as "an independent publishing company with big ideas," Square One offers titles on health, parenting, self-help, finance, and memoir. A deep knowledge of the subject matter you are addressing should be evident in your query.

Freelance Potential: Publishes 15 titles annually: 65% developed from unsolicited submissions; 35% by authors who are new to the publishing house; 55% by previously unpublished writers. Receives 100 queries monthly.

Nonfiction: Self-help and how-to books for adults. Topics: pregnancy, childbirth, infant care, food and nutrition, history, parenting, social issues, health and fitness, religious.

Titles: *Does Your Baby Have Autism?*, by Philip Teitelbaum PhD and Osnat Teitelbaum. *Enough, Inigo, Enough*, by Janet Dorman (ages 1–6).

Submissions and Payment: Guidelines and catalogue available at website. Query with a cover letter explaining the concept of your book, why you wrote it, and its intended audience; detailed table of contents; brief overview of the book; and author bio. Accepts hard copy. SASE. Responds in 4–6 weeks. Publication period varies. Royalty.

Woodbine House

6510 Bells Mill Road, Bethesda, MD 20817
www.woodbinehouse.com

Acquisitions Editor: Nancy Gray Paul

Woodbine House is a publisher specializing in books about children with special needs. Its titles cover everything from ADHD, autism, celiac disease, Down syndrome, and early intervention. The books from Woodbine House target parents, children, therpists, health care providers, and teachers.

Freelance Potential: Publishes 9 titles annually.

Fiction: Concept books, story picture books. Topics: developmental and intellectual disabilities, mental health issues.

Nonfiction: Guides and reference books for parents and professionals. Topics: autism spectrum disorders, Down syndrome, Tourette syndrome, executive dysfunction, and other developmental disabilities.

Titles: *Andy and His Yellow Frisbee*, by Mary Thompson (grades K–5). *I Like Berries, Do You?* by Majorie W. Pitzer M.Ed (ages 0–4).

Submissions and Payment: Guidelines and catalogue available at website. For nonfiction, query with table of contents, 2–3 sample chapters, an annotated list of competitive titles with an explanation of how your book differs, potential markets, author qualifications, published or unpublished writing samples, and estimated length and completion date. For children's fiction, send complete manuscript, including a few representative illustrations. Accepts hard copy only. Accepts simultaneous submissions if identified. SASE. Responds in 3 months. Publication in 18 months. Payment policy varies

Wyatt-MacKenzie Publishing

15115 Highway 36, Deadwood, OR 97430
www.wymacpublishing.com

Publisher: Nancy Cleary

This award-winning publisher has published hundreds of products over the last 17 years with a special focus on mom writers. Along with traditional publishing, Wyatt-MacKenzie also has self-publishing, imprint, and editorial consulting services available.

Freelance Potential: Publishes 5–8 titles annually.

Fiction: Adult. Genres: contemporary, mystery, realistic.

Nonfiction: Adult. Topics: parenting, child development, social issues, business, careers, multicultural, health, relationships, biography.

Titles: *Soul to Soul Parenting: A Guide to Raising a Spiritually Conscious Family*, by Annie Burnside. *10 Daily Questions to Be a Better Parent,* by Ruth Fett, MSC.

Submissions and Payment: Guidelines and catalogue available at website. Accepts proposals from agented writers as well as unsolicited submissions. Accepts hard copy and email to nancy@wyattmackenzie.com (put "Major Release" in subject line). Response time, publication period, and payment policy varies.

Regional Publishing for Children & Families

Regional publishing is a niche that, while narrow in terms of geographic area, can be quite broad in genres and categories. And many regional publishers offer books for children, teens, and families.

These companies tend to be small presses, and many publish in the obvious categories: regional nonfiction, regional history, regional fiction, historical fiction. But in the pages of this section you will also find companies that look for YA fiction, mysteries, picture books, and early readers that focus on the Southwest or Hawaii or Maine, activity books, folklore, graphic novels, biographies, and much more.

Look for a small press in your region, or one that you know well, and see how conducive its list might be to your writing aspirations.

Alazar Press

2201 Orchard Lane, Carroboro, NC 27510
www.alazar-press.com

Publisher Rosemarie Gulla

An imprint of Royal Swan Press, this North Carolina-based publisher focuses on engaging young people with ideas. It publishes quality books for children of all ages.

Freelance Potential: Publishes about 1–2 titles annually. Receives 1–2 queries monthly.

Fiction: Early readers, middle-grade, YA. Genres: religious, mystery, real life, historical, adventure, humor.

Nonfiction: Concept books, middle-grade, YA. Topics: religion, history, multicultural.

Titles: *The Artist and the King*, by Julie Fortenberry, (ages 5–8). *Walk Together Children - Black American Spirituals* Volume One, by Ashley Bryan (ages 7–12).

Submissions and Payment: Catalogue available at website. Query with outline. Accepts email queries to alazar.press@gmail.com. Accepts simultaneous submissions. Responds in 2 months. Publication period and policy varies.

Allium Press of Chicago

1530 Elgin Avenue, Forest Park, IL 60130. www.alliumpress.com

Editor

Founded in 2009, this small, independent press features literary fiction, mysteries, thrillers, and young adult fiction—all with a Chicago connection. At this time, Allium Press of Chicago is not accepting submissions.

Freelance Potential: Publishes 3–5 titles annually: 70% by authors new to the publishing house, 50% by previously unpublished authors.

Fiction: YA, adult. Genres: historical fiction, literary fiction, mystery, regional, thrillers.

Titles: *Her Mother's Secret*, by Barbara Polikoff (YA). *A Bitter Veil*, by Libby Fischer Hellman (Adult)

Submissions and Payment: Submissions have been temporarily suspended. Check website for updates. Send email to submissions@alliumpress.com. Response time, 3–6 months.

Bess Press

3565 Harding Avenue, Honolulu, HI 96816. www.besspress.com

Editor

This publisher is constantly seeking authors, artists, photographers, and organizations that are developing works concentrating on Hawaii and the Pacific. Its interest lies in unique material that serves both the trade and education categories. It does publish a limited number of children's books each year.

Freelance Potential: Publishes 8–12 titles annually: 10–25%

developed from unsolicited submissions; 10–25% assigned. Receives 15–30 queries monthly.

Fiction: Concept books, board books, early picture books, story picture books, color and activity books, graphic novels. Genres: regional, historical, educational, folklore.

Nonfiction: Concept books, board books, early picture books, chapter books, YA. Topics: Hawaiian and Pacific Island culture, language, history, natural history, literature, biography.

Titles: *Hush Little Keiki*, by Kim Vukovich (ages 0–5). *From Aloha to Zippy's*, Puakea Nogelmeir (ages 0–4).

Submissions and Payment: Guidelines available. Query only with title, genre, target audience, and a short (4–6 sentences) description of the work. Accepts email queries to submission@ besspress.com and hard copy. Accepts simultaneous submissions. Responds in 4 weeks if interested, and will request full submission at that time. Publication in 6–18 months. Royalty, 10–20%; advance.

John F. Blair, Publisher

1406 Plaza Drive, Winston-Salem, NC 27103. www.blairpub.com

Acquisitions Committee

John F. Blair features titles that focus on the southeastern region of the United States. Topics for nonfiction titles include history, travel, folklore, and biographies. Fiction offerings are few, and must have a tie-in with the American Southeast. It publishes a small number of children's and young adult books, but many titles from its adult list will be of interest to young adult readers.

Freelance Potential: Publishes 5–10 titles annually: 25–50% developed from unsolicited submissions; 10–25% assigned; 1–10% by agented authors.

Fiction: Story picture books, middle grade, YA. Genres: historical, regional, folklore, stories from the southeastern U.S.

Nonfiction: YA. Topics: history, travel, biography, nature, all as related to the southeastern U.S.

Titles: *Longleaf*, by Roger Reid (YA). *The Salvation of Miss Lucretia*, by Ted M. Dunagan (ages 10+).

Submissions and Payment: Guidelines and catalogue available at website. For fiction, send first two chapters (or 30 pages) along with a cover letter, synopsis, brief market analysis, and author biography/ publishing credits. For nonfiction, query with cover letter briefly describing the book, outline and/or introduction, 30 pages of text, market analysis, and author biography/publishing credits. Accepts email to: editorial@blairpub.com and hard copy. SASE for response. Responds in 2 months. Publication period and payment policy vary.

Breakwater Books

1 Stamp's Lane, P.O. Box 2188, St. John's, Newfoundland A1C 6E6 Canada. www.breakwaterbooks.com

Managing Director: Kim Pelley

This publisher was founded on the principle of preserving the unique culture and stories of Newfoundland and Labrador and the Maritime provinces. Its catalogue includes children's books, poetry, and adult fiction and nonfiction. All books must be about or set in this region of Canada.

Freelance Potential: Publishes 12–16 titles annually. Receives 1–2 queries monthly.

Fiction: Picture books, early readers, story picture books, chapter books, middle-grade, YA. Genres: contemporary, historical, regional, multicultural, adventure, folklore.

Nonfiction: Middle-grade, YA. Topics: regional, history.

Titles: *Little Snowshoe*, by Ellen Bryan Obed (ages 5–8). *Life Lines: The Lanier Phillips Story*, by Christine Welldon (YA).

Submissions and Payment: Guidelines and catalogue available at website. For picture books, send complete manuscript with cover letter indicating genre, subject matter, intended audience, and author biography. For novels and nonfiction, query with synopsis, first 10–15 pages of manuscript, and cover letter with same information as listed above. Accepts hard copy only. SAE/IRC. Responds in 6 months. Publication in 1 year. Royalty, 10%.

Caitlin Press Inc.

8100 Alderwood Rd, Halfmoon Bay, BC, V0N 1Y1, Canada
www.caitlin-press.com

Publisher: Vici Johnstone

Caitlin Press publishes books that reflect the diverse cultures, histories, and concerns of British Columbia, bridging the gap between the urban and the rural communities. Its catalogue includes fiction, nonfiction, poetry, and a limited number of titles for children or young adults.

Freelance Potential: Publishes 5 titles annually.

Fiction: Early readers, middle-grade, YA, adult. Genres: short fiction and children's literature.

Nonfiction: Early readers, middle-grade, YA, adult. Topics include regional history, memoir, nature, cookbooks, and anthologies.

Titles: *The Adventures of Grey-Dawn,* by "The Ghostwriter" (ages 8–12). *Friends from the Sea,* by Todd Lee (ages 5–8).

Submissions and Payment: Catalogue available at website. Canadian authors only. Query with synopsis. Accepts email queries to vici@caitlin-press.com. Response time varies. Payment policy and rates vary.

Cinco Puntos Press

701 Texas Avenue, El Paso, TX 79901. www.cincopuntos.com

Editor: Lee Byrd

For more than 25 years, the bilingual fiction and nonfiction titles from Cinco Puntos have focused on the history and folklore of the U.S./Mexico border region, the southwestern U.S., and Mexico. Also published are books about Latino and Mexican culture. Its list features books as well as poetry and graphic novels for children and young adults. To ensure the book is a good fit, authors must call the editor to discuss the project before submitting anything.

Freelance Potential: Publishes 10 titles annually.

Fiction: Board books, picture books, early readers, chapter books, middle-grade, YA. Genres: contemporary, historical, regional, multicultural, graphic novels.

Nonfiction: Middle-grade, YA. Topics: regional history; Latino, Chicano, Mexican biographies.

Titles: *Grandma Fina and Her Wonderful Umbrella*, by Benjamin Alire Saenz (ages 4–8). *Double Crossing*, by Eve Tal (YA).

Submissions and Payment: Guidelines and catalogue available at website. Accepts phone calls to Lee Byrd at 915-838-1625 to discuss potential projects; manuscript must be completed prior to calling. No unsolicited queries or manuscripts before speaking with editor. Publication in 18–36 months. Royalty.

Creative Book Publishing

P.O. Box 8660, St. John's, Newfoundland A1B 3T7 Canada
www.creativebookpublishing.ca

Editor: Donna Francis

Creative Book Publishing looks to advance Newfoundland and Labrador's publishing sector by producing works of literary and cultural excellence, and by actively promoting its authors and their books in national and international markets. It publishes children's books and young adult literature under its Tuckamore Books imprint.

Freelance Potential: Publishes 10–14 titles annually. Receives 60 unsolicited manuscripts monthly.

Fiction: Toddler books, picture books, early readers, story picture books, chapter books, middle-grade, YA. Genres: contemporary, historical, regional, multicultural, coming-of-age.

Titles: *At Nanny's House,* by Susan Pynn Taylor (ages 5–8). *A Moose Goes a-Mummering*, by Lisa Dalrymple (ages 5–8).

Submissions and Payment: Canadian authors only. Guidelines and catalogue available at website. Send complete manuscript with cover letter indicating genre and intended audience; author résumé and publishing credits; synopsis of proposed work; brief market overview; and submission checklist printed from online submissions guide. Accepts hard copy. SASE. Response time, publication period, and payment policy vary.

Dancing Cat Books

c/o Cormorant Books, 10 St. Mary Street, Unit 615, Toronto, ON M4Y 1P9. www.dancingcatbooks.com

Publisher: Barry Jowett

Dancing Cat Books, an imprint of Cormorant Books, publishes

author-driven literary fiction, nonfiction and poetry for middle grade readers and young adults. It is not currently open to picture book submissions. Dancing Cat Books accepts submissions from Canadian authors only.

Freelance Potential: Publishes 5–10 titles annually.

Fiction: Picture books, early readers, middle-grade, YA. Genres: adventure, fantasy, contemporary, historical, mystery, fairy tales, stories about nature and animals, poetry.

Nonfiction: Picture books, early readers, middle-grade, YA. Topics: Canadian history, biography, nature, science, social skills.

Titles: *Home Truths*, by Jill Maclean (YA). *The Dead Man's Boot*, by Eric Murphy.

Submissions and Payment: Guidelines and catalogue available at website. Not accepting picture book submissions at this time. Send complete ms with synopsis, author bio. Accepts hard copy. SASE. Responds within 6 months. Publication period and payment policy varies.

Douglas & McIntyre

P.O. Box 219, Madeira Park, BC V0N 2H0
www.douglas-mcintyre.com

Editorial Board

Douglas & McIntyre is one of Canada's pre-eminent independent publishers. In 2013, it was acquired by Harbour Publishing. It accepts submissions from Canadian authors only.

Freelance Potential: Publishes 60 titles annually.

Fiction: Picture books, middle-grade, YA. Genres: contemporary, stories about the environment and animals.

Nonfiction: Early readers, story picture books, middle grade, YA. Topics: the environment, ecology, natural science, inspirational.

Titles: *Of Myths and Sticks,* by Kevin Gibson (YA). *Big City Bees,* by Maggie de Vries (ages 5–8).

Submissions and Payment: Guidelines and catalogue available at website. Accepts hard copy and email submissions to submissions@douglas-mcintyre.com. Publication period and payment policy vary.

Down East Books

P.O. Box 679, Camden, ME 04843
www.downeast.com

Books Editor

Down East is a multimedia company focused on the state of Maine—its history, people, environment, and lifestyle. Among Down East's offerings are children's fiction and nonfiction for toddlers through middle-graders, with an emphasis on picture books. All books must be about or set in Maine.

Freelance Potential: Publishes 28 titles (4–6 juvenile) annually: 20% developed from unsolicited submissions; 20% by agented authors; 20% by authors who are new to the publishing house. Receives 200–300 queries monthly.

Fiction: Toddler books, early picture books, story picture books, middle-grade. Genres: contemporary, regional, historical.

Nonfiction: Toddler books, early picture books, early readers, story picture books. Topics: Maine wildlife and history.

Titles: *Andre the Famous Harbor Seal*, by Fran Hodgkins (ages 4–8). *Lost Trail,* by Donn Fendler (ages 9–12).

Submissions and Payment: Guidelines and catalogue available at website. Query only with 1-page description of book, short author biography and qualifications, and first 2 pages of book (1,000 words maximum). Prefers email queries to submissions@downeast.com; will accept hard copy. No SASE; materials not returned. Response time varies. Publication in 2 years. Royalty, 9–12%; advance, $300–$600.

Harbour Publishing

P.O. Box 219, 4437 Rondeview Road, Madeira Park, British Columbia V0N 2H0 Canada
www.harbourpublishing.com

Acquisitions

Established in 1974, Harbour Publishing is based on British Columbia's Sunshine Coast. Along with its many topics for adults, the catalogue from Harbour also features books for children and teens. Its titles appeal to a wide range of age groups, and all are authored by Canadian writers.

Freelance Potential: Publishes 20 titles annually. Receives 84 queries monthly.

Fiction: Picture books, chapter books, middle-grade, YA. Genres: contemporary, regional, historical.

Nonfiction: Picture books. Topics: British Columbia, the Yukon, regional history, nature.

Titles: *The Airplane Ride*, by Howard White (ages 3+). *Boys, Girls & Body Science: A First Book About Facts of Life*, by Meg Hickling (ages 8–12).

Submissions and Payment: Canadian authors only. Guidelines and catalogue available at website. Query with cover letter, outline, author biography, publication credits, and sample chapter. Accepts hard copy only. SASE. Receipt of manuscript will be acknowledged within 2 months. Publication period varies. Royalty; advance, negotiable.

Hendrick-Long Publishing

10635 Tower Oaks, Suite D, Houston, TX 77070
www.hendricklongpublishing.com

Publisher: Michael Long

Hendrick-Long specializes in books with a Texas historical focus for children and young adults. It welcomes proposals from authors who can help keep alive the love of Texas and its people.

Freelance Potential: Publishes 4 titles annually: 100% developed from unsolicited submissions; 50% by authors who are new to the publishing house. Receives 50 queries monthly.

Fiction: Middle-grade. Genres: historical, regional, folklore.

Nonfiction: Activity books, early readers, middle-grade, YA. Topics: animals, natural history, geography, biography, folklore, all as they relate to Texas.

Titles: *Explorers in Early Texas*, by Betsy Warren (ages 8–12). *Indians Who Lived in Texas*, by Betsy Warren (ages 8–12).

Submissions and Payment: Catalogue available at website. Send query letter, summary, outline, and sample chapter. Accepts hard copy. Accepts simultaneous submissions if identified. SASE. Responds in 6 months. Publication in 2 years. Royalty; advance.

Heyday Books

P.O. Box 9145, Berkeley, CA 94709
www.heydaybooks.com

Acquisitions Editor, Children's Submissions

Heyday is an independent publisher that promotes widespread awareness and celebration of California's many culltures, landscapes, and boundary-breaking ideas. Books should foster an understanding of California history, nature, arts, or culture.

Freelance Potential: Publishes 25 titles annually.

Fiction: Picture books. Genres: contemporary, multicultural, regional, historical, stories about California.

Nonfiction: Activity books, picture books, middle-grade, YA. Topics: California history, culture, nature.

Titles: *Adopted by Indians: A True Story*, by Thomas Jefferson Mayfield (ages 8–12). *Aesop in California*, by Doug Hansen (ages 6–10).

Submissions and Payment: Guidelines and catalogue available at website. Send complete manuscript for picture books. For all others, query with brief description of book, 3 sample chapters, and table of contents (with chapter-by-chapter summary). All submissions should include letter of author introduction and qualifications, along with market description. Accepts hard copy. SASE. Responds in 3 months. Publication period varies. Advance; royalty.

Islandport Press

P.O. Box 10, Yarmouth, ME 04096. www.islandportpress.com

Senior Editor Children's Books: Melissa Kim

Founded in 1999, Islandport Press focuses on books about Maine,

New Hampshire, and Vermont. Its titles are not just set in one of those states--books must be about those states: their cultures, characteristics, and the people who live in them. They have an active children's list and they prefer to work directly with authors, although they will accept manuscript submissions from agents.

Freelance Potential: Unavailable.

Fiction: Story picture books, picture books, early reader, chapter books, middle grade, YA. Genres: adventure, mystery, animals, nature, coming of age, contemporary, real life, fantasy, all about and set in Maine, New Hampshire, or Vermont.

Nonfiction: Story picture books, picture books, early readers, middle grade, YA. Topics: animals, the outdoors, nature, history, people, places, and activities of Mane, New Hampshire, and Vermont.

Titles: *A Little Brown Bat Story*, by Melissa Kim (ages 4–8). *Hold This!*, by Carolyn Cory Scoppettone (ages 3–7).

Submissions and Payment: Catalogue available at website. Guidelines available. Send complete ms with cover letter and brief author bio. Prefers hard copy. SASE. Accepts simultaneous submissions if identified. Responds in 3–6 months. Publication period and payment policy unknown.

Mountain Press Publishing

P.O. Box 2399, Missoula, MT 59806. www.mountain-press.com

Publisher: John Rimel
Managing Editor: Jennifer Carey

Mountain Press Publising Company publishes books on western U.S. history, natural history, and non-technical earth science and ecology, as well as a line of children's books. Books for children and young adults should introduce readers to the factual wonders of the natural world or to historical topics.

Freelance Potential: Publishes 5–10 titles annually: 25–50% developed from unsolicited submissions; 1–10% by agented authors; 50–75% by authors who are new to the publishing house; 50–75% by previously unpublished writers. Receives 10–25 queries monthly.

Nonfiction: Early picture books, early readers, story picture books, chapter books, middle-grade, YA. Topics: natural history, geology, biography, earth science, western U.S. history.

Titles: *Evidence from the Earth*, by Ray Murray (YA). *Mammals on Montana*, by Kerry R. Foresman.

Submissions and Payment: Catalogue and guidelines available at website. Query with résumé, author bio, outline or table of contents, proposal package, 1 or 2 sample chapters, bibliography, copies of artwork you plan to use, market report, and detailed cover letter; see website for info to include. Accepts hard copy. SASE. Responds in 6–8 weeks. Publication in 2–3 years. Royalty, 12%.

NewSouth Books

P.O. Box 1588, Montgomery, AL 36102-1588
www.newsouthbooks.com

Managing Editor: Brian Seidman

This Alabama-based publishing company specializes in regional books of national interest. It publishes quality works of nonfiction, fiction, and poetry with a special interest on regional history, biography, folklore, African American, and Native American. It's Junebug imprint offers regional-based titles for children. At press time, it was closed for submissions, but it was looking to change this policy in 2016.

Freelance Potential: Currently has about 150 active titles on the Junebug list and NewSouth list combined.

Fiction: Picture books, chapter books, middle-grade, YA. Genres: adventure, historical, folklore, fairy tales, fantasy, mystery.

Nonfiction: Picture books, chapter books. Topics: the South, history, culture.

Titles: *Alef-Bet: A Hebrew Alphabet Book*, by Michelle Edwards (ages 4–8). *Ernest's Gift*, by Kathryn Tucker Windham (ages 0–4).

Submissions and Payment: Guidelines and catalogue available at website. Not currently accepting submissions. Check website for changes to this policy. Response time, publication period, and payment policy vary.

Nimbus Publishing

P.O. Box 9166, Halifax, Nova Scotia B3K 5M8 Canada
www.nimbus.ca

Managing Editor: Patrick Murphy

The largest English-language publisher east of Toronto, Nimbus Publishing produces more than 30 titles each year on a range of topics relevant to the Altantic Provinces. Children's picture books and fiction, literary nonfiction, social and cultural history and current events related to Nova Scotia, New Brunswick, Prince Edward Island, and Newfoundland.

Freelance Potential: Publishes 35 titles annually: 35% developed from unsolicited submissions; 5% by agented authors; 25% by authors who are new to the publishing house; 25% by previously unpublished writers. Receives 20 queries monthly.

Fiction: Board books, toddler books, early readers, story picture books, chapter books, middle-grade, YA. Genres: contemporary, regional, historical, multicultural, adventure, folklore.

Nonfiction: Toddler books, early readers, story picture books, middle-grade. Topics: Atlantic Canada's geography, history, and environment.

Titles: *Mabel Murple*, by Sheree Fitch (ages 4–8). *Last Summer in Louisbourg*, by Claire Mowat (ages 9+).

Submissions and Payment: Guidelines and catalogue available at website. Query with cover letter, description of book and its market, short author bio, detailed table of contents or outline, and first 3–4 chapters or approximately 50 pages. Accepts hard copy. Accepts simultaneous submissions. No SASE; materials not returned. Responds in 2–6 months. Publication in 1–2 years. Royalty; advance. Flat fee.

North Country Books

220 Lafayette Street, Utica, NY 13502
www.northcountrybooks.com

Publisher: Rob Igoe, Jr.

Founded in 1965, North Country publishes and distributes quality books and related products for New York State and northern New England. History, biography, folklore, children's nature books, and cookbooks are all a part of its catalogue.

Freelance Potential: Publishes 7 titles annually: 100% developed from unsolicited submissions; 45% by authors who are new to the publishing house; 15% by previously unpublished writers. Receives 4–6 unsolicited manuscripts monthly.

Fiction: Early picture books, story picture books, chapter books. Genres: contemporary, historical, folklore, nature.

Nonfiction: Early picture books, early readers, middle-grade. Topics: New York history, nature, biographies.

Titles: *The Woodman's Boy*, by April Blanchard (YA). *The Adirondack Kids: Mystery of the Missing Moose*, by Justin and Gary Van-Riper (ages 5–10).

Submissions and Payment: Guidelines and catalogue available at website. Send complete manuscript with letter of inquiry that includes a brief overview of the book, author biography and other background that relates to the topic of submission, copies of illustrations or photographs, proposed market, and competition analysis. Accepts hard copy. Accepts simultaneous submissions if identified. SASE. Responds if interested. Publication in 2–5 years. Royalty.

North Star Press of St. Cloud

P.O. Box 451, St. Cloud, MN 56302-0451
www.northstarpress.com

Editor: Anne Rasset

North Star Press is a family business with nearly half a century's commitment to quality in books, relationships, and service and the publishing of books that matter. It is currently seeking submissions for junior readers, young adults, and books on the subjects of Midwest regional fiction, history, and outdoors.

Freelance Potential: Publishes about 45 titles annually:

Fiction: Chapter books, middle-grade, YA. Genres: contemporary, historical, mystery, paranormal.

Nonfiction: Chapter books, middle-grade, YA. Topics: regional history, nature, biographies.

Titles: *Searching for Raven*, by Jerry Hines (ages 8–12). *The Ridge*, by Nick Hupton (YA).

Submissions and Payment: Guidelines and catalogue available

at website. Query with subject, word count, market analysis and author bio, including previous publishing credits. Accepts hard copy, email to info@northstarpress.com, and phone calls (320-558-9062). Accepts simultaneous submissions if identified. SASE. Response time varies; allow at least 2 weeks before inquiring. Publication period and payment policy, unavailable.

Ooligan Press

Portland State University, P.O. Box 751, Portland, OR 97207
www.ooliganpress.pdx.edu

Acquisitions Committee

This general trade publisher is rooted in the rich literary tradition of the Pacific Northwest. Ooligan Press aspires to discover works that reflect the values and attitudes that inspire so many to call the Northwest their home. It accepts submissions for young adult and adult books that are regionally significant to the Northwest.

Freelance Potential: Publishes 3 titles annually: 100% by authors who are new to the publishing house, 66% by previously unpublished writers. Receives 50 queries monthly.

Fiction: YA. Genres: historical, regional, contemporary.

Titles: *Forgive Me If I've Told You This Before*, by Karelia Stetz-Waters (YA). *The Ninth Day*, by Ruth Tenzer Feldman (YA).

Submissions and Payment: Guidelines and catalogue available at website. Send query with brief summary of work, description of intended audience and potential market, and short paragraph about author and publishing history or proposal with cover letter containing above info plus a table of contents and 40–60 consecutive pages of the manuscript through Submishmash. Accepts queries only by email to acquisitions@ooliganpress.pdx.edu (no attachments). Will request full manuscript if interested. Responds in 2–3 months. Publication period and payment policy vary.

Pelican Publishing

1000 Burmaster Street, Gretna, LA 70053. www.pelicanpub.com

Editor in Chief: Nina Kooij

Established in 1926, Pelican is the largest independent book pubisher in the South. Its catalogue is comprised of children's book, history, cooking and regional titles.

Freelance Potential: Publishes 65 titles annually: 15% by agented authors; 50% by authors who are new to the publishing house; 30% by previously unpublished writers. Receives 2,500 queries yearly.

Fiction: Early readers, middle-grade. Genres: historical, regional.

Nonfiction: Concept books, early picture books, early readers, middle-grade. Topics: arts, history, biography, current events, regional history and facts.

Titles: *Blue Bonnet at Johnson Space Center*, by Mary Brooke Casad (ages 8–12). *The Adventure of Roopster Roux*, by Lavaille Lavette (ages 7–10).

Submissions and Payment: Guidelines and catalogue available at website. Query with synopsis/outline, one or two sample chapters, anticipated length, intended audience, promotional ideas, and résumé. Send complete manuscript for picture books only (1,100-word limit). Availability of artwork increases chance of acceptance. Accepts hard copy only. No simultaneous submissions. SASE. Responds to queries in 1 month, to manuscripts in 3 months. Publication in 9–12 months. Royalty.

Pineapple Press

P.O. Box 3889, Sarasota, FL 34230. www.pineapplepress.com

Executive Editor: June Cussen

Founded in 1982 by June and David Cussen, Pineapple Press publishes quality books that bring Florida to life for readers nationwide. Most of its catalogue is nonfiction on the subjects of travel, nature, history, and art in Florida. It does publish a limited number of children's books and literary novels as well.

Freelance Potential: Publishes 18 titles annually: 75% developed from unsolicited submissions; 45% by authors who are new to the publishing house; 5% by previously unpublished writers. Receives 100 queries monthly.

Fiction: Story picture books, chapter books, middle-grade, YA. Genres: folklore, mystery, historical.

Nonfiction: Early readers, story picture books, middle-grade.

Topics: Florida-related biography, history, sports, wildlife, nature, environment.

Titles: *Solomon,* by Marilyn Bishop Shaw (ages 8+). *The Dogs of Proud Spirit,* by Melanie Sue Bowles (10+).

Submissions and Payment: Guidelines and catalogue available at website. For fiction, query with cover letter describing author, manuscript, and title; 1-page synopsis; and sample chapters, including the first. For nonfiction, query with cover letter describing manuscript, author qualifications, and title; table of contents; sample chapters (including introduction); proposed market; other published books on the topic; and an explanation of how your project differs. Accepts hard copy. Accepts simultaneous submissions if identified. SASE. Responds in 2 months. Publication in 12–18 months. Royalty.

Plexus Publishing

143 Old Marlton Pike, Medford, NJ 08055
www.plexuspublishing.com

Editor in Chief: John B. Bryans

This regional publisher is based in New Jersey. In addition to regional titles, its catalogue includes books in the fields of biology and ecology.

Freelance Potential: Publishes 4 titles annually: 25% developed from unsolicited submissions; 50% by authors who are new to the publishing house; 25% by previously unpublished writers. Receives 12–25 queries monthly.

Fiction: Adult titles, some with YA appeal. Genres: contemporary, historical, mystery, adventure, folklore.

Nonfiction: Adult titles, some with YA appeal. Topics: biography; regional field guides; New Jersey history, natural resources, seashore, wildlife, recreation, tourism, travel, unique locations.

Titles: *Dinosaurs in the Garden*, by R. Gary Raham. *Jacket: The Trials of a New Jersey Criminal Defense Attorney*, by John Hartmann.

Submissions and Payment: Catalogue available at website. Query with synopsis, table of contents, and 3 sample chapters. Accepts hard copy. SASE. Responds in 2 months. Publication in 10 months. Royalty, 12%.

Rio Chico Books for Children

P.O. Box 5250, Tucson, AZ 85703. www.rionuevo.com

Editor: Theresa Howell

An imprint of Rio Nuevo Publisher, Rio Chico published its first children's titles in 2011. Its award-winning books focus on arts and crafts, children's literature, cooking, hisotry, Native America, and travel. Its list so far consists of picture books, and most titles must have a southwestern or western theme.

Freelance Potential: Publishes about 4 books a year.

Fiction: Picture books. Genres: animals, nature, southwestern and western subjects.

Nonfiction: Picture books. Topics: the West.

Titles: *Boots and Burgers: An Arizona Handbook for Hungry Hikers,* by Roger Naylor (YA). *Cowgirl and Her Horse,* by Jean Ekman Adams (ages 2+).

Submissions and Payment: Guidelines and catalogue available at website. Send complete manuscript with suggestions for illustrations if necessary to understand the text. Accepts email to theresah@rionuevo.com; no attachments, put manuscript in the body of the email. Responds in 3 months. Publication period and payment policy vary.

Ronsdale Press

3350 West 21st Avenue, Vancouver, British Columbia V6S 1G7 Canada. www.ronsdalepress.com

Children's Acquisition Editor: Veronica Hatch

Since 1988 Ronsdale Press has been dedicated to publishing books from across Canada that offer Canadians new insights into themselves and their country. It publishes a limited number of children's titles each year.

Freelance Potential: Publishes 12 titles annually: 25–50% developed from unsolicited submissions; 5% by agented authors; 20% by authors who are new to the company; 20% by previously unpublished writers. Receives 10–25 queries monthly.

Fiction: Middle-grade, YA. Genres: Canadian historical, contemporary, and multicultural fiction; stories featuring real-life contemporary problems.

Nonfiction: High/lo, reluctant readers, middle-grade, YA. Topics: Canadian history, biographies, subjects of interest to girls or boys, poetry.

Titles: *Adrift in Time*, by John Wilson (YA). *Chasing a Star*, by Norma Charles (YA).

Submissions and Payment: Canadian authors only. Guidelines and catalogue available at website. Query or send complete manuscript with résumé. Accepts hard copy only. Accepts simultaneous submissions if identified. SASE. Responds in 2–3 months. Publication in 1 year.

Texas Tech University Press

1120 Main Street, Second floor, Box 41037, Lubbock, TX 79409
http://ttupress.org

Editor in Chief: Judith Keeling

Texas Tech University Press produces an acclaimed fiction series for middle-grade readers and young adults, as well as a variety of nonfiction and scholarly titles for adults, a wide range of general interest topics as well as those with themes and topics relating to Texas, the American West, and the Great Plains. See website for current needs.

Freelance Potential: Publishes 30 titles annually. Receives 25–30 queries monthly.

Fiction: Middle-grade, YA. Genres: regional, historical, folklore.

Nonfiction: Middle-grade, YA. Topics: biography, history of the American Southwest, sports, science.

Titles: *Perspectives in Interdisciplinary and Integrative Studies,* by Patrick C. Hughes, Juan S. Munoz, and Marcus N. Tanner (educators). *Forbidden Fashions*, by Isabella Campagnol (YA–A).

Submissions and Payment: Guidelines and catalogue available at website. Send proposal with 2- to 4-page outline or annotated table of contents indicating the nature and scope of each chapter; introduction; 2 sample chapters; and a cover letter with working title, manuscript length, description of illustrations (if any), market comparison, brief autobiographical summary or CV with author qualifications, and the nature and scope of research done. Accepts hard copy only. SASE. Responds in 2 months. Publication in 1–2 years. Royalty, 10%.

Wayne State University Press

The Leonard N. Simons Building, 4809 Woodward Avenue, Detroit, MI 48201-1309
http://wsupress.wayne.edu

Acquisitions Editors: Kathryn Wildfong and Annie Martin

This university press is a leading publisher of books about the Great Lakes, Judaica, and African American studies. It disseminates research, advances education, and serves the local community. It also publishes regional titles for young readers.

Freelance Potential: Publishes 35 titles (1 juvenile) annually: 5% by agented authors. Receives 15+ queries monthly.

Nonfiction: Early picture books, middle-grade, YA. Topics: history, natural history, and biographies relevant to the Great Lakes region.

Titles: *Under Michigan*, by Charles Ferguson Barker (ages 6+). *Great Girls in Michigan History*, by Patricia Majher (ages 10+).

Submissions and Payment: Guidelines and catalogue available at website. Query with description of work, table of contents with chapter synopsis, details of proposed project, author biography and credentials, and 1–2 sample chapters. Accepts hard copy and email to k.wildfong@wayne.edu. SASE. Responds in 12 weeks. Publication in 12–18 months. Royalty.

Religious Publishing for Children & Families

Religious publishing embraces books of almost every kind, from the earliest board books to young adult fiction, from biblical education to inspiring adolescents in faith or spirituality. Since the last decades of the last century, religious publishing has expanded mightily. It also moved well beyond a reputation for rather narrow and, truth be told, often second-rate books.

Today, religious publishing is like any other segment of the industry. Much of it is very high quality, and some companies cover many, many subjects. Other companies take a tight focus on particular religious topics and genres, and require that their books reflect specific tenets.

Look here for what interests you: mainstream companies open-ended in their need for religious, spiritual, or inspirational books for children and adults, or more denominational publishers with beliefs and goals that match your own, and your writing interests.

Abingdon Press

201 Eighth Avenue South, P.O. Box 801, Nashville, TN 37202-0801
www.abingdonpress.com

Manuscript Submissions

For more than 200 years, Abingdon Press has continued a tradition in religious publishing for cross denominational boundaries with thought-provoking and enjoyable books.

Freelance Potential: Publishes about 10 titles annually. Receives 50 queries monthly.

Fiction: Chapter books, middle-grade, YA. Genres: religious, mystery, real life, historical, adventure, humor.

Nonfiction: Board books, middle-grade, YA. Topics: religion, holidays, education, theology, activities, puzzles.

Titles: *A Blessing on the Way*, by Sue Christian (families). *The Christian World of The Hobbit*, by Devin Brown (grades 6–12).

Submissions and Payment: Guidelines available at website. Only accepts fiction submissions from agents and writers met at writers conferences by the editor. Query with outline and 1–2 sample chapters (30 pages maximum). All curriculum writing is done on assignment by active members of the United Methodist Church. Accepts email to submissions@umpublishing.org. No simultaneous submissions. Responds in 2 months. Publication in 2 years. Royalty.

ACTA Publications

4848 North Clark Street, Chicago, IL 60640. www.actapublications.com

Acquisitions Editor

ACTA Publications offers books and video resources for Catholic religious education and marriage preparation. Books on grief and bereavement and spirituality are also are part of its mix.

Freelance Potential: Publishes about 15 titles annually: most developed from unsolicited submissions and by agented authors. Receives 12 queries monthly.

Nonfiction: Story picture books, YA. Topics: religion, parenting, education, divorce, grief, self-help, contemporary social issues, theology, history—all with a Christian theme.

Titles: *Yes, It Is So!* (youth ministry). *A Child's Book of the Mass,* by Betsy Puntel and Hannah Roberts (ages 5–10).

Submissions and Payment: Guidelines and catalogue available at website. Query with table of contents, sample chapter, and author credentials, and cover letter that describes the audience for your book. Accepts hard copy only. Accepts simultaneous submissions if identified. SASE. Responds in 8–12 weeks. Publication time varies. Royalty, 10%.

Ambassador International

427 Wade Hampton Boulevard, Greenville, SC 29609
www.ambassador-international.com

Publisher: Samuel Lowry

Ambassador International is a publisher with a Christian world view. It publishes a rang of titles and genres including children's books, cookbooks, fashion, histry, and memoir. 30% self-, subsidy-, co-venture, or co-op published material.

Freelance Potential: Publishes 60 titles annually: 50–75% developed from unsolicited submissions; 25–50% assigned; 25% by agented authors; 30% by authors who are new to the publishing house; 45% by previously unpublished writers. Receives 25–50 queries, 75–100 unsolicited manuscripts monthly.

Fiction: Early readers, story picture books, chapter books, middle-grade, YA. Genres: coming-of-age, fantasy, graphic novels, historical, inspirational, mystery, regional, real life/problems, religious.

Nonfiction: Early readers, story picture books, chapter books, middle-grade, YA. Topics: biography, factual/info, inspirational, reference, self-help, real life/problems, religious, parenting.

Titles: *The Double Cousins and the Mystery of Custer's Gold,* by Miriam Jones Bradley (ages 8+). *Jesus and the Children of Galilee,* by Belinda Ford Kramer (YA).

Submissions and Payment: Guidelines and catalogue available at website. Query with overview/table of contents, approximate word count, completion date, illustrations, special features, target audience, possible reviewers, 2 sample chapters, a description of previous writing experience, and platforms. Prefers email queries with Word attachments to publisher@emeraldhouse.com or through website; will accept hard copy. Accepts simultaneous submissions. SASE. Responds in 30 days. Publication in 3–6 months. Royalty, 15–20%.

AMG Publishers

6815 Shallowford Road, Chattanooga, TN 37421
www.amgpublishers.com

Acquisitions: Rick Steele

This evangelical, nondenominational, mission-focused publishing house specializes in Bible-related nonfiction and fiction for middle-grade and young adult readers, as well as adults. Its nonfiction titles include reference books and resources for religious educators and parents. It has been expanding its juvenile and YA fiction offerings, as well as adult Bible studies and devotionals.

Freelance Potential: Publishes about 30 titles (12 juvenile) annually: 50% by agented authors; 20% reprint/licensed properties; about 30% by authors who are new to the publishing house; about 30% by previously unpublished writers. Receives 100 queries monthly.

Fiction: Chapter books, middle-grade, YA. Genres: fantasy, contemporary with Christian themes.

Nonfiction: Middle-grade, YA, adult. Topics: Bible study materials, devotionals, inspirational, history, real life, parenting, family life.

Titles: *Angela's Answer,* by Pat Matuszak (YA). *Simone's Secret*, by Pat Matuszak (YA).

Submissions and Payment: Guidelines and catalogue available at website. Query with brief book description including proposed page count, target audience, and author credentials. Accepts email queries to ricks@amgpublishers.com. Response time and publication period vary. Royalty; advance.

Parents, Divisions, Imprints

Living Ink Books, See page 412

Ancient Faith Publishing

P.O. Box 748, Chesterton, IN 46304
http://ancientfaith.com

Children's Acquisitions Editor: Jane Meyer

Ancient Faith Publishing offers Orthodox Christian books for children and adults. Its mission is to embrace the fullness of the Orthodox faith, encourage discipleship of believers, equip the faithful for ministry, and evangelize the unchurched. Its middle-grade/YA fiction reflects an Orthodox Christian worldview and lifestyle but is not moralistic or pedantic. It only considers submissions by Eastern Orthodox Christians with specifically Orthodox subject matter.

Freelance Potential: Publishes 1–4 titles annually: 50–75% developed from unsolicited submissions; 25–50% by authors who are new to the publishing house; 25–50% by previously unpublished writers. Receives 1–10 queries, 1–10 unsolicited manuscripts monthly.

Fiction: Toddler books, picture books, early picture books, story picture books, middle-grade, YA. Genres: coming-of-age, historical fiction, multicultural, real life/problems. All fiction must have strong Orthodox content, showing God at work in children's lives, or the Orthodox Christian worldview and lifestyle.

Nonfiction: Toddler books, early picture books, story picture books, middle-grade, YA. Genres: church life or history, lives of saints, Bible stories, biographies, holidays, practical theology about living out the Orthodox faith in contemporary life.

Titles: *A Child's Guide to Divine Literacy*, by Megan Gilbert (ages 2–10). *A Gift for Matthew*, by Nick Muzekari (ages 5–10).

Submissions and Payment: Guidelines and catalogue available at website. Query with brief description of the book, intended audience, author qualifications, projected word count, and completion date. Accepts email queries only with "CP Submission" and your surname in the subject line (Word or RTF attachments), to jmeyer@conciliarmedia.com. Accepts simultaneous submissions. Responds to queries in 1 month, requested manuscripts in 6 months. Publication period, 12–24 months. Royalty.

Ave Maria Press

P.O. Box 428, Notre Dame, IN 46556
www.avemariapress.com

Acquisitions Department

In business since 1865, Ave Maria Press is owned by thr United States Province of the Congregation of Holy Cross. Its imprints include Sorin Books, Forest of Peace, Christian Classics, and Spiritual Book Associates. While it does publish for young adults based on Christian faith, it does not accept submissions targeting young children.

Freelance Potential: Publishes about 40 titles annually: a very few developed from unsolicited submissions; some by agented authors; a very few by authors who are new to the publishing house. Receives 15 queries, 25+ manuscripts monthly.

Nonfiction: YA. Topics: catechism, Christian living, prayer, relationships, religion, sacraments, spirituality, education, youth ministry.

Titles: *Day By Day,* by Thomas McNally, CSC (YA). *Sex, Love, and You,* by Tom and Judy Likona (YA).

Submissions and Payment: Guidelines and catalogue available at website. Query with cover letter that contains a description of the book, intended audience, competition analysis, estimated length of the book, and author qualifications; a prospectus; table of contents; introduction; and 1 or 2 sample chapters; or send the complete manuscript. Accepts hard copy and email submissions for queries only (no complete manuscripts) to submissions@mail.avemariapress.com. Accepts simultaneous submissions if identified. Does not return unsolicited materials. Responds in 6–8 weeks. Publication in 1 year. Payment policy varies.

Baker Publishing Group

Baker Publishing Group, 6030 East Fulton Road, Ada, MI 49301
www.bakerpublishinggroup.com

Editor

This Christian publisher is made up of several divisions, including Baker Books, Bethany House, Revell Books, and other academic and theological divisions. It publishes work that represents historic Christianity and serve the diverse interests and concerns of evangelical readers. Bethany House publishes Christian fiction, children's fiction and nonfiction, and books on family, health, theology, and devotionals.

Freelance Potential: Publishes hundreds of books annually.

Fiction: Middle-grade, YA, adult. Genres: animals, religious, holidays, girls, people and places, sports. For adults: Christian, romance, historical, contemporary, fantasy, men's, women's, psychological, suspense, humor, mysteries.

Nonfiction: Middle-grade, YA, adult. Topics: religion, Bible stories, biography, history, family, home, health, crafts, cooking, current events, education, parenting, pets, relationships, self-help, sports.

Titles: *The Mandie Collection*, by Lois Gladys Leppard (ages 8–12). *The Upside-Down Day*, by Beverly Lewis (ages 6–10).

Submissions and Payment: Baker Publishing accepts unsolicited manuscripts only through agents; at conferences where Baker staff participates; or through the manuscript services Authonomy. com, Writer's Edge (www.writersedgeservice.com), or Christian Manuscript Submissions, an online service of the Evangelical Christian Publishers Association (www.christian-manuscriptsubmissions.com). Response time and publication period vary. Royalty, 15% of net.

Parents, Divisions, Imprints

Bethany House Publishers, See page 388
Revell, See page 423

B & H Kids

One Life Way Plaza, Nashville, TN 37234.
www.bhpublishinggroup.com

Submissions

This children's imprint from B & H Publishing is dedicated to "help kids develop a lifelong relationship with Jesus and to empower parents to guide them in their spiritual growth." Bible storybooks, study guides, Bible-centered fiction and nonfiction, and movie tie-ins are featured on its lists. The imprint accepts submissions through literary agents.

Freelance Potential: Publishes 20 books annually.

Fiction: Story picture books, early readers, YA. Genres: Bible stories, inspirational, romance.

Nonfiction: YA. Topics: theology, the Bible, prayer, contemporary issues, history, current events, devotionals, real life/problems, evangelizing, missions.

Titles: *Teen to Teen*, by Patti M. Hummel (YA). *365 Devotions for Girls* (ages 10+).

Submissions and Payment: Agented authors only. Guidelines available to agents by email to ManuscriptSubmission@lifeway.com. Also offers self-publishing arrangements via CrossBooks (www.crossbooks. com). Responds in 3 months. Publication in 12–18 months. Royalty; advance.

B & H Publishing

One LifeWay Plaza, Nashville, TN 37234-0188
www.bhpublishinggroup.com

Submissions

This non-profit publisher is made up of people who are passionate about taking God's Word to the world. It publishes Bible-centered material that positively impacts the hearts and minds of people—inspiring them to build a life-long relationship with Jesus Christ.

Freelance Potential: Publishes 100 books annually. Receives 30 unsolicited manuscripts monthly.

Fiction: Story picture books, early readers, YA. Genres: Bible stories, inspirational, romance.

Nonfiction: YA. Topics: theology, the Bible, prayer, contemporary issues, history, current events, devotionals, real life/problems, evangelizing, missions, family.

Titles: *Blotch*, by Andy Addis (ages 8–12). *Can You Relate?*, by Vicki Courtney (YA).

Submissions and Payment: Agented authors only. Guidelines available to agents by mail. Also offers self-publishing arrangements via CrossBooks (www.crossbooks.com). Responds in 3 months. Publication in 12–18 months. Royalty; advance.

Parents, Divisions, Imprints

B & H Kids, See page 385

Barbour Publishing

P.O. Box 719, 1810 Barbour Drive, Uhrichsville, OH 44683
www.barbourbooks.com

Submissions Editor

This conservative, evangelical Christian publisher offers religious and inspirational fiction and nonfiction for toddlers through teens. It also publishes biblical reference books for a variety of ages, and books for adults. Faithfulness to the Bible and Jesus Christ is central to all Barbour books. Fiction submissions must come via an agent, but the company is open to author queries for nonfiction.

Freelance Potential: Publishes about 150 titles (30 juvenile) annually.

Fiction: Toddler books, story picture books, early readers, middle-grade, YA. Genres: historical, adventure, mystery, Bible stories.

Nonfiction: Story picture books, middle-grade, YA. Topics: holidays, biography, the Bible, inspiration, prayer, self-help, real life, sports, puzzles, activities, devotionals.

Titles: *Meek and Mild*, by Olivia Newport (YA). *Lydia's Charm*, by Wanda E. Brunstetter.

Submissions and Payment: Guidelines available at website. Fiction, agents only. Nonfiction, send book proposal. Query with résumé, synopsis, and 3 sample chapters. Accepts email queries only to submissions@barbourbooks.com. Accepts simultaneous submissions, if identified. Responds in 4–6 months. Publication period varies. Royalty; advance.

Beacon Hill Press

P.O. Box 419527, 2923 Troost Avenue, Kansas City, MO 64141
www.beaconhillbooks.com

Submissions: Rene McFarland

Beacon HIll Press is a leading provider of Wesleyan Christian books, Bible studies, and Bible commentaries. Its mission is to provide inspiration and support with biblically sound materials that are relevant to the church's changing needs.

Freelance Potential: Publishes about 40 titles annually: about 20% developed from unsolicited submissions; 25% by authors who are new to the publishing house; 25% by previously unpublished writers. Receives many queries and unsolicited manuscripts monthly.

Nonfiction: YA, books for parents and teachers. Topics: Church of the Nazarene theology, the Bible, church history, self-help, parenting, spiritual growth, Christian living.

Titles: *Broken Children, Grown-Up Pain*, by Paul Hegstrom (parents). *101 Ways to Grow a Healthy Sunday School*, by Stan Toler (educators).

Submissions and Payment: Guidelines available at website and via email request to crm@nph.com. Catalogue available at website. Send a proposal with a thesis statement; author biography with your credentials on the chosen subject (such as education, career, life experience); a description of how the book differs from others in the marketplace; chapter titles and a synopsis for each; 2–3 complete chapters; projected word count of completed manuscript; and projected date of completion. Responds to queries in 1 month, to manuscripts in 3–6 months. Publication in 12–18 months. Payment policy varies.

Bethany House Publishers

Baker Publishing Group, 6030 East Fulton Road, Ada, MI 49301
www.bethanyhouse.com

Submissions Editor

This leading publisher of Christian of fiction and nonfiction books helps Christians apply biblical truths in all areas of life. Although it no longer publishes titles specifically for children, it does offer many books that would be of interest to young adult readers. Bethany House is part of the Baker Publishing Group, whose other divisions include Baker Books, Baker Academic, Brazos Press, Chosen Books, Cambridge Bibles, God's Word Translation, and Revell.

Freelance Potential: Publishes approximately 75 titles annually: 100% by agented authors or authors using Christian submission services; 20% by authors who are new to the publishing house; 13% by previously unpublished writers. Receives 30 queries monthly.

Fiction: Adult/YA. Genres: historical, Amish, contemporary, romantic, suspense, fantasy, inspirational.

Nonfiction: Adult/YA. Topics: devotionals, the Bible, history, biography, personal growth, Christian living, theology, Christian classics.

Titles: *In Jesse's Shoes*, by Beverly Lewis (ages 5–8). *Addicted to God*, by Jim Burns (YA).

Submissions and Payment: Guidelines and catalogue available at website. Accepts manuscripts only through agents, conferences where Baker staff participates, or the manuscript services Writer's Edge (www.writersedgeservice.com) or Christian Manuscript Submissions, an online service of the Evangelical Christian Publishers Association (www.christianmanuscriptsubmissions.com). Response time, publication period, and payment policy vary.

Parents, Divisions, Imprints

Baker Publishing Group, See page 384

Bondfire Books

7680 Goddard Street, Suite 220, Colorado Springs, CO 80920
www.bondfirebooks.com

Submissions

This electronic publisher features fiction and nonfiction by today's top writing talent, from established voices to up-and-comers. It works on "a straight partnership model" with authors, offering copyediting, cover design, digitization, metadata, search optimization, marketing, and accounting, and a 50% royalty split.

Freelance Potential: Actively seeking submissions of new and out-of-print books. A "significant percentage," but not all, of Bondfire's authors are agented.

Nonfiction: Adult. Topics: parenting, religion, inspirational.

Titles: *What Every Child Needs,* by Eiisa Morgan and Carol Kuykendall. *Dear Abba: Morning and Evening Prayer,* by Brennan Manning.

Submissions and Payment: Guidelines and catalogue available at website. Send submission including author bio, publishing credits, a brief (150-word) overview of the book, and sample chapter or proposal via form at website. Response time and publication period vary. Royalty, 50% with 5-year contract.

R. H. Boyd Publishing

6717 Centennial Blvd, Nashville, TN 37209
www.rhboydpublishing.com

Submissions

This publisher produces Christian, primarily Baptist, literature, including children's books, religious education and ministry materials, African American heritage titles, historical titles, books on family, and music. The company offers publishing contracts to help authors publish for a fee. 30% Self-, subsidy-, co-venture, or co-op published material.

Freelance Potential: Publishes many titles annually, in books and periodical religious education materials.

Fiction: Picture books, early readers, chapter books, middle-grade, YA. Genres: Bible stories, historical, real life, inspirational, poetry.

Nonfiction: Story picture books, early readers, chapter books, middle-grade, YA. Topics: biography, education, history, religious, the Bible, environment, self-help, contemporary issues, real life/problems, coloring and activity books.

Titles: *101 Games That Keep Kids Coming,* by Jolene L. Roehlpartain (ages 3–12). *All-in-One Bible* (ages 5–10).

Submissions and Payment: Guidelines and catalogue available at website. Query with table of contents and sample chapters; or send complete manuscript to receive a proposal from the company for a publishing arrangement in which the author pays for editorial, design, distribution, and other services. Accepts hard copy. SASE. Freelancers who are members of a National Baptist congregation and wish to write Sunday school curriculum should write to 6717 Centennial Boulevard, Nashville, TN 37206 or send an email to nbpb1@rhboyd.com. Responds in 2–4 months. Publication period varies.

Bridge-Logos Foundation

17750 NW 115th Avenue, Building 200, Suite 220, Alachua, FL 32615
www.bridgelogos.com

Acquisitions Editor: Peggy Hildebrand

Bridge Logos is a Christian publisher that offers inspirational fiction and nonfiction titles for children, teens, and adults. Its titles cover Christian living, social issues, evangelism, and theology. It is currently looking for children's books, and books on families and marriage, in addition to other categories. 40% self-, subsidy-, co-venture, or co-op published material.

Freelance Potential: Publishes 20–24 titles annually: 15% by agented authors, 40% by authors new to the publishing house, 40% by previously unpublished writers. Receives 75 queries, 50 mss yearly.

Fiction: Picture books, chapter books, YA. Genres: fantasy, contemporary, historical, inspirational, multicultural, religious, romance, science fiction, westerns.

Nonfiction: Picture books, early readers, YA. Topics: creation, theology, biography, religious, inspirational, real life/problems, self-help.

Titles: *God Made Dad & Mom,* by Amber Dee Parker (ages 5–8). *Mary Jones and Her Bible,* by Mary Ropes ((grade 4–8).

Submissions and Payment: Guidelines and catalogue available at website. Query or send complete manuscript with proposal letter (no more than 5 pages) that includes summary and approximate word count, market analysis, and author biography, including professional background and previously published works; and $100 evaluation fee. Also offers an in-depth editorial review for $200. Prefers email queries with Word attachments to manuscripts@bridgelogos.com; payment must be mailed ahead. Accepts hard copy. SASE. Responds in 4–8 weeks. Publication in 1 year. Payment policy varies.

Canon Press

www.canonpress.com

Submissions Editor

Located in Idaho, this small press publishes products that sketch a vision of a whole life—a whoole culture: a life ful of beauty, tradition, education, community, and celebration. Its books reflect the life that God would like us to live.

Freelance Potential: Unavailable.

Fiction: Early readers, story picture books, middle grade, YA. Genres: religious, adventure, mystery, folktales, and real life problems.

Nonfiction: Middle grade, YA. Topics: biography, self-help, religious.

Titles: *Blah Blah Black Sheep*, by N. D. Wilson (ages 4–8). *A House for Many: Q & A*, by Joshua Appel (YA).

Submissions and Payment: Catalogue available. Query with proposal. Accepts email to submissions@conaripress.com. Responds only if interested. Publication period and payment policies vary.

Cedar Fort

2373 West 700 South, Springville, UT 84663
www.cedarfort.com

Acquisitions Manager

Uplifting fiction and nonfiction for the LDS audience are the primary focus of this publisher. Imprints include Council Press (historical western fiction and nonfiction); Front Table Books (cookbooks), Hobble Creek Press (Dutch oven/outdoor cooking); Sweetwater Books (fiction); and Plain Sight Publishing (nonfiction).

Freelance Potential: Publishes 158 titles annually: 50-75% developed from unsolicited submissions; approximately 6% by agented authors; 66% by authors who are new to the publishing house; 57% by previously unpublished writers. Receives 75+ manuscripts monthly.

Fiction: Chapter books, middle-grade, YA. Genres: adventure, fantasy, contemporary, coming of age, historical, humor, realistic, multicultural, romance, sports, political thrillers.

Nonfiction: YA. Topics: history, religion, self-help, biography, crafts, games/puzzles, health, holidays, nature, cookbooks, gardening, LDS doctrine. Also publishes books for adults.

Titles: *A to Z Coobook for Kids,* by Jacque Wick (ages 6+). *Shedding Light on the Dark Side: Defeating the Forces of Evil (A Guide for Youth and Young Adults),* by Stephen J. Stirling (YA).

Submissions and Payment: Guidelines and catalogue available at website. Query with synopsis, table of contents, manuscript submissions form, and first 3 chapters; or send complete manuscript with résumé, author bio, and manuscript submission form from website. Prefers hard copy. Accepts email to submissions@cedarfort.com. Accepts simultaneous submissions. Response time, 2-4 months. Publication period, 10–12 months. Royalty, escalated scale.

Christian Focus Publications

Geanies House, Fearn, Tain, Ross-shire IV20 ITW Scotland, United Kingdom. www.christianfocus.com

Children's Editor: Catherine Mackenzie

Christian Focus Publications is all about the message of the gospel; the message of God's word communicated in the Bible. Its CF4K imprint is devoted to producing books for children, including Sunday school and home school titles.

Freelance Potential: Publishes about 80 titles (40 juvenile) annually: 1–10% developed from unsolicited submissions; 1–10% by agented authors; 1–10% reprint/licensed properties; 1–10% by authors who are new to the publishing house; 1–10% by previously unpublished writers. Receives 20 queries, 20 unsolicited manuscripts monthly.

Fiction: Toddler books, early picture books, story picture books, early readers, chapter books, middle-grade, YA. Genres: contemporary, religious, real life/problems, historical.

Nonfiction: Toddler books, early readers, story picture books, chapter books, middle-grade, YA. Topics: the Bible, biographies, devotionals, puzzles, activities.

Titles: *The Very First Christman*, by Catherine MacKenzie (ages 4–5). *Living Water in the Desert,* by Rebecca Davis (ages 8–14).

Submissions and Payment: Guidelines and catalogue available at website. Query with author information sheet (online), table of contents, synopsis, and 3 sample chapters. Send complete manuscript for works under 10 chapters. Prefers email to catherine.mackenzie@christianfocus.com. Accepts hard copy. Does not return manuscripts to authors outside of the U.K. Responds in 3–6 months. Publication period and payment policy vary.

Concordia Publishing House

3558 South Jefferson Avenue, St. Louis, MO 63118-3968
www.cph.org

Executive Director of Editorial: Rev. Paul T. McCain

Concordia Publishing House provides books and other resources that are faithful to the Scriptures and the Lutheran Confessions to families, congregations, and church school teachers. Its children's and YA list features books on religion, faith, prayer, and reliance on God to face life's challenges. It also publishes some Spanish titles.

Freelance Potential: Publishes 50–75 titles annually: all on assignment. Receives 120 queries monthly.

Fiction: Middle-grade, YA. Genres: Contemporary, coming of age, religious, real life.

Nonfiction: Early picture books, early readers, story picture books, middle-grade, YA. Topics: faith, religious holidays, prayer, spirituality, Bible studies, social issues, biography. Also publishes religious education resources and devotionals.

Titles: *Faith on the Edge: Off the Edge: Faith, Science and the Future,* by Adam Francisco (YA). *How You Are Changing: For Girls 9–11 Learning About Sex*, by Jane Graver (ages 9–11).

Submissions and Payment: Guidelines available at website. It is not currently accepting unsolicited manuscripts for children's picture books. For other categories, submit a proposal package that includes a cover letter, résumé, summary, outline or table of contents, sample chapter, and the names of 2 people with credentials to review the work. Accepts email to sarah.steiner@cph.org (Word or PDF attachments only). To be considered for work-for-hire projects, submit credentials to CPH Development Editor. Response time, publication period, and payment policy vary.

Covenant Communications

920 East State Road, Suite F, P.O. Box 416, American Fork, UT 84003 www.covenant-lds.com

Managing Editor: Kathryn Jenkins Gordon

Covenant publishes many kind of books including adult fiction and nonfiction, children's books, and holiday books, all representing the values espoused by The Church of Jesus Christ of Latterday Saints. Its books lift and inspire readers of all ages.

Freelance Potential: Publishes 80 titles (6 juvenile) annually: 100% developed from unsolicited submissions; 25% by authors who are new to the company; 25% by previously unpublished writers. Receives 100 unsolicited manuscripts monthly.

Fiction: Concept books, toddler books, early picture books, middle-grade. Genres: adventure, suspense, inspirational, historical.

Nonfiction: Concept books, toddler books, story picture books. Topics: Bible stories, history, religion, regional, biography, activity, photo-essays, reference books.

Titles: *Seek and Ye Shall Find: Life of Jesus*, by Val Chadwick Bagley (ages 5–10). *Beautiful Savior,* by Greg Olson (ages 10+).

Submissions and Payment: Guidelines and catalogue available at website. Send complete manuscript; cover letter indicating fiction or nonfiction, the intended audience, what makes the proposed book distinct, and the LDS elements of your work; author biography, especially in relation to the book topic; and author questionnaire (downloadable from the website). Prefers email submissions with Word attachments to submissions@covenant-lds.com. Responds in 4–6 months. Publication in 6–12 months. Payment policy varies.

Crossway

1300 Crescent Street, Wheaton, IL 60187. www.crossway.org

Editorial Administrator: Jill Carter

Gospel-centered, Bible-centered books that honor the Savior and serve his church fill the catalogue of Crossway Books. It publishes titles for all ages to help people understand the massive implcations of the gospel and the truth of God's Word.

Freelance Potential: Publishes 80 titles (2 juvenile) annually: 1–5% reprint or licensed properties; 1% by authors who are new to the publishing house. Receives about 5 queries and unsolicited mss monthly.

Nonfiction: Story picture books, YA. Topics: religion, contemporary Christian issues, Christian living, biblical studies, parenting.

Titles: *The Biggest Story: How the Snake Crusher Brings Us Back to the Garden*, by Kevin DeYoung (ages 8–11). *Tell Me the Story*, by Max Lucado (ages 8–12).

Submissions and Payment: Guidelines and catalogue available at website. Email queries to submissions@crossway.org. Do not send manuscripts. Responds within a month to request a proposal, if interested. Publication period and payment policy vary.

CSS Publishing

5450 North Dixie Highway, Lima, OH 45807. www.csspub.com

Acquisitions Editor

CSS produces books and supplemental material that focuses on the "ready-to-use" ministry needs of congregations. Among the variety of material it publishes includes resources for working with youth, children's object lessons and sermons, lectionary-based resources for worship, preaching, group study and drama. It does not publish books for children.

Freelance Potential: Publishes 20–25 titles annually: most developed from unsolicited submissions; 1–10% by authors who are new to the publishing house; 1–10% by previously unpublished writers. Receives 10–20 queries, 10 unsolicited manuscripts monthly.

Nonfiction: Christian education materials, program planners, children's sermons, children's object lessons, pastoral aids. Topics: religious education, the Bible, prayer, worship, parenting, family life.

Titles: *Teaching the Mystery of God to Children*, by Judy Gattis Smith. *The Sacrament of Holy Communion,* by Patti Thisted Arthur.

Submissions and Payment: Guidelines and catalogue available

at website. Mail query with 1- to 2-page summary, author bio, marketing information about the proposed audience and how it may be reached, and 1–2 sample chapters. Also accepts email queries to editor@csspub.com, with no attachments; will respond if interested. Publication in 1 year. Payment policy varies.

Deseret Book Company

P.O. Box 30178, Salt Lake City, UT 84130
www.deseretbook.com

Manuscript Acquisitions: Liz Alley

This publisher is committed to supporting the mission of The Church of Jesus Christ of Latter-day Saints by providing scriptures, books, music, and other products that strengthen individuals, families, and our society. Deseret Book Company publishes adult and children's fiction and nonfiction that reflect church values.

Freelance Potential: Publishes 150 titles (70 juvenile) annually: about 6% developed from unsolicited submissions; 12% by authors who are new to the publishing house. Receives 40 queries, 80 unsolicited manuscripts monthly.

Fiction: Early picture books, story picture books, YA. Genres: fantasy, mystery, romance, contemporary, historical, inspirational, religious.

Nonfiction: Early picture books, board books, story picture books, chapter books, YA. Topics: activity, biography.

Titles: *Tennis Shoes Adventure Series: Gadiantons and the Silver Sword*, by Chris Heimerdinger (ages 12+). *Embark*, by John Bytheway (YA).

Submissions and Payment: Guidelines and catalogue available at website. Query with outline/table of contents, and 2–3 sample chapters; or send complete manuscript. Accepts hard copy or online submissions through the website. SASE. Responds in 3–4 months. Publication in 6–12 months. Royalty, 5–12% of retail.

Eerdmans Books for Young Readers

2140 Oak Industrial Drive NE, Grand Rapids, MI 49505
www.eerdmans.com/youngreaders

Acquisitions Editor

This imprint of Wm. B. Eerdmans Publishing Company features a wide variety of titles for children, including a number with religious subjects or inspirational themes. The publisher puts a premium on engaging characters, good humor, and delightful storylines. Its goal is to produce quality literature for a new generation of readers. Eerdmans is now expanding its list of YA titles. Also of interest are stories that celebrate diversity, stories of historical significance, and stories that relate to contemporary social issues.

Freelance Potential: Publishes 12–18 titles annually: 1–10% developed from unsolicited submissions; 25–50% by agented authors; 50–75% by authors who are new to the publishing house; 10–25% by previously unpublished writers. Receives 1–25 queries, 75–100 unsolicited manuscripts monthly.

Fiction: Toddler books, early picture books, early readers, story picture books, chapter books, middle-grade, YA. Genres: adventure, multicultural, historical, folktales, coming-of-age, nature, sports, real life.

Nonfiction: Picture books, middle-grade, YA. Topics: history, religion, social issues, biography.

Titles: *Animal Beauty,* by Kristin Roskifte (ages 5–9). *Soldier Bear*, by Bibi Dumon Tak and Philip Hopman (ages 4–12).

Submissions and Payment: Guidelines and catalogue available at website. Query with synopsis and at least 3 sample chapters, or send complete manuscript (required for picture books) with a cover letter. Accepts hard copy only. Accepts simultaneous submissions if identified. SASE for manuscript receipt only. Responds in 4 months if interested; materials not returned. Publication period varies. Royalty; advance.

Parents, Divisions, Imprints

Concordia Publishing House, See page 393

Focus on the Family Book Publishing

8605 Explorer Drive, Colorado Springs, CO 80920
www.focusonthefamily.com

Director: Larry Weeden

Focus on the Family is a global Christian ministry dedicated to helping families thrive. Its book development division publishes books for families and a children's fiction series called Imagination

Station, a spinoff of Focus on the Family Adventures in Odyssey radio dramas. In nonfiction, Focus on the Family is currently publishing books of advice on parenting, marriage, and topics for women and seniors. In fiction, it is also looking for books on family issues that promote traditional values. Fiction must be set in the years between 1900 and the present day.

Freelance Potential: Publishes 15 titles (about 3 juvenile) annually: all by agented authors or from writers' conference requests; very few are by new or previously unpublished writers. Receives about 15 queries monthly.

Fiction: Chapter books. Genres: religious, social skills.

Nonfiction: Middle-grade, YA, adult. Topics: family advice, marriage, parenting, relationships, encouragement for women, life challenges.

Titles: *Adventures in Odyssey: Countdown to Christmas Advent Collection. Speak Love: Making Your Words Matter,* by Annie F. Downs (YA). *120 Bible Stories Activity Book,* (ages 5+).

Submissions and Payment: Agented queries only, or by request from a Focus on the Family editor at a writers' conference. Guidelines available. Response time varies. Publication in 18 months. Payment policy varies.

Forward Movement

412 Sycamore Street, Cincinnati, OH 45202–4011
www.forwardmovement.org

Managing Editor

A ministry of the Episcopal Church, Forward Movement has been inspiring disciples and empowering evangelists around the world since 1935. Its catalogue is filled with books and merchandise that encourage spiritual growth and congregations.

Freelance Potential: Publishes about 30 titles annually: about 15% developed from unsolicited submissions; 15% by authors who are new to the publishing house; 30% by previously unpublished writers. Receives 2 unsolicited manuscripts monthly.

Nonfiction: Early readers, middle-grade, YA, adult. Topics: religion, the Bible, devotionals, parenting, church, prayer, holidays, healing.

Titles: *Can You Find Jesus?,* by Philip D. Gallery (ages 4–8). *The Bible Challenge,* edited by Rev. Marek P. Zabriskie.

Submissions and Payment: Guidelines and catalogue available at website. Sample pamphlet available. Send complete manuscript with cover letter or proposal including author bio, intended audience, and scope of the work. Accepts email to editorial@forwardmovement.org. Responds in 1 month. Publication period varies. Flat fee.

Franciscan Media

28 West Liberty Street, Cincinnati, OH 45202–6498
www.franciscanmedia.org

Product Development Director: Mary Carol Kendzia

This well-established Catholic publisher seeks to help Christians grow closer to God by creating inspiring and innovative products in the spirit of St. Francis. It does not publish children's books but some titles will be of interest to young adults and parents.

Freelance Potential: Publishes 20–30 titles annually: 25–35% by authors who are new to the publishing house; 10–15% by previously unpublished writers. Receives 15–25 queries monthly.

Nonfiction: YA, adult (parents, ministers, religious education teachers). Topics: Christian living, personal growth, faith, the sacraments, Scripture, prayer, spirituality, the saints, marriage, family, parenting, Catholic life and identity, Franciscanism, saints, Catholic heroes, contemporary issues, social issues, church history, parish life.

Titles: *The Sign of the Carved Cross,* by Lisa M. Hendey (ages 5–8). *Raising God-First Kids in a Me-First World,* by Barbara Curtis.

Submissions and Payment: Guidelines available at website. Query with cover letter that indicates the topic, working title, approximate length, audience, and competition; table of contents; outline or chapter-by-chapter synopsis; 1–2 sample chapters; author biography; any endorsements; a description of your platform (social media, blog, speaking engagements, etc.); and promotion and marketing ideas. Prefers submissions through online form at website or by email to mckendzia@franciscanmedia.org. Accepts hard copy. SASE. Responds in 2 months. Publication in 1–2 years. Royalty, 10%.

Parents, Divisions, Imprints

Servant Books, See page 426

Friends United Press

101 Quaker Hill Drive, Richmond, IN 47374. www.fum.org/shop

Editor

This Quaker publisher produces books that reflect the denomination's beliefs and heritage. While most of its offerings are designed for adults, the company publishes a number of titles that are appropriate for middle-grade and young adult readers, as well as religious curricula. It is always interested in books on peace and social justice.

Freelance Potential: Publishes 2–5 books annually: some developed from unsolicited submissions. Receives 4–5 queries monthly.

Fiction: Middle-grade, YA. Genres: historical, religious.

Nonfiction: Middle-grade, YA. Topics: Quaker history, theology, the Bible, biography, spirituality, peace, justice, African American culture, the Underground Railroad.

Titles: *Stepping in the Light: Life in Joy and Power,* by Howard R. Macy (YA). *The Good and Beautiful Community,* by James Bryan Smith.

Submissions and Payment: Guidelines and catalogue available at website. Submit cover letter, proposal, and 2–3 sample chapters. Accepts hard copy and electronic submissions to friendspress@fum.org (Word attachments). SASE. Responds in 3 to 6 months. Publication in 1 year. Royalty, 7.5%.

Gefen Kids

6 Hatzvi Street, Jerusalem 94386 Israel
www.gefenpublishing.com

Editor: Ilan Greenfield

Gefen Publishing, a leading Israeli publisher, has a line of children's books that includes English-language fiction and nonfiction. Some of its adult books may also appeal to a young adult audience. All of its books have subjects of interest to a Jewish readership. Gefen Books is the company's U.S. distribution partner.

Freelance Potential: Publishes 20 titles (4–5 juvenile) annually: most developed from unsolicited submissions. Receives 20 queries, 10+ unsolicited manuscripts monthly.

Fiction: Story picture books, chapter books, YA. Genres: religious, Jewish holidays, folktales, historical, social issues.

Nonfiction: Story picture books, early readers, YA. Topics: Jewish holidays, history, Jewish lifestyle, the Holocaust, contemporary issues.

Titles: *Elisha Davidson and the Letters of Fire*, by M. Rhonda Attar and Chaim Natan Firszt (YA–A). *Children of Israel,* by Althea Gold.

Submissions and Payment: Guidelines and catalog available at website. Send complete manuscript with cover letter, table of contents, 1- to 2-page synopsis, author bio, and audience description. Accepts hard copy. Accepts simultaneous submissions. SASE. Responds in 6 months. Publication period and payment policy vary.

Group Publishing

1515 Cascade Avenue, Loveland, CO 80539. www.group.com

Managing Editor: Jennifer Hooks

The mission at Group Publishing is to create experiences that help people grow in relationships with Jesus and each other. Its catalogue is filled with titles that represent that the Bible is the inspired, authoritative Word of God.

Freelance Potential: Publishes 20-30 titles annually: 10-25% developed from unsolicited submissions; 50-75% assigned; less than 10% by agented authors; 10-25% by authors who are new to the publishing company; less than 10% by previously unpublished writers. Receives 4-6 manuscripts monthly.

Nonfiction: Christian educational resources for all ages. Topics: children's sermons and worship ideas, Bible lessons and activities, crafts, devotions, games, plays and skits, leadership, volunteer management, spiritual growth, counseling, the media, current events and social issues, messages, music, retreats, parenting, technology, family ministry.

Titles: *Veggie Tales Sunday School* (ages 3–7). *100 Best Ideas to Turbocharge Your Preschool Ministry* (religious educators).

Submissions and Payment: Catalogue available at website. Query with outline, 2–3 sample chapters, and sample activities; or send complete manuscript as a Word attachment to cmmsubmission@group.com. Also accepts hard copy. SASE. No simultaneous submissions. Responds in 4-8 weeks. Publication period varies. Royalty, rate varies. Flat fee.

Hachai Publishing

527 Empire Boulevard, Brooklyn, NY 11225. www.hachai.com

Editor: Devorah L. Rosenfeld

Hachai Publishing. produces children's books that play a vital role in Jewish homes. It seeks books that convey the Jewish experience through engaging and well-crafted stories that impart a love of Hashem and an understanding of Judaism. Its books convey the traditional Jewish experience of both modern times or long ago.

Freelance Potential: Publishes 5–10 titles annually: 50–75% developed from unsolicited submissions; 25–50% assigned; 1–10% by agented authors. Receives 20 queries, 20 unsolicited manuscripts monthly.

Fiction: Early picture books, early readers, story picture books, chapter books. Genres: Jewish historical, folklore, adventure.

Nonfiction: Early picture books, story picture books, early readers, chapter books. Topics: the Torah, holidays, prayer, biography, mitzvos, middos, Jewish history.

Titles: *If I Went to the Moon,* by Sara Blau (ages 6–8). *Bracha Do You Know?,* by Ariella Stern (ages 0–4).

Submissions and Payment: Guidelines and catalogue available at website. No animal stories. Query with outline and sample chapter; or send complete manuscript. Accepts hard copy and email to editor@ hachai.com (no attachments). SASE. Responds in 2–6 months. Publication in 18–36 months. Flat fee.

Horizon Publishers

191 North 650 East, Bountiful, UT 84010-3628
www.ldshorizonpublishers.com

Manuscript Acquisition Editors: Duane Crowther, Jean Crowther

Horizon publishes across several subject areas, including outdoor life, family preparedness, family life, crafts, writing skills, and music, but many of its books are directed toward the Latter-day Saints market. For children and teens, it wants religious education materials and fiction with LDS values. It is currently closed to submissions; check website for updates.

Freelance Potential: Publishes 20–30 titles annually: most developed from unsolicited submissions and by assignment. Receives 1 unsolicited submission monthly.

Fiction: Early readers, middle-grade, YA. Genres: LDS faith, inspirational, romance, adventure, holidays.

Nonfiction: Chapter books, middle-grade, YA. Topics: Latter-day Saints life, the Mormon faith, church history, spirituality, social issues, activities, holidays, cooking, stitchery, camping, scouting, outdoor life.

Titles: *300 Questions to Ask Your Parents Before It's Too Late*, by Alder Shannon (YA). *Campfire Verses—25 Tales to Share Around the Campfire*, by Ted C. Hindmarsh (all ages).

Submissions and Payment: Guidelines and catalogue available at website. Currently closed to submissions. Check website for changes to this policy. Publication in 6–12 months. Royalty, 10% of wholesale.

InterVarsity Press

P.O. Box 1400, Downers Grove, IL 60515. www.ivpress.com

Academic Editor, General Editor

For more than 70 years, InterVarsity Press has been publishing thoughtful Christian titles. It focuses on general interest books, Bible studies, and study guides for religious education. InterVarsity is an interdenominational publisher and therefore does not publish on strictly denominational issues. It only publishes books by pastors, professors, or previously published authors.

Freelance Potential: Publishes about 110 titles annually: very few developed from unsolicited submissions; about 10% by agented authors; about 30% by authors who are new to the publishing house. Receives 110–120 queries monthly.

Nonfiction: YA, adult (educators, college students, parents). Topics: religion, education, how-to, reference, contemporary issues, Christian lifestyle, the Bible, the church, history, theology, doctrine, prayer, science.

Titles: *How to Read Job*, by John H. Walton. *Making Neighborhoods Whole*, by Wayne Gordon and John M. Perkins.

Submissions and Payment: Guidelines and catalogue available at website. Query with résumé, chapter-by-chapter summary, and 2 sample chapters to the Academic Editor if you are associated with a college or seminary; to the General Editor if you are a pastor or previously published author. Manuscripts may also be submitted through www.christianwritersubmissions.com or Writer's Edge, www.writersedgeservice.com. Accepts hard copy. Accepts simultaneous submissions, if identified. SASE. Response time, 12 weeks. Publication period and payment policy vary.

Jewish Lights

Sunset Farm Offices, Route 4, P.O. Box 237, Woodstock, VT 05091
www.jewishlights.com

Vice President, Editorial: Emily Wichland

Books that reflect the Jewish wisdom tradition, and the search for meaning, for people of all faiths and backgrounds are the mainstay of this publisher. It emphasizes materials about Jewish unity and community, and Judaism's relevance in everyday life. The children's catalogue includes nonfiction titles on Jewish holidays and traditions, spiritual issues, social issues, and guidance.

Freelance Potential: Publishes about 25 titles annually: 60% by authors who are new to the publishing house. Receives 80 queries, 35 unsolicited manuscripts monthly.

Fiction: Story picture books, early readers, chapter books, middle-grade, YA. Genres: graphic novels, religious, multicultural, Bible stories, Jewish customs, holidays, social issues, real life/problems.

Nonfiction: Toddler books, early readers, story picture books, middle-grade, YA. Topics: religion, inspirational, self-help, the Bible, social issues.

Titles: *Adam and Eve's New Day,* by Sandy Eisenberg Sasso (ages 4–8). *The Adventures of Rabbi Harvey,* by Steve Sheinkin (ages 10–14).

Submissions and Payment: Guidelines and catalogue available at website. Query with cover letter, table of contents, introduction to the book, 2 sample chapters, and marketing plan for promotion. Send complete manuscript for picture books only. Accepts hard copy only and simultaneous submissions, if identified. SASE. Responds in 3–6 months. Publication in 1 year. Payment policy varies.

Jewish Publication Society

2100 Arch Street, 2nd Floor, Philadelphia, PA 19103
www.jewishpub.org

Editor: Rabbi Barry Schwartz

The oldest publisher of Jewish books in the United States, the Jewish Publication Society embraces Jewish heritage and culture, and seeks to enhance Jewish literacy with great books.

Freelance Potential: Publishes about 12 titles annually. Receives 40–50 queries monthly.

Nonfiction: Adult. Topics: the Bible, Jewish ethics, scholarship, Midrash, interfaith, history.

Titles: *Abraham Joshua Heschel,* by Or Rose (ages 9–12). *Best Jewish Books for Children and Teens: A JPS Guide*, by Linda Silver (parents).

Submissions and Payment: Guidelines and catalogue available at website. Send a 1-page query that includes: a brief description of the book, target audience, author qualifications, market analysis of other works on the same topic, résumé. Accepts hard copy and email to bschwartz@jps.org. SASE. Response time, publication period, and payment policy vary.

JourneyForth

1700 Wade Hampton Boulevard, Greenville, SC 29614-0060
www.journeyforth.com

Acquisitions Editor: Nancy Lohr

JourneyForth publishes fiction and nonfiction for children from preschool through high school. under its JourneyForth Youth imprint. It also offers Bible studies and Christian living books for teens and adults. All manuscripts must be written from a Christian worldview. Current needs include mysteries for tweens and early chapter books. It is not currently accepting picture book submissions.

Freelance Potential: Publishes 5–10 titles annually: 1–10% developed from unsolicited submissions; 1–10% by agented authors; 1–10% by authors who are new to the publishing house; 1–10% by previously unpublished writers. Receives 10–25 queries, 10–25 unsolicited mss monthly.

Fiction: Chapter books, middle-grade, YA. Genres: historical, biblical, Christian, mystery, contemporary, folktales, fantasy.

Nonfiction: Chapter books, middle-grade, YA, adult. Topics: spiritual growth, biography, Christian living, Bible study.

Titles: *A King for Brass Cobweb*, by Dawn L. Watkins (ages 6–7). *A Father's Promise,* by Donnalynn Hess (ages 9–12).

Submissions and Payment: Guidelines and catalogue available at website. For nonfiction, query. For fiction, query with cover letter including target audience and author bio, and first 5 chapters. Accepts hard copy and email to journeyforth@bju.edu. See website for specific guidelines for each genre. Accepts simultaneous submissions if identified. SASE. Responds in 12 weeks. Publication in 12–18 months. Royalty, advance.

The Judaica Press

123 Ditmas Avenue, Brooklyn, NY 11218. www.judaicapress.com

Editor: Norman Shapiro

For more than 50 years, The Judaica Press has been publishing impressive titles that hold true to the ideals of authentic Judaism and its traditions. Its motto, "Jewish Books that Matter" represents the standard set by this company. It publishes titles for children under its JP Kids imprint.

Freelance Potential: Publishes 20–25 titles annually: about 25% by authors who are new to the publishing house. Receives about 10 queries, 10 unsolicited manuscripts monthly.

Fiction: Board books, early picture books, early readers, story picture books, chapter books, middle-grade, YA. Genres: historical, religious, contemporary, mystery, folktales, Jewish holidays and heritage.

Nonfiction: Story picture books, early readers, YA. Topics: Jewish traditions, Torah stories, the Hebrew language, crafts, hobbies, holidays.

Titles: *Penina's Doll Factory,* by Miriam Walfish (ages 8–12). *What Do You See on Rosh Hashanah and Yom Kippur?*, by Bracha Goetz.

Submissions and Payment: Guidelines and catalogue available at website. Send complete manuscript with cover letter that summarizes manuscript and states intended purpose and audience. Email to submissions@judaicapress.com. Availability of artwork improves chance of acceptance. Responds in 3 months. Publication in 1 year. Royalty.

Judson Press

P.O. Box 851, Valley Forge, PA 19482-0851. www.judsonpress.com

Editor: Rev. Rebecca Irwin-Diehl

The publishing arm of the American Baptist Churches USA, Judson publishes ecumenically and specializes in practical books for church leaders and Christians. Titles for children are mostly non-curriculum educational materials and ministry resources, and a few inspirational titles.

Freelance Potential: Publishes 10–12 titles annually: about 60% developed from unsolicited submissions; 10% by agented authors; 5% reprint/licensed properties; 50% by authors who are new to the publishing house; 30% by previously unpublished writers. Receives 20-25 queries monthly.

Nonfiction: Education and youth ministry titles. Topics: religion, history, social issues, real life/problems, theology, education, devotionals.

Titles: *I'll Do the Right Thing,* by Jean Alicia Elster (ages 6–10). *Jordan's Hair,* by Ed and Sonya Spruill (ages 5–8).

Submissions and Payment: Guidelines, including current needs, and catalogue available at website. Query with cover letter that indicates the working title, a summary of 3–5 sentences, and target audience; proposal with annotated table of contents; related/competing titles, market analysis; marketing plan; résumé; and 25 manuscript pages that include the first chapter (send complete manuscript for picture books only). Accepts hard copy and email to acquisitions@judsonpress.com (Word attachments). SASE. Responds in 3–6 months. Publication in 12–18 months. Royalty, 10%.

Kar-Ben Publishing

241 First Avenue North, Minneapolis, MN 55401
www.karben.com

Publisher: Joni Sussman

This division of Lerner Publishing Group produces children's books exclusively on Jewish themes, such as Jewish holidays, Bible stories, folktales, and stories reflecting the rich diversity of contemporary Jewish life. Its titles are targeted to children from pre-K up through 6th grade. It looks for books with a combination of Jewish theme, reader appeal, and liveliness of language.

Freelance Potential: Publishes 15–18 titles annually: 50–75% developed from unsolicited submissions; 10-20% assigned; 1–10% by agented authors; 25–50% by authors who are new to the publishing house; 10–25% by previously unpublished writers. Receives 25–50 unsolicited manuscripts monthly.

Fiction: Jewish-themed concept books, toddler books, early picture books, story picture books, chapter books. Genres: folklore, life-cycle stories, tales from the Torah, Jewish identity, holiday stories.

Nonfiction: Board and activity books, early picture books, and early reader books with Jewish subjects. Topics: Jewish identity, traditions, holidays, history, doctrine, Israel, the Jewish experience, prayer books.

Titles: *Seder in the Desert*, by Jamie Korngold (ages 4–6). *The Whispering Town*, by Jennifer Elvgren (ages 7–11).

Submissions and Payment: Guidelines and catalogue available at website. Send complete manuscript. Prefers email with Word attachment to editorial@karben.com. Accepts hard copy. SASE. Simultaneous submissions accepted if identified. Responds in 6–8 weeks. Publication period varies. Flat fee and/or advance, royalty.

Parents, Divisions, Imprints

Lerner Publishing Group: See page 277

Kregel Publications

P.O. Box 2607, Grand Rapids, MI 49501-2607. www.kregel.com

Acquisitions Editor

The mission of Kregel Publications as an evangelical publisher is to develop and distribute trusted, biblically based resources that lead individuals to know and serve Jesus Christ. Its backlist includes more than 900 titles including books on Christian education, contemporary issues, Christian living and Bible studies.

Freelance Potential: Publishes about 75 titles (1-8 juvenile) annually: 65% by agented authors; 1–10% reprint/licensed properties; 25% by authors who are new to the publishing house; 1–10% by previously unpublished writers. Receives 18 queries monthly.

Fiction: Board books, story picture books, early readers, chapter books, middle-grade, YA. Genres: Bible stories, adventure, prayer, religion, holidays, folktales, activity.

Nonfiction: Board books, story picture books, early readers, middle-grade, YA. Topics: the Bible, religion, holidays, family, Christian parenting, Christian lifestyle.

Titles: *Would You Like to Know the Story of Easter?*, by Tim Dowley and Eira Reeves (ages 4–10). *The Midnight Visitor*, by Juliet David and Jo Parry (ages 4–8).

Submissions and Payment: Catalogue available at website. Accepts queries from agents. No unsolicited manuscripts. Reviews manuscripts through the manuscript screening services Writer's Edge (www.writersedgeservice.com) and Christian Manuscript Submissions (www.christianmanuscriptsubmissions.com). Royalty.

Legacy Press

P.O. Box 261129, San Diego, CA 92196. www.legacypresskids.com

Submissions: Daniel Miley

A division of Rose Publishing, Legacy Press specializes in Christian-themed and Bible study materials. It also publishes fiction and nonfiction for children, activity books, and resources for religious education teachers. Its titles are meant to help children grow in their faith and become closer to God. All books should exalt the presence of Jesus in our lives in a fun yet meaningful way.

Freelance Potential: Publishes 10 titles each year: 80% developed from unsolicited submissions; 10% by agented authors; 10% reprint/licensed properties; 50% by authors who are new to the publishing house; 50% by previously unpublished writers. Receives 10 queries monthly.

Fiction: Toddler books, story picture books, early readers, chapter books, middle-grade. Genres: adventure, mystery, contemporary, animals, social issues—all with a Christian theme.

Nonfiction: Sunday school activity workbooks, devotionals, chapter books, middle-grade. Topics: the Bible, holidays, cooking, crafts, fashion, social issues, hobbies, sports, real life/problems, activities.

Titles: *Gotta Have God* (ages 2–5). *The Christian Girl's Guide to Your Mom* (ages 8–12).

Submissions and Payment: Guidelines available at website.

Query with table of contents and 2–5 chapters, author bio, and audience analysis. Accepts hard copy only. SASE. Responds in 10–20 weeks. Publication period varies. Royalty; advance, $500+.

Lighthouse Publishing

251 Overlook Park Lane, Lawrenceville, GA 30043
www.lighthousebooks.com

Submissions Department

The goal of Lighthouse Publishing is to provide high-quality original works at the lowest possible prices. It's titles range from children's books, to business/technical manuals, to self-help books. 30% self-, subsidy-, co-venture, or co-op published material.

Freelance Potential: Publishes 50–55 titles annually: 95% developed from unsolicited submissions; 10–15% by agented authors; 70% by authors who are new to the publishing house, 30–35% by previously unpublished writers. Receives 200 manuscripts yearly.

Fiction: Story picture books, early readers, chapter books, middle-grade. Genres: fantasy, mystery, social issues, inspirational.

Nonfiction: YA, adult. Also publishes church school materials and devotionals. Topics: the Bible, history, religion, evolution, social issues, real life/problems.

Titles: *Candy Moon*, by Londa Hayden (ages 5–8). *If Rocks Could Speak,* by Holly Smalley (6+).

Submissions and Payment: Guidelines available at website. Send complete manuscript with a synopsis of the book, a brief outline of each chapter, and résumé. Accepts email submissions only (Word or RTF attachments) to iandyoverett@lighthouseebooks.com. Responds in 3–6 weeks. Publication in 4–6 months. Royalty, 50% of net.

Liguori Publications

1 Liguori Drive, Liguori, MO 63057-9999. www.liguori.org

Editorial Director

This Catholic book and magazine publisher promotes outreach to Catholics of all ages. The goal is to help them understand and celebrate the role of God in their lives and joyfully practice their faith. Liguori's children's books include titles that introduce God, the Bible, and prayer, and help young readers navigate contemporary social issues. The company also publishes religious education materials and some titles in Spanish.

Freelance Potential: Publishes 40 titles annually: several developed from unsolicited submissions.

Nonfiction: Toddler books, early readers, middle-grade, YA. Topics: prayer, catechism, Catholicism, the saints, celebrations, holy days, youth ministry, family, divorce, chastity, contemporary issues.

Titles: *10 Things Pope Francis Wants You to Know about the Family*, by Joshua J. McElwee (families). *Your Child's First Confession*, by Rosemary Gallagher (parents).

Submissions and Payment: Guidelines and catalogue available at website. Send proposal with overview, tentative title, outline, sample table of contents, sample chapter, author bio, completion timeline, market analysis, and competition report. Accepts hard copy and email submissions to manuscript_submission@liguori.org. SASE. Responds in 6 weeks. Publication in 9–18 months. Royalty.

Lion Children's Books

Wilkinson House, Jordan Hill Road, Oxford OX2 8DR
United Kingdom. www.lionhudson.com

Editorial Administrator: Jessica Tinker

An imprint of Lion Hudson, Lion Children's Books publishes books that reflect Christian values or are inspired by a Christian worldview. Its list includes fiction and nonfiction titles that address the needs of an audience ranging from infants to teens. It is not accepting any fiction submissions at this time, however. The company publishes books that introduce children to God and the Bible, and books that foster an awareness of the world.

Freelance Potential: Publishes 45 titles annually: only a few developed from unsolicited submissions or agented authors; 2% reprint/licensed properties. Receives 80 queries monthly.

Fiction: Early picture books, concept books, toddler books, chapter books, YA. Genres: fairy tales, inspirational, social issues, adventure.

Nonfiction: Toddler books, early picture books, early readers, story picture books, middle-grade, YA. Topics: religion, current events, history, nature, social issues, health and fitness.

Titles: *Are You Sad, Little Bear?*, by Rachel Rivett and Tina Macnaughton (ages 4–8). *Candle Bible for Me*, by Juliet David and Mark Jones (ages 2–4).

Submissions and Payment: Guidelines and catalogue available at website. Query with cover letter, synopsis, and résumé. Accepts hard copy. SAE/IRC. Responds in 3 months, if interested. Publication period and payment policy vary.

Living Ink Books

AMG Publishers, 6815 Shallowford Road, Chattanooga, TN 37421
www.amgpublishers.com

Acquisitions: Rick Steele

This imprint of AMG Publishers produces exciting, Christian-themed fiction for middle-grade and young adult readers. Its focus is on books that help the reader get into the Bible. Its books are inspiring, and full of action and emotion.

Freelance Potential: Publishes about 10 juvenile and 3–5 adult titles annually. Receives 100 queries monthly.

Fiction: Middle-grade, YA adult. Genres: fantasy, dystopian, historical, mystery, adventure—all with Christian themes.

Titles: *The Curse of the Seer*, by Daniel Schwabauer (ages 8-13). *Omega Dragon*, by Bryan Davis (ages 13+).

Submissions and Payment: Guidelines and catalogue available at website. Query with brief description of the book, proposed market, proposed page count, and author biography; query should be no longer than 1 page. Accepts hard copy and email queries to ricks@amgpublishers.com. If interested, a proposal will be requested. Response time and publication period vary. Royalty; advance.

Parents, Divisions, Imprints

AMG Publishers, See page 382

Master Books

P.O. Box 726, Green Forest, AR 72638. www.masterbooks.net

Assistant Editor: Craig Froman

Part of New Leaf Publishing Group, this imprint focuses on Christians needing to understand the times to know what the church ought to do. It is interested in educational materials for kindergarten through grade 12, homeschooling materials, and inspirational books on faith. It also publishes a small amount of fiction. New Leaf Publishing's other imprint offering children's titles is New Leaf Press.

Freelance Potential: Publishes 20–30 titles annually: 10–25% developed from unsolicited submissions; 50–75% assigned; 10–25% by agented authors; 25–50% by authors new to the publishing company; 25–50% by previously unpublished writers. Receives 25–50 queries, 50–75 manuscripts monthly.

Fiction: Concept books, chapter books, middle-grade, YA. Genres: religious, inspirational.

Nonfiction: Picture books, middle-grade, YA. Topics: science, biography, education, inspirational, real life/problems, social issues, sports, animals, reference materials.

Titles: *N is for Noah: Trusting God and His Promises*, by Ken and Mally Ham (grades preK-2). *The Ecology Book* (Wonders of Creation Series), by Tom Hennigan and Jean Lightner (grades 5–12).

Submissions and Payment: Catalogue available at website. Email proposal form at website as an attachment to submissions@newleafpress.net, or print out and mail. Accepts simultaneous submissions if identified. Responds in 3 months and will request complete manuscript if interested. Publication in 9-12 months. Royalty.

Parents, Divisions, Imprints

New Leaf Press, See page 415

Thomas Nelson Children's Books and Education ✐

501 Nelson Place, P.O. Box 141000, Nashville, TN 37214
www.thomasnelson.com

Acquisitions Editor

Since its establishment in Edinburgh, Scotland, more than 200 years ago, Thomas Nelson's publishing program has been guided by two goals—to honor God and to serve people. It offers books for very young children to young adults under its Tommy Nelson imprint. This Christian publisher's mission is to inspire the world with works of fiction and nonfiction on a wide variety of topics. Both are owned by HarperCollins Christian Publishing. Common to all of its products are biblical themes, Christian values, and quality writing. 2% self-, subsidy-, co-venture, or co-op published material.

Freelance Potential: Publishes about 40 titles annually: 100% by agented authors. Receives 85+ submissions monthly.

Fiction: Toddler books, early picture books, early readers, story picture books, middle-grade. Genres: religious, real life/problems, contemporary, inspirational, action/adventure, fantasy, social issues.

Nonfiction: Concept books, early readers, story picture books middle-grade, YA, devotionals, Bible storybooks. Topics: the Bible, Christianity, Christian living, inspirational, biography, books of interest to girls, books of interest to boys.

Titles: *Say & Pray Bible,* by Diane Stortz (ages 1-4). *My ABC of God Loves Me,* by Thomas Nelson (ages 0–5).

Submissions and Payment: Catalogue available at website. Accepts proposals through literary agents only. Also recommends www.christianmanuscriptsubmissions.com. Response time and publication period vary. Royalty; advance.

Parents, Divisions, Imprints

Tommy Nelson Kids, See page 174

New Hope Publishers

P.O. Box 12065, Birmingham, AL 35202-2065
www.newhopepublishers.com

Publisher: Andrea Mullins

They are about mission living, specializing in titles for women—their service, testimony, families, and community. New Hope Publishers also has some titles on its list for children and young adults. It offers inspirational, self-help, and spiritual books, along with Christian education materials. New Hope looks for books that inspire and challenge Christians to do God's work and help readers live out Christ's love in their homes and in their communities.

Freelance Potential: Publishes about 25 titles annually: 50% by agented authors.

Fiction: YA, adult. Genres: inspirational, historical, romance, adventure.

Nonfiction: PreK, middle-grade, YA, adult. Topics: spiritual growth, religion, contemporary issues, real life/problems, prayer, women's issues, parenting, relationships, mission life, Christian living, Bible study, religious education materials.

Titles: *Ladies In Waiting for Little Girls,* by Jackie Kendall and Dede Kendall (ages 4–10). *Intertwined,* by Jennifer Slattery (YA/adult).

Submissions and Payment: Catalogue available at website. No queries or unsolicited submissions. It recommends the manuscript screening service, Christian Manuscript Submissions (www.christianmanuscriptsubmissions.com). Response time and publication period vary. Royalty. Flat fee.

New Leaf Press

P.O. Box 726, Green Forest, AR 72638. www.nlpg.com

Assistant Editor: Craig Froman

Believing in the power of the printed page to move people towards Christ, New Leaf Press, an imprint of New Leaf Publishing Group, specializes in nonfiction religious books for children, young adults, parents, and teachers. It offers a broad range of inspirational titles for families and ministries, including books on Christian values and Bible stories, as well as gift books, church leadership resources, and children's Bibles. It is currently not accepting children's fiction.

Freelance Potential: Publishes 20–25 titles annually: 10–25% developed from unsolicited submissions; 25–50% assigned; 10–25% by agented authors; 25%–50% by authors who are new to the publishing house; 10–20% by previously unpublished writers. Receives 50–75 queries and manuscripts monthly.

Fiction: Currently not accepting children's fiction.

Nonfiction: Concept books, picture books, middle-grade, YA. Topics: the Bible, Christian living, history, education, current events, animals, sports, biography, career/college, science, social issues.

Titles: *The Answers Book for Kids, Volumes 5 & 6,* by Ken Ham and Bodie Hodge (ages 8–12). *Children's Atlas of God's World,* by Craig Froman (ages 8–14).

Submissions and Payment: Guidelines available at website. Must use submission form on website with query letter. Prefers submissions via email with Word attachments, to submissions@newleafpress.net. Accepts simultaneous submissions if identified. Responds in 3 months. Publication in 9-12 months. Royalty.

Parents, Divisions, Imprints

Master Books, See page 412

O Books

Laurel House, Station Approach, Alresford, Hampshire SO24 9JH United Kingdom. www.o-books.com

Editor: Trevor Greenfield

Aiming to inform and help you on this journey through life, this company, an imprint of John Hunt Publishing, takes its name from the symbol of the world, oneness, and unity. It publishes books for children and adults on religion and spirituality from all angles—psychology, culture, and self-help. 2% self-, subsidy-, co-venture, or co-op published material.

Freelance Potential: Publishes 200 titles annually: 25% developed from unsolicited submissions; 10% by agented authors; 30% by authors who are new to the publishing house; 20% by previously unpublished writers. Receives 500 queries monthly.

Fiction: Early readers, story picture books, chapter books, middle-grade, YA. Genres: religious, spiritual, adventure, fantasy, historical, fairy tales, folktales, contemporary.

Nonfiction: Story picture books, chapter books, middle-grade, YA. Topics: spirituality, religion, meditation, prayer, astrology, social issues, animals.

Titles: *From Darkness to Diva*, by Skye High (YA–A). *It's About You!,* by Chris W.E. Johnson (YA–A).

Submissions and Payment: Guidelines and catalogue available at website. Query with proposal form at website and sample chapters. Response time varies. Publication in 18 months. Royalty. Flat fee.

Our Sunday Visitor

200 Noll Plaza, Huntington, IN 46750. www.osv.com

Acquisitions Editor

Responding to peoples' needs, this nonprofit publisher produces trade books, periodicals, and religious education products that reinforce the Roman Catholic perspective. It publishes titles for children, young adults, parents, and church school teachers. Our Sunday Visitor also publishes religious education curricula serving kindergarten through grade eight, including the materials published by Harcourt Religion, which OSV purchased a few years ago. OSV looks for books and subjects that are engaged with the contemporary world yet are still faithful to what the Catholic Church teaches.

Freelance Potential: Publishes 20 titles annually: 10–15% by authors who are new to the publishing house. Receives 10–12 queries monthly.

Nonfiction: Concept books, story picture books, chapter books, middle-grade, YA. Topics: family issues, parish life, the Bible, sacraments, religion, theology, holidays, prayer, devotionals, real life/problems, social issues, Catholic identity and practices, lives of saints, contemporary issues, educational materials.

Titles: *Where Is That in the Bible,* by Patrick Madrid (YA–A). *The Beatitudes for Children*, (grades K-3).

Submissions and Payment: Catalogue available at website. Query with proposal that includes: cover letter with working title, manuscript length, anticipated completion date, market comparison, and explanation of why your book is unique; 2- to 4-page chapter outline, including projected illustrations or other features; author biography; and 1–2 sample chapters. Email to booksed@osv.com. Also accepts hard copy. Accepts simultaneous submissions, if identified. SASE. Responds in 6 weeks. Publication in 1+ years. Royalty; advance. Flat fee.

Pacific Press Publishing

1350 North Kings Road, Nampa, ID 83687. www.pacificpress.com

Acquisitions Editor: Scott Cady

With a sole purpose to uplift Jesus Christ in communicating biblical teachings, health principles and family values, Pacific Press publishes a wide variety of Christian books with a Seventh-day Adventist perspective. Its aim is to help readers develop a relationship with God. Books are in complete harmony with the Bible and are meant to encourage and uplift readers in the struggles of life as well as prepare them for eternal life with God.

Freelance Potential: Publishes 30–40 titles annually: 10–25% developed from unsolicited submissions; 50–75% assigned; 10–25% by authors who are new to the publishing house; less than 10% by previously unpublished writers.

Fiction: Early readers, chapter books, middle-grade, YA. Topics: real life/problems, adventure, historical.

Nonfiction: Toddler books, chapter books, middle-grade, YA, activity/puzzle books. Topics: biography, holidays, inspirational, religious nonfiction on Seventh-day Adventist beliefs and key figures.

Titles: *A Friend for Zipper,* by Heather Grovet (ages 9-12). *The Schoolhouse Burned Twice,* by B.A. Larsen (ages 9–12).

Submissions and Payment: Guidelines and catalogue available at website. Query with one-sentence thesis of main idea, summary of the book, intended audience, author qualifications, chapter outline, and how far along the manuscript is. Accepts hard copy (SASE), fax to (208) 465-2531, or email to booksubmissions@ pacificpress.com. Responds in 1–3 weeks. Publication in 12–18 months. Royalty, advance.

P & R Publishing

P.O. Box 817, Phillipsburg, NJ 08865. www.prpbooks.com

Acquisitions Editor: Melissa Craig

Dedicated to publishing excellent books that promote "biblical understanding and Godly living, " P & R's list ranges from academic works advancing biblical scholarship to popular books that help lay readers grow in Christian thought and service. For middle-grade and YA readers, the publisher offers Christian and inspirational fiction and Christian-themed nonfiction on life issues.

Freelance Potential: Publishes about 40 titles (4–8 juvenile) annually: 35–50% by authors who are new to the publishing house; 1–20% by previously unpublished writers. Receives 15–25 queries monthly.

Fiction: Middle-grade, YA. Genres: inspirational, religious, fantasy, historical, adventure.

Nonfiction: Middle-grade, YA. Topics: Christian living, counseling, theology, religion, education, the Bible, apologetics, Christian issues, ethics, women's issues.

Titles: *Unleash: Quest for Truth Book 3*, by Brock Eastman (ages 9–14). *Am I Called*, by George W. Robertson (YA–A).

Submissions and Payment: Catalogue and guidelines available at website. Query with submissions form at website by email to editorial@prpbooks.com. Responds in 1–3 months. Publication period varies. Royalty.

Pauline Books & Media

50 St. Paul's Avenue, Boston, MA 02130-3491. www.pauline.org

Children's Editors: Marlyn Evangelina Monge, FSP, Jaymie Stuart Wolfe

The editors of Pauline Books & Media particularly welcome proposals for books that help form a child in their faith and affirm the dignity of the person the child is to become. It is the publishing arm of the Daughters of St. Paul, and offers material for all ages, from children to adults. Its Pauline Kids and Pauline Teens titles offer wholesome and entertaining reading, help children develop strong Christian values, and inspire hope. It seeks engaging picture book concepts for toddlers and primary readers, as well as manuscripts for beginning, intermediate, preteen, and teen readers. Pauline Books also publishes select Spanish and bilingual titles. All material should be relevant to the lives of young readers and in accord with Catholic teaching and practice.

Freelance Potential: Publishes 20 titles annually: 10% developed from unsolicited submissions; 15% reprint/licensed properties; 20% by authors who are new to the publishing house; 20% by previously unpublished writers. Receives 20–35 queries monthly.

Fiction: Toddler books, early picture books, story picture books, early readers, chapter books, middle-grade, YA. Genres: Bible stories, religion, inspirational, historical fiction, graphic novels, fantasy, fairy tales, science fiction, myths, romance, all with a Catholic perspective.

Nonfiction: Toddler books, chapter books, middle-grade, YA. Topics: religious education, religious coloring/activity books, church holidays, values, prayer, faith, spirituality, saints, sacraments, the Bible, contemporary issues.

Titles: *Forever You: A Book About Your Soul and Body,* by Nicole Lataif (ages 4–7). *Mission Libertad,* by Lizette M. Lantigua (ages 11–14).

Submissions and Payment: Guidelines available at website. Query with cover letter containing synopsis and 2 sample chapters. Send complete manuscript for board books and picture books. Accepts hard copy, and email with Word attachments to editorial@paulinemedia. com. Accepts simultaneous submissions, if identified. SASE. Responds within 3 months. Publication in 2–3 years. Royalty, 5–10% of net; advance, $200–$500.

Paulist Press

997 Macarthur Boulevard, Mahwah, NJ 07430.
www.paulistpress.com

Submission Editor

Since 1865, Paulist Press has published the best of Catholic thought at the intersection of faith and culture, using all contemporary media to communicate relgious truths and to support people in their search for a greater meaning. It publishes books for children, young adults, and adults on faith, history, social issues, and personal growth.

Freelance Potential: Publishes 60–75 titles annually: 10% by agented authors; 50–75% assigned; 30% by authors who are new to the publishing house; 1% by previously unpublished writers. Receives 25–50 queries, 25–50 unsolicited manuscripts monthly.

Nonfiction: Early picture books, story picture books, middle-grade, YA. Topics: prayer, saints, modern heroes, Bible stories, Catholic viewpoints on current issues.

Titles: *Dorothy Day: Champion of the Poor*, by Elaine Murray Stone (ages 8+). *Finn's Marching Band,* by Rachelle Evensen (ages 2–5).

Submissions and Payment: Guidelines and catalogue available at website. Send complete manuscript for picture with résumé and cover letter that summarizes the story, states the intended age group and category (see website for list), estimated length and completion date, market analysis, and author promotion ideas. Picture book submissions must include sample illustrations. Prefers email to submissions@paulistpress.com, cc: dcrilly@paulistpress. com (Word attachments); will accept hard copy. SASE. Responds in 2+ months. Accepts simultaneous submissions if identified. Publication period varies. Royalty.

The Pilgrim Press

700 Prospect Avenue, Cleveland, OH 44115-1100
www.ucc.org/the-pilgrim-press

Editorial Director: Kim Sadler

Trying to remain attentive to God's creative movement in the
world, Pilgrim Press is the publishing division of the United Church
of Christ. Many of its titles are used as part of religious education
programs. It is currently interested in submissions in the following
categories: spiritual health and wellness, leadership and congregations, pastoral ministry, and worship. Pilgrim Press looks for
authors who can write clearly and concisely and who have the credentials to write on the topic they propose.

Freelance Potential: Publishes 40 titles annually: about 50%
developed from unsolicited submissions; 1–10% by agented
authors; about 25% by authors who are new to the publishing
house; 1–10% by previously unpublished writers. Receives 20+
queries monthly.

Nonfiction: Middle-grade, YA, adult. Topics: spiritual health and
wellness, leadership and congregations, pastoral ministry, worship, social issues, multicultural, ethnic, religious education.

Titles: *Finding God in the Graffiti: Empowering Teenagers Through
Their Stories,* by Frank Rogers (YA). *God's Blue Earth: Teaching
Kids to Celebrate the Sacred Gifts of Water,* by Randy Hammer and
Suzanne Blokland (ages 7–10).

Submissions and Payment: Detailed guidelines and catalogue
available at website. Send an email to proposals@thepilgrimpress.
com for a proposal questionnaire. Responds in 9–12 months. Flat
fee for work-for-hire projects.

Rainbow Publishers

P.O. Box 261129, San Diego, CA 92196. www.rainbowpublishers.com

Submissions: Daniel Miley

Believing that the Bible is the true, inspired word of God Rainbow
Publishers publishes books for use in Christian religion classes or for
teaching religion at home to children ages 2 to 12 are the focus of
this publisher. Its aim is to help teachers and parents lead children
to stronger relationships with Jesus Christ. Rainbow Publishers spe-

cializes in reproducible, flexible, and age-appropriate Bible teaching books that are of value to Christian Ministries. It is always seeking fresh ideas that capture the imagination yet stay true to Bible teaching.

Freelance Potential: Publishes about 16 titles annually. Receives 8–10 queries monthly.

Nonfiction: Christian education resource materials, preK–grade 6. Topics: the Bible, Christianity, crafts, activities, puzzles, hobbies.

Titles: *Instant Bible Lessons for Toddlers: Jesus Teaches Me: Volume 2,* by Mary Davis (ages 2–4). *5 Minute Sunday School Activities: Forever Faithful,* by Karen Wingate (ages 5–10).

Submissions and Payment: Guidelines and catalogue available at website. Query with résumé, table of contents, 2–5 sample chapters, intended audience, and market/competition analysis. Accepts hard copy. Accepts simultaneous submissions, if identified. SASE. Responds in 10–20 weeks. Publication in 1–3 years. Flat fee.

Randall House

114 Bush Road, P.O. Box 17306, Nashville, TN 37217
www.randallhouse.com

Acquisitions Editor: Michelle Orr

When it comes to discipleship one size does not fit all. Randall House publishes Sunday school resources for children of all ages, parenting titles, and fiction and nonfiction on Christian themes. Owned by the National Association of Free Will Baptists, its materials are Bible-based and promote the cause of Christ.

Freelance Potential: Publishes 15 titles annually: 20% developed from unsolicited submissions; 15% by agented authors; 20% by authors who are new to the publishing house; 15% by previously unpublished writers. Receives 80–100 queries monthly.

Fiction: Story picture books, early readers, chapter books, middle-grade, YA. Genres: fantasy, adventure, social issues, religion.

Nonfiction: Church school curriculum materials for preK–grade 12, story picture books, early readers, middle-grade, YA. Topics: holidays, religion, the Bible, social issues, theology, family.

Titles: *52 Creative Family Time Experiences,* by Timothy Smith (adult). *The Smart Stepdad,* by Ron L. Deal (adult).

Submissions and Payment: Catalogue available at website. Query with proposal that includes the book's purpose and primary and secondary audience, author biography, market and competition analysis, annotated outline/table of contents, 3–4 sample chapters, estimated manuscript length, suggested illustrations, and experts who will endorse the book. Accepts hard copy, or email queries to michelle.orr@randallhouse.com. Accepts simultaneous submissions, if identified. SASE. Responds in 10–12 weeks. Publication in 12–14 months. Royalty, 10–14%; advance, $1,000–$2,000.

Resource Publications

160 East Virginia Street, #170, San Jose, CA 95112. www.rpinet.com

Publisher/Editor: William Burns

Resource Publications is an independent communications company that strives to help people reach their fullest potential, specializing in materials for professionals and volunteers in religious education and liturgical ministry. For children, it publishes books on faith formation, Christian topics, and children's liturgy. It is interested in titles that confront leading issues of the day.

Freelance Potential: Publishes 5–10 titles annually: 10–25% developed from unsolicited submissions; 10-25% assigned. Receives 6–10 queries monthly.

Nonfiction: Middle-grade, YA. Topics: prayer, religion, catechism, faith, meditations, the sacraments, spirituality, contemporary issues.

Titles: *Evangelizing Unchurched Children*, by Therese M. Boucher (adult). *Modern Liturgy Answers the 101 Most-Asked Questions About Liturgy*, by Nick Wagner.(YA/adult)

Submissions and Payment: Guidelines and catalogue available at website. Accepts queries and complete manusript. Submit project proposal form at website along with a table of contents and writing sample (introduction or chapter). Accepts hard copy and email to editor@rpinet.com. Responds in 6–8 weeks. Publication in 9 months. Royalty, 8% of net.

Revell

Baker Publishing Group, 6030 East Fulton Road, Ada, MI 49301
www.revellbooks.com

Editor

Revell has been a division of Baker Publishing Group since the 1990s, but it has a history of more than 125 years as a Christian publisher. It publishes books that represent historic Christianity. Its books are both practical and inspirational.

Freelance Potential: Publishes hundreds of books annually.

Fiction: Middle-grade, YA, adult. Genres: religious, holidays, people and places, sports, animals. For adults: Christian, romance, historical, contemporary, fantasy, men's, women's, psychological, suspense, humor, mysteries.

Nonfiction: Middle-grade, YA, adult. Topics: religion, Bible stories, biography, history, family, home, health, crafts, cooking, self-help, education, parenting, pets, relationships, sports.

Titles: *The Chase,* by Kyle and Kelsey Kupecky (adult). *Your Love and Marriage*, by Willard F. Harley, Jr (adult).

Submissions and Payment: Accepts manuscripts only through agents; conferences where Baker staff participates; or the manuscript services Authonomy.com, Writer's Edge (www.writersedgeservice.com), or Christian Manuscript Submissions (www.christianmanuscriptsubmissions.com). Response time and publication period vary. Royalty, 15% of net.

Parents, Divisions, Imprints

Baker Publishing Group, See page 384

Rose Publishing

4733 Torrance Boulevard, # 259, Torrance, CA 90503
www.rose-publishing.com

Acquisitions Editor: Lynette Pennings

Helping believers love God by deepening their understanding of who God is, Rose Publishing, keeps with the conservative, evangelical Christian perspective, producing easy-to-use Bible study and reference materials, including visual aids such as charts and timelines.

Freelance Potential: Publishes about 25 titles annually: 1–10% by authors who are new to the publishing house.

Nonfiction: Church school and Bible reference books, pamphlets, and digital materials for children of all ages, and adults. Topics: the Bible, history, prayer, devotionals, religion, apologetics.

Titles: *Decision Making: Discerning the Will of God,* by June Hunt (Adult). *Rose Atlas of Then and Now Bible Maps with Biblical Backgrounds and Culture,* by Paul H. Wright (adult).

Submissions and Payment: Catalogue available at website. Submit manuscripts through ChristianManuscriptSubmissions.com. Responds in 2–3 months. Publication in 18 months. Flat fee.

Saint Mary's Press

702 Terrace Heights, Winona, MN 55987-1320. www.smp.org

Product Development Administrator: Linda Waldo

Saint Mary's Press's mission is to enliven the hearts and minds of young Catholics, ages 10 to 19, with the Good News of Jesus Christ. It publishes materials for schools, parishes, and families, including religious education textbooks, parish curriculum, and youth ministry resources. It does not publish young adult fiction.

Freelance Potential: Publishes 30 titles (15 juvenile) annually: 20% by authors who are new to the publishing house. Receives 20 queries monthly.

Fiction: Middle-grade. Genres: Folktales, drama, religion, inspirational.

Nonfiction: Middle-grade, YA. Topics: spirituality, Christianity, Catholic faith and life, sacraments, the Bible, contemporary issues, social issues, social justice, morality. Also publishes titles for adults who teach or minister to youth; Bibles; and supplemental resources.

Titles: *The Catholic Faith Handbook for Youth,* (ages 13+). *Breakthrough! The Bible for Young Catholics,* (ages 11–14).

Submissions and Payment: Guidelines available at website. Query with cover letter that includes author biography and publishing credits; information sheet with product description (and results if it has already been tested), audience, competition, design features, promotion ideas, estimated length, and estimated completion date; and manuscript sample, with title, table of contents, introduction, and sample chapter or activity. Accepts hard copy, or email to submissions@smp.org. Accepts simultaneous submissions, if identified. SASE. Responds in 2 months. Publication in 12–18 months. Royalty or work-for-hire.

Servant Books

Franciscan Media, 28 West Liberty Street, Cincinnati, OH 45202
http://www.americancatholic.org

Director of Product Development: Claudia Volkman

With its missions of spreading the gospel of Jesus Christ, helping Catholics live in accordance with that gospel, and promoting renewal in the church, this imprint of Franciscan Media publishes books of interest to young adults, parents, and religious educators. It seeks titles with a conversational style that offer practical advice.

Freelance Potential: Publishes 15–20 titles annually: 1–10% reprint/licensed properties; 30–40% by authors new to the publishing house; 10–15% by previously unpublished writers.

Nonfiction: YA. Also publishes books for parents and teachers. Topics: Christian living, the sacraments, Scripture, prayer, spirituality, popular apologetics, church teaching, Mary, the saints, charismatic renewal, marriage, family life, popular psychology.

Titles: *Tweet Inspiration: Faith in 140 Characters (or Less)*, by Mark Hart (YA). *Seven Lonely Places, Seven Warm Places: The Vices and Virtues for Children*, by April Bolton (ages 7–10).

Submissions and Payment: Guidelines available. Query with cover letter that indicates the topic, working title, approximate length, audience, and competition; table of contents; outline or chapter-by-chapter synopsis; 1–2 sample chapters; author biography; any endorsements; a description of your platform (social media, blog, speaking engagements, etc.); and promotion and marketing ideas. Accepts submissions through online form at website, email to servanteditor@franciscanmedia.org, and hard copy. SASE. Responds in 2 months. Publication in 1–2 years. Royalty, 10%; advance, $1,000.

Parents, Divisions, Imprints

Franciscan Media, See page 399

Standard Publishing

8805 Governor's Hill Drive, Suite 400, Cincinnati, OH 45249
www.standardpub.com

Editor, Children's Ministry Resources: Ruth Frederick

Having one purpose, to bring the Bible alive, Standard Publishing provides books and other Christian resources that meet church and family needs in the area of children's ministry. Its titles are true to the Bible and are meant to inspire, educate, and motivate people to create a growing relationship with Christ. It is not currently accepting fiction or poetry submissions.

Freelance Potential: Publishes 20–30 titles annually: less than 5% developed from unsolicited submissions; 10–25% assigned; 1–10% by agented authors; 1–10% by previously unpublished writers. Receives 10–15 queries and unsolicited manuscripts monthly.

Fiction: Picture books, middle-grade. Genres: parables, stories that help children understand the meaning behind biblical passages, Christian values, faith in daily life, adventure, mystery, rhyme.

Nonfiction: Board books, activity books, early picture books, early readers, story picture books, middle-grade. Also publishes teacher, parent, and leadership resources, children's classroom resources, devotionals, and materials geared toward smaller churches. Topics: Bible stories, religion, faith, Christianity, Christian values, outreach.

Titles: *First Virtues*, by Dr. Mary Manz Simon (ages 3–7). *God Said and Moses Led,* by Jennifer Holder (ages 4–8).

Submissions and Payment: Guidelines available at website. Query with introduction and 2 sample chapters or send complete manuscript. For all submissions, include summary of book, age category, genre, author qualifications, and platforms. Accepts email submissions with Word attachments to ministrytochildren@standardpub.com and simultaneous submissions if identified. Responds in 6 months. Publication in 18 months. Payment policy varies.

Targum Press

250 44th Street suite #B2, Brooklyn NY 11232. www.targum.com

Editor

One of today's leading Jewish publishers, Targum is a Jewish publishing company offering a wide variety of Jewish literature and nonfiction titles on Jewish holidays, law, philosophy, as well as commentary on the Torah, Mishnah, and Talmud. Included on its list are children's books and ones for young adults. It is interested in seeing any submissions that would be of interest to Orthodox Jewish audience.

Freelance Potential: Unavailable.

Fiction: Story picture books, early readers, chapter books, middle- grade, YA. Genres: contemporary, religious, social issues, holiday, adventure, historical.

Nonfiction: Story picture books, middle-grade, YA. Topics: Bible stories, Jewish religion, social issues, history.

Titles: *Watching My Words,* by Rabbi Ze'ev Greenwald (ages 7–11). *A Second Look,* by Sara Weiderblank (Adult).

Submissions and Payment: Guidelines and catalogue available at website. Send complete manuscript and cover letter with author credentials and contact information. Accepts hard copy and email submissions to editor@targum.com. SASE. Response time, publication period and payment policy varies.

Teach Services

7 Swetwater Lane, P. O. Box 954, Ringgold, GA 30736–0954
www.teachservices.com

President: Timothy Hullquist

The goal of Teach Services is to encourage and strengthen indoviduals around the world through the distribution of books that point readers to Christ. Its secondary mission is to make more Adventist materials available in the areas of health and Christian living.

Freelance Potential: Publishes 60–80 titles annually: 5% by agented authors, 90% by auhtors who are new to the publishing house, 80% by previously unpublished writers. Receives 10–25 queries, 10–25 unsolicited manuscripts monthly.

Fiction: Early readers, chapter books, middle-grade. Genres: adventure, mystery, historical, religious, Bible stories, values.

Nonfiction: Early readers, chapter books, middle-grade, YA. Topics: Bible study, church doctrine and history, prayer, youth and children's ministry, health, education, spiritual growth, biography.

Titles: *Best Buddies*, by Juanita Hamil (ages 5–8). *Bells of the Blue Pagoda*, by Jean Carer Cochran (YA).

Submissions and Payment: Guidelines and catalogue available at website. Query with outline, target audience, author bio; or send complete manuscript with form at website. Prefers email

(Word attachments) to publishing@teachservices.com. Accepts simultaneous submissions if identified. Responds in 2 weeks. Publication in 4–6 months. Royalty, 10%.

Tyndale House

351 Executive Drive, Carol Stream, IL 60188
www.tyndale.com

Acquisitions Director, Children & Family: Katara Washington Patton

Founded 50 years ago as a means of publishing The Living Bible, Tyndale now publishes Christian fiction, nonfiction, and various editions of the Bible. Its children's list includes fiction and non-fiction with a Christian perspective. Tyndale House does not accept unsolicited manuscripts or queries. It only reviews submissions through literary agents or by previous Tyndale authors.

Freelance Potential: Publishes about 15 titles annually: 100% by agented authors. Receives 20 queries monthly.

Fiction: Toddler books, story picture books, middle-grade. Genres: mystery, adventure, social issues, holidays, religion.

Nonfiction: Toddler books, story picture books, early readers, middle-grade, YA. Topics: the Bible, religion, spirituality, the Christian faith, real life/problems, devotionals, contemporary issues. Also publishes parenting books and Bibles.

Titles: *Your Best Destiny*, by Wintley Phipps (Adult). *Passages Volume 1: The Marus Manuscripts,* by Paul McCusker (ages 8+).

Submissions and Payment: Agented authors only. No unsolicited manuscripts. Publication period varies. Royalty; advance. Flat fee.

Unity House

Unity House, 1901 Northwest Blue Parkway, Unity Village, MO 64065-0001. www.unityonline.org

Editorial Assistant: Sharon Sartin

An open-minded, spiritual community, Unity School of Christianity bases its teachings on metaphysical interpretation of scriptures with an emphasis on practical application. This imprint publishes nonfiction adult books, some of which may appeal to a YA audience, that contribute to Unity's mission of empowering people to realize and express their divine potential for healthy, prosperous, and meaningful lives. Writers should be Unity-licensed teachers, ministers, or others whose works are inspired by Unity principles and teachings.

Freelance Potential: Publishes about 6 titles annually: most by authors who are new to the publishing house. Receives 35–40 queries monthly.

Nonfiction: YA, adult. Topics: spirituality, parenting, contemporary issues, inspirational, self-help, Unity teachings.

Titles: *Spiritual Economics,* by Eric Butterworth (adult). *The Many Faces of Prayer,* by *Dr. Thomas Shepherd* (adult).

Submissions and Payment: Guidelines and catalogue available at website. Unity House is not currently accepting submissions for new books at this time. Check the website for changes to this policy.

URJ Press

633 Third Avenue, New York, NY 10017-6778
www.urjbooksandmusic.com

Editor in Chief: Michael H. Goldberg

Aiming to encourage lifelong learning about what it means to be Jewish, this publishing arm of the Union for Reform Judaism produces an array of children's books dedicated to Jewish history, values, and traditions. It also offers educational resource materials for Torah and Hebrew study.

Freelance Potential: Publishes 25 titles annually: about 15% developed from unsolicited submissions; 15% by authors who are new to the publishing house; 30% by previously unpublished writers. Receives 8–10 queries, 25 unsolicited manuscripts monthly.

Fiction: Early picture books, story picture books, YA. Genres: religious, historical, all with Jewish themes.

Nonfiction: Toddler books, early picture books. Also publishes textbooks and educational resource materials for grades K–12, and parenting titles. Topics: Jewish history, holidays, the Holocaust, Hebrew language, Jewish culture, social issues.

Titles: *Jewish U: A Contemporary Guide for the Jewish College Student,* by Scott Aaron (YA). *Big Book of Great Teaching Ideas, For Jewish Schools, Youth Groups, Camps, and Retreats,* by Shirley Barish (Adult).

Submissions and Payment: Guidelines and catalogue available at website. Complete New Book Proposal form at website and submit via website, or fax to 212-650-4119, or mail. Response time and publication period vary. Royalty; advance.

Warner Press

1201 East Fifth Street, P.O. Box 2499, Anderson, IN 46012
www.warnerpress.org

Acquisitions Editor: Robin Fogle

With the goal of equipping the Church for ministry, this publishing house produces a wide variety of materials that communicate the message of Jesus Christ, including children's books and resources for religious education, as well as church bulletins and boxed card assortments.

Freelance Potential: Publishes about 4–6 children's picture books annually: 75–100% developed from unsolicited submissions by authors who are new to the publishing house. Receives 25–50 queries, 10–25 unsolicited manuscripts monthly.

Fiction: Picture books, chapter books, early readers, middle-grade. Genres: religious, fantasy, adventure, books directed at boys, books directed at girls, stories with biblical themes.

Nonfiction: Early readers, middle-grade, activity books. Topics: the Bible, religious holidays and history, Christianity. Also publishes reference books for parents and teachers.

Titles: *Going Live in 3-2-1,* by Tina Houser (ages 7–1). *Holly Jean and the Box in Granny's Attic,* by Bonnie Compton Hanson (ages 9–12).

Submissions and Payment: Guidelines and catalogue available at website. Query with story published credentials. Prefers email to rfogle@warnerpress.org. No simultaneous submissions. Response time varies. Publication in 12 months. Payment policy varies.

WaterBrook Multnomah Publishing Group 🔑

12265 Oracle Boulevard, Suite 200, Colorado Springs, CO 80921
www.waterbrookmultnomah.com

Submissions Editor

Committed to creating products that both intensify and satisfy the elemental thirst for a deeper relationship with God, the evangelical division of Random House, WaterBrook Multnomah offers books for Christian living and spiritual growth. Its list includes books for children and inspirational novels for young adults. Among its offerings for adults are titles on parenting, love, and relationships—all from a Christian perspective.

Freelance Potential: Publishes 65–70 titles annually. Receives 45–50 queries monthly.

Fiction: Story picture books, YA. Genres: religious, inspirational, romance, adventure, contemporary, fantasy.

Nonfiction: YA. Topics: religion, Christianity, personal faith, social issues, relationships, devotionals. Also publishes parenting titles.

Titles: *Messy Grace*, by Caleb Kaltenbach (Adult). *The Orphan King,* by Sigmund Brouwer (ages 9––12).

Submissions and Payment: Catalogue and author resources available at website. Accepts queries and proposals through literary agents only. Responds in 6–10 weeks. Publication in 1 year. Royalty; advance.

Parents, Divisions, Imprints

Penguin Random House Group, See page 184

Weiser Books

655 Third Street, Suite 400, San Francisco, CA 94107
www.redwheelweiser.com

Acquisitions Editorial Coordinator: Pat Bryce

Aiming to inspire and nourish the body, mind and soul, Weiser Books publishes titles about esoteric or occult teachings from traditions around the world, on topics such as consciousness, new science, Wicca, spirituality, and astrology. Other books cover self-help and recovery, nutrition and health, and lifestyle. It does not publish children's titles, but some of its books may be of interest to teens.

Freelance Potential: Publishes 30 titles annually: 15% developed from unsolicited submissions; 15% by agented authors. Receives 100+ queries monthly.

Nonfiction: Adult, of interest to YA. Topics: new consciousness, new science, coming Earth changes, magic, Wicca, Western mystery traditions, tarot, yoga, occult, astrology, paranormal, health, lifestyle, spirituality.

Titles: *Angels Legacy*, by Morgana Starr (Adult). *Astrology for Lovers*, by Liz Greene (Adult).

Submissions and Payment: Guidelines and catalogue available at website. Query with cover letter that includes an author biography and brief description of proposed work; proposal with a book overview, table of contents, market/audience analysis, marketing and promotion ideas, author qualifications, and 2–3 sample chapters; and sample photos or art if appropriate. Accepts hard copy, or email to submissions@rwwbooks.com (Word or PDF attachments). Accepts simultaneous submissions if identified. SASE. Responds in 3 months. Publication in 18 months. Royalty; advance.

Wisdom Tales

World Wisdom, Inc. P.O. Box 2682, Bloomington, IN 47402-2682
www.worldwisdom.com

Production Director: Stephen Williams

With titles that are meant to "share the wisdom, beauty, and values of traditional cultures and peoples from around the world with young readers and their families," World Wisdom, publishes books on philosophy, religion, and belief systems of many cultures. Its mission is to bring books on similar topics to children and young adults.

Freelance Potential: Publishes 5–10 titles annually.

Fiction: Picture books, middle-grade. Genres: folktales, legends, historical, multicultural.

Nonfiction: Picture books, middle-grade, YA. Genres: religious, inspirational, philosophy, history, culture, multicultural.

Titles: *The Compassionate Warrior*, edited by Elsa Marston and Barbara Petzon (YA). *Angels*, by Alexis York Lumbard (ages 2–4).

Submissions and Payment: Guidelines and catalogue available at website. Send manuscript submission application at website with complete manuscript through webpage. Accepts hard copy. SASE. Responds in 4 months if interested. Publication period and payment policy vary.

Zonderkidz

5300 Patterson Avenue Southeast, Grand Rapids, MI 49530
www.zondervan.com

Acquisitions

A world leading Bible publisher, Zondervan/HarperCollins is the parent company of Zonderkidz, a publisher of Christian board books, picture books, storybook Bibles, chapter books, middle-grade and young adult titles, and Bibles for teens. Nonfiction on topics such as naturesports, religion, and crafts appears on its list, along with fiction of most genres. It is not accepting new children's or YA proposals currently.

Freelance Potential: Publishes 150 titles (60 juvenile) annually: most by agented authors. Receives 60–72 queries yearly.

Fiction: Board books, picture books, storybook Bibles, early readers, chapter books, middle-grade, YA. Genres: social issues, religion, Christian values, fantasy, adventure, inspirational, real life/problems.

Nonfiction: Board books, picture books, storybook Bibles, early readers, chapter books, middle-grade, YA. Topics: nature, sports, religion, crafts, the Bible, biography, prayer, religion, inspirational.

Titles: *101 Bible Stories from Creation to Revelation,* by Dan Andreasen (ages 6–9). *Alone Yet Not Alone: Their Faith Became Their Freedom,* by Tracy Leininger Craven (ages 8+).

Submissions and Payment: Catalogue available at website. Currently not accepting proposals for childrens and teen books. Check website for updates and current needs. Response time 6–8 weeks. Publication in 2–3 years. Royalty.

Publishing of Interest to Children & Teens

While the prime goal of *Book Markets for Children's Writers 2016* is to provide the best information on publishers of books for children and teens, some authors may be interested in a wider field. This section sheds light on a number of publishers that offer books children and teens may find of interest, even if they aren't directly targeted to them. Some of the categories here are study skills and exam preparation, educational or reference books for older readers, crime stories, science fiction for a general audience, role-playing games, environmental topics, outdoor recreation, and many others.

The section also includes publishers for adults that offer a limited number of children's or teen titles, and are open to submissions.

Abrams ComicArts

115 West 18th Street, 6th Floor, New York, NY 10011
www.abramsbooks.com; Abramscomicarts.com

Editorial

Abrams ComicArts publishes groundbreaking graphic novels and illustrated books about the creators and the history of comics art, animation, and cartoons.

Freelance Potential: Publishes about 6–12 titles annually. Fiction: YA/Adult. Genres: graphic novels.

Nonfiction: YA/Adult. Topics: history, pop culture, biography as related to comic arts and animation.

Titles: *Will Eisner: Champion of the Graphic Novel,* by Paul Levitz; *Trashed,* by Derf Backderf.

Submissions and Payment: Guidelines and catalogue available at website. Accepts hard copy submissions only. No SASE; materials not returned. Responds in 6 months if interested. Publication period varies. Royalty; advance.

Parents, Divisions, Imprints

Abrams Books for Young Readers, See page 380

Adams Media

57 Littlefield Street, Avon, MA 02322. www.adamsmedia.com

Book Proposals

Adams Media Corporation publishes a broad range of non-fiction topics including business and careers, parenting, pets and self-help. It welcomes submissions from new, experienced, and agented authors.

Freelance Potential: Publishes 250 titles annually.

Nonfiction: YA. Topics: humor, inspirational, self-help, examprep, how-to. Also publishes books for adults on business, cooking, home improvement, parenting, personal finance, women's issues, wedding planning, crafts and hobbies, travel, writing.

Titles: *Your Illistrated Guide to Being One with the Universe*, by Yumi Sakugawa. *Mean Chicks, Cliques and Dirty Tricks: A Real Girl's Guide to Getting Through it All*, by Erika V. Shearin Karres, Ed.D

Submissions and Payment: Catalogue available at website. Query/proposal with description of intended market, an explanation of why someone would want to buy the book, summary of your background, detailed table of contents, and a sample chapter. Accepts hard copy. SASE. No electronic submissions. Do not send full manuscripts. Electronic submissions: AdamsMedia-Submissions@fwmedia.com Responds only if interested. Publication period varies. Royalty.

Angry Robot Books

Lace Market House, 54–56 High Pavement, Nottingham, NG1 1 HW, United Kingdom. www.angryrobotbooks.com

Editor: Amanda Rutter

Angry Robots publishes standalone and series titles that cross genres of fantasy, science fiction, and cyberpunk. Though it's titles are geared toward adults, many of its books are of interest to young adults. Check website for submission periods and guidelines.

Freelance Potential: Unavailable.

Fiction: YA. Genres: science fiction, fantasy, paranormal, contemporary, crime, thrillers.

Titles: *Zenn Scarlett*, by Christine Schoon (12+). *The Almost Girl*, by Amalie Howard (YA).

Submissions and Payment: Guidelines and catalogue available at website. Does not accept unsolicited manuscripts but will post special calls for submissions. Check website for opening and closing dates. Accepts submissions from agents only. Response time 3–6 months. Publication period, and payment policy vary.

Ashland Creek Press

2305 Ashland St., Ashland, OR 97520
www.ashlandcreekpress.com

Editor: Midge Raymond

Ashland Creek Press is dedicated to publishing books with a world view. Its titles cover the environment, animal protection, ecology, and wildlife combined with compelling writing.

Freelance Potential: Publishes 4–6 titles annually; 20 were by agented authors, 100% were by authors who are new to the publishing house, 25% by previously unpublished writers.

Fiction: YA, adult. Genres: environmental literature, fantasy, contemporary, mystery.

Nonfiction: YA, adult. Topics: travel, the environment, ecology, wildlife, sports.

Titles: *Strays*, by Jennifer Caloyeras (YA). *The Last Mile*, by Blair Richmond (YA).

Submissions and Payment: Guidelines and catalogue available at website. Send first 50 pages of manuscript; a 1- to 2-page synopsis (including word count); and author bio listing all publishing experience, awards, and credits. Accepts submissions via the website only, using the service Submittable. Responds in 1–3 months. Publication period and payment policy vary.

Beckham Publications

P.O. Box 4066, Silver Spring, MD 20914-4066
www.beckhamhouse.com

Acquisitions Editor

Fiction and nonfiction books that focus on multicultural and cutting edge topics. Its catalogue features a few titles for juveniles as well as adults. The company also offers joint venture and self-publishing services.

Freelance Potential: Publishes 60 titles (4 juvenile) annually: 85% developed from unsolicited submissions. Receives 16 unsolicited manuscripts monthly.

Fiction: Story picture books. Genres: multicultural, spiritual. Also publishes novels for adults.

Nonfiction: Topics: parenting, education, business, personal finance, and biography. Also publishes poetry collections.

Titles: *The Second First Lady,* by Vanessa W. Snyder. *Never Easy, Always Necessary,* by Dwight L. Ford.

Submissions and Payment: Guidelines and catalogue available at website. For adult nonfiction, send an outline, table of contents, 2 sample chapters, target audience, and author biography. For adult fiction, send complete manuscript with outline. For juvenile works, send complete manuscript with illustrations. Prefers email to submit@beckhamhouse.com (Word attachments); will accept hard copy. SASE. Responds in 6 weeks. Publication in 2 months. Royalty.

Behler Publications

1211 Lincoln Highlands Drive, North Fayette, PA 15108
www.behlerpublications.com

Editor: Lynn Price

Primarily a publisher of nonfiction titles about going from ordinary to extraordinary. Focuses on personal journeys with social relevance. It looks for books that will make readers say, "I'm a better/ more thoughtful/smarter person for having read this book." Manuscripts for fiction are occasionally reviewed.

Freelance Potential: Publishes 12 titles annually. Receives 200 queries monthly.

Nonfiction: Adult. Topics: inspirational themes.

Titles: *A Chick in the Cockpit,* by Erika Armstrong. *Finding Dad: From "Love Child" to Daughter,* by Kara Sundlum.

Submissions and Payment: U.S. authors only. Guidelines and catalogue available at website. Not accepting fiction submissions at this time. Query with proposal that includes: overview and purpose of the book; target audience; market and competition analysis; marketing, promotion, and publicity suggestions and author's planned contribution to these; completion schedule for the book; and the first 3 chapters. Accepts email only to acquisitions@ behlerpublications.com (Word attachments). Response time and publication period vary. Royalty, 10%.

Black Rose Writing

P.O. Box 1540, Castroville, TX 78009
www.blackrosewriting.com

Acquisitions Editor

This independent publishing house strongly believes in developing personal relationship with their authors. The Texas-based company doesn't see authors as clients or numbers, but rather as individual people. All of it's titles showcase originality.

Freelance Potential: Publishes 150+ electronic titles annually: 20% by agented authors, 60% by authors who are new to the publishing house, 20% by prevously unpublished writers. Receives 50 queries monthly.

Nonfiction: Standardized tests and reference books, curriculum materials, teacher/parent references, and visual/perceptual training aids. Topics: speech/language, occupational therapy, rehabilitation, special education, school psychology.

Fiction: Early reader, middle grade, YA. Genres include: real-life problems, mystery, romance, fantasy, contemporary fiction.

Nonfiction: Middle grade and YA. Topics include: nature, biography, travel.

Titles: *The Dream Travelers*, by Cindi Elli (ages 8–12). *Tell Me a Story Mama Bear*, by Lynne Carol Austin (ages 4–8).

Submissions and Payment: Catalogue and guidleines available at website. Query with synopsis for proposed book with author bio (no attachments). Children's submissions must include all artwork. Accepts email queries to creator@blackrosewriting.com. Accepts simultaneous submissions. Responds to queries in 3–6 weeks. Payment rate and policy varies.

Chaosium

719 East Murray Street, Rockport, TX 78382-2349
www.chaosium.com

Submissions

This publisher offers fiction and anthologies, role-playing games and resource publications, as well as board and card games. They are currently undergoing reorganization.

Freelance Potential: Publishes 15 titles annually: 40% by authors who are new to the publishing house; 20% by previously unpublished writers. Receives 5 queries monthly.

Fiction: YA, adult. Genres: fantasy, horror.

Nonfiction: Monographs, role-playing games with fantasy themes.

Titles: *Eldritch Chrome* (anthology). *Cthulhu Invictus* (anthology).

Submissions and Payment: Catalogue and contest announcements available at website. For Basic Roleplaying and Call of Cthulhu submissions, send query with introduction letter outlining your idea, with a summary paragraph for each chapter or adventure, target completion date, the aim of the book, writing sample, and any special knowledge you have on a topic; and a completed release form (found at website). Accepts hard copy and email to dustin@chaosium.com. Response time varies. Publication in 1–2 years. Flat fee, 3¢–5¢ a word.

Conari Press

665 Third Street, Suite 400, San Francisco, CA 94107
www.Redwheelweiser.com

Acquisitions Editorial Coordinator: Pat Bryce

Conari Press, an imprint of Red Wheel, publishes on topics ranging from spirituality, personal growth, and relationships to women's issues, parenting, and social issues. Their mission is to "publish quality books that will make a difference in people's lives."

Freelance Potential: Publishes 45 titles annually: 20% developed from unsolicited submissions; 80% by agented authors. Receives 100 queries monthly.

Nonfiction: YA, adult. Topics: health, nutrition, spirituality, personal growth, parenting, social issues, women's issues, relationships, recovery, 12-step programs.

Titles: *Mindfulness, Meditation, and Mind Fitness*, by Joel and Michelle Levy. *Being Present: A Book of Daily Reflections*, by David J. Kuntz.

Submissions and Payment: Guidelines and catalogue available at website. Prefers query with cover letter that includes an author bio and brief description of proposed work; proposal with a book overview, table of contents, market/audience analysis, marketing and promotion ideas, author qualifications, and 2–3 sample chapters; and sample photos or art if appropriate. Accepts complete manuscript. Accepts hard copy, or email to submissions@

rwwbooks.com (Word or PDF attachments). Accepts simultaneous submissions if identified. SASE. Responds in 3 months. Publication in 18 months. Royalty; advance.

DAW Books

375 Hudson Street, New York, NY 10014. www.dawbooks.com

Submissions Editor: Peter Stampfel

For 40+ years, this publishing house is exclusively devoted to the creation and marketing of science fiction and fantasy novels. While it does not publish stories for children, or even directly target young adults, many of its books appeal to teen readers. DAW Books offers both paperback and hardcover mass-market books, and many of its novels are published as part of a series. It is committed to discovering and nurturing new talent.

Freelance Potential: Publishes 35 titles annually. Receives 150 unsolicited manuscripts monthly.

Fiction: YA. Genres: science fiction, fantasy.

Titles: *Faces,* by E.C. Blake. *Mirror Sight,* by Kristen Britain.

Submissions and Payment: Guidelines and catalogue available at website. Send complete manuscript with cover letter and word count. Accepts hard copy. No short stories. No simultaneous submissions. SASE for response only; manuscript not returned. Responds in 3 months. Publication period varies. Royalty; advance.

Dragon Hill Publishing

5474 Thibault Wynd NW, Edmonton, Alberta T6R 3P9 Canada
www.dragonhillpublishing.com

Editorial Director

The titles from Dragon Hill target young adults and teens seeking a better understanding of themselves and their place in the community. This company also publishes biographies and self-help guides.

Freelance Potential: Publishes 4 titles annually: 100% assigned; 50% by authors who are new to the publishing house. Receives 3+ queries monthly.

Nonfiction: Self-help, multicultural titles. Topics: biography; self-improvement; culture, traditions, sports, and history of Canada.

Titles: *The Ferbey Four,* by Terry Jones. *Running Uphill,* by Fil Fraser.

Submissions and Payment: Guidelines and catalogue available at website. Send proposal with table of contents; 2–3 sample chapters; sample illustrations; résumé; description of competitive titles; and a cover letter describing your book, its unique features, target audience, and reasons why you should write it. Accepts email to submissions@ dragonhillpublishing.com and hard copy. SAE/IRC. No multiple submissions. Response time varies. Publication in 6–12 months. Flat fee.

Dzanc Books

5220 Dexter, Ann Arbor, MI 48103. www.dzancbooks.org

Editors: Dan Wickett & Steve Gillis

A not-for-profit publisher of innovative and award-winning literary fiction including short story collections and novels. Also runs a writers-in-residence program, instructional writing workshops, and an annual short story competition.

Freelance Potential: Publishes 6 titles annually: 65% developed from unsolicited submissions; 35% by agented authors. Receives 100 queries monthly.

Fiction: Short story collections and novels.

Nonfiction: Creative nonfiction and poetry collections.

Titles: *Calloustown,* by George Singleton. *Kafka's Son,* by Curt Leviant.

Submissions and Payment: Guidelines and catalogue available at website. For fiction or literary nonfiction, query with 1–2 sample chapters (no more than 35 pages). or send complete manuscript. For short stories, send complete manuscript with $20 reading fee. Accepts submissions via online submission form. Responds in 5–6 months. Publication period varies. Royalty; advance.

Eastgate Systems

134 Main Street, Watertown, MA 02472. www.eastgate.com

Acquisitions Editor: Mark Bernstein

This publisher specializes in stand-alone hypertext technology and publishes hypertext, fiction and non-fiction. Eastgate's fiction and nonfiction titles are directed toward young adult and adult readers. It also publishes poetry.

Freelance Potential: Publishes 2 titles annually. Receives 25 unsolicited manuscripts monthly.

Fiction: YA, adult. Genres: suspense, adventure, coming-of-age, Westerns, romance.

Nonfiction: YA, adult. Topics: culture, literary criticism, science, history, philosophy, poetry collections.

Titles: *Afternoon,* by Michael Joyce. *Patchwork Girl,* by Shelley Jackson.

Submissions and Payment: Guidelines and catalogue available at website. Send complete manuscript. Accepts submissions on CD-ROM or DVD; or email to info@eastgate.com directing editors to your URL. Accepts simultaneous submissions if identified. SASE. Responds in 4–6 weeks. Publication in 1 year. Royalty, 15%; advance.

Ebooksonthe.net

Write Words, Inc., 2934 Old Route 50, Cambridge, MD 21613 www.writewordsinc.com; www.ebooksonthe.net

Publisher: Arline Chase

Ebooksonthe.net produces fiction titles in a number of genres for middle-grade readers and young adults as well as adults. Its offerings include ebooks and paperback books that appeal to a global audience. It is actively seeking manuscripts in the romance, mystery, and action-adventure genres.

Freelance Potential: Publishes 72 titles annually: 65% by authors who are new to the publishing house; 25% by previously unpublished writers. Receives 50 queries monthly.

Fiction: YA. Genres: contemporary, historical, inspirational, science fiction, romance, mystery.

Titles: *Wanted: Royal Princess Wife and Mother,* by Anna Dynowski (16+). *Lost Spirit: A Hannah Griswold Mystery,* by Robert Kanehl (ages 12+).

Submissions and Payment: Guidelines and catalogue available at website. Send a 3-paragraph query with title, genre, word count, and synopsis (first paragraph); target audience and explanation of why it will interest them (second paragraph); and brief author biography and writing experience (third paragraph). Accepts email queries only to arline@mail.com. Responds in 1 week. Publication in 3 months. Royalty, 40% for ebooks sold from its company website, 15% for paperback books; 50% for ebooks sold on subsidiary websites (such as Amazon).

Ecopress

Finney Company, 5995 149th Street West, Suite 105
Apple Valley, MN 55124. www.ecopress.com

President: Alan E. Krysan

This imprint of the Finney Company has a goal of improving the quality of lifelong learning worldwide. It will only consider submissions that are educational.

Freelance Potential: Publishes 4 titles (1 juvenile) annually: 75% developed from unsolicited submissions; 75% by authors who are new to the publishing house; 50% by previously unpublished writers. Receives 10 queries monthly.

Fiction: YA. Themes: environmental.

Nonfiction: YA, adult environmental guides, resource books, narratives. Topics: bicycling, canoeing, hiking, rivers, fishing.

Titles: *My Little Book of Burrowing Owls,* by Irvin Marston. *Reef Rescue,* by India Evans (ages 12–18).

Submissions and Payment: Guidelines available at website. Query with a description of manuscript and author qualifications, 1-page overview, table of contents, introduction, 3 sample chapters, and description of target markets. Accepts hard copy. Accepts simultaneous submissions. SASE. Responds in 10–12 weeks. Publication in 6–18 months. Royalty, 10%.

Etopia Press

1643 Warwick Ave., #124, Warwick, RI 02889
www.etopiapress.com

Submission Editor

Etopia Press specializes in all types of romance novels, from sweet YA romances to erotic fiction. Titles are published in both print and digital formats.

Freelance Potential: Publishes 75–100 titles annually. 3% by agented authors; 29% by authors who are new to the publishing house; 22% by previously unpublished writers. Receives 20 unsolicited submissions monthly.

Fiction: YA. Genres: fantasy, contemporary, historical, science fiction, thriller, paranormal, fantasy and urban fantasy, romance.

Titles: *Sunlight*, by C. L. Bledsoe (YA). *Blood She Read*, by Sara Hubbard (YA).

Submissions and Payment: Guidelines and catalogue available at website. Send cover letter with word count, author info (include social media accounts and previous publication credits), and short blurb about the book; complete ms, and a short synopsis (1-2 pages for novellas, 2-3 pages for novels). Accepts email submissions only with RTF attachments to submissions@etopia-press.net. Accepts simultaneous submissions. Responds in 4–8 weeks. Publication period unknown. Royalty, 40% on e-books; advance, $100–$1,000.

The Feminist Press

The Graduate Center, 365 Fifth Avenue, Suite 5406, New York, NY 10016. www.feministpress.org

Associate Editor: Anjoli Roy

Nonprofit publisher of fiction and nonfiction by and about women and other underrepresented groups. It seeks out innovative books to support personal transformation and social justice. Books for young readers are among the catalogue's titles.

Freelance Potential: Publishes 15–20 titles annually: 10% developed from unsolicited submissions; 75% reprint/licensed properties; 60% by authors who are new to the publishing house. Receives 100+ queries monthly.

Fiction: Middle-grade, YA. Genres: multicultural, historical.

Nonfiction: Middle-grade, YA. Topics: memoirs, biography, historical references about women-related issues.

Titles: *Stella Dallas,* by Olive Higgins Provty. *Therese and Isabelle,* by Violette Leduc.

Submissions and Payment: Guidelines and catalogue available at website. Send proposal with sample chapter, author biography, and email address or SASE to receive a reply. Prefers hard copy; will accept email queries to editor@feministpress.org (include "Submission" in subject line). Materials are not returned. Response time and publication period vary. Royalty; advance.

Fernwood Publishing

32 Oceanvista Lane, Black Point, NS B0J 1B0, Canada
www.fernwoodpublishing.ca

Submissions Editor

Fernwood Publishing believes in publishing books that challenge the status quo and imagine ways to move forward toward a more socially just world. Its books are widely used in course texts for colleges and universities, and are often read by young adults. 10% subsidy.

Freelance Potential: Publishes about 40 titles annually: 60% by authors who are new to the publishing house, 25% by previously unpublished writers. Receives 25–50 unsolicited manuscripts monthly.

Fiction: Board books, early picture books, early readers, picture books, story picture books. Genres: contemporary, animal stories., social issues, social skills.

Titles: *Indigenous Nationhood: Empowering Grassroots Citizens,* by Pamela Palmater (YA–A). *Settler: Idenitity and Colonialism in 21st Century Canada*, by Emma Battell Lowman and Adam J. Barker.

Submissions and Payment: Catalogue and guidelines available at website. Submit book proposal of no more than 4–5 pages with tentative table of contents and potential audience. Accepts hard copy and email submissions to editorial@fernpub.ca. Payment policies and rates vary.

Folklore Publishing

11414 - 119 St NW, Edmonton, AN T5G 2X6, Canada
www.folklorepublishing.com

Publisher: Faye Boer

Folklore Publishing was founded in 2002 with a mandate to publish well-written, accessible histories drawn from North America. The publisher has a Canadian focus.

Freelance Potential: Publishes 3–10 titles annually: 10% developed from unsolicited submissions; 25% by authors who are new to the publishing house; 25% by previously unpublished writers. Receives 15 queries, 5–10 unsolicited manuscripts monthly.

Nonfiction: Middle-grade, YA, adult. Topics: Canada-related history, biography, humor.

Titles: *Angelina Jolie*, by Edgar McFaye (YA-A). *A Woman's Guide to Fifty Shades of Canadian Men,* by David MacLennan.

Submissions and Payment: Guidelines and catalogue available at website. For completed manuscripts, send résumé detailing your interests and passions, an overview of your manuscript and its marketability, a chapter-by-chapter synopsis, and 2–3 sample chapters (up to 75 pages). To be considered for work-for-hire projects, send résumé detailing your interests and passions, and 3 nonfiction writing samples, preferably about a topic of interest to Canadians. Accepts hard copy and email to submissions@folklorepublishing.com (Word or PDF files). SAE/IRC. Response time varies. Publication in 6–12 months. Fee for services contract.

Istoria Books

www.istoriabooks.com

Founders: Matthew, Libby, and Hannah Sternberg

This print and digital publisher offers mystery, historical, and inspirational titles. It is also interested in romance, women's fiction, mystery/thriller, sci-fi/fantasy, short stories and young adult fiction. It is open to unpublished and published authors, with or without agents. The editors value creativity, and are open to breaking genre boundaries.

Freelance Potential: Looking for new authors.

Fiction: YA, adult. Genres: mystery, historical, inspirational, literary, romance, women's, thrillers, science fiction, fantasy, short stories.

Titles: *Jimmy's Girl,* by Stephanie Gertler. *Dragon Lady,* by Gary Alexander.

Submissions and Payment: Currently closed to author submissions. Only accepting recommendations from current authors or literary agents. Query to istoriabooks@gmail.com, with "Query" and the genre indicated in the subject line. In the body of the email, include the genre, a 1-paragraph summary of the book, writing credentials, and contact information. Manuscript must be complete. Response time varies. Author and publisher split royalties.

Loving Healing Press

5145 Pontiac Trail, Ann Arbor, MI 48105-9627
www.lovinghealing.com

Senior Editor: Victor R. Volkman

Loving Healing Press is a small independent press, not a vanity publisher, that has published for 12 years. Its titles for adults and children focus on life's issues, with a strong focus on children's and parenting subjects, such as developmental disorders and cyber bullying, as well as trauma and healing for all ages. Loving Healing Press is open to first-time authors.

Freelance Potential: Publishes about 12 titles annually.

Nonfiction: Story picture book, middle-grade, YA, adult. Topics: health, trauma, mental health, family, social issues, self help.

Titles: *The Windsor Beauties: Ladies of the Court of Charles II,* by Lewis Melville. *Life Skills: Improve the Quality of Your Life with Metapsychology,* by Marian K. Volkman.

Submissions and Payment: Guidelines and catalogue available at website. Asks authors to consider submitting your proposal through the online manuscript service, www.BowkerManuscript-Submissions.com. Reopened to unsolicited submissions in July 2015. Current authors are always exempt from any solicitation restrictions. Query with outline of book listing all chapters, 1–4 sample chapters, statement of market and marketing plans, and estimate of total length of manuscript and date of completion. Accepts email to info@lovinghealing.com (Word files). Response time, publication period, unknown. Royalty.

Mage Publishers

1032 29th Street NW, Washington, DC 20007
www.mage.com

Submissions Editor: Amin Sepehri

Mage is an independent press founded in 1985 which publishes books of Persian literature and culture in English. Its list includes translations, historical texts, and contemporary works written in English. For children, it publishes books about Persian folktales, legends, and history. It is interested in receiving more children's book proposals on Persian history, notable figures, and culture.

Freelance Potential: Publishes 4–6 titles annually: 20% by authors who are new to the publishing house. Receives 4 queries monthly.

Fiction: Children's tales and legends from Persia.

Nonfiction: YA. Topics: Persian literature, culture, history, life. Also publishes books for adults on Persian cooking, architecture, music, history, poetry, literature.

Titles: *My Uncle Napoleon: A Comic Novel,* by Irai Pezeshkad, translated by Dick Davis. *Savushun,* by Simin Daneshvar.

Submissions and Payment: Guidelines and catalogue available at website. Only books on Persian culture will be considered. Send query outlining book and brief biographical statement. Accepts email to as@mage.com (attention: Amin Sepehri). Responds in 6–8 weeks. Publication in 9–15 months. Royalty; advance.

Naturegraph Publishers

P.O. Box 1047, Happy Camp, CA 96039. www.naturegraph.com

Owner: Barbara Brown

Naturegraph's mission is to publish books for a better world that are well-written and thoroughly researched. Its titles give knowledge and awareness of nature in all its myriad form, and increase understanding and appreciation of Native American heritage and culture. Naturegraph is not currently accepting submissions.

Freelance Potential: Currently suspended publication. Check website for updates.

Fiction: YA. Genre: Native American folklore.

Nonfiction: YA. Topics: Native American wildlife, birds, crafts, environment, hiking, backpacking, outdoor skills, rocks and minerals, marine life, natural history.

Titles: *Where the Wild Things Live,* by Dan Story. *Packing with Burros,* by Dave Daney.

Submissions and Payment: Guidelines and catalogue available at website. Not currently accepting submissions. Check website for changes in this policy.

Orbit Books

Hachette Book Group, 237 Park Avenue, 16th Floor, New York, NY 10017. www.orbitbooks.net

Editorial Department

Orbit Books, an imprint of Hachette Book Group, focuses on the science fiction and fantasy with imprints in the UK, US and Australia. They publish across the spectrum of sci-fi and fantasy from urban fantasy to sweeping epic thrillers. While most titles are geared toward adult readers, some are suitable for young adults. Orbit Books will consider the work of new writers, but accepts submissions only from writers who are represented by literary agents.

Freelance Potential: Publishes 40 titles annually.

Fiction: YA. Genres: science fiction, fantasy.

Titles: *The Last Days of Jack Sparks,* by Jason Arnopp. *Zero-G,* by Rob Boffard.

Submissions and Payment: Accepts submissions from agented authors only. Responds in 2–6 months. Publication period varies. Royalty; advance.

Parents, Divisions, Imprints

Hachette Book Group, See page 134

Overtime Books

1469 Galt, #7, Montreal, Quebec J4Z 2J1 Canada
www.overtimebooks.com

President: J. Alexander Poulton

This publisher specializes in sports-related books for older teens and adults; books written by sports fan aimed at other sports fans. Prospective authors should have a passion for the sport in question as well as a journalism background. Overtime Books is looking for good baseball, basketball, hockey and golf writers, as well as strong generalists.

Freelance Potential: Publishes 6 titles annually: 50% developed from unsolicited submissions; 15% by authors who are new to the publishing house; 15% by previously unpublished writers. Receives 10 queries monthly.

Nonfiction: YA. Topics: athletes, Olympics, hockey, auto racing, skateboarding, snowboarding, golf, wrestling, soccer, and Canadian sports.

Titles: *Skateboarding,* by Thomas Peacock. *Canadians in the Summer Olympics,* by J. Alexander Poulton

Submissions and Payment: Guidelines and catalogue available at website. Query with clips or send complete manuscript with résumé. Accepts hard copy and email to submissions@overtime-books.com. SAE/IRC. Responds to queries in 2 weeks, to manuscripts in 3–6 months. Publication in 6–12 months. Flat fee.

Samhain Publishing

577 Mulberry Street, Suite 1520, Macon, GA 31201
www.samhainpublishing.com

Editorial Assistant: Imogen Howson

Samhain Publishing is an international publisher of ebook and traditional print fiction, proud to partner more than 600 authors of romance and horror fiction. With five to seven new releases each week, our store now includes more than 2200 titles. The company considers itself "an author-friendly publisher which exists to bring readers all types of stories, from the usual to the out-of-the-box."

Freelance Potential: Publishes 200–300 titles annually: 1–10% developed from unsolicited submissions; 1–10% by agented authors; 1–10% by authors who are new to the publishing house; 10–25% by previously unpublished writers. Receives about 10 queries, 75–100 manuscripts monthly.

Fiction: Does not currently publish YA, but its Retro Romance and horror lines, as well as fantasy, urban fantasy, and science fiction titles (all with strong romantic elements) may be of interest to teens. Samhain also publishes adult erotica.

Titles: *Bloodhunt*, by Lucien Diver. *Grimm's End*, by Shiloh Walker.

Submissions and Payment: Guidelines and catalogue available at website. Prefers complete manuscript to editor@amhainpublishing.com (Word attachments) with a synopsis; accepts synopsis and first 3 chapters. Accepts simultaneous submissions, if identified. Responds in 3–4 months. Publication in 6–12 months. Royalty, 30–40% of retail.

Seal Press

1700 Fourth Street, Berkeley, CA 94710. www.sealpress.com

Senior Editor: Brooke Warner

Seal Press publishes books with the goal of informing women's lives. Our authors are radical and original thinkers, professionals with a distinct point of view, gutsy explorers, truth-tellers, and writers who engender laughter, tears, inspiration, and transformation. Based in Berkeley, California and a member of the Perseus Books Group.

Freelance Potential: Publishes 25 titles annually: 10% developed from unsolicited submissions. Receives 50 queries monthly.

Fiction: YA, adult. Genres: romance, multicultural fiction, fantasy, social issues.

Nonfiction: YA. Topics: health, sexuality, abuse, politics, travel, other women's issues. Also publishes parenting titles and books for adults.

Titles: *Yogalosophy*, by Mandy Ingber. *Replacement Child*, by Judy L. Mandel.

Submissions and Payment: Guidelines, current call for submissions and catalogue available at website. It is not accepting fiction submissions at this time. For nonfiction, send query with writing sample, working title, brief description of your book's mission and overall concept, table of contents, outline with chapter summaries, status of project, book length, list of competitive titles and a description of how your book differs, target audience, marketing strategy, and author bio. Accepts hard copy. SASE. Responds in 6–8 weeks. Publication period and payment policy vary.

Second Story Press

20 Maud Street, Suite 401, Toronto, Ontario M5V 2M5 Canada
www.secondstorypress.ca

Editorial Manager

This publisher is dedicated to feminist-inspired books for adults and young readers. It works almost exclusively with Canadian authors, seeking books that feature strong female characters and explore themes of social justice, human rights, equality, and ability issues. Their list spans adult fiction and nonfiction; children's fiction, nonfiction and picture books; and YA fiction and nonfiction.

Freelance Potential: Publishes 15 titles (10 juvenile) annually: 40% by authors who are new to the publishing house; 15% by previously unpublished writers. Receives 20 queries, 25 unsolicited manuscripts monthly.

Fiction: Story picture books, chapter books, middle-grade, YA. Genres: mystery, historical, contemporary, multicultural.

Nonfiction: Middle-grade, YA. Topics: history, nature, the environment, contemporary social issues, family life, ethics. Also publishes parenting titles.

Titles: *Branded by the Pink Triangle,* by Ken Setterington (YA). *Pure,* by Karen Krossing (YA).

Submissions and Payment: Preference given to Canadian authors. Guidelines and catalogue available at website. Query with outline and sample chapters; or send complete manuscript. Include author bio and publishing credits with all submissions. Accepts hard copy. SAE/IRC. Responds in 6–9 months. Publication period varies. Royalty; advance.

Three O'Clock Press

425 Adelaide Street West, Suite 200, Toronto, Ontario M5V 3C1 Canada. www.threeoclockpress.com

Submissions Editor

This publisher combined its Sumach Press and Women's Press Literary imprints under one umbrella to add a unique voice to Canadian publishing. It is a feminist publisher of both fiction and nonfiction titles written by and for women. The young adult titles reflect the diversity of Canadian youth particularly young women and queer-identified youth.

Freelance Potential: Publishes 10 titles annually.

Fiction: YA, adult. Genres: mystery, literary, fantasy, historical.

Nonfiction: YA, adult. Topics: environment, education, parenting, women's health, women's, social and political issues, disabilities.

Titles: *Feast of Lights,* by Ellen S. Jaffe (YA). *Healer's Touch,* by Anne Gray (YA).

Submissions and Payment: Not currently accepting unsolicited submissions. Guidelines and catalogue available at website. Query only with outline, author bio, and no more than 2 sample chapters. Accepts hard copy. Accepts simultaneous submissions if identified. SAE/IRC. Responds in 4 months. Publication period and payment policy vary.

TouchWood Editions

103-1075 Pendergast Street, Victoria, British Columbia V8V 0A1 Canada. www.touchwoodeditions.com

Associate Publisher: Ruth Linka

Publishes titles about the people, places, landscape, food, art and culture of the pacific Northwest. Includes cookbooks, food and lifestyle titles, visual art, mysteries and other fiction and nonfiction. It only publishes Canadian authors.

Freelance Potential: Publishes 15 titles annually: 35% developed from unsolicited submissions; 15% by agented authors; 5% reprint/licensed properties; 25% by authors who are new to the publishing house; 25% by previously unpublished writers. Receives 16 manuscripts monthly.

Fiction: Adult. Genres: mystery, suspense, historical fiction. Nonfiction: Adult. Topics: Western Canada-related biography, cookbooks, creative nonfiction, regional travel guidebooks.

Titles: *Last Dance in Shediac: Memories of Mum, Molly Lamb Bobak,* by Anny Scoones. *High Rider,* by Bill Gallagher.

Submissions and Payment: Guidelines and catalogue available at website. Only publishes Canadian authors. Send complete manuscript with brief summary of the book and how it fits with TouchWood's publishing program; author bio and publication history; short synopsis; target audience; marketing plan; and art (CD or DVD). For nonfiction, also include table of contents. Accepts email to edit@touchwoodeditions.com (Word attachments; send each component in separate document), and hard copy. SAE/IRC. Accepts simultaneous submissions if identified. Responds in 3–6 months. Publication period and payment policy vary.

Turtle Press

P.O. Box 34010, Santa Fe, NM 87594-4010
www.turtlepress.com

Acquisitions Committee

Turtle Press is a leading producer of books and videos for martial arts students and instructors as well as law enforcement personnel and those interested in self-defense and personal protection. Books that are appropriate for students still welcome. Authors knowledgeable about the martial arts are encouraged to send a query.

Freelance Potential: Publishes 10 titles annually: 30% developed from unsolicited submissions; 30% by authors who are new to the publishing house; 20% by previously unpublished writers. Receives 40 queries monthly.

Fiction: Chapter books, middle-grade. Genres: adventure, martial arts-related stories.

Nonfiction: Chapter books, YA. Topics: martial arts, Eastern philosophy, fitness, health, sports, self-improvement. Also publishes books for martial arts teachers and martial arts students.

Titles: *Fight Back: A Women's Guide to Self-Defense That Works,* by Loren W. Christiansen and Lisa Place. *Capoeira Illustrated,* by Dimitris Papadopoulos.

Submissions and Payment: Guidelines and catalogue available at website. Query with an outline or summary, table of contents, 2–4 sample chapters (including chapter one), market potential, author credentials, sample photos or artwork, and availability of manuscript, all on disk. Accepts hard copy. SASE. Responds in 2–4 weeks. Publication period varies. Royalty, 10%; advance, $500–$2,000.

Twilight Times Books

P.O. Box 3340, Kingsport, TN 37664. www.twilighttimesbooks.com

Publisher: Lida Quillen

Produces both electronic and print titles across numerous genres including science fiction and fantasy. Some titles may be of interest to teens. Also publishes in the historical, mystery, romance and fantasy genres. Twilight's backlist contains children's books but it has not published any recently. It is currently interested in acquiring more juvenile titles.

Freelance Potential: Publishes 15 titles annually: 50% developed from unsolicited submissions; 10% by authors who are new to the publishing house; 10% by previously unpublished writers. Receives 150+ queries monthly.

Fiction: YA. Genres: historical, literary, science fiction, fantasy, mystery, suspense.

Nonfiction: YA. Topics: self-improvement, how-to, humor.

Titles: *Don't Let the Wind Catch You,* by Aaron Paul Lazar (YA). *Listen to the Ghost,* by Beverly Stowe McClure.

Submissions and Payment: Guidelines and catalogue available at website. See guidelines for latest submission periods. Query with cover letter, synopsis, first chapter, and marketing plan. Accepts email queries to publisher@twilighttimesbooks.com (no attachments). Responds in 3–4 weeks during submission period. Publication period varies. Royalty.

Watson-Guptill

1745 Broadway, New York, NY 10019. www.watsonguptill.com

Senior Acquisitions Editor

For more than 70 years, Watson-Guptill (now part of Ten Speed Press) has a legacy of publishing hard-working and influential illustrated art books. Their list covers fine art and practical art instruction in traditional disciplines such as drawing, painting, sculpture, and printmaking. They publish modern books focused on artistic pursuits such as craft, collage, comics, cartooning, manga, and animation.

Freelance Potential: Publishes 75 titles annually: 30% by agented authors.

Nonfiction: Middle-grade, YA. Topics: fine arts, drawing, painting, sculpture, cartooning, animation, graphic design, crafts, dramatic arts, music, photography, makeup artistry, architecture, interior design.

Titles: *The Time Garden,* by Daria Song. *Pop Manga,* by Camilla D'Errico and Stephen W. Martin

Submissions and Payment: Guidelines and catalogue available at website. No unsolicited submissions at this time. Agented authors only. Response time and publication period vary. Royalty; advance.

Whiskey Creek Press

P.O. Box 51052, Casper, WY 82605-1052
www.whiskeycreekpress.com; www.start-publishing.com

Executive Editor: Melanie Billings

Whiskey Creek Press publishes fiction and nonfiction titles as well as ebooks. Their emphasis is on genre fiction including romance, science fiction, thrillers and adventure. Most titles are aimed at adults but some titles might appeal to teens as well.

Freelance Potential: Publishes 150–200 titles (60–75 titles for new imprint, Wee Creek Press) annually. Receives 100+ unsolicited manuscripts monthly.

Fiction: Story picture books, middle-grade, YA, adult. Genres: science fiction, mystery, adventure, fantasy, romance, contemporary, real life/real problem.

Titles: *Blood in Trust,* by Laura A. Ellison (YA). *Dance of the Bull Rider*, by Gary Clark (YA).

Submissions and Payment: Guidelines and catalogue available at website. Send complete manuscript (60,000–80,000 words for adult submissions) with a cover letter outlining the book, author credentials including past publishing history, and word length; 1- to 2-page synopsis including character description, plot, conflict, and resolution; 1-paragraph sketch of storyline and your motivation for writing the manuscript; and a 1-page business plan detailing promotion plans and past marketing experience. Accepts email submissions to subs@whiskeycreekpress.com; and for Wee Creek, submissions to submissions@weecreekpress.com. No simultaneous submissions. Responds in 3–4 months. Publication period varies. Royalty.

YMAA Publication Center

P.O. Box 480, Wolfeboro, NH 03894. www.ymaa.com

Director: David Ripianzi

This publishing arm of Yang's Martial Arts Association offers books and instructional videos on Qigong and Chinese martial arts. Its nonfiction titles cover martial arts theory and practice as well as history, and philosophy. It also publishes martial arts fiction though not children's stories.

Freelance Potential: Publishes 8 titles annually: 25% by agented authors; 10–15% by authors who are new to the publishing house. Receives 8+ queries monthly.

Fiction: YA, adult. Topics: martial arts.

Nonfiction: YA, adult. Topics: martial arts instruction, Qigong, Oriental philosophy.

Titles: *A Sudden Dawn,* by Goran Powell (martial arts fiction). *101 Reflections on Tai Chi Chuan,* by Michael Gilman.

Submissions and Payment: Guidelines and catalogue available at website. For nonfiction, query with target audience, specific reader benefits, 1-page synopsis, author biography, and publishing experience. For fiction, also include first 30 pages. Accepts email to davidr@ymaa.com (Word and PDF files) and hard copy. SASE. Responds in 1–3 months. Publication in 12–18 months. Royalty, 10%.

Agents

Agents have become a more central part of publishing children's books, especially at major trade publishers. As the industry shifted in recent years, quite a few respected, long-term children's editors and publishers have joined literary agencies or opened their own.

At some point, almost all book writers consider whether or not to look for an agent. Some successful authors never work with an agent, while others would not be without one to take care of selling, negotiations, and contracts. But a good manuscript will find its home with or without an agent, if you are committed to finding the right publisher for your work.

How to find an agent: To begin, review the listings of children's book agents in the following pages to see which might be likely candidates to represent your work.

Other sources for lists of agents include the standard publishing reference, *Literary Marketplace* (LMP); the Association of Authors' Representatives (www.aar-online.org) member list; the SCBWI Agents Directory (free to members); and the *2016 Guide to Literary Agents* (F + W Publications), which offers valuable information on how to work with agents. The website Agent Query (www.agentquery.com) is a free searchable database of agents that includes specific information about each, including past and present clients and special interests. Be sure that any agent you contact works with children's writers.

Like publishers, most literary agencies today have websites where you can find individual agents' special interests, guidelines for submissions, and even forms to use to attach your manuscript.

What an agent does: Before taking you on as a client, an agent will review your work editorially. Although agents are willing to take on unpublished writers—they want to find the next great children's writer—an author should aim to impress an agent, just like an editor, by demonstrating commitment to the craft and a professional approach to writing. The primary work of an agent is to contact publishers, market your material, negotiate for rights and licenses, and review financial statements.

How to contact an agent: If the agent has a website, go online for specific contact requirements. If not, send a well-written, professional cover letter describing your work and background, accompanied by an outline or synopsis and sample chapter. Most agents will accept simultaneous submissions, as long as you inform them that you're querying other agents, and perhaps publishers, as well. Remember to tailor your query to individual agents just as you would to publishers.

Fees: Be careful about agent fees. Some charge for readings and critiques, even without taking you on as a client. Compare the fees and the commissions to similar agents if you do enter into a contract. A typical rate is 15 percent for domestic sales, 20 percent for foreign.

What you need to know: Once you have an agent interested in representing you, compile a list of questions to ask before agreeing. These might include:

- Why do you like my work?
- What should I expect of you, and you of me?
- What are the terms of the contract, including its duration?
- What is your track record, i.e., how many books have you sold?
- How does communication between us take place, via phone, email, or both?
- What can I do to help sell my work?
- What is required to end the agreement if it doesn't work out?

Adams Literary

7845 Colony Road, C4 #215, Charlotte, NC 28226
www.adamsliterary.com

Agents: Tracey Adams, Josh Adams, Samantha Bagood

A boutique agency, Adams specializes in juvenile publishing from picture books to YA novels. It is a place where authors, artists, editors and publishers come together to create outstanding books for children of all ages.

Categories & Submissions: Timeless, character-driven picture books; literary stories; fantasy adventure; high-concept speculative fiction; humor. Only accepting picture books from author-artists. Currently not accepting new submissions.

Contract & Payment: One-page agreement, standard commission, 15% domestic; 20% foreign and film/television.

Miriam Altshuler Literary Agency

53 Old Post Road North, Red Hook, NY 12571
www.miriamaltshulerliteraryagency.com

Agent: Miriam Altshuler, Reiko Davis

Specializing in literary and commercial fiction, narrative nonfiction, and children's books, MALA clients benefit from the personalized attention of an intimate, editorially driven office, and from more than thirty years of publishing experience.

Categories & Submissions: YA (including fantasy and dystopian) and middle-grade and, very selectively, picture books. Focuses on literary commercial fiction and nonfiction, memoirs, and narrative nonfiction. Considers how-to, self-help, and spiritual books for adults if they focus on women, children, mothering, or relationships. No romance, mysteries, horror, screenplays, or poetry. Query with a brief author bio, synopsis, and first chapter. Include an email address for response. No unsolicited manuscripts. Accepts electronic submissions to query@maliterary.com (no attachments). Responds if interested but cannot guarantee any response.

Contract & Payment: Commission, 15% domestic; 20% foreign.

Anderson Literary Management

12 West 19th Street, New York, NY 10011
http://www.andersonliterary.com/

Agents: Kathleen Anderson, Adam Friedstein, Jessie Kunhardt, Tess Taylor

This agency represents authors who are truth-tellers as well as story-tellers. They foster long-term relationships based on integrity, sound business practices, mutual respect, and companionship. Areas of interest include nonfiction such as literary journalism, psychology, history, science, and current affairs as well as wide ranging fictional works in the categories of women's, historical, humorous, and thrillers.

Categories & Submissions: No science fiction, cookbooks, gardening, craft books or children's picture books. For fiction, mail a query letter, brief synopsis, and up to the first 50 pages. For non-fiction, mail a query letter, proposal, and up to the first 3 chapters. SASE. Responds in 5 minutes to 6 weeks.

Contract & Payment: Represents and negotiates all rights in all media, throughout the world.

The Bent Agency

19 W. 21st St., #201, New York, NY 10010
www.thebentagency.com

Agents: Jenny Bent, Susan Hawk, Molly Ker Hawn, Gemma Cooper, Victoria Lowes, Heather Flaherty, Louise Fury, Beth Phelan, Brooks Sherman

The Bent Agency represents writers of a broad range of children's, YA, and adult books including fiction, commercial fiction, nonfiction, and picture books. All agents have represented best-selling authors and are eager to make talented author's dreams a reality.

Categories & Submissions: Middle-grade and YA fiction and nonfiction, including mysteries, historical fiction, fantasy, science fiction, realism, humor, and boy books. Story—strong plotting—is key. No poetry, textbooks, sports, or reference. Query with information on your writing background, what the book is about and why you're the one to write it, and the first 10 pages. See website for individual agents' email addresses (no attachments) and submit to one agent at a time. Accepts email submissions only. Accepts simultaneous submissions. Responds in 1 month.

Contract & Payment: Standard.

Meredith Bernstein Literary Agency

2095 Broadway, Suite 505, New York, NY 10023
www.meredithbernsteinliteraryagency.com

Agent: Meredith Bernstein

The Meredith Bernstein Literary Agency is a boutique agency that has developed its reputation as a place where an author experiences a unique and interactive relationship. It seeks out new talent in fiction and nonfiction and has taken many authors on to best-selling careers.

Categories & Submissions: YA fiction, commercial and literary fiction, romance, mystery and thrillers. Bernstein looks for commercial nonfiction in many categories, including parenting, science, travel, women's issues, memoirs and others. Mail query with SASE or submit online via website. Responds in 2–5 weeks.

Contract & Payment: One-page agreement with an agency clause. Commission, 15% domestic; 20% foreign.

The Book Group

20 W. 20th Street, Suite 601, New York, NY 10011
http://www.thebookgroup.com/

Agents: Julie Barer, Faye Bender, Brettne Bloom, Elisabeth Weed

The Book Group represents a wide range of distinguished authors, including critically acclaimed and bestselling novelists, celebrated writers of children's literature, and award-winning historians, food writers, memoirists and journalists.

Categories & Submissions: No poetry or screenplays. Send query letter with all relevant information, along with 10 sample pages. Email to submissions@thebookgroup.com (no attachments). No paper or phone queries. Response time varies.

Contract & Payment: Not available.

Andrea Brown Literary Agency

1076 Eagle Drive, Salinas, CA 93905
www.andreabrownlit.com

Agents: Andrea Brown, Laura Rennert, Caryn Wiseman, Jennifer Rofé, Kelly Sonnack, Jennifer Laughran, Jamie Weiss Chilton, Jennifer Mattson, Lara Perkins

An innovative West Coast agency representing children's books exclusively. Andrea Brown's agents also have East Coast publishing backgrounds as well as editing, academia, business, and many more. They are proud to be able to offer the personal attention of a small agency but the clout of a larger one.

Categories & Submissions: Picture books, chapter books, middle-grade, and YA. For picture books, paste complete manuscript. Illustrators should send 2-3 illustrations samples and link to online portfolio. Fiction, first 10 pages. For nonfiction, send proposal and sample chapter. For graphic novels, send summary and 2–3 sample page spreads. Include previous publishing experience, if applicable, with all queries. Accepts email only. Put "query" in the subject line. See website for individual agents' areas of expertise and email addresses. No attachments. Accepts simultaneous submissions if identified. Responds in 6–8 weeks if interested.

Contract & Payment: Commission, 15% domestic; 25% foreign.

The Chudney Agency

72 North State Rd, Suite 501, Briar Cliff Manor, NY 10510
www.thechudneyagency.com

Agent: Steven Chudney

This small, independent agency specializes in books for children and young adults. It will also consider taking on adult titles, especially if they may be of interest to young adults.

Categories & Submissions: Children's and YA fiction. Will consider juvenile nonfiction. Query with proposal package and 4–6 sample chapters. Children's books, include full text and 3.5 illustrations. Accepts queries by email. Responds in 2–4 weeks.

Contract & Payment: Offers written contract, binding for one year. Agent receive 15% on domestic sales.

Don Congdon Associates, Inc.

110 Williams St., Suite 2202, New York, NY 10038
www.doncongdon.com

Agents: Don Congdon, Christina Concepcion, Michael Cogndon, and Katie Grimm

Founded in 1983, this literary agency represents a diverse list of authors with everything from bestsellers to emerging talent.

Categories & Submissions: Middle-grade and YA fiction and nonfiction, as well as books for adults. Query to appropriate editor with 1 page synopsis and 1 chapter. Accepts hard copy and email submissions to appropriate agent. See website for information on its agents and what they are currently seeking.

Contract & Payment: Unavailable.

The Connor Literary Agency

2911 W. 71st Street, Minneapolis, MN 55423
http://connorliteraryagency.webs.com

The Connor Literary Agency is a full-service literary agency serving writers throughout the world. It was established in 1985 in New York City and now has offices in both New York and Minneapolis. CLA has placed authors with the most prestigious commercial and literary publishing houses including HarperCollins, Grand Central Publishing, Random House, Sourcebooks, Crown and more. Our list has included bestsellers and ground-breakers.

Categories & Submissions: Picture books, YA fiction; historical, literary, mainstream fiction. Query with 1 page synopsis. Accepts hard copy or submissions through the website.

Contract & Payment: Offers written contract binding for one year. Agent receives 15% commission on domestic sales.

Curtis Brown, Ltd.

10 Astor Place, New York, NY 10003-6935
www.curtisbrown.com

Agents: Ginger Clark, Katherine Fausset, Holly Frederick, Peter Ginsberg, Elizabeth Harding, Steve Kasdin, Ginger Knowlton, Timothy Knowlton, Laura Blake Peterson, Maureen Walters, Mitchell Waters, Noah Ballard, Kerry D'Agostino, Holly Frederick

Curtis Brown, Ltd. represents a wide variety of established and emerging authors of all YA and children's genres, including film, translation, and illustrations.

Categories & Submissions: Picture books, juvenile, middle-grade, YA fiction and nonfiction. Genres: contemporary, literary, multicultural, mystery, historical, humor, fantasy, adventure. Visit individual agent pages for submission requirements for each agent.

Contract & Payment: Written contract. Commission, 15% domestic; 20% foreign.

Laura Dail Literary Agency

350 Seventh Ave, Suite 2003, New York, NY 10001
www.ldlainc.com

Agents: Laura Dail, Tamar Rydzinski, Diane Cahill

Since 1996, the Laura Dail Literary Agency has represented many authors whose books have made the New York Times bestseller list.

Categories & Submissions: Picture books, middle-grade, YA fiction and nonfiction. Query with synopsis and make them want to read more. Accepts email queries to queries@ldlainc.com. Include "Query" in the subject line of the email. Response time varies.

Contract & Payment: Unavailable.

Liza Dawson Associates

350 Seventh Avem Suite 2003, New York, NY 10001
www.lizdawsonassociates.com

Agents: Liza Dawson, Caitlin Blasdell, Anna Olswanger, Monica Odom, Hannah Bowman

This full-service agency is based in New York City. Its agents are former publishers that ensure their material stands out. We represent first-time novelists and those with established careers.

Categories & Submissions: Young adult. Accepts email queries to Caitlin Blasdell for YA submission at querycaitlin@ lizadawsonassociates.com. Responds with request for synopsis if interested.

Contract & Payment: Offers written contract. Agent receives 15% commission.

The Jennifer DeChiara Literary Agency

31 East 32nd Street, Suite 300, New York, NY 10016
www.jdlit.com

Agents: Jennifer DeChiara, Stephen Fraser, Marie Lamba, Linda Epstein, Roseanne Wells, Vicki Selvaggio

This full service agency was named one of the top 25 agencies in the country by Writer's Digest. The Jennifer DeChiara Literary Agency represents children's books for all ages, including picture books, middle-grade, and young adult novels, as well as adult fiction and nonfiction. It is open to any and all genres. See each agent's submission guidelines for type of manuscripts they are seeking.

Categories & Submissions: Picture books, middle-grade, and YA. Each agent has his or her own guidelines, submission requirements, and contact methods and information. See website for details.

Contract & Payment: Standard contract; 15% commission.

DeFiore and Company

47 East 19th Street, Third Floor, New York, NY 10016
www.defioreandco.com

Agents: Brian DeFiore, Adam Schear, Meredith Kaffel Simonoff, Laurie Abkermeier, Matthew Elblonk, Caryn Karmatz Rudy, Rebecca Strauss, Lisa Gallagher, Nicole Tourtelot, Ashley Collom, Colin Farstad

Covering a broad range of fiction genres and general interest nonfiction books, the company represents dozens of authors and experts, including #1 *New York Times* bestsellers, award winning fiction writers for adults and children, important nonfiction authors, thinkers and practitioners, and new voices in all areas of writing.

Categories & Submissions: Picture books, middle-grade, and YA. Query with brief summary of the book, short description why you're writing the project, author bio/credentials, and the first five pages of the manuscript for fiction. Accepts email to submissions@defioreandco.com (no attachments) or to individual agents. See website for email addresses. Accepts hard copy. SASE. Responds in 4 weeks.

Contract & Payment: Unknown.

Joelle Delbourgo Associates

101 Park St, 3rd floor, Montclair, NJ 07042
www.delbourgo.com

Agents: Joelle Delbourgo, Jacqueline Flynn, Carrie Cantor

This boutique agency represents a broad range of authors writing for the adult market, as well as middle grade and young adult fiction and nonfiction.

Categories & Submissions: Middle grade, YA. and adult novels. Query to specific agent. Complete information is available at the website. Accepts simultaneous submissions.

Contract & Payment: Standard contract. Agent receives 15% commission on domestic sales.

Donadio & Olson, Inc.

121 W. 27th St., Suite 704, New York, NY 10001
www.donadio.com

Agents: Neil Olson, Edward Hibbert, Carrie Howland

This full service agency was named one of the top 25 agencies in the country by *Writer's Digest*. The Jennifer De Chiara Literary Agency represents children's books for all ages, including picture books, middle-grade, and young adult novels, as well as adult fiction and nonfiction. It is open to any and all genres. See each agent's submission guidelines for type of manuscripts they are seeking.

Categories & Submissions: Picture books, middle-grade, and YA. Each agent has his or her own guidelines, submission requirements, and contact methods and information. See website for details.

Contract & Payment: Standard contract; 15% commission.

Dunham Literary

110 William Street, Suite 2202, New York, NY 10038-3901
www.dunhamlit.com

Agents: Jennie Dunham, Bridget Smith

Dunham Literary represents writers of children's books and illustrations for all ages and adult literary fiction and nonfiction. It welcomes first-time writers, and looks to develop writers' careers, not just books. The Rhoda Weyr Agency is now a division of Dunham Literary.

Categories & Submissions: Picture books, middle-grade, and YA. No short stories, chapbooks, or novellas nor screenplays. Query by mail or email to query@dunhamlit.com (no attachments). SASE. In one page, describe plot, themes, your credentials, and how you learned of the agency. If interested, an agent will request a manuscript or proposal, biography, synopsis, and market statement.

Contract & Payment: Exclusive representation; agency clause. Commission, 15% domestic; 20% foreign; 15% dramatic.

Dunow, Carlson, & Lerner Agency

27 W. 20th St., Suite 1107, New York, NY 10011
www.kdclagency.net

Agents: Jennifer Carlson, Amy Hughes, Arielle Datz, Hery Dunow, Ellen Hosier, Eleanor Jackson, Julia Kenny, Betsy Lerner, Edward Necarlsumer, Jr., and Yishai Seidman

The agency represents literary and commercial fiction, narrative nonfiction, memoir, popular culture and young adult fiction. In addition to representing publishing rights, the agency works with established networks of co-agents to represent translation rights in all foreign territories in addition to film, television, and audio rights.

Categories & Submissions: YA fiction. and adult memoir, pop culture, Query by hard copy or email to mail@dclagency.com (no attachments) Responds if interested.

Contract & Payment: Unavailable.

Dystel & Goderich Literary Management

One Union Square West, Suite 904, New York, NY 10003
www.dystel.com

Agents: Jane Dystel, Miriam Goderich, Michael Bourret, Stacey Glick, Jim McCarthy, Lauren E. Abramo, Jessica Papin, John Rudolph, Michael Hoogland, Rachel Stout, Sharon Pelletier, Amy Bishop, Eric Myers, Kemi Faderin

This agency offers representation for picture books, middle-grade and young adult authors. It prides itself on being a full service provider and following projects through from inception to publication and beyond. The primary goal of the agency was and is to offer not just financial and contractual advice to its clients, but also editorial guidance and support. Dystel & Goderich stresses that it takes unsolicited queries very seriously and has discovered several talented writers in its slush pile.

Categories & Submissions: Picture books, middle-grade, and YA. Send cover letter, outline or brief synopsis with word count if possible, and sample chapter. Accepts hard copy and email to specific agent (no attachments). SASE. Submit to only one agent; see website for current needs and email addresses. Accepts multiple queries to other agencies. Responds in 6–8 weeks.

Contract & Payment: Commission, 15%.

East West Literary Agency

1158 26th Street, Suite 462, Santa Monica, CA 90403
www.eastwestliteraryagency.com

Agents: Deborah Warren

East West Literary Agency is a boutique agency that facilitates hands-on, personalized service and attention to authors and their books. They provide career management for established and first-time authors and their breadth of experience in many genres enable them to meet the demands of a diverse clientele.

Categories & Submissions: Picture books, juvenile fiction and nonfiction, middle-grade, and YA fiction. Query with cover letter that includes publishing credits, first 3 chapters, table of contents, and 1-page synopsis. Include complete manuscript for picture books. Currently not accepting unsolicited queries.

Contract & Payment: Written contract. Commission, 15% domestic; 25% foreign.

Ethan Ellenberg Literary Agency

155 Suffolk St., #2R, New York, NY 10002
http://ethanellenberg.com

Agents: Ethan Ellenberg, Evan Gregory, Bibi Lewis

Ethan Ellenberg Literary Agency is an independent full-service agency with robust sales all over the world. The agency is a member of the Association of Authors Representatives, an affiliate member of the Science Fiction and Fantasy Writer's of America, and an associate member of the Society for Children's Book Writers and Illustrators, The Romance Writers of America, and the Mystery Writers of America.

Categories & Submissions: Interested in all kinds of commercial fiction, including thrillers, mysteries, children's, romance, women's fiction, ethnic, science fiction, fantasy and general fiction. Literary fiction must have a strong narrative. In nonfiction, we are interested in current affairs, history, health, science, psychology, cookbooks, new age, spirituality, pop-culture, adventure, true crime, biography and memoir. Do not represent poetry. All submissions must include a query letter. For fiction, a 1-2 page synopsis and the first 50 pages of your manuscript. For nonfiction, a proposal. For picture books, the complete manuscript and 4-5 sample illustrations pasted into the body of the email. Illustrators, 4-5 sample images pasted into the body of the email and a link to your online portfolio. Send all information to agent@ethanellenberg.com. Accepts regular postal mail. If interested, will respond within 2 weeks.

Contract & Payment: Not available.

The Fielding Agency

269 S. Beverly Dr., #341, Beverly Hills, CA 90212
www.fieldingagency.com

Agent: Whitney Lee

This full service agency that represents a select number of authors domestically and also handles the foreign rights for titles on behalf of many prominent literary agencies.

Categories & Submissions: Picture books, YA fiction and titles for adults in the categories of romance, fantasy, humor, suspense, and adventure. Query with synopsis and author bio. Accepts hard copy. SASE.

Contract & Payment: Agents receive 15% commission for domestic sales; 20% commission on foreign sales. Offers written contract, 9–12 months.

FinePrint Literary Management

115 West 29th Street, 3rd Floor, New York, NY 10001
www.fineprintlit.com

Agents: Peter Rubie, Stephany Evans, June Clark, Janet Reid, Penny Moore, Laura Wood

This agency represents a wide range of literary and commercial fiction and some nonfiction for adults and children. Accepting new and established writers. Their expertise covers traditional and e-book publishing and subsidiary rights.

Categories & Submissions: Middle-grade, YA fiction and non-fiction. Genres include character-driven picture books, contemporary fiction, historical, fantasy, literary, boy-oriented YA, humor, paranormal, mainstream fiction, books that tackle social issues or taboos, romance. Match the genre to the agent profiles available on the website and submit a query and first 2 chapters for fiction; query, proposal, and sample chapters for nonfiction. Some agents prefer mail, some email (no attachments). See website for details.

Contract & Payment: Standard 1-year contract initially, but the agency strives to represent authors for their careers and through multiple projects. Commission, 15%.

Flannery Literary

1140 Wickfield Ct., Naperville, IL 60563
www.flanneryliterary.com

Agent: Jennifer Flannery

Based in Chicago, Flannery Literary represents writers of books for children and young adults. Its primary goal is putting good books in the hands—and hearts—of young readers. The agency is always looking for a fresh new voice.

Categories & Submissions: Early readers, middle grade and young adult fiction. Query. Accepts hard copy. SASE. Responds in 2 weeks.

Contract & Payment: Agent receives 15% commission on domestic sales; 20% commission on foreign sales. Offers written contract.

Fletcher & Company

78 Fifth Avenue, 3rd Floor, New York, NY 10011
www.fletcherandco.com

Agents: Christy Fletcher, Melissa Chinchillo, Grainne Fox, Rebecca Gradinger, Lisa Grubka, Donald Lamm, Sylvie Greenberg

Co-founded by agent Christy Fletcher in 2003, Fletcher & Co. is a full service literary management and production company dedicated to writers of upmarket nonfiction as well as literary fiction.

Categories & Submissions: YA fiction and nonfiction. Query with brief synopsis. Accepts hard copy or email to info@fletcherandco.com (no attachments). Responds if interested.

Contract & Payment: Unavailable.

Sheldon Fogelman Agency

10 East 40th Street, Suite 3205, New York, NY 10016
www.sheldonfogelmanagency.com

Agents: Sheldon Fogelman, Janine Le, Amy Stern

Founded in 1975, this agency was the first to specialize in children's book authors. As a full service agency, Sheldon Fogelman Agency has the resources and knowledge to assist their clients in all aspects of their creative lives from contract negotiation and rights management to editorial input and long term career planning.

Categories & Submissions: All genres and types of children's books, from picture books to YA. Send a 1-page letter with a brief synopsis, credentials, and where you learned of the agency; indicate simultaneous submissions. Also send first 3 chapters for novels, or complete manuscript for picture books. Accepts hard copy and email to submissions@ sheldonfogelmanagency.com (Word attachments). SASE. Responds in 6 weeks.

Contract & Payment: Not available.

Folio Literary Management, LLC

The Film Center Building, 630 Ninth Ave., Suite 1101, New York, NY 10036. www.foliolit.com

Agents: John Cusick, Erin Harris, Molly Jaffa, Katherine Latshaw, Marcy Posner, Melissa Sarver White, Emily Van Beek

This literary agency has a subdivision called Folio Jr., which is dedicated to representing today's most stellar children's book authors and artists. The agency places both fiction and nonfiction with major publishers throughout the U.S. and around the world.

Categories & Submissions: Picture books, middle grade, YA fiction and nonfiction. Query to appropriate agent. Agent bio and current needs are listed on the website. Responds if interested.

Contract & Payment: Unavailable.

Foundry Literary + Media

33 West 17th Street, PH, New York, NY 10011
www.foundrymedia.com

Agents: Hannah Brown Gordon, Brandi Bowles, Mollie Glick, Anthony Mattero, Peter McGuigan, Kristen Neuhaus, Yfat Reiss Gendell, Chris Park, Peter Steinberg, Roger Freet, Richie Kern, Jess Regel.

A full-service agency, Foundry represents clients from books to foreign publishing, film and TV, merchandise, online media, and beyond. The Foundry team is relentless in finding new and diverse ways for our clients to reach wider audiences throughout the entire publication process.

Categories & Submissions: Picture books through YA, as well as adult commercial and literary fiction and nonfiction. Query with author bio, synopsis, and first 3 chapters for fiction; sample chapters and table of contents for nonfiction. Address one agent; see website for submission method preferences and email addresses. Responds in 8 weeks if interested.

Contract & Payment: Not available.

Frances Collin, Literary Agent

P.O. Box 33, Wayne, PA 19087
www.francescollin.com

Agent: Frances Collin

Representing more than 90 clients France Collin considers both fiction and nonfiction for adults, young adults, and middle grade readers.

Categories & Submissions: Middle-grade and YA fiction and nonfiction, as well as books for adults. Query describing project (no attachments) Accepts email to queries@francescollin.com Response time varies.

Contract & Payment: Offers written contract. Agent receives 15% commission on domestic sales.

Sarah Jane Freymann Literary Agency

59 W. 71st St., Suite 9B, New York, NY 10023
www.sarahjanefreymann.com

Agents: Sarah Jane Freymann, Steve Schwartz, Katherine Sands, Jessica Sinsheimer

Sarah Jane Freymann has been a literary agent since the 1970s. She and her team have a strong affinity for narrative fiction, and represent world-renowned naturalists, award-winning journalists, and memoirists. It also represents a growing number of edgy young adult fiction titles.

Categories & Submissions: YA fiction, literary and commercial fiction for adults, self-help, memoirs, cookbooks. Query with author bio, pitch letter and first 10-pages of manuscript. Accepts email to submissions@sarahjanefreymann.com (no attachments). Responds if interested.

Contract & Payment: Agent receives 15% commission on domestic sales; 20% on foreign sales. Offers written contract.

Rebecca Friedman Literary Agency

110 Wall Street, New York, NY 10005
www.frfliterary.com

Agents: Rebecca Friedman, Kimberly Brower, Rachel Marks

This full-service agency represents a wide-range of fiction and nonfiction authors. The agency is always looking for great stories told with strong voices.

Categories & Submissions: YA fiction and contemporary romance, women's fiction, journalistic nonfiction and memoir. Query with first chapter. Accepts email queries to appropriate editor; check website for what individual agents are looking for. No attachments. Responds in 6–8 weeks.

Contract & Payment: Unavailable.

Full Circle Literary, LLC

7676 Hazard Center Dr., Suite 500, San Diego, CA 92108
www.fullcircleliterary.com

Agents: Stephanie Von Borstel, Adriana Dominguez, Taylor Martindale Kean, Lilly Ghahremani

This agency offers a full circle approach to literary representation. Its team has diverse experience in book publishing including editorial, marketing, publicity, legal and rights.

Categories & Submissions: Picture books, middle grade and YA fiction, as well as fiction and nonfiction for adults. Query with first ten pages for fiction; with one sample chapter for nonfiction. Accepts email submissions to submissions@fullcircle.com or through the submission form on the website. Responds if interested.

Contract & Payment: Agent receives 15% commission on domestic sales; 20% on foreign sales. Offers written contract.

Nancy Gallt Literary Agency

273 Charlton Ave., South Orange, NJ 07079
www.nancygallt.com

Agents: Nancy Gallt, Marietta B. Zacker

This agency focuses on developing and finding the right home for
the work of some of the most talented writers in the children's book
industry. It aims to bring to life stories and artwork that help young
readers throughout the world become life-long reading enthusiasts.

Categories & Submissions: Picture books, early readers, middle grade and young adult fiction. Send complete ms through the
website or by hard copy. SASE. Responds if interested.

Contract & Payment: Agent receives 15% commission on
domestic sales; 20% on foreign sales. Offers written contract.

Barry Goldblatt Literary LLC

320 7th Avenue, #266, Brooklyn, NY 11215
www.bgliterary.com

Agent: Barry Goldblatt

Barry Goldblatt had many years in the publishing industry working at
publishers including Penguin and Orchard Books. He represents authors
of high-quality children's, middle grade, and young adult fiction.

Categories & Submissions: Picture books, early readers, middle
grade, and YA fiction. Query with synopsis, and first five pages
of the manuscript. Include the word "query" in the subject line.
Accepts email queries to query@bgliterary.com (no attachments).
Responds if interested.

Contract & Payment: Agent receives 15% commission on
domestic sales; 20% on foreign sales.

Go Literary

www.go-lit.com

Agent: Amaryah Orenstein

Go Literary aims to give a voice to a broad range of perspectives across the literary spectrum. It is actively seeking fiction and nonfiction that features a strong narrative and that tackle big issues in engaging, accessible ways.

Categories & Submissions: Early readers, middle grade, and young adult fiction and nonfiction titles.' Adult fiction and nonfiction. Query with synopsis and biographical sketch. Accepts queries by email only to submissions@go-lit.com. Responds in 3–4 weeks.

Contract & Payment: Agent receives standard commission. Offers written contract.

Irene Goodman Literary Agency

27 West 24th Street, Suite 700B, New York, NY 10010
www.irenegoodman.com

Agents: Irene Goodman, Miriam Kriss, Barbara Poelle, Rachel Ekstrom, Beth Vesel, Danny Baror, Heather Baror, Steve Fisher

This large agency has been in business for almost 40 years. It represents over 100 authors in the categories of young adult and adult fiction, including historical, thrillers, mysteries, and women's titles, and nonfiction with an emphasis on pop culture, memoir, music, social issues, parenting, and lifestyle topics. See the website for agents currently looking for middle-grade and YA fiction. Currently do not represent poetry, inspirational fiction, screenplays, or picture books.

Categories & Submissions: Middle-grade and YA fiction and nonfiction. Does not represent picture books. Email query with first 10 pages of manuscript, synopsis (3–5 paragraphs), and author bio in the body of the email to the agent of your choice. See website for interests and addresses of individual agents. Responds in 6–8 weeks if interested.

Contract & Payment: Simple, 1-page agreement. Standard 15% commission.

Sanford J. Greenburger Associates

55 Fifth Avenue, New York, NY 10003
www.greenburger.com

Agents: Brenda Bowen, Faith Hamlin, Courtney Miller-Callihan, Heide Lange, Daniel Mandel, Matt Bialer, Nicholas Ellison, Chelsea Lindman, Lindsay Ribar, Rachael Dillon Fried, Thomas Miller, Bethany Buck

This is a large, prestigious agency that has represented Theodore Dreiser and Antoine de Saint-Exupéry, and currently represents such global bestselling authors and artists as Dan Brown, Robin Preiss Glasser, Christopher Moore, Patrick Rothfuss, and Brad Thor. Also among the agency's current clients are writers of fiction, non-fiction, genre books, and original ebooks; author and artists of children's books; and a small number of poets and essayists.

Categories & Submissions: Children's books. All genres. Send query letter, first 3 chapters (for fiction) or book proposal (for non-fiction), synopsis, and author bio. If emailing, put letter in body of email and other items as Word attachments. See website for agent listings and interests, email addresses, and specific guidelines; many do not accept hard copy. Bowen wants full manuscripts for picture books and prefers email to bb@sjga.com. Responds in 6–8 weeks if interested. No screenplays.

Contract & Payment: Commission, 15% domestic; 20% foreign.

Janklow & Nesbit

445 Park Avenue, New York, NY 10022-2606
www.janklowandnesbit.com

Agents: Morton Janklow, Lynn Nesbit, Luke Janklow, Emma Parry, Anne Sibbald, Cullen Stanley, PJ Mark, Paul Lucas, Richard Morris, Kirby Kim, Stefanie Lieberman

Janklow & Nesbit's approach has always been focused on client advocacy and meticulous attention to detail. This prestigious literary agency has prided itself on offering the care and personal attention associated with a boutique agency and the clout and expertise of a big firm.

Categories & Submissions: Picture books, young readers, middle-grade, YA fiction and nonfiction. Email brief query with sample chapters and first 10 pages below query to submissions@janklow.com. Accepts hard copy. SASE.

Contract & Payment: Not available.

Harvey Klinger, Inc.

300 West 55th Street, Suite 11V, New York, NY 10019
www.harveyklinger.com

Agents: Harvey Klinker, Sara Crowe, David Dunton

"Celebrating over 30 years representing the best in quality adult and children's fiction and non-fiction." Harvey Klinger represents only adult books; other agents take on children's book projects. The company is always looking for new voices, both published and unpublished, but only takes on a small number of new authors in any given year.

Categories & Submissions: Middle-grade, YA in all categories. Query should be short and to the point. Include a short synopsis, author bio, and the first five pages of your manuscript. Do not send full manuscript unless requested. Indicate simultaneous submissions. Agent bios and emails available at website. No attachments. Crowe accepts email or electronic queries only. Responds in 2–4 weeks if interested.

Contract & Payment: Simple, to-the-point contract. Commission, 15% domestic; 25% foreign.

Knight Agency

570 East Avenue, Madison, GA 30650
www.knightagency.net

Agents: Deidre Knight, Pamela Harty, Lucienne Diver, Elaine Spencer, Nephele Tempest, Melissa Jeglinski, Travis Pennington

The Knight Agency philosophy is simple: what you give is what you get. As such, they are dedicated to cultivating prosperous, long-term writing careers by giving clients unparalleled service. Their team of talented agents have placed more than 2,000 titles with all major traditional and online publishers.

Categories & Submissions: Picture books, middle-grade, graphic novels, and YA. No books for younger children. Also specializes in romance, women's fiction, literary fiction, mysteries, science fiction, fantasy, and multicultural and inspirational fiction and nonfiction for adults. Email only to submissions@ knightagency.net. No attachments. Each query should be sent to individual agents listed on website. Response time is 6-8 weeks.

Contract & Payment: Commission, 15% domestic; 20–25% foreign.

KT Literary

9249 S. Broadway, #200-543, Highlands Ranch, CO 80129
www.ktliterary.com

Agents: Kate Testerman, Sara Megibow, Renee Nyen

"Books aren't just what we do, they're who we are." Located in Highlands Ranch, a Denver, CO suburb, KT Literary believes in the power of new technology to connect authors and readers. They leverage their decade of experience in New York publishing to the foothills of the Rocky Mountains where any major publishing house is just a phone call or email away.

Categories & Submissions: Middle-grade and YA as well as new adult, romance, erotica, science fiction, and fantasy. No picturebooks at this time. All agents accept email queries to individual emails. Please see website. Send query with first 3 pages of manuscript in the body of the email (include "Query" and the title of the manuscript in the subject line). Responds in 2 weeks.

Contract & Payment: Not available.

Leshne Agency

16 West 23rd Street, New York, NY 10010
www.leshneagency.com

Agents: Lisa Leshne, Sandy Hodgman, Asja Parrish
The Leshne Agency is a full-service literary and talent management agency, representing writers, artists, and entertainers looking to grow their brand across all forms of traditional and digital media. With over 25 years of experience in newsprint, online media, and entertainment consultant experience, Leshne is positioned to off guidance on long-lasting success.

Categories & Submissions: The Leshne Agency is seeking authors across all genres: narrative, memoir, and prescriptive non-fiction, with a particular interest in sports, wellness, business, political and parenting topics. They will also look at truly terrific commercial fiction and young adult and middle-grade books. They are NOT interested in screenplays or scripts. All materials must be submitted via email and include QUERY and the title of your manuscript in the subject line. Everything must be in the email body, no attachments. Include a synopsis, table of contents, and 10 sample pages. Also provide your author bio, previous publications, and total word count.

Contract & Payment: Not available.

Levine Greenberg Rostan Literary Agency, Inc. ⭐

307 Seventh Avenue, Suite 2407, New York, NY 10001
www.levinegreenberg.com

Agents: Jim Levine, Stephanie Rostan, Melissa Rowland, Victoria Skurnuck, Danielle Svetcov, Keery Sparks, Monika Verma, Shelby Boyer

This agency's mission is to represent people rather than projects. Most of its titles are published by imprints of the major houses, but they also work with many independent presses.

Categories & Submissions: Middle grade, and YA fiction and nonfiction titles. Query with no moore than 50 pages of ms. Accepts submissions through the website or by email to submit@lgrliterary.com. Include individual agent's name if appropriate. Responds if interested.

Contract & Payment: Agent receives 15% commission on domestic sales; 20% on foreign sales. Offers written contract.

Lowenstein Associates

115 East 23rd Street, 4th floor, New York, NY 10010
www.lowensteinassociates.com

Agents: Barbara Lowenstein, Mary South

Founded in 1976 by Barbara Lowenstein, this agency represents a variety of authors from New York Times bestsellers to Pulitzar Prize nominees.

Categories & Submissions: Accepts YA fiction and nonfiction, as well as adult titles. Fiction: query with first 10 pages in the body of the email (no attachments). Nonfiction, query with table of contents and proposal (no attachments). Accepts submissions to assistant@bookhaven.com. Responds if interested.

Contract & Payment: Agent receives 15% commission on domestic sales; 20% on foreign sales. Offers wrtten contract.

Maass Literary Agency

121 W. 27th Street, Suite 801, New York, NY 10001
www.maassagency.com

Agents: Donald Maass, Jennifer Jackson, Cameron McClure, Stacia Decker, Amy Boggs.

This literary agency has represented more than 150 novelists and sells more than 100 novels every year to leading publishers in th U.S. and overseas.

Categories & Submissions: Early readers, middle grade, YA. Query with synopsis, genre, word count, and first 5 pages of ms. Accepts email queries to individual agents. See website for information on agents and the types of books they are interested in. Responds if interested.

Contract & Payment: Agent receives 15% commission on domestic sales; 20% on foreign sales. Offers wrtten contract.

MacGregor Literary

P.O. Box 1316, Manzanita, OR 97130
http://macgregorliterary.com

Agents: Chip MacGregor, Amanda Luedeke, Erin Buterbaugh, Holly Lorincz

MacGregor Literary has over 20 years of experience representing bestsellers from the New York Times, USA Today, Wall Street Journal, Publishers Weekly, and others. They have a commitment to their authors from conception to publication and help them focus on long-term careers, not "just books." Their new agent, Erin Buterbaugh, loves focusing on children's, middle-grade, and YA fiction.

Categories & Submissions: Currently not accepting unsolicited submissions and will not return unsolicited material even with SASE.

Contract & Payment: Not available.

Mansion Street Literary Management

www.mansionstreet.com

Agents: Jean Sagendorph, Michelle Witte

This young agency is rapidly growing with new authors of both fiction and nonfiction. It specializes in children's books, cookbooks, and craft books.

Categories & Submissions: Early reader, middle grade, YA fiction and nonfiction. Query with no more than 10 pages. (no attachments) Accepts submissions to specific agents. Visit the website for a list of agents and their current interests. Responds if interested.

Contract & Payment: Agent receives 15% commission on domestic sales; 20% on foreign sales. Offers wrtten contract.

Mary Evans, Inc.

242 E. Fifth St., New York, NY 10003
www.maryevansinc.com

Agents: Mary Evans, Julie Kardon, Mary Gaule.
This New York literary agency works with authors on picture books, middle grade and young adult fiction. It also represents a wide range of nonfiction books.

Categories & Submissions: Picture books, middle grade, YA fiction. Review the website for specific agents and their specialties. Query with a brief synopsis and resume. Accepts hard copy or email to info@maryevansinc.com. Responds in 6–8 weeks.

Contract & Payment: Unavailable.

Dee Mura Literary

P.O. Box 131, Massapequa Park, NY 11762
www.deemuraliterary.com

Agents: Dee Mura, Kimiko Nakamura, Kaylee Davis

A full-service literary management company, Dee Mura Literary specializes in a hands-on, collaborative expertise, which enables it to guide writers through every step of the publishing process. It is interested in the long term goals of its authors. Both Kimiko Nakamura and Kaylee Davis are interested in YA and new adult fiction.

Categories & Submissions: Action/adventure, animals, anthropology, archeology, arts & photography, biography, business, chick lit, comedy/humor, contemporary fiction, cooking, conservation & environmental issues, current affairs, entertainment, erotica, ethnic & Jewish, finance, fantasy, gay & lesbian, literary, government, health, historical, home & garden, inspirational, medical, memoirs, middle grade, military, mind & body, mystery, narrative nonfiction, new adult, New Age, outdoors & nature, paranormal, parenting & families, popular culture, psychology, religion/spirituality, romance, satire, science, science fiction, self-help & motivational, sports, thrillers & espionage, travel, women's lit, young adult. No poetry, no screenplays. Email only with short description, author bio, synopsis, and sample writing (25 pages for fiction, an excerpt of the proposal for nonfiction).

Contract & Payment: Unavailable.

Jean V. Naggar Literary Agency

216 East 75th Street, Suite 1E, New York, NY 10021
www.jvnla.com

Agents: Jean Naggar, Jennifer Weltz, Alice Tasman, Elizabeth Evans, Laura Biagi

The Jean V. Naggar Literary Agency was born from grassroots in 1978 with no staff, no capital, and 10 unpublished authors. Almost 40 years later, they now represent writers from every genre and have been published in over 50 countries around the world.

Categories & Submissions: See website for agents' individual preferences. Email query and form at website. See specific guidelines, but generally, include a brief description of the work, brief biography, and the first 2 manuscript pages in the body of the email. No attachments. Accepts simultaneous submissions if identified.

Contract & Payment: Commission, 15%.

Nelson Literary Agency

1732 Wazee Street, Suite 207, Denver, CO 80202
www.nelsonagency.com

Agents: Kristin Nelson

This Denver agency is full-service and hands-on in its representation of adult and children's books, and other media. They've represented many *New York Times* and *USA Today* bestsellers, and are open to new authors.

Categories & Submissions: Middle-grade, YA, and adult. Genres include science fiction, fantasy, romance, commercial fiction, women's fiction, and literary fiction with a commercial bent. nonfiction, memoir, screenplays, short-story collections, poetry, children's picture books or early reader chapter books, or material for the Christian/inspirational market. Email query letter to query@nelsonagency.com for completed works of fiction. Do not send sample pages, synopses, links, or attachments. Responds in 5–10 days.

Contract & Payment: Commission, 15% domestic; 25% foreign; 20% film rights.

Pippin Properties

110 West 40th Street, Suite 1704, New York, NY 10018
www.pippinproperties.com

Agents: Holly M. McGhee, Elena Giovinazzo, Heather Alexander, Courtney Stevenson

Founded in 1998, Pippin is devoted primarily to picture books, middle-grade fiction, and YA novels, but it does represent adult projects on occasion. They place nearly every project they take on by working closely with the author all the way from the marketing plan to their long term careers.

Categories & Submissions: Picture books, middle-grade, YA. All genres. Email query letter with first chapter or complete manuscript for picture books, synopsis of work, author background and/or publishing history, and any other relevant information to info@pippin-properties.com (no attachments). Responds in 3 weeks if interested.

Contract & Payment: Not available.

Prospect Agency

551 Valley Road, PMB 377, Upper Montclair, NJ 07043
www.prospectagency.com

Agents: Emily Sylvan Kim, Teresa Keitlinski, Rachel Orr, Becca Stumpf, Carrie Pestritto, Linda Camacho

Prospect Agency is an independent New York based literary agency. Agents collaborate to offer skilled editorial and artistic advice while advocating for clients in the publishing marketplace. They represent both adult and children's books and seek to work with authors and illustrators who will contribute to the vibrant literary landscape.

Categories & Submissions: Picture books, juvenile, middle-grade, YA, and adult fiction. Genres: contemporary, literary, urban fantasy, science fiction, mysteries, thrillers, romance, women's fiction. Query with 3 chapters or complete manuscript for picture books, synopsis, contact information, credits, writing education. Upload via the website only. No mail or email. Accepts simultaneous submissions. Responds in 3 months if interested.

Contract & Payment: At-will agreement. Commission, 15%.

Red Fox Literary

129 Morro Avenue, Shell Beach, CA 93449
www.redfoxliterary.com

Agents: Abigail Samoun, Karen Grencik, Danielle Smith

This is a boutique agency specializing in children's books, from picture books through YA titles. It was formed in 2011 by Abigail Samoun and Karen Grencik. It is currently looking for stories about real life and real people, where character development is front and center. At present, it is only accepting submissions from conference attendees and professional references.

Categories & Submissions: Picture books, juvenile, middle-grade, YA; fiction and nonfiction. All genres. Currently only accepting submissions from authors who have presented at conferences which the agents have attended, or by referral.

Contract & Payment: Not available.

Red Sofa Literary

2163 Grand Avenue #2, St. Paul, MN 55105
www.redsofaliterary.com

Agents: Dawn Frederick, Jennie Goloboy, Laura Zats, Amanda Rutter, Bree Ogden

Red Sofa Literary is the celebration of the quirky, eclectic ideas, realizing the best ones come via engaging conversations over good coffee while sometimes relaxing in a colorful lounger. Their mission is to celebrate a life of reading and geek culture, where brains always win over the brawn.

Categories & Submissions: Middle-grade fiction, graphic novels, YA fiction and nonfiction. Query letter first before sending entire book or sample. No email attachments. Will respond in 4-6 weeks.

Contract & Payment: Standard agency contract and commission.

Rodeen Literary Management

3501 North Southport #497, Chicago, IL 60657
www.rodeenliterary.com

Agent: Paul Rodeen

Rodeen Literary is a boutique agency focusing on career management for experienced and aspiring authors specializing in children's book authors and illustrators.

Categories & Submissions: Actively looking for picture books, early readers, middle-grade fiction and nonfiction, graphic novels, comic books, YA fiction and nonfiction. Send cover letter, contact information, full text for picture books, and up to 50 pages for novels and nonfiction to submissions@rodeenliterary.com. Submissions sent via mail will not be accepted. Accepts simultaneous submissions if identified. Responds if interested.

Contract & Payment: Not available.

Sadler Children's Literary

www.sadlerchildrensliterary.com

Agent: Jodell Sadler

This literary boutique agency focuses on the craft of learning fun and working with writers and illustrators to create, beautiful, memorable books for young readers.

Categories & Submissions: Picture books, early readers, middle grade, and YA fiction and nonfiction titles. Accepts submissions through the website only. Responds if interested.

Contract & Payment: Unavailable.

Susan Schulman Literary Agency

454 West 44th Street, New York, NY 10036
http://schulmanagency.com/

Agents: Susan Schulman, Emily Uhry, Christine LeBlond

This boutique agency represents children's books, juvenile fiction, and adult fiction and nonfiction—particularly related to women's issues. Schulman looks for writers who "have thoroughly familiarized themselves with what constitutes good writing in their chosen genre," and welcomes new voices. Though it accepts unsolicited submissions, it obtains most of its clients through recommendations, solicitations, and conferences.

Categories & Submissions: Picture books, juvenile, middle-grade, YA; fiction and nonfiction. All genres. Send query letter, résumé, outline, 3 sample chapters for fiction; query letter, résumé, at least 1 chapter for nonfiction. Accepts hard copy with SASE or email to schulmanqueries@yahoo.com.

Contract & Payment: Agency agreement available for review. Commission, 15% domestic; 20% foreign.

Scovil Galen Ghosh Literary Agency

276 Fifth Avenue, Suite 708, New York, NY 10001
www.sgglit.com

Agents: Russell Galen, Jack Scovil, Danny Baror, Anna Ghosh, Ann Behar

This agency's list is eclectic and diverse, and the agents are open to any kind of book that is "first-rate." At any given moment they could be working on a first sale for an exciting new author or an eight-figure deal for a veteran of the New York Times bestseller list, or anything in between. Ann Behar is the juvenile publishing specialist. She looks for strong, distinct voices, vibrant characters, and beautiful writing. The agency is open to first-time authors.

Categories & Submissions: Children's and YA books for all ages. Also represents all genres of adult fiction and nonfiction. Email an "unadorned, unaccompanied" query letter to annbehar@sgglit.com (no attachments). Regular mail is accepted (no SASE, include email address for response), but email is preferred.

Contract & Payment: Not available.

Serendipity Literary

305 Gates Avenue, Brooklyn, NY 11216
www.serendipitylit.com

Agents: Regina Brooks, Karen Thomas, Dawn Michelle Hardy, Foladé Bell, Nadeen Gayle, Chelcee Johns

Children's and YA publishing is a specialty of this boutique agency, now in business more than a dozen years. President and lead agent Regina Brooks is very open to first-time authors with talent, and also represents authors of adult fiction and nonfiction. Check the website for other agents' preferences.

Categories & Submissions: Picture books to YA, fiction and nonfiction. Currently not accepting picture books, but check website for updates. Use the website form to provide information and upload a submission. It asks for the components of a query letter, including the title, premise, manuscript length, your writing background, long-term writing plans, a 1-page synopsis that details the plot and theme, and the first 50 pages or 3 chapters of your manuscript. The website also offers guidance on nonfiction proposals. Responds in 4–6 weeks. No submissions by regular mail.

Contract & Payment: Commission, 15% domestic; 20% foreign.

Stimola Literary Studio

308 Livingston Court, Edgewater, NJ 07020
www.stimolaliterarystudio.com

Agents: Rosemary B. Stimola, Allison Remcheck

Stimola Literary Studio is a full service literary agency devoted to representing authors and author/illustrators of fiction and nonfiction, preschool through young adult, who bring unique and substantive contributions to the industry.

Categories & Submissions: Picture books, middle-grade, YA; fiction and nonfiction. Current needs include picture books; middle-grade humor; middle-grade/YA mysteries; YA thrillers, supernatural, and science fiction; multicultural teen fantasy; graphic novels; nonfiction with adult crossover appeal; cookbooks. No Revolutionary or Civil War historical fiction, poetry, or institutional books. Send a 1-page query with synopsis, credentials, and what makes the book distinctive. Use email form on website. Responds only if interested.

Contract & Payment: Commission, 15% domestic, 20% foreign.

Stonesong

270 West 39th Street, #201, New York, NY 10018
http://stonesong.com

Agents: Alison Fargis, Judy Linden, Emmanuelle Morgen, Maria Ribas, Leila Campoli

Stonesong agents represent authors of middle-grade and YA fiction and nonfiction, as well as adult authors. Among the specific interests of various agents is children's fiction "that blurs the line between literary and commercial." They also have a custom publishing division and a book production/packaging division.

Categories & Submissions: Middle-grade, YA; fiction and nonfiction. Query to a specific agent (see website for categories each handles) with the first chapter or first 10 pages of your manuscript. Accepts email to submissions@stonesong.com.

Contract & Payment: Not available.

The Strothman Agency

63 E. 9th St., 10X, New York, NY 10003
www.strothmanagency.com

Agents: Wendy Strothman, Lauren E. MacLeod

The Strothman Agency represents middle-grade and YA fiction and nonfiction, as well as many categories of adult books. The agency is very selective but advocates for their authors through-out the entire publishing cycle. Lauren MacLeod is interested in contemporary and humorous books, middle-grade, and various YA genres, including thrillers, mysteries, horror, contemporary, romance, and chick lit.

Categories & Submissions: Middle-grade and YA; adult history, science, current affairs, nature/environment, narrative nonfiction, arts, travel, business, memoirs. No commercial fiction, romance, picture books, poetry or self-help. Send electronic submissions only to strothmanagency@ gmail.com. Include a query letter out-lining your qualifications and experience, a synopsis of your work, and the genre and word count of your manuscript. For fiction, include 2–10 pages of your manuscript in the body of the email; no attachments. Do not send entire manuscript unless requested. Responds in 3–4 weeks if interested.

Contract & Payment: Commission, 15% domestic; 20% foreign.

Talcott Notch Literary Agency

2 Broad Street, Second Floor, Suites 1, 2, & 10, Milford, CT 06460
www.talcottnotch.net

Agents: Gina Panettieri, Paula Munier, Rachael Dugas, Sara Sulaiman

Walcott Notch represents a very eclectic mix of authors and proj-ects. Original thought, original research, unique concepts and ground-breaking new approaches are the earmarks that set our books apart. Currently looking for middle-grade and YA fiction and non-fiction. No picture books at this time.

Categories & Submissions: Middle-grade and YA fiction; con-temporary, fantasy, science fiction, mystery/thriller, paranormal, romance. Query only (1-2 pages that tells genre, word count, brief overview of plot and main characters) with first ten pages of man-uscript. Prefers email to specific agents; see website for addresses and interests. Accepts hard copy. SASE. Responds in 4 weeks.

Contract & Payment: Unknown.

Transatlantic Literary Agency

2 Bloor Street East, Suite 3500, Toronto, Ontario, Canada M4W 1A8
http://transatlanticagency.com/

Agents: David Bennett, Sandra Bishop, Shaun Bradley, Marie Campbell, Jesse Finkelstein, Samantha Haywood, Fiona Kenshole, Stephanie Sinclair, Amy Tompkins, Trena White

Transatlantic Agency is a full service literary agency covering adult trade, children's and young adult authors, and illustrators They represent all aspects of publishing rights including book-to-tv/film. They curate author's careers and maintain close relationships with editors across the world.

Categories & Submissions: Picture books, middle-grade, graphic novels, YA; fiction and nonfiction. Each agent has specific current interests and submission guidelines; see website.

Contract & Payment: Not available.

Trident Media Group

41 Madison Ave., 36Fl, New York, NY 10010
www.tridentmedia.com

Agents: Robert Gottlieb, Kimberly Whaen, Scott Miller, Dan Strone, Alyssa Eisner Henkin, Melissa Flashman, Ellen Levine

This prominent New York literary agency represents more than 1,000 bestselling and emerging authors in a range of fiction and nonfiction.

Categories & Submissions: Fiction, Nonfiction. Query through the website to one lierary agent only. Include a one paragraph bio, brief plot synopsis, and contact information. No simultaneous submissions for 30 days.

Contract & Payment: Agent receives 15% for domestic sales; 20% for foreign sales. Offers written contract.

Wernick & Pratt

www.wernickpratt.com

Agents: Marcia Wernick, Linda Pratt, Emily Mitchell

Wernick & Pratt focuses exclusively on children's books of all genres, from very early picture books through YA literature and everything in between. Marcia Wernick and Linda Pratt were long-time agents at the Sheldon Fogelman Agency before branching out on their own. They love to focus on the people and not just the books.

Categories & Submissions: Interested in all children's book projects, fiction and nonfiction with particular emphasis on picture books, humorous chapter books, and middle-grade and YA novels, both literary and commercial. Not interested in picture books of more than 750 words, work targeting the educational market, or fiction about the American Revolution, Civil War, or World War II. Send query letter with contact information, 1-page synopsis, and author's background and publishing history. Include 3 chapters for novel submissions; 2 manuscripts for picture book submissions. Indicate if submission is exclusive (preferred) or non-exclusive. Accepts email only to sumbmissions@ wernickpratt.com and indicate the agent to whom you are submitting. Responds if interested.

Contract & Payment: Not available.

Contests

Selected Contests & Awards

Contests are an excellent mechanism for writers to practice their craft, and promote their writing and reputation among editors and readers. Winning an award for a published book can increase sales, sometimes dramatically; receiving the Newbery or Caldecott Award can double the number of books sold, and generates more interest in other books created by winning authors and illustrators.

Whether you enter a contest for unpublished writers or submit your published book for an award, your book will be read by established writers and qualified editors. Participating in a competition can increase recognition of your writing and possibly open more doors for selling your work. Some publishers, in fact, use contests to find new writers.

If you enter a contest and do not win, look for the winning entry when it is published. Read it to see how your work compares with the competition.

To be considered for the contests and awards that follow, your entry must fulfill all the requirements. Many contests accept unpublished manuscripts, while some require published works. Note special entry requirements, such as whether the submission must come from you or your publisher, whether you need to be a member of the sponsoring organization, or if you are limited in the number of entries you can send. Be sure to submit your entry in the standard manuscript submission format.

For each listing, we've included the address, a description, the entry requirements, the deadline, and the prize. In some cases, the deadlines were not available at press time. Visit the indicated websites to request entry forms and detailed guidelines, which usually specify the current deadline.

Abilene Writers Guild Monthly Contest

P.O. Box 2562, Abilene, TX 79604
www.abilenewritersguild.org

Open to Guild members only, this themed monthly contest offers awards in 10 categories, among them children's stories for readers ages 3 to 8, young adult novels, inspirational fiction, and poetry. There is also an annual contest not restricted to members.

Length: Prose, 1,000 words. Poetry, 50 lines. See website for other length restrictions.

Requirements: Submissions must be original and unpublished. One entry per category. No entry fee. Accepts hard copy to Jill Henderson, P.O. Box 7501, Abilene, TX 79608 (with month of submission noted on envelope). SASE. Accepts email submissions to jiffi123@live.com, AWG Contest "Month" in subject line (Word) attachments. Author's name should not appear on manuscript. A cover letter should indicate the author's name, address, telephone, and email in the upper left corner, and the word or line count in the upper right corner.

Prizes: First-place winners in each category receive $15. Second- and third-place winners in each category receive $10 and $5, respectively.

Deadline: Entries must be postmarked by the tenth day of the month.

Arizona Authors Association Literary Contest

6145 West Echo Lane, Glendale, AZ 85302
www.azauthors.com

Worldwide writers are welcome to submit to this annual contest, however special categories are offered to Arizona state residents. Unpublished essays, novels, short stories, and poems along with published fiction, children's literature, and nonfiction will be considered.

Length: Varies for each category.

Requirements: Entry fees range from $15–$30, depending on category. Send 3 copies of each entry or 2 copies of published book with completed entry form, found on the website. Manuscripts are not returned; published books are donated. Visit the website or contact the contest coordinator for complete submission guidelines for each category.

Prizes: For all categories: First prize, $100; second prize, $50; third prize, $25; and publication or feature in Arizona Literary Magazine and additional promotional listings.

Deadline: Entries must be postmarked between January 1 and July 1.

Atlantic Writing Competition

Writers' Federation of Nova Scotia, 1113 Marginal Road, Halifax, Nova Scotia B3H 4P7 Canada
www.writers.ns.ca/atlantic-writing-competition/submission-procedures.html

New writers residing in Atlantic Canada are being sought to submit this competition, unpublished short stories, poetry, plays, writing for children, magazine articles, essays, and young adult novels will be accepted.

Length: Varies for each category.

Requirements: Entry fees for novels, $35; all other categories, $25. WFNS members receive a $5 discount. Published authors may not enter the competition in any genre in which they have been published. Limit one entry per category. Writers are asked to choose a pen name and include it on each manuscript page. Submit 2 copies of the manuscript with brief biography and writing credits. Accepts hard copy. Guidelines available at website.

Prizes: First- through third-place winners in each category receive awards ranging from $300 to $50.

Deadline: January 7.

Autumn House Poetry, Fiction, and Nonfiction Contests

Autumn House Press, 87 ½ Westwood Street, Pittsburgh, PA 15211
www.autumnhouse.org/contest-submissions/

Autumn House Press is sponsoring their annual contest once again. Novels, novellas, short stories, short-shorts, in either fiction or nonfiction, as well as poetry are all invited to submit for consideration.

Length: Poetry collections, 50–80 pages. Fiction and nonfiction, 200–300 pages.

Requirements: Entry fee, $30. Accepts hard copy or email to autumnh420@gmail.com (include attachment). Visit the website for complete competition guidelines. Include an SASE for contest results.

Prizes: Winning entries receive publication, a $1,000 advance, and a $1,500 travel grant. All entries are considered for publication by Autumn House.

Deadline: June 30.

AWP Award Series

Association of Writers & Writing Programs, George Mason University, 4400 University Ave, MSN 1E3, Fairfax, VA 22030
www.awpwriter.org/contests/awp_award_series_overview

The annual AWP competition is an evaluation "of writers, for writers, by writers," and his open to all writers. Four awards are given out, Grace Paley Prize for Short Fiction, Donald Hall Prize for Poetry, AWP Prize for Creative Nonfiction and the AWP Prize for the Novel Manuscripts that have been previously published in their entirety, including self-publication, are not eligible.

Length: Poetry, at least 48 pages; short story and creative nonfiction collections, 150–300 pages; novels, at least 60,000 words. Requirements: Entry fee, $20 for AWP members; $30 for non-members. Upload manuscript to awp.submittable.com/submit

Prizes: Winners receive awards ranging from $2,500 to $5,500, and publication of their book by the University of Pittsburgh Press, University of Massachusetts Press, University of Georgia Press, or New Issues Press.

Deadline: Entries accepted between January 1 and February 28.

Doris Bakwin Award

Carolina Wren Press, 120 Morris Street, Durham, NC 27701
http://carolinawrenpress.org/submissions/contests

The Doris Bakwin Award is given for unpublished prose fiction (a short stories collection or a novel) or memoir by women authors. Its sponsor, Carolina Wren Press, publishes adult and children's titles by writers who are historically underrepresented.

Length: Fiction and nonfiction, 150–500 pages; poetry, 48–72 pages.

Requirements: Reading fee, $20. Multiple entries are accepted. Send the first 50–60 pages of fiction or nonfiction manuscript and a CD or flashdrive containing entire manuscript; 2 copies of complete poetry manuscript. Accepts hard copy and simultaneous submissions. SASE for contest results only. Visit the website for updated guidelines.

Prizes: $1,000 and publication by Carolina Wren Press.

Deadline: March 15.

Geoffrey Bilson Award for Historical Fiction for Young People

The Canadian Children's Book Centre, 40 Orchard View Boulevard, Suite 217, Toronto, Ontario M4R 1B9 Canada
www.bookcentre.ca/awards/geoffrey_bilsson_award_historical_fiction_young_people

Presented for outstanding historical fiction for young readers by a Canadian author, this award values work that is historically accurate and based on primary research. The award winner is decided by a jury selected by the Canadian Children's Book Centre.

Length: Novels; no specific length requirements.

Requirements: No entry fee. Books must be published between January 1 and December 31 of the previous year. Send 5 copies of each title with a submission form to Meghan Howe.

Prize: $5,000.

Deadline: February (see website for exact date).

The Black River Chapbook Competition

Black Lawrence Press, 115 Center Avenue, Aspinwall, PA 15215
www.blacklawrence.com/submissions-and-contests/
the-black-river-chapbook-competition/

For their semiannual competition, Black Lawrence Press will accept unpublished chapbooks of short stories or poems. These genre limitations are there to receive and publish the best writing of today.

Length: 16–36 pages.

Requirements: Entry fee, $15. Accepts submissions and fees electronically through Submittable. Also accepts simultaneous submissions.

Prizes: $500, book publication, and 25 copies of the book.

Deadline: Spring: April 1–May 31. Fall: September 1–October 31.

The Boston Globe–Horn Book Awards

The Horn Book, 56 Roland Street, Suite 200, Boston, MA 02129
www.hbook.com/boston-globe-horn-book-awards/

These prestigious awards honor the best in literature for children and teens in the United States of America. A three-judge committee evaluates in three categories: picture books, nonfiction, and fiction/poetry.

Length: No length requirements.

Requirements: No entry fee. Publishers may submit multiple books, 1 copy of each to all three judges (see website for names and addresses). A list of books submitted should be sent to Katrina Hedeen at Horn Book, Inc. Books must have been published between June 1 and May 31 of the preceding year. No reprints, textbooks, audiobooks, ebooks, or manuscripts are eligible.

Prizes: Winner receives $500 and an engraved silver bowl.

Deadline: May 15.

Ann Connor Brimer Book Award for Atlantic Canadian Young People

Lara McAllister, Woodlawn Public Library, c/o Halifax Public Libraries, 60 Alderney Drive, Dartmouth, NS B2Y 4P8 www.atlanticbookawards.ca/awards/ann-connor-brimer-award

The Nova Scotia Library Association and the Writer's Federation of Nova Scotia sponsors this annual contest to give recognition to published writers residing in Atlantic Canada who have contributed so much to children's literature.

Length: No length requirement. Book must be intended for children up to the age of 15.

Requirements: Author needs to be living and a resident of Atlantic Canada. Book being nominated must have been published in the calendar year of the contest. Mail 5 copies of the book and complete nomination form from website to Matthew McCarthy. For more information, call (902) 490-5792 or email mccarthm@halifax.ca.

Prizes: $2,000 and assistance with travel expenses to attend the award ceremony.

Deadline: October 20.

Randolph Caldecott Medal

American Library Association, 50 East Huron Street, Chicago, IL 60611 www.ala.org/awardsgrants/awards/6/apply

The Caldecott is an annual award earned by the American artist who produced the most impressive original picture book of the previous year. Winners display excellence of execution in art primarily, but also show masterful depiction of story, theme, concept, setting, mood, and recognition of the child audience. Length: No length requirements.

Requirements: Must be an American picture book written in English. Submit 2 copies, 1 to the Association for Library Service to Children office and 1 to the committee chair.

Prizes: The winner is announced at the ALA Midwinter Meeting and presented with the medal at an awards banquet.

Deadline: December 31 of the publication year.

California Book Awards

The Commonwealth Club of California, 555 Post Street, San Francisco, CA 94102www.commonwealthclub.org/events/special-events/california-book-awards

Since 1931, The California Book Awards have honored California writers and publishers who demonstrate exceptional literary merit. Awards are given in 8 categories, including juvenile literature (to age 10) and young adult literature (ages 11–16).

Length: No length requirements.

Requirements: Entries must be written by a California resident and published in the award year. Authors or publishers may mail 6 copies of the book with an entry form, found at the website. Prizes: Medals are awarded in each category.

Deadline: December 22.

Edgar Awards

Mystery Writers of America, 1140 Broadway, Suite 1507, New York, NY 10001
www.mysterywriters.org

The Edgar Awards, considered the most prestigious in the mystery/crime/suspense genres, are sponsored by the Mystery Writers of America. These awards, presented annually, include prizes adult categories, and for best juvenile mystery (preK–grade 7) and best young adult mystery (grades 8–12).

Length: Varies for each category.
Requirements: No entry fee required. Books, TV shows, films, and short stories in the suspense, intrigue, crime, and mystery genres are able to compete to win the Edgar Awards if they were published initially in the United States during the previous calendar year.. Submit with entry form on website, via fax, or by mail. See website for specific category requirements. Accepts electronic entries via website, hard copy, and fax to 212-888-8107. See guidelines for details.

Prizes: An Edgar and cash award, presented at an annual banquet. The following is the list of publication/release dates, followed by their corresponding Deadlines:
    January – March, March 31
    April, May 29

May, June 30
June, July 31
July, August 28
August, September 30
September, October 30
October – December 31, November 30.

Margaret A. Edwards Award

American Library Association, Young Adult Library Services Association, 50 East Huron Street, Chicago, IL 60611
www.ala.org/yalsa/edwards

The Margaret A. Edwards Award honors an author and his or her body of work for making a significant and lasting contribution to young adult literature. It recognizes "an author's work in helping adolescents become aware of themselves and addressing questions about their role and importance in relationships, society, and in the world."

Length: No length requirements.

Requirements: The author must be living at the time of the nomination. Nominations for the award may be submitted by young adult librarians and teenagers.

Prizes: $2,000 and a citation presented during the annual ALA conference.

Deadline: November 1.

The Eloquent Quill International Book Award

P.O. Box 3362, Rapid City, SD 57709
www.clcawards.org/Eloquent-Quill.html

The Eloquent Quill International Book Award recognizes the best in novellas, novels, and chapter books written for young adults and children. Books will be judged on their literary quality and how well they promote character, vision, creativity, and learning. Self-published books and eBooks are eligible. Books may be nominated by authors, publishers, or agents.

Length: No length requirements. All books must possess an ISBN.

Requirements: Entry fee: $45. Send nomination form (on website), entry fee, and 5 copies of the book. Accepts hard copy and electronic entries via form on website.

Prizes: A medal, certificate, and embossed seals for winning book.

Deadline: Early Entry Deadline, May 1. Final Award Application Deadline, August 15.

The Enchanted Page International Book Award

P.O. Box 3362, Rapid City, SD 57709
www.clcawards.org

This award has been created to honor one distinguished children's story picture book. Books should be literary and promote character, vision, creativity, and learning. Self-published books are eligible; eBooks are not. Books may be nominated by authors, publishers, or agents.

Length: No length requirements. All books must possess and ISBN.

Requirements: Entry fee: $45. Send nomination form (on website), entry fee, and 5 copies of the book. Accepts hard copy and electronic entries via form on website.

Prizes: A medal, certificate, and embossed seals for winning book.

Deadline: Early Entry Deadline, May 1. Final Award Application Deadline, August 15.

Shubert Fendrich Memorial Playwriting Contest

Pioneer Drama Service, P.O. Box 4267, Englewood, CO 80155
www.pioneerdrama.com

This annual contest supports the very best in drama of the highest quality for community, educational and children's theaters.. It is sponsored by Pioneer Drama Service, a full-service publisher of more than 850 plays and musicals. The contest is open to playwrights who have not yet been published by Pioneer Drama Service.

Length: Running time 20 to 90 minutes.

Requirements: No entry fee. Send complete manuscript with 100- to 200-word synopsis, cast list, running time, CD/score for musicals, set designs, proof of production or staged reading, and age of intended audience. Accepts hard copy to Submissions Editor and email submissions to playwrights@pioneerdrama. com. SASE. Accepts multiple submissions. See website for further guidelines.

Prizes: Winners are announced on June 1. Prizes include a publication contract and a $1,000 advance.

Deadline: Ongoing.

Don Freeman Grant-in-Aid

Society of Children's Book Writers & Illustrators, 8271 Beverly Boulevard, Los Angeles, CA 90048
www.postgraduatefunding.com/award-464

This grant was created by the SCBWI to foster picture book artists' growth in understanding the genre. SCBWI members and associate members are eligible.

Length: No length requirements.

Requirements: Applicants should supply either a book dummy with 2 illustrations (1 color and 1 black & white) and the picture book text, or 10 completed illustrations (at least 8 in color). The book dummy should show your ability to convey story mood, show action and pacing, and reveal characters. Include 4 copies of the application. Do not send original artwork. Accepts electronic submissions only to sarahbaker@scbwi.org; put "Don Freeman Grant" in subject line. See website for more details.

Prizes: One grant of $1,500 is awarded annually, as is a runner-up grant of $500.

Deadline: Submissions for application requests should be by June 15th, and February 10th, completed applications should be submitted.

Theodor Seuss Geisel Award

American Library Association, 50 East Huron Street, Chicago, IL 60611
www.ala.org

The annual Geisel Award named for the legendary "Dr. Seuss" gives recognition to the author and illustrator of the best beginning reader book in the United States for the previous year. Winning books provide a "stimulating and successful reading experience" for preschool to second-grade readers, through excellence of plot, rhythm, language, sensibility, and illustration.

Length: 24 to 96 pages.

Requirements: Applicants must be citizens or residents of the U.S. Submit 1 copy to the ALA office and 1 to the award committee chair.

Prizes: Bronze medal and plaque presented at the annual ALA conference.

Deadline: December 31.

Genesis Contest

American Christian Fiction Writers
www.acfw.com/genesis

American Christian Fiction Writers, both members and nonmembers are eligible to participate in this annual contest, under the condition that they have not been published any young adult or adult fiction in the past seven years.. Manuscripts in various genres including young adult, contemporary, suspense/thriller, historical fiction, and women's fiction will be considered.

Length: Projected final word count of 45,000 words minimum; no maximum.

Requirements: Entry fee, $35 for members; $95 for nonmembers. Multiple entries are allowed. Enter with the online form only; include the first 15 pages of the manuscript and 1-page synopsis in the same file. Accepts multiple entries. See guidelines at website for specific category email contacts. No hard copy submissions.

Prizes: Winners receive a plaque, a gold pin, one hour of telephone mentoring time with a published author, and first choice for an editor/agent appointment at the annual ACFW conference.

Deadline: March 15.

Elizabeth George Foundation Awards

P.O. Box 1429, Langley, WA 98260
www.elizabethgeorgeonline.com/

Founded by the best-selling mystery novelist Elizabeth George, the foundatuon awards grants to unpublished writers of fiction, poets, and emerging playwrights. It also supports organizations for disadvantaged youth, gives scholarships to MFA programs, and supports writing research and attendance at writers' conferences and retreats.

Length: N/A.

Requirements: Processing fee, $25. Request brochure to begin the process and send package of materials that includes a letter describing the project; the amount requested to complete it and the budget for the project; a curriculum vitae; 5 professional references; and either a complete first chapter of the applicant's book, a complete short story, a selection of poetry or published chapbook, or a one-act play. Accepts hard copy only.

Prize: One year of support.

Deadline: First step of process, July 1. Second step of process, November 1.

Golden Kite Awards

Society of Children's Book Writers & Illustrators,
8271 Beverly Boulevard, Los Angeles, CA 90048
www.scbwi.org/awards/golden-kite-award/

The SCBWI presents the Golden Kite Awards, which is an annual recognition of the talented authors and illustrators in children's literature. These individuals come from the genres: fiction, nonfiction, picture book text, and picture book illustration.

Length: Varies for each category.

Requirements: Current SCBWI members are eligible, and may enter themselves or be entered by their publishers. All entries must be in final form, having been published and copyrighted within the calendar year. Send 4 copies with a letter indicating the category. Picture books may be submitted for both text and illustrations; in that case, 8 copies are required.

Prize: $2,500.

Deadline: November 25, 2015.

Institute for Writers Writing Contests ⭐

The Institute for Writers
www.instituteforwriters.com

The Institute for Writers sponsors quarterly writing contests encouraging both new and experienced writers to hone their skills and and have the opportunity to receive a critique by an industry expert. All entrants are eligible to attend the webinar where the contest winners will be presented and critiqued. Past contests include poetry and PreK writing.

Length: Varies for each category.

Requirements: Entry fee, $19. Entries are accepted through the website submission form following payment of the entry fee.

Prize: Cash awards, publication on the Institute for Writers website, and a personalized critique of the winning entries are awarded to winners.

Deadline: Varies for each contest. Visit the website for complete details information.

The Barbara Karlin Grant

Society of Children's Book Writers & Illustrators, Barbara Karlin Grant Committee, c/o Q. L. Pearce, 884 Atlanta Court, Claremont, CA 91711. www.scbwi.org

The Society of Children's Book Writers & Illustrators presents this award in memory of Barbara Karlin, a celebrated author of numerous picture books. She believed that writers of picture book text deserved support and encouragement for their contribution to the unique art form that is the picture book.

Length: 8 pages.

Requirements: One SCBWI grant submission per applicant. Send 6 copies of the completed application and 6 copies of the picture book manuscript (text only) along with a 1-paragraph cover letter and a synopsis of the book.

Prizes: Grant of $2,000; runner-up grant, $500.

Deadline: Entries are accepted between March 1 and March 31.

Ezra Jack Keats New Writer Award

The de Grummond Children's Literature Collection, Box 5148, Hattiesburg, MS 39406
www.lib.usm.edu/degrummond/ezra_keats/keats_writer.html

The Ezra Jack Keats New Writer Award is given every year to honor new authors in the children's books realm. It seeks picture books that portray the universal qualities of childhood, a strong and supportive family, and the multicultural nature of the world.

Length: No length requirements.

Requirements: Author must have published no more than 3 books. Submitted title must be published in award year.

Prizes: $1,000 and silver medal.

Deadline: December 15.

Coretta Scott King Book Award

American Library Association, 50 East Huron Street, Chicago, IL 60611
www.ala.org/emiert/2016-coretta-scott-king-book-awards-submission-form

The Coretta Scott King Award is an annual recognition of the best African-American authors and illustrators of children's books and young adult literature. The recipients honor and encourage the expression in the literary and artistic representation of the black experience in the United States and appreciation of all people's contribution to the American Dream. The John Steptoe New Talent

Award is to affirm new talent; the winner cannot have more than 3 published works. Check the guidelines for category information.

Length: No length restrictions.

Requirements: Must be written/illustrated by an African American, and published in the U.S. in the preceding year. Submit entry form online to ALA Office and instructions will then be sent regarding where to send copies of the book.

Prizes: $1,000 award and plaque are conferred at the Coretta Scott King Award Breakfast at the annual ALA conference.

Deadline: December 1.

The Astrid Lindgren Memorial Award

Swedish Arts Council, P.O. Box 272 15, 102 53 Stockholm, Sweden
www.alma.se/en/Nominations

Outstanding authors, illustrators, and oral storytellers are honored with the Astrid Lindgren Memorial Award is presented to those individuals who are authors, illustrators, and oral storytellers of the highest caliber whose works create interest in young adult and children's literature in the global consciousness. This Swedish Arts Council distributes the award.

Length: No length restrictions.

Requirements: Books are nominated by an international panel of authors and others with a strong knowledge of children's literature.

Prize: A total of $685,000 is awarded to one or several authors.

Deadline: May 15.

Los Angeles Times Book Prizes

http://events.latimes.com/bookprizes

In 1980, teacher, editor, novelist and famed book critic for the LA Times, Robert Kirsch passed away, he was the originator of an idea from which the Book Prizes were conceived. The late Art Seidenbaum, a highly successful teacher, television host, as well as writer and editor of books and newspapers created the Book Prize program. The Los Angeles Times book prizes have grown to 10 single-title categories, including young adult literature and graphic novels, in an effort to promote literacy and education to people across Southern California. The most recent winner for YA literature was Ask the Passengers, by A. S. King (Scholastic).

Length: No length restrictions.

Requirements: Books published in English in the award year are eligible. Nominations originate from a select panel of judges.

Prize: $500 cash prize.

Deadline: N/A.

The Lumen Award for Literary Excellence

P.O. Box 3362, Rapid City, SD 57709
www.clcawards.org/Lumen-Award-for-Literary-Excellence.html

The Lumen Award honors a nonfiction book written for young adults or children as part of the Literary Classics International Book Awards. Books will be judged on the quality of their writing and how well they promote character, vision, creativity, and learning. Self-published books and eBooks are eligible. Books may be nominated by authors, publishers, or agents.

Length: No length requirements. All books must possess and ISBN.

Requirements: Entry fee: $45. Send nomination form (on website), entry fee, and 5 copies of the book. Accepts hard copy and electronic entries via form on website.

Prizes: A medal, certificate, and embossed seals for winning book.

Deadline: May 1.

Maryland Writers' Association Contests

3 Church Circle, #165, Annapolis, MD 21401
www.marylandwriters.org

The Maryland Writers' Association offers two contests, the Novel

Contest: Great Beginnings, focusing on the first 7,000 words of a novel; check website for list of categories. It also has a Short Works Contest, which accepts entries in the categories of fiction, nonfiction, and poetry.

Length: Novels, first 7,000 words. Short works contest, to 3,000 words; poetry, to 50 lines.

Requirements: Entry fees to be determined; members will receive a discount. Check website for updated information. Entries must be original and not currently under contract. Accepts electronic submissions only via the website. For more info on the Novel Contest email: novel@marylandwriterscontest.com; for the Short Works contest, email: shortworks@marylandwriterscontest.com. Visit the website for complete guidelines.

Prizes: First prize: $200, a certificate, and free attendance to MWA's Writer's Conference; second- and third-place prizes are $100 and $50 and certificates.

Deadline: Novels: May 15 to June 30; Short works: June 30 to July 30.

Milkweed Prize for Children's Literature

1011 Washington Avenue South, Suite 300, Minneapolis, MN 55415-1246. www.milkweed.org

The publication of high-quality middle-grade fiction is the ultimate goal of this annual competition, held by Milkweed Editions. Entries for readers ages 8 to 13 should reflect humane values and cultural understanding.

Length: 90–200 typewritten pages.

Requirements: All manuscripts submitted to Milkweed by writers the company has not previously published are considered for the prize. Picture books and story collections are not eligible. Follow Milkweed's regular submission guidelines at the website. Prefers electronic submissions via Submission Manager at the website. Accepts hard copy to appropriate category editor. SASE.

Prizes: Publication and $10,000.

Deadline: Unavailable

The William C. Morris YA Debut Award

American Library Association, 50 East Huron Street, Chicago, IL 60611. www.ala.org/yalsa/morris-award

William C. Morris was an active supporter of literature of great esteem written for young adults and children, and this award recognizes authors publishing their first young adult novel in the current year. The book must have teen appeal and be strong in all components: story, voice, setting, accuracy, style, characters, theme, and design. Popularity and message of the book are not criteria.

Length: No restrictions.

Requirements: Entries may be nominated by the committee or come from the field. Publishers, authors, agents, or editors may not nominate their own titles. Nomination form on website. See website for details.

Prizes: Winner is endorsed by the American Library Association and may place a seal showing award on the cover of their book.

Deadline: December 1.

Mythopoeic Fantasy Award for Children's Literature

306 Edmon Low Library, Oklahoma State University, Stillwater, OK 74078. www.mythsoc.org

The Mythopoeic Fantasy Award for Children's Literature gives recognition to those books written in the same vein as C.S. Lewis and J.R.R. Tolkien in the middle grade, young adult, picture book, and early readers genre. To qualify, these books had to have been published in the previous year.

Length: No length requirements.

Requirements: Members of the Mythopoeic Society nominate books, and a membership committee selects winners. Authors who are members of the society may not nominate their own titles. For complete contest information email the awards administrator at awards@mythsoc.org.

Prize: A statuette.

Deadline: February 28.

National Book Award for Young People's Literature

National Book Foundation, 90 Broad Street, Suite 604, New York, NY 10004
www.nationalbook.org/nba_process.html#.VIATmaRoTu0

Publishers submit books for the prestigious The National Book Awards accept books that are examples of original work in the following genres: young people's literature, nonfiction, fiction, and single-author collections. Stories or essays for young readers are also welcome to be considered. The publishers of such works make submissions in any of the aforementioned types of writing.

Length: Full-length books.

Requirements: Entry fee, $125. All books must have been published in the U.S. between December 1 and November 30 in the year of the contest, and written by a U.S. citizen. Self-published books are eligible as long as the author/publisher also publishes titles by other authors. Retellings of folktales, myths, or fairy tales are not eligible. Submit book and entry form.

Prizes: $10,000 and a crystal sculpture. Four finalists receive $1,000 each.

Deadline: Entry form must be postmarked by June 3. Books must be received by July 15.

Newbery Award

American Library Association, 50 East Huron Street, Chicago, IL 60611
www.ala.org/alsc/awardsgrants/ bookmedianewberymedal/ newberymedal

The Newbery Award is an annual award given to an author to recognize a distinguished contribution to the realm of children's literature in America. The Newbery Award was the first to honor children's books.in all of the world.. It values interpretation of theme, clarity and accuracy, plot development, well-delineated characters and setting, and appropriate style.

Length: No length requirements.

Requirements: No entry fee. All entries must have been published in the U.S. in the preceding year. Authors must be U.S. citizens or residents. Send 1 copy to the ALSC office and 1 copy to the award committee chair with a cover letter if you wish.

Prize: The Newbery Medal is awarded to the winner. Honor books may also be named.

Deadline: December 31.

New Voices Award

Lee & Low Books, 95 Madison Avenue, Suite #1205, New York, NY 10016
www.leeandlow.com/writers-illustrators/new-voice-award

Lee & Low Books honors picture book manuscripts by writers of color that address the needs of children of color with this annual award. Fiction, nonfiction, or poetry, all submissions need to present stories that can be readily identifiable to readers ages 5 through 12 and equally important, they must promote mutual understanding.

Length: To 1,500 words.

Requirements: Open to U.S. residents of color who have not published a picture book. No folklore or animal stories. No entry fee. Limit 2 entries per competition. Include cover letter, brief biographical note with cultural and ethnic information, publication history, if any, and manuscript. Accepts hard copy. No simultaneous submissions.

Prizes: $1,000 and a standard publishing contract. An honor grant of $500 is also awarded.

Deadline: Submissions accepted between May 1 and September 30.

Scott O'Dell Award for Historical Fiction

Roger Sutton, Horn Book, 56 Roland Street, Suite 200, Boston, MA 02129
www.scottodell.com/pages/scottodellawardforhistoricalfiction.aspx

Late legendary author Scott O'Dell created this award to recognize others, but predominantly new writers who are focusing their abilities on historical fiction for children and young adults. Ultimately he hoped to interest young readers in learning more about the history that has shaped our country and our world.

Length: No length requirements.

Requirements: Eligible historical fiction must have been published in the calendar year of the contest; target young readers; be set in the Americas; be published by a U.S. publisher; and be written in English by a U.S. citizen. Send submission form and 1 copy of the book to the committee chairman, and 1 copy to the 2 committee members. For information, email Chair Roger Sutton at rsutton@hbook.com; put "O'Dell Award" in the subject line.

Prize: $5,000.

Deadline: Ongoing.

On-The-Verge Emerging Voice Award

Society of Children's Book Writers & Illustrators, 8271 Beverly Boulevard, Los Angeles, CA 90048
www.scbwi.org/awards/grants/on-the-verge-emerging-voices-grant/

Martin and Sue Schmitt of the 455 Foundation introduced this award in 2012 by sponsoring a grant. It was conceived to encourage diversity in children's books' voices. It is given to two writers or illustrators of children's picture books or novels from an ethnic and/or cultural background that is traditionally underrepresented in children's literature in the U.S. The manuscript must be an original work in English, written for young people and not under contract.

Length: No length requirements.

Requirements: Send complete manuscript, with 250-word synopsis, 250-word autobiographical statement and career summary, and explanation of why your work will bring forward and underrepresented voice (250 words). Applicants must be over 18, unpublished and should not have agent representation. Accepts email entries only to Voices@scbwi.org (Word attachments; PDF for manuscripts). See website for details.

Prizes: All-expense paid trip to SCBWI Winter Conference in New

York, NY, a press release to publishers, a ear of free membership to SCBWI and an SCBWI mentor for a year.

Deadline: November 15.

Orbis Pictus Award for Outstanding Nonfiction for Children

National Council of Teachers of English, Orbis Pictus Committee Chair, 1111 West Kenyon Road, Urbana, IL 61801-1096
www.ncte.org/awards/orbispictus

The Orbis Pictus Award recognizes the very best in children's nonfiction in the United States for books geared toward kindergarten through eighth grade.. The winning titles are factually accurate, balanced, well-structured, attractive and readable, stimulating, rich in language, and appealing to a range of ages.

Length: No length requirements.

Requirements: Nominations may come from NCTE members or the educational community. Nonfiction or informational books intended to share information are eligible. Textbooks, historical fiction, folklore, and poetry are not. Books must have been published in the U.S. during the previous calendar year. To nominate, send a letter with book information and a short explanation on why you like the book.

Prize: A medal is presented at the annual NCTE convention. Up to 5 honor books are also recognized.

Deadline: December 31.

Pacific Northwest Writers Association Literary Contests

PMB 2717, 1420 NW Gilman Boulevard, Suite 2, Issaquah, WA 98027. www.pnwa.org

Pacific Northwest Writers Association holds this annual contest to award the best in 12 categories including chapter books, middle-grade books, and young adult. Only original, unpublished material in English is eligible for submission.

Length: Varies for each category; see website.

Requirements: Entry fee, $35 for PNWA members; $50 for nonmembers. Multiple entries are accepted. See guidelines for specific requirements for each category. Send 3 copies of all manuscript materials and entry form on website. Accepts submissions through the website only.

Prizes: First place in each category, $700, the Zola Award, and an opportunity to attend the Agents and Editors Reception at the PNWA summer conference; second place, $300. All entries receive two critiques. Finalists (8 in each category) receive special recognition at the conference.

Deadline: February 19.

Please Touch Museum Book Award

Memorial Hall, Fairmount Park, 4231 Avenue of the Republic, Philadelphia, PA 19131
www.pleasetouchmuseum.org/education/book-award/

The Please Touch Museum Book Award stands apart from the rest as it is the only award given by a children's museum. It is recognition of books that encourage a child to have a life filled with a passion for reading by having a showcase of illustration and are highly imaginative.

Length: No length restrictions.

Requirements: American authors only. Books must be published between September 1 and August 31 of the preceding year. Entries are accepted in 2 categories: ages 3 and under, and ages 4–7. Send 4 copies to Attn: Heather Boyd at the above address.

Prize: Award presented at ceremony.

Deadline: October 1.

San Antonio Writers Guild Annual Contest

P.O. Box 100717, San Antonio, TX 78201-8717
www.sawritersguild.submittable.com/submit

This contest, open to all writers, offers five different categories in poetry, fiction and nonfiction. First, second, and third place winners receive prizes for unpublished work.

Length: Novel, first chapter or up to first 5,000 words. Short story, 4,000 words. Flash fiction, 1,000 words. Nonfiction memoir/personal essay, 2,500 words. Poetry, up to 3 poems, 40 lines maximum per poem.

Requirements: Entry fee, $10 for SAWG members; $20 for nonmembers. Multiple entries are accepted in up to 3 different categories.

Prizes: First place, $150. Second place, $75. Third place, $50. Any contestant receiving a perfect score from an outside (professional) judge receives an additional $250.

Deadline: Entries must be postmarked by the first Thursday of October.

SCBWI Work-in-Progress Grants

Society of Children's Book Writers & Illustrators, 4727 Wilshire Boulevard, Suite 301 Los Angeles, CA 90010www.scbwi.org/awards/grants/work-in-progress-grants/

The SCBWI awards annual grants to help children's book writers to complete projects of numerous varieties. These include: a general work-in-progress, a contemporary novel for young people, nonfiction research, the multicultural or minority perspective, and for an unpublished author.

Length: 750-word synopsis and 2,500-word writing sample from the relevant manuscript.

Requirements: No entry fee. Open to members only. Applications accepted online only as PDFs. Send 4 copies of application, synopsis, and writing sample all as one PDF document (15 pages maximum) to:wip@scbwi.org. Instructions, complete guidelines, and application forms are available at website. For questions, email Grant Coordinator Kayla Heinen at kayla.heinen@scbwi.org.

Prizes: Cash grants of $2,000 and $500 in each category.

Deadline: Application period is March 1 to March 31.

Schneider Family Book Award

American Library Association, 50 East Huron Street, Chicago, IL 60611
www.ala.org/awardsgrants/schneider-family-book-award

The Schneider Family Book Award gives recognition to those authors and illustrators whose work artistically conveys an adolescent or child's emotional, physical, or mental disabilities. It includes 3 categories: birth through age 10, middle school (ages 11 to 13), and teens (ages 13 to 18). In fiction, the person with the disability may be the protagonist or a secondary character. Nonfiction is also considered.

Length: No length requirements.

Requirements: Work must be published in English during the preceding two years of the contest year. Submit 1 copy of the book and application to the ALA Governance Office and 1 copy each of the book and application to the 7 jury members (see website for contact information).

Prizes: $5,000 and a plaque for first place in each age category.

Deadline: December 1.

Seven Hills Literary & Penumbra Poetry Contest

2910 Kerry Forest Parkway D-4-357, Tallahassee, FL 32309
www.sevenhillsreview.submittable.com/submit

The Tallahassee Writers Association holds numerous contests annually including one for the graphic short story started in 2015, short story, creative nonfiction, young adult novel excerpt, adult novel excerpt, flash fiction, poetry, and haiku. Additionally, on alternating years, the TWA also has a competition for children's picture books. for children's picture books, ages 4 to 8, and in alternate years, a children's chapter book competition, in addition to contests for adult short stories, creative nonfiction, and flash fiction.

Length: Children's chapter books (ages 6–12), to 2,500 words. excerpt, plus short synopsis. Children's picture books, 1,500 word maximum. Short stories, creative nonfiction, to 2,500 words. Flash fiction, to 500 words.

Requirements: Entry fee, $12 for TWA members; $17 for non-members. Accepts electronic submissions only through Submittable. All entries must be unpublished. For questions, email Donna Meredith at meredithds@comcast.net.

Prizes: First prize, $100; second prize, $75; third prize, $50. Winners are published in Seven Hills Review.

Deadline: August 31.

Lee Smith Novel Prize

Carolina Wren Press, 120 Morriss Street, Durham, NC 27701
http://carolinawrenpress.org/submittable.com/submit

With a goal of "exploring and expanding the definition of Southern literature," this contest is open to unpublished novels written by authors from, living in, or writing about the American south. Authors need to meet only one (not all three) of these qualifications to have their work considered.

Length: Minimum, 50,000 words.

Requirements: Fee, $20 per entry. All novels must be in English and written by one person. Submit electronically through link at website: https://carolinawrenpress.submittable.com/submit. Send complete ms and cover letter with author bio and list of previously published works. Accepts simultaneous submissions.

Prizes: $1,000 and publication by Carolina Wren Press.

Deadline: November 30.

Kay Snow Writing Contest

Willamette Writers, 2108 Buck Street, West Linn, OR 97068
www.willamettewriters.org/submit-your-writing/kay-snow-writing-contest

The Kay Snow Writing Contest gives writers a push to attain their professional goals, but also helps out student writers. Many awards are given out over various categories: nonfiction, screenwriting, juvenile fiction, and fiction. It offers awards in several categories including juvenile writing, fiction, nonfiction, and screenwriting. All material submitted must be previously unpublished.

Length: Varies for each category.

Requirements: Entry fee, $10 for WW members; $15 for non-members. Student writers (18 and under), no fee. Submit 2 copies of each entry with registration form and a 3x5 card that includes author name, contact information, book title, and category. Author's name must not appear on manuscript. For complete contest information or questions, email wilwrite@ willamettewriters.com.

Prizes: Awards range from $300 to $10 in each category. The Liam Callen award, $500, is presented to the best overall entry.

Deadline: Entries must be postmarked by April 30.

SouthWest Writers Contests

SouthWest Writers, 3200 Carlisle Blvd NE, Suite 114, Albuquerque, NM 87110
www.southwestwriters.com/contest/bimonthly-writing-contest/

SouthWest Writers holds bimonthly contests every year for numerous genres including; young adult, middle grade, picture books, and nonfiction. See the website for changing specifications.

Length: Varies for each category.

Requirements: Entry fees vary. SWW members receive a discount. See website for specific submission guidelines by contest and category. Submit 2 copies of each entry and an entry form. Author's name should appear on entry form only. Multiple entries are accepted. Accepts hard copy.

Prizes: Prizes range from $1,500 for the annual contest to $150 to $25 for bimonthly contests.

Deadline: May 1 (for annual contest).

John Steptoe Award for New Talent

American Library Association, 50 East Huron Street, Chicago, IL 60611
www.ala.org/emiert/cskbookawards/johnsteptoe

The John Steptoe Award in affiliation with the Coretta Scott King Awards recognizes new talent in writing and illustration whose children's books are a depiction of the African-American experience. It focuses on original books that otherwise might not be formally acknowledged because they fall outside other award criteria.

Requirements: Entrants may not have more than 3 published works. Must be written/illustrated by an African American, and published in the U.S. in the preceding year. Submit entry form online to ALA Office and instructions will then be sent regarding where to send copies of the book.

Prize: A plaque is awarded at the annual ALA conference.

Deadline: December 1.

Surrey International Writers' Conference Writing Contest

SiWC Writing Contest, Suite 544, 151-10090 152nd Street, Surrey, BC V3R 8X8. www.siwc.ca/2015-writing-contest-rules

The Surrey International Writers' Conference Writing Contest is open to unpublished writers 18 and up, and gives awards for poetry, short story, writing for young people, an nonfiction.

Length: Nonfiction and writing for young people, to 1,500 words. Short stories, 2,500–5,000 words. Poetry, to 100 lines.

Requirements: Entry fee, $15. Multiple entries are accepted. Accepts hard copy and email entries to contest@siwc.ca (no attachments). Author's name should not appear on the manuscript. Include a cover letter with author's name, contact info, word length, and competition category. For questions, email kc dyer at contest@siwc.ca. Visit the website for complete contest information.

Prizes: First-place winners in each category, $1,000. Honorable mentions, $150. Winning entries are printed and sold as an anthology.

Deadline: Submissions accepted from April 1 to September 18.

Sydney Taylor Manuscript Competition

P.O. Box 1118, Teaneck, NJ 07666
www.jewishlibraries.org/content.php?page=STMA_Rules

The Sydney Taylor Manuscript Award from its inception was set-up to provide encouragement to Jewish children's book authors for ages 8-13. The stories should be ones that promote and enhance knowledge of Judaism and appeal to Jewish and non-Jewish readers alike.

Length: 64–200 pages.

Requirements: No entry fee. One entry per competition. Short stories, plays, and poetry are not eligible. Send 6 copies with application and release form found on website, and a cover letter that includes a short personal statement, manuscript summary, and author biography or résumé. Accepts email to stmacajl@aol.com (PDF attachment) or CD (no hard copy).. SASE for receipt confirmation only. See website for complete rules. For questions, contact Aileen Grossberg, Competition Coordinator at 973-744-3836 or by email.

Prize: $1,000 and the opportunity to have the winning manuscript read by an experienced literary agent.

Deadline: September 30.

Three-Day Novel Contest

201-111 West Hastings Street, Vancouver, British Columbia V6B 1H4 Canada
www.3daynovel.com/rules/

The Three-Day Novel Contest has been put on Labor Day weekend (usually the first weekend in September) by Three-Day Books since 1977. There are no genre or setting limitations of any kind.. Entrants start writing at midnight Friday, and must stop by midnight Sunday and then submit their manuscript. Writing may take place anywhere.

Length: No limitations; typical entries average 100 typed, double-spaced pages.

Requirements: Fee, $50 (Canadian) to preregister, and if desired, submit a brief outline. Entrants may collaborate with one other author. Submit manuscripts by mail or online, along with a signed witness statement stating that the entrant followed contest rules. See the website for more complete contest information. Send questions to info@3daynovel.com.

Prizes: First prize, a publication contract with 3-Day Books. Second prize, $500; third prize, $100.

Deadline: Register up until midnight the day before the contest starts; submissions must be received by the Friday after Labor Day.

Times/Chicken House Children's Fiction Competition 🌐

2 Palmer Street, Frome, Somerset, BA11 1DS, England
http://chickenhousebooks.com/submissions/

The Times/Chicken House Children's House Children's Fiction competition is held annually. It is open to unpublished novelists, as well as published poets, and picture book and short story authors. All entries should be lively and entertaining, as well as of the highest quality writing. All contest entries should target children ranging from 7–18. Only complete manuscripts will be accepted.

Length: 30,000–80,000 words.

Requirements: £15. Send complete ms and cover letter with an explantation of why your novel would appeal to children, brief author bio, 1-page synopsis of the novel, and a chapter-by-chapter plot plan outlining the major events of each chapter. Accepts hard copy only. For questions, email tina@doublecluck.com.

Prize: Winner receives a publishing contract with Chicken House including a royalty advance of £10,000, plus representation from a top children's literary agent.

Deadline: December 18.

E. B. White Read Aloud Awards

333 Westchester Avenue, Suite S202. White Plains, NY 10604
www.bookweb.org/btw/awards.ICBA.html

The E.B. White Read Aloud Awards aim to represent the books that adhere to the high standards set by acclaimed author E.B. White for his children's books and hold universal appeal as "read-alouds.". The contest has two categories: picture books and older readers.

Requirements: Books must be nominated by an ABC bookseller and have been published in the preceding year. The author must be living. Dynamic writing, engaging themes, and universal appeal are the main criteria for nomination. Picture books, early readers, young adult titles, and poetry are accepted. Visit the website for complete award guidelines.

Prizes: A crystal book engraved with the E. B. White Medal seal and book title are awarded at the ABA Celebration of Bookselling luncheon. Six shortlist books receive E. B. White Read Aloud Honors.

Deadline: April 30.

Laura Ingalls Wilder Award

Association for Library Service to Children, 50 East Huron Street, Chicago, IL 60611
www.alaorg/alsc/awardsgrants/bookmedia/wildermedia/wilderterms/wildermedaltrms

The Laura Ingalls Award is presented every year to either an illustrator or author who demonstrates a contribution to American children's literature that will endure over the years..

Requirements: Nominations are made by ALSC members, and the winner is selected by a team of children's librarians. Criteria for judging includes whether the books have been notable examples of the genre they represent, or have forged a new direction in children's books.

Prize: A medal is presented at the annual ALA conference.

Deadline: Unavailable.

Write Now New Plays Competition and Workshop

Childsplay, Sybil B. Harrington Campus for Imagination and Wonder at Mitchell Park, 900 South Mitchell Drive, Tempe, AZ 85281 www.writenow.co/competition/write-now-submission/

The Write Now New Plays Competition and Workshop awards competition is open to playwrights that are involved in the biennial Childsplay Write Now Workshop. The goal is to push writers to develop artistic theatrical scripts for grades K-12. The award was formerly called the Waldo and Grace Bonderman Youth Theatre Playwriting Competition.

Length: No length restrictions.

Requirements: Unpublished scripts, even those that have been commissioned, are eligible as long as they have never been professionally produced. Playwrights must be 18 or older. One submission per playwright. Send submission; a synopsis that includes a list of unusual effects and technical requirements; cast list noting age, sex, and possible doublings; and entry form via website. For questions or more info, send email to jmillinger@childsplayaz.org.

Prizes: At least four finalists will be invited to participate in the full workshop process and have a reading for their script at the Write Now gathering. Semi-finalists will be invited to read excerpts of their scripts at the gathering.

Deadline: July 31.

Writers-Editors Network Writing Competition

CNW Publishing, Editing & Promotion Inc., P.O. Box A, North Stratford, NH 03590. www.writers-editors.com

The Writers-Editors Network Writing Competition is held annually and is open to authors of unpublished children's literature, unpublished poetry, published and unpublished fiction, and published and unpublished nonfiction. Additionally, children's literature entrants maybe self-published and fall under the following categories: short story, book chapter, poem, or nonfiction article.

Length: Maximum 5,000 words.

Requirements: Entry fee, $3–$10 for CNW members; $5–$20 for nonmembers. Send submission with entry form found online. Accepts email to contestentry@writers-editors.com and hard copy. Multiple entries are accepted; each entry requires a separate entry form. Author's name should not appear on manuscript. Visit the website for category-specific guidelines. Send an SASE for winners list.

Prizes: First place, $100. Second place, $75. Third place, $50.

Deadline: March 15.

Writers' League of Texas Book Contest

611 South Congress Avenue, Suite 200A-3, Austin, TX 78704
www.writersleague.org

The Writers' League of Texas gives recognition to Texan authors published or self-published in the previous year in categories including young adult and middle grad fiction, poetry, picture books, nonfiction, adult fiction. Authors do not need to be members of the Texas Writers' League to enter.

Length: No length restrictions.

Requirements: $40 per title for non-members; $30 per title for members. Send 2 copies of the book with entry form found on the website and proof of Texas residency. Multiple entries accepted; each must have separate entry form and fee. Send an SASE or visit the website for guidelines. For questions, email sara@writersleague.org.

Prizes: Winners are given $750, an award, and an appearance at the Writers' League of Texas Third Thursday panel at BookPeople in Austin, TX.

Deadline: April 30.

Writers' League of Texas Manuscript Contest

611 South Congress Avenue, Suite 200A-3, Austin, TX 78704
www.writersleague.org/

The Writers' League of Texas holds this contest for unpublished manuscripts in the following genres: children/middle-grade (no picture books), mainstream fiction, thriller/action-adventure, mystery, romance, science fiction/fantasy, historical fiction, young adult fiction, and nonfiction. Authors do not need to be members of the Texas Writers' League to enter.

Length: 2,500 words.

Requirements: $30 per entry for non-members; $20 per entry for members. Send payment and entry form from website by mail. After receipt, instructions will be sent to submit 250-word synopsis and the first 2,500 words of the manuscript electronically. Visit the website for more details. For questions, email sara@writersleague.org.

Prizes: Private meeting with a literary agent and recognition at the WLT Agents Conference, including the reading of the winning submissions in each category.

Deadline: March 1.

YALSA Award for Excellence in Nonfiction for Young Adults

American Library Association, Young Adult Library ServicesAssociation, 50 East Huron Street, Chicago, IL 60611
www.ala.org/yalsa/nonfiction

The YALSA Award for Excellence in Nonfiction for Young Adults is an annual award sponsored by the American Library Association. It is presented to the very best nonfiction book written for teens. Only books published in the previous year are eligible for submission into this award competition. The criteria is based upon accessibility for ages 12-18, as well as subject and treatment.

Length: No length restrictions.

Requirements: Committee members nominate titles. All print forms of nonfiction, including graphic formats, are eligible if the

book is intended for a YA audience, and the book was published in the U.S. in the preceding contest year.

Prizes: The winning title and four honor titles will be announced at a presentation held during the ALA Midwinter Meeting.

Deadline: Entries are accepted between November 1 and October 31.

The Zebulon

c/o Pikes Peak Writers, P.O. Box 64273, Colorado Springs, CO 80962www.pikespeakwriters.com/contest

The Zebulon is an award geared to assist writers to focus on marketable projects, and how to get the most out of feedback. It is open annually for the following categories of book-length fiction: urban fantasy, science fiction/fantasy, romance/women's, mystery/suspense, mainstream/literary, and middle-grade/young adult.

Length: First 2,500 words.

Requirements: Open to both published and unpublished authors but the work being submitted must not have been previously published. Entry fee, $20. May submit up to 2 entries per category. Send query first; if accepted author will be asked to submit first 2,500 words and a synopsis of the work (500 words). Accepts electronic submissions only to pgcontest@gmail.com.

Prizes: First place winners in each categor receive free registration to Pikes Peak Writers Conference or $100. Second place, $40. Third place, $20.

Deadline: Submissions accepted from September 16 to November 1.

Charlotte Zolotow Award

Cooperative Children's Book Center, 600 North Park Street, Room 4290, Madison, WI 53706
www.ccbc.education.wisc.edu/books/zolotow.asp

The Charlotte Zolotow Award is a tribute to the highly acclaimed children's book editor and author. The award is given to the very best picture book in fiction, nonfiction, and folklore published in the United States from the previous year and is presented by the Cooperative Children's Book Center in Wisconsin.

Length: No length restrictions.

Requirements: Book must be published in the preceding year and be appropriate for readers under age 7. Publishers send 1 copy to the award committee chair and if desired, additional copies to the entire committee; judges may consider any eligible book that comes to their attention from other sources.

Prize: Bronze medallion.

Deadline: December 15.

Indexes

2016 Market News

New Listings: Publishers, Agents, Contests

Alazar Press
Allosaurus
Angry Robot Books
Appleseed
Autumn Publishing
Bridge Books
Bellerophon Books
Bilingual Books for Kids
Black Bed Sheet Books
Black Rose Writing
Bloomsbury Spark
The Book Group
Brandylane
Caitlin Press Inc.
Canon Press
Carson-Dellosa Publishing
  Company
Cengage Learning
Chudney Agency
Clean Reads
Don Congdon Associates, Inc.
Connor Literary Agency
Laura Dail Literary Agency
Dancing Cat Books
Liza Dawson Associates
Joelle Delbourgo Associates
Donadio & Olson, Inc.
Dunow, Carlson, & Lerner
  Agency
Epic Press
Epic Press Impulse
Fernwood Publishing
The Fielding Agency
Flannery Literary
Fletcher & Company
Folio Literary Management, LLC
Frances Collin, Literary Agent
Sarah Jane Freymann Literary
  Agency

Rebecca Friedman Literary
  Agency
Full Circle Literary, LLC
Nancy Gallt Literary Agency
Barry Goldblatt Literary LLC
Go Literary
HarperTrophy
Heinemann Raintree
Hungry Tomato
Imprint
Institute for Writers Writing
  Contests
Jolly Fish Press
Levine, Greenberg Rostan
  Literary Agency, Inc.
Little Creek Books
Lowenstein Associates, Inc.
Donald Maass Literary Agency
Mansion Street Literary
  Management
Marimba Books
Mary Evans, Inc.
Mighty Media Press
PageSpring Publishing
Pavilion Children's Books
Pinter & Martin
The Poisoned Pencil
Pro-Ed
Ramsey & Todd
Ripple Grove Press
Sadler Children's Literary
Sky Pony Press
Skyscape
Sourcebooks Fire
Stripes Publishing
Teen Crave
Teen Crush
Treehouse Publishing Group
Trident Media Group
Two Lions

2016 Market News: Deletions

The following publishers have been removed from this year's directory because they have ceased publishing, are unresponsive, or have proven too small a niche or too little interested in books for or of interest to children, teens, parents, or educators.

Abrams Appleseed: See **Appleseed**

All Classic Books

Amazon Breakthrough Novel Award

Amazon Children's Publishing: See **Skyscape** and **Two Lions**

Anova: See **Pavilion Books**

Astraea: See **Clean Reads**

Behrman House

Cheerios New Author Contest

Concordia

Dunham Literary

Egmont

Eschia Books

Fire: See **Sourcebooks Fire**

Frances Foster Books

Gale/Cengage: See **Cengage**

Graphic Universe

Harcourt Religion Publishers

Harper Voyager

Hartlyn Kids

Learning Resources

Morning Glory Press

National Children's Book of the Year Award

Palari Books

Palm Kids Publishing

PCI: See **Pro-Ed**

Razorbill

ReferencePoint Press

Scarletta: See **Mighty Media Press**

Strange Chemistry: See **Angry Robot Books**

Walker Books for Young Readers

Category Index

To help you find the appropriate market for your query or manuscript, we have compiled a selective index of publishers according to the types of books they currently publish. If you do not find a category that exactly fits your material, try a broader term that covers your topic. For example, if you have written a middle-grade biography, look for both Middle-Grade Nonfiction *and* Biography. If you have written a young adult mystery, look under Mystery/Suspense *and* YA Fiction. Always check the publisher's listing for explanations of specific needs.

Action/Adventure

Activity

Animal Fiction

Arts

Board Books

Boys

Contemporary Fiction

Crafts/Hobbies

Cultures/Anthropology

Current Events/ Politics

Fairy Tales

Family/Parenting

Fantasy

Health/Fitness

Historical Fiction

Holidays/Seasonal

Horror

How-to

Humor, Fiction

Humor, Nonfiction

Inspirational Fiction

Inspirational Nonfiction

Middle-Grade Fiction

Middle-Grade Nonfiction

Multicultural Nonfiction

Mystery/Suspense

Mythology

Nature Fiction

Nature/Outdoors

Paranormal Fiction

Picture Books, Nonfiction

Poetry

Pop Culture

PreK Fiction

PreK Nonfiction

Realistic Fiction

Real Life/Problem-Solving

Reference

Regional Fiction

Regional Nonfiction

Romance

Science

Social Issues

Sports Nonfiction

Technology

Young Adult Nonfiction

Publisher, Agent & Contest Index